Communications in Computer and Information Science

2716

Series Editors

Gang Li , *School of Information Technology, Deakin University, Burwood, VIC, Australia*
Joaquim Filipe, *Polytechnic Institute of Setúbal, Setúbal, Portugal*
Zhiwei Xu, *Chinese Academy of Sciences, Beijing, China*

Rationale

The CCIS series is devoted to the publication of proceedings of computer science conferences. Its aim is to efficiently disseminate original research results in informatics in printed and electronic form. While the focus is on publication of peer-reviewed full papers presenting mature work, inclusion of reviewed short papers reporting on work in progress is welcome, too. Besides globally relevant meetings with internationally representative program committees guaranteeing a strict peer-reviewing and paper selection process, conferences run by societies or of high regional or national relevance are also considered for publication.

Topics

The topical scope of CCIS spans the entire spectrum of informatics ranging from foundational topics in the theory of computing to information and communications science and technology and a broad variety of interdisciplinary application fields.

Information for Volume Editors and Authors

Publication in CCIS is free of charge. No royalties are paid, however, we offer registered conference participants temporary free access to the online version of the conference proceedings on SpringerLink (http://link.springer.com) by means of an http referrer from the conference website and/or a number of complimentary printed copies, as specified in the official acceptance email of the event.

CCIS proceedings can be published in time for distribution at conferences or as post-proceedings, and delivered in the form of printed books and/or electronically as USBs and/or e-content licenses for accessing proceedings at SpringerLink. Furthermore, CCIS proceedings are included in the CCIS electronic book series hosted in the SpringerLink digital library at http://link.springer.com/bookseries/7899. Conferences publishing in CCIS are allowed to use our online conference service (Meteor) for managing the whole proceedings lifecycle (from submission and reviewing to preparing for publication) free of charge.

Publication process

The language of publication is exclusively English. Authors publishing in CCIS have to sign the Springer CCIS copyright transfer form, however, they are free to use their material published in CCIS for substantially changed, more elaborate subsequent publications elsewhere. For the preparation of the camera-ready papers/files, authors have to strictly adhere to the Springer CCIS Authors' Instructions and are strongly encouraged to use the CCIS LaTeX style files or templates.

Abstracting/Indexing

CCIS is abstracted/indexed in DBLP, Google Scholar, EI-Compendex, Mathematical Reviews, SCImago, Scopus. CCIS volumes are also submitted for the inclusion in ISI Proceedings.

How to start

To start the evaluation of your proposal for inclusion in the CCIS series, please send an e-mail to ccis@springer.com

William Yurcik

Editor

Cybersecurity in Healthcare

First Annual HealthSec 2024
Salt Lake City, UT, USA, October 14, 2024
Proceedings

 Springer

Editor
William Yurcik
Centers for Medicare & Medicaid Services (CMS)
Baltimore, MD, USA

ISSN 1865-0929   ISSN 1865-0937 (electronic)
Communications in Computer and Information Science
ISBN 978-3-032-13799-9   ISBN 978-3-032-13800-2 (eBook)
https://doi.org/10.1007/978-3-032-13800-2

This Springer imprint is published by the registered company Springer Nature Switzerland AG
The registered company address is: Gewerbestrasse 11, 6330 Cham, Switzerland

If disposing of this product, please recycle the paper.

Preface

The Cybersecurity in Healthcare (HealthSec 2024) Workshop was held in Salt Lake City, Utah, USA on Monday October 14, 2024, co-located with the ACM Conference on Computer and Communications Security (CCS). The goal of our HealthSec Workshop is to foster an interdisciplinary community of researchers focused on cybersecurity in healthcare. To our knowledge this inaugural workshop was the first ACM or IEEE research forum to include credentialed medical doctors with expertise or roles in healthcare cybersecurity!

The history of cybersecurity in healthcare includes notable research forums. USENIX hosted six "HealthTech" conferences from 2010-2015 which emphasized cybersecurity research. In 2009, the ACM CCS held a "SPIMACS" workshop with the theme of security and privacy in medical and home-care systems. While these initial research forums focused on theoretical cybersecurity contributions, the community was too small to sustain a regular annual forum. Now, in 2024, the "Cybersecurity in Healthcare" research community has grown significantly, with practical issues like hospital ransomware outages, genetic data handling, medical device approvals, and virtual health services being at the forefront. Toward our goal of establishing a sustained, ongoing, annual research forum, we assembled a large and talented workshop program committee with 82 members including credentialed medical doctors.

A common experience shared by many of the researchers in this research space is that it is difficult to find a forum for their work since almost no cybersecurity forums include program committee members with the backgrounds necessary to appropriately understand, appreciate, and/or critically peer review their work. This has led to many cases of excellent research contributions not finding a publication outlet - HealthSec to the rescue!

HealthSec 2024 attracted submissions and participation from Australia, Brazil, Canada, Germany, India, Israel, Singapore, UK, and the USA. HealthSec 2024 had two different paper categories: regular papers and position papers. Research papers with demonstrated results were given priority. Position papers provide a unique opportunity for leaders in the field to identify new directions for research and development, bring in important ideas from other fields, and share perspectives from decades of experience.

HealthSec 2024 accepted 16 papers in total, 11 regular papers and 5 position papers, presented in 6 different sessions – (1) an opening session with notable general papers (3 papers), (2) a Cyberprotection of Medical Imaging Session (2 papers), (3) a Cyberprotection of Hospitals Session (4 papers), (4) a Cyberprotection of Medical Devices Session (2 papers), (5) a Specialized Healthcare Protection Session (4 papers), and (6) a post-workshop discussion on Healthcare Cybersecurity Legal Issues [1 paper]. This volume contains revised versions of all accepted HealthSec 2024 papers (with two exceptions) including feedback received during workshop interactions. Unrevised and condensed versions of the papers have been published in the ACM proceedings. All papers in this volume have been substantially revised following feedback at the conference.

The HealthSec 2024 program committee produced 90 paper reviews for 28 submitted papers. All paper submissions were non-blinded. Every submitted paper received at least 3 peer reviews, with some papers receiving as many as 6 peer reviews. Peer reviewers had an option to reveal/not reveal their identity so while most papers were single-blinded (reviewer identity not revealed), in the interest of building a constructive community some paper authors received non-blinded feedback.

The HealthSec 2024 organizers take enormous pride in our peer review process which provides invaluable, constructive, and supportive peer review unavailable from any other research forum! In all cases, peer review was either incorporated into the finished paper and/or peer review substantially improved the submitted paper. Several papers were specifically shepherded and eventually brought to publication quality and acceptance by a volunteer member of the program committee. External reviewers contributed their expertise to peer review papers on topics outside of the program committee's expertise. Peer review of papers from members of the HealthSec 2024 program committee and organizing committee were handled with conflict protection within the HotCRP.com paper review system and/or external peer reviews were handled by program committee members without conflicts via email.

HealthSec 2024 had a paper acceptance rate of 57% (16/28). Making final paper acceptance decisions was difficult, with several papers referred to as "not quite ready for publication this year – please resubmit next year". Outstanding program committee members who should be recognized include

Paper Shepherd: Allen Householder/CMU SEI CERT
Paper Shepherd: Eugene Vasserman/Kansas State University
Paper Shepherd: Simson Garfinkel/BasisTech, LLC (intensive shepherding)
Peer Reviewer: Dan Geer/In-Q-Tel (impactful reviews)
Peer Reviewer: Debra Bruemmer/MedSec (intensive reviews)
Paper Session 2 Chair: Aashish Sharma/LBNL
Paper Session 3 Chair: C. Scott Kruse/Texas State University

In closing, the HealthSec 2024 Workshop was a complete success as the largest CCS 2024 Workshop, with as many as 60 attendees at its peak! This success was the direct result of the extraordinary teamwork involved in its planning and execution. Let me attempt to name our assembled team begging forgiveness in advance for possibly leaving an important contribution unnamed. I would personally like to thank the Health-Sec 2024 Workshop Vice-Chairs for their constant support, the entire HealthSec 2024 Workshop program committee for going above and beyond making this such a valuable and insightful event experience, the organizers of the larger ACM CCS 2024 conference forum who provided excellent logistical support, CCS 2024 hospitality host (the University of Utah and especially Luis Garcia), ACM SIGSAC organizational sponsorship, and a special thank you to the CCS 2024 Workshop Organizers Aurore Fass/CISPA and Christophe Hauser/Dartmouth for your advocacy in making this workshop possible. Commitment to excellence was truly evident in every aspect of HealthSec 2024!

November 2025   William Yurcik

Organization

Chair

William Yurcik — Centers for Medicare & Medicaid Services, USA

Vice-Chairs

Gregory Pluta — University of Illinois at Urbana-Champaign, USA
Toan Luong — MITRE, USA
Luis Garcia — University of Utah, USA

Program Committee

Jenny Amos — University of Illinois Urbana-Champaign, USA
Spiros Antonatos — Aegis Technologies, USA
Zahid Anwar — North Dakota State University, USA
Stefan Axelsson — Stockholm University, Sweden
James Barlow — Yahoo, Inc., USA
Roelof Boonstra — Physician Software Systems, USA
Debra Bruemmer — MedSec, USA
Christopher Bunnell — UniteGPS, USA
Roy Campbell — University of Illinois at Urbana-Champaign (Emeritus), USA
George Cantwell — University of Cambridge, UK
Guenevere Chen — University of Texas at San Antonio, USA
Sung Choi — University of Central Florida, USA
Michael Collins — University of Southern California Information Sciences Institute, USA
Christian Dameff — University of California San Diego Health, USA
Marek Druzdzel — Bialystok University of Technology, Poland
Robert F. Erbacher — U.S. Army Research Laboratory (ARL), USA
Wade Fagen-Ulmschneider — University of Illinois Urbana-Champaign, USA
Francisco Fonseca — BitSight Technologies Inc., USA
Allan Friedman — Cybersecurity and Infrastructure Security Agency, USA
Deborah Frincke — Sandia National Laboratories, USA

Kevin Fu	Northeastern University, USA
Simson Garfinkel	Basis Technology Corp., USA
Michael T. Gastner	Singapore Institute of Technology, Singapore
Carrie Gates	Bank of America Corporation, USA
Dan Geer	In-Q-Tel Inc., USA
Carl Gunter	University of Illinois Urbana-Champaign, USA
Jaiwei Han	University of Illinois Urbana-Champaign, USA
Dan Harkness	Argonne National Laboratory, USA
Ragib Hasan	University of Alabama at Birmingham, USA
Colton Hood	George Washington University Hospital, USA
Tadd Hopkins	BitSight Technologies Inc., USA
Allen Householder	Carnegie Mellon University Software Engineering Institute, USA
Haochen Huang	Whova Inc., USA
Cynthia Irvine	Naval Postgraduate School, USA
Anupam B. Jena	Harvard Medical School, USA
Eric Johnson	Vanderbilt University, USA
James Joshi	University of Pittsburgh, USA
Nikolai Joukov	modelizeIT Inc., USA
Nadir Kiyanclar	Oracle Corporation, USA
Gregory Koenig	Arkstro Inc., USA
Scott Kruse	Texas State University, USA
Kiran Lakkaraju	Sandia National Laboratories, USA
Tom Linehan	BitSight Technologies Inc., USA
Kwan-Liu Ma	University of California Davis, USA
John McHugh	AssuranceLabs Inc., USA
Fabio Miranda	Insper Institute of Education and Research, Brazil
Forrest Xin Meng	DragonPass International Ltd., Singapore
Ethan Miller	University of California Santa Cruz, USA
Jacki Monson	Sutter Health, USA
Suvda Myagmar	Salesforce Inc., USA
Peter G. Neumann	SRI International, USA
Stephen North	Infovisible Inc., USA
Godwin Odia	Applied Health Informatics LLC, USA
Rhonda O'Kane	BitSight Technologies Inc., USA
Sean Peisert	Lawrence Berkeley National Laboratory, USA
Eric Perakslis	Pluto Health Inc., USA
Kate Pierce	Fortified Health Security, USA
Jim Prewett	University of New Mexico, USA
Ronald Pulivarti	National Institute of Standards and Technology, USA
Raj Rajagopalan	Resideo Technologies Inc., USA

Ram Ramadoss	Avera Health, USA
Esa M. Rantanen	Rochester Institute of Technology, USA
Daniel Reed	University of Utah, USA
Will Ricciardi	BitSight Technologies Inc., USA
Jeremy Rossi	Binary Data Engineering LLC, USA
Avi Rubin	Harbor Labs Inc., USA
Marcus Sachs	Center for Internet Security, USA
Rami Saydjari	Ronin Institute for Independent Scholarship, USA
Sami Saydjari	Dartmouth College, USA
Stuart Schechter	Harvard University, USA
Andreas Schick	U.S. Food and Drug Administration, USA
Naomi Schwartz	Medcrypt Inc., USA
Cigdem Sengul	Brunel University London, UK
Aashish Sharma	Lawrence Berkeley National Laboratory, USA
Bryan Smith	Boldend Inc., USA
Natalie Sullivan	George Washington University Hospital, USA
Jeff Tully	University of California San Diego Health, USA
Eugene Vasserman	Kansas State University, USA
Jun Wang	Rackspace Technology Inc., USA
David Wiegandt	Sandia National Laboratories, USA
Christopher Worsham	Massachusetts General & Harvard Medical School, USA
Felix Wu	University of California Davis, USA
Xiaoxin Yin	Airbnb Inc., USA
Erez Zadok	Stony Brook University, USA

Additional Reviewers

Adam Shostack	University of Washington, USA
Daphne Yao	Virginia Tech University, USA

Contents

Opening Papers Discussion

Computer-Related Healthcare Risks – Updated! 3
Peter G. Neumann and William Yurcik

Cybersecurity Threats to U.S. Hospitals: Focus on Emergency Departments 19
Natalie Sullivan, Laura Tilley, and William Yurcik

Extending Analogies and Applying Public Health Models to Cybersecurity 33
O. Sami Saydjari, Josiah Dykstra, and Douglas Hough

Cyberprotection of Medical Imaging

Towards Better Adversarial Defense on Lung CT Nodule Classification
Models with Feature Enhancement 67
Yunzheng Zhu, Yuan Tian, and Aichi Chien

The Security of Deep Learning Defenses in Medical Imaging 86
Moshe Levy, Guy Amit, and Yisroel Mirsky

Cyberprotection of Hospitals

Cybersecurity Measurability: Three Magnified Vulnerabilities of USA
Healthcare 113
William Yurcik, Andreas Schick, Stephen North, Michael T. Gastner,
Fabio Roberto de Miranda, Rodolpho da Silva Avelino,
Andre Filipe de Moreas Batista, Gregory Pluta, and Ian Brooks

Evaluating Interoperability of Medical Communication Protocols
via Differential Testing 130
Prashant Anantharaman, Vishnupriya Varadharaju,
Carlos Guerrero Alvarez, Danylo Borodchuk, Aamish A. Beg,
Rebecca Shapiro, Andrew Gettinger, Sean W. Smith,
and Michael E. Locasto

MedBlockSync: A Blockchain Solution for Multi-institutional Healthcare 160
Jorge Castillo, Kwabena Aboagye-Otchere, and Qian Chen

Security and Privacy Framework for Cloud-Based Remote Patient
Monitoring and In-place Sensor-Based Care 188
  Sai Shreya Nuguri, Subrahmanya Chandra Bhamidipati,
  Anirudh Kambhampati, Karan Karthik, Aneesh Calyam,
  Mahesh Karthik Duvvuri, Mauro Lemus Alarcon, and Prasad Calyam

Cyberprotection of Medical Devices

On the Security of RL–Based Artificial Pancreas Systems 217
  Preston Chang, Veena Krish, and Amir Rahmati

Systems-Theoretic and Data-Driven Security Analysis in ML-Enabled
Medical Devices 232
  Gargi Mitra, Mohammadreza Hallajiyan, Inji Kim,
  Athish Pranav Dharmalingam, Mohammed Elnawawy, Shahrear Iqbal,
  Karthik Pattabiraman, and Homa Alemzadeh

Specialized Healthcare Protection – Genetic Data, Rural Services, & Senior Living

Collaborative, Privacy-Preserving Genomic Research: A Vision
and Real-World Deployment 267
  Zahra Rahmani, Zebin Yun, Nahal Shahini, Nadav Gat, Yuzhou Jiang,
  Ofir Farchy, Yaniv Harel, Vipin Chaudhary, Erman Ayday,
  and Mahmood Sharif

What Are the Hazards in Providing of Remote Health Services in Rural
Australia and How Can We Manage Them? 284
  Ashley Brooks and Arnab Majumdar

Computer Security Issues in Continuing Care Retirement Communities:
A Resident's Perspective 301
  John McHugh and William Yurcik

Author Index 327

Opening Papers Discussion

Computer-Related Healthcare Risks – Updated!

Peter G. Neumann[1] and William Yurcik[2]

[1] SRI Computer Science Lab, Menlo Park, CA 94025, USA
neumann@csl.sri.com
[2] Centers for Medicare and Medicaid Services (CMS), Baltimore, MD 21244, USA
william.yurcik@cms.hhs.gov

Abstract. This paper is an updated summary with feedback of a paper originally presented at the ACM HealthSec Workshop held in Salt Lake City October 2024 [4]. The content is computer-related risks to healthcare documented within the book [6] and the ACM Forum on Risks to the Public on Computers and Related Subjects, which was created by the first author in 1985 and has been continuously moderated by him since then. The complete set of RISKS archives is dual-hosted online and specific issues referred to as (R vol no) can be obtained directly in the searchable site in Newcastle UK [7]. The paper style provides direct references to hundreds of events which have occurred over several decades.

Computer-related risks in healthcare include data breaches, provider outages interrupting continuity of care via ransomware and denial-of-service attacks, system malfunctions, unauthorized access, data loss, data corruption, insider threats, and supply chain attacks. All of these risks can lead to patient harms ranging from minor inconvenience all the way to patient death.

By identifying the events and describing the conditions that have brought us to our current state, broader patterns emerge beyond isolated occurrences, from which we can learn to better understand the present to improve in the future.

Keywords: healthcare risks and damages · system and subsystem trustworthiness · safety · security · integrity · reliability · survivability · usability · real-time behavior · assurance

1 Introduction

The first author has assembled the largest worldwide online collection of computer-related risk events and categorized these events thematically specific to healthcare risks– predominantly from the past five years of RISKS but comprehensively going back decades. Included are human safety and security issues (e.g., healthcare providers experiencing cyberattacks), a wide variety of healthcare privacy issues, COVID-related problems, and other miscellaneous risks, along with interspersed italicized comments from the authors about the risk referenced in each category.

W. Yurcik—The views presented herein do not represent the views of the Federal Government.

W. Yurcik (Ed.): HealthSec 2024, CCIS 2716, pp. 3–18, 2026.
https://doi.org/10.1007/978-3-032-13800-2_1

Almost everything today seems to have opposing applicability, in the sense of having both up-sides and down-sides, with many different risks emerging in both cases. However, awareness of the risks by both system developers and the general public is typically very poor and would benefit from reaching more widely. Not only are the risks widely ignored overall, the notion of ground-truth seems to have disappeared when it comes to conspiracy theories and rampant disinformation. The risks of misinformation and willful disinformation are not a new challenge, but recently have been seriously exacerbated with the accelerating use of artificial intelligence and Chatbots.

Risks seem to be getting wildly out of control, particularly with respect to computers involved in healthcare, hospital and clinical uses of artificial intelligence, self-driving vehicles, and other life-critical or mission-critical automated and semi-automated systems. From a computer perspective, we desperately need evidence-based assurance rather than over-hyped assertions that we should simply trust the developers and operating managers. Otherwise, the integrity and credibility of our rampantly increasing overdependence on untrustworthy technology may cause a collapse of trust in our technology. Undoubtedly, avoiding systemic failures may require radical changes in how computer science and system engineering should be taught and practiced, along with corresponding oversight, and consequentially much heavier penalties for failures.

The first author's research has been inspired by the Albert Einstein Principle – "that everything should be made as simple as possible, but no simpler".[1]*[8] It is just one of many important principles that are needed to make our computer-related healthcare into a more robust, safe, and secure discipline. This has served as a fundamental principle for the first author since he had a long discussion on complexity with Albert Einstein at home in November 1952.*

In numerous cases, it is the violation of the "no simpler" part, ignoring obscure corner-cases whose triggering can result in disasters. In healthcare, the no-simpler might be related to the stark difference between allopathic medicine (western) and holistic/functional medicine (which treats causes rather symptoms). It is often the source of systemic failures and rampant system security/safety flaws.

---

[1] That literal oral quote was precisely what we talked about during most of our discussion of complexity during my two and one-quarter hours with Albert Einstein on the morning of 8 November 1952. I had previously seen it simplified without the word 'made' in The Reader's Digest and questioned him about it. Albert insisted that the word 'made' was very relevant in any constructive act. I subsequently verified with Helen Dukas (his associate) that she was unable to find his oral directly quoted in print, as suggested by the Robinson citation [8]. Mrs. Dukas also mentioned when she invited me to meet Albert Einstein that he adored my mother Elsa Schmid (Neumann), who had made a wonderfully insightful mosaic portrait of Albert in 1944–45, a photo of which is on my website < https://www.csl.sri.com/~neumann/einstein3-bu.jpg > along with a letter he wrote to my mother thanking her after visiting the mosaic in my father's art gallery New Art Circle in NYC in 1945: "The viewing of your mosaic portrait has been an artistic experience for me that I shall never forget. I am happy that through my very existence I have been the inspiration for the origin of such a work. In this portrait is perfectly expressed exactly that which is so completely missing in modern man -- inwardness and contemplation, detachment from the here and now. It is a riddle to me how it is possible to achieve such a delicate and strong expression with this inflexible material." (signed A. Einstein).

Holistic thinking in healthcare is not just thinking out of the box – it is realizing that there never was a box in the first place, as diagnosing and treating problems are often open-ended.

In the near future, global warming and environmental hazards are likely to have a terrible impact on healthcare in countries where there is little electricity, and in developed countries where power failures will require massive cogeneration plants to ensure power system survivability in crises.

Overall, we must also be aware of human foibles – e.g., being blinded or legally-bound by so-called best practices which in-reality are lowest-common-denominator guides and nowhere near where best practice should be. We must also avoid over-endowing uses of technology to solve non-technological problems, simplistic legislation, charlatans, frauds, and other recurring risks.

2 Systemic Trustworthiness Requirements: Risks Regarding Human Safety, Integrity, Security, Privacy, Reliability, Real-Time Response, and More

Everything in our lives seems to be increasingly interconnected with other problems: healthcare is influenced by climate change, locust swarms, melting icebergs, failing bird flocks, bird flu, and previously unseen migration patterns, the dolphin and whale groundings, pollution, Tonga-Hunga Ha'apai eruption, underground explosions, and so on. The lack of trustworthiness is outrageous, ad infinitum. Thus, we need more holistic thinking, where so many factors are involved in healthcare and human well-being. Nevertheless, although we focus mostly on first-order risks to healthcare – we also note some of the collateral risks.

Air pollution is linked to irreversible sight loss. (R 32 49) Forever chemicals are widespread in U.S. drinking water. (R 32 46) Glyphosate was found in samples from a French infertility clinic raising questions about controversial chemical's impact on fertility. More than 55% of sperm samples from a French infertility clinic contained high levels of glyphosate, the world's most common weedkiller, raising further questions about the chemical's impact on reproductive health and overall safety, noted on 24 May 2024. Rainwater everywhere on Earth unsafe to drink due to forever-chemicals. (R 33 38-39) A weekend-long Iowa fertilizer spill killed 750K fish in Iowa and Missouri over a 60-mile stretch of rivers. (R 34 12) As Tom Lehrer wrote in the song "Pollution - Don't Drink the Water, and Don't Breath the Air." Brain-altering bioweapons and DNA surveillance: Experts are already preparing for the next biological threat. (R 32 49) Scientists propose lithium to cope with high-risk condition in future fusion facilities. (R 32 49) A hole in the International Space Station made by a meteorite the size of a grain of sand. (R 33 27) Nuclear waste. Toxic dumps. Computer fabrication effluents. GPS spoofing. Cyber-attacks could jeopardize global food supplies, they are already affecting shipping through the Suez Canal. (R 33 23).

3 Medical Device Failures

The Therac-25 is the seminal case for medical device failure. Therac was a radiation therapy device that alternated as a high-intensity research machine. The Therac-20 had a physical interlock that prevented the switch over from research mode to therapy mode from causing any damage. However programmers of the Therac-25 software forgot the hardware interlock in the Therac-20 resulting in multiple deaths and patient harms. Professor Nancy Leveson was very influential in investigating, discovering, and documenting the root cause of this event [2, 3].

3.1 Medical and IoT Devices Vulnerable to Attack

Researchers at Forescout's Vedere Labs cybersecurity intelligence team and CyberMDX cybersecurity service provider discovered seven vulnerabilities, known collectively as "Access:7" in more than 150 Internet of Things (IoT) devices made by over 100 companies.[10] Three of the critical bugs allowed attackers to gain full control of devices by remotely executing malicious code. The remainder, rated moderate to high in severity, allow attackers to steal data or execute denial-of-service attacks. The flaws were found in multiple versions of PTC Axeda agent and PTC Desktop Server, which are used in many IoT devices to enable remote access and management. All versions of the Axeda technology below 6.9.3 are affected. PTC has released patches for the vulnerabilities. (R 33 09) Medical and IoT devices are almost all vulnerable to attack. (R 33 09).

3.2 FDA Warning Links Heart Pump to 49 Deaths

A troubled Impella heart pump that has now been linked to 49 deaths and dozens of injuries worldwide will be allowed to remain in use, despite the FDA's decision to issue an alert about the risk that it could puncture a wall of the heart. The FDA said Abiomed (the manufacturer of the device, acquired by Johnson & Johnson in 2022) should have notified the agency more than two years before that, when the company first posted an update on its website about the perforation risk. "To say that you're addressing 49 deaths by saying 'be careful' is not addressing the problem at all." Rita Redberg, UCSF cardiologist and professor. (R 34 12).

3.3 Other Problematic Medical Devices

Bluetooth-related flaws threaten dozens of medical devices, including pacemakers. (R 31 59) Oximeters used to be designed for equity. What happened? (R 32 70) Blood oxygen monitors face scrutiny from FDA panel. (R 33 51) 'Painless' glucose monitors are popular, but with little evidence that they help most diabetes patients. (R 32 55) More than 200 people with diabetes injured after software issue drained insulin pump batteries, shut down unexpectedly due to a problem with a connected mobile app, Class 1 Recall. (R 34 24) Study finds variations in quantitative MRI scanner measurements. (R 32 75) Get This Thing Out of My Chest: A life-sustaining heart pump was taken off the market after years of problems and FDA inaction. Thousands of people are now stuck with it embedded in their hearts. Those who already have the heart pump, also known as the HVAD, can't simply get it removed or replaced. The required surgery is typically considered more dangerous than leaving it in. (R 33 01) Vulnerability of insulin pumps. (R 33 46) Surprisingly many risky infusion pumps? Are you part of the IoT? (R 33 08) Four vulnerabilities discovered in popular infusion pumps, WiFi batteries. (R 33 44) Risks of CPAP machines: CPAP murder mystery regarding the advent of remotely controllable ones with minimal security? (R 33 12).

A High-Risk Medical Device Didn't Meet Federal Standards. The Government Paid Millions for More. (R 33 02) More than half of medical devices have critical vulnerabilities. (R 33 03) Their Bionic Eyes Are Now Obsolete and Unsupported: Patient had to find out second-hand that the company had abandoned the technology and was on the verge of going bankrupt. While his two-implant system is still working, he doesn't know how long that will be the case. (R 33 06) Top Philips executive approved sale of defective breathing machines by distributors, with tests showing health risks. (R 33 92) Wearable fitness trackers could interfere with cardiac devices, study finds. (R 33 63) Your Medical Devices Are Getting Smarter: Can the FDA Keep Them Safe? Unfortunately, the historical record is spotty. (R 33 89) Crushed to death by robot in South Korea. (R 33 93–94) Biometric devices sold on eBay reportedly contained sensitive U.S. military data. (R 33 59) CoolSculpting: fat-freezing procedure left supermodel Linda Evangelista 'disfigured'. (R 32 89) Implantable AI system developed for early detection and treatment of illnesses. (R 32 84) Most medical imaging devices run outdated operating systems. (R 31 62) Do-It-Yourself artificial pancreas given approval by team of experts. (R 32 93) Fixing medical devices that are biased against race or gender. (R 32 71).

Defibrillation fiasco: In an incident in Houston TX a student died when the school defibrillator failed. When the authorities checked, all of Houston's 150 school devices failed to operate correctly. Built-in designed self-checking failed miserably in the absence of testing. (R 34 47).

4 Healthcare Cyber-Attacks

Ransomware is the latest form of disruption of entire sets of networked computer communication systems especially for healthcare providers. Here are a few recent outages and the concomitant risks, however, there are many other forms of attacks.

4.1 Ransomware Attacks Show Flaws in Cybersecurity Persist

The recent cyberattack on the billing and payment colossus Change Healthcare revealed just how serious the vulnerabilities are throughout the U.S. healthcare system and alerted industry leaders and policymakers in the urgent need for better digital security. (R 34 12) *They clearly have not been reading RISKS for any of the past 40 years!* Alarms over healthcare cyberattacks are getting louder (R 33 45) Corporate Greed Made the Change Healthcare Cyberattack Worse (R 34 17) UnitedHealth Top Executive Slammed Over Cyberattack (R 34 24) London Hospitals Face Major Disruptions After Cyberattack: ransomware cyberattack on Synnovis significantly disruptive (R 34 29) Patients of a Vermont hospital are left in the dark after a cyberattack (R 32 39) Steamship Authority targeted in ransomware attack, unable to make reservations for several weeks to/from Martha's Vineyard and Nantucket – serious implications on ambulances, hospitals, etc. (R 32 70) Ransomware attacks on hospitals take toll on patients. (R 33 51) Ransomware attacks have entered a heinous new phase. (R 33 66) Cybercriminal group claims responsibility for ransomware attack as hospital CEO says recovery will take weeks. (R 33 92) Paying ransom for data stolen in cyberattack bankrolls further crime, experts caution. (R 33 94) Ransomware forces 3 hospitals to turn away all but the most critical patients. (R 31 45) Ransomware and cyber-insurance. (R 32 71) Company shuts down because of ransomware, leaves 300 without jobs just before holidays. (R 31 53) We Have Met the Ransomware Enemy, and It Is (Partly) Us! (R 32 71)) Secret chats show how Cybergang became a ransomware powerhouse. (R 32 69) How to Negotiate with Ransomware Hackers. (R 32 70).

4.2 Healthcare Cyber-Incident Reporting

Illumina Cybersecurity Vulnerability May Present Risks for Patient Results and Customer Networks: Letter to Healthcare Providers. (R 33 25) Companies would need to report substantial attacks within 72 h and ransom payments within 24 h [9]. (R 34 13) Cybersecurity insurance, if you can get it. (R 32 70) Cybersecurity Framework Profile for Ransomware Risk Management – Preliminary Draft. (R 32 71) Healthcare giant comes clean about recent hack and paid ransomware. (R 34 22) Health-care hack spreads pain across hospitals and doctors nationwide. (R 34 09).

4.3 Infrastructure Utility Outages

Healthcare is dependent on many utility infrastructures – electricity, water, transportation, heating and ventilation systems, food supply, and most recently increasingly dependence on the Internet. Power outages have periodically been a problem. During a massive east-coast power outage in 1965, the first author was on the ninth floor of the MIT Project Mac computer room when the disk units all made a slurping noises shutting down simultaneously. Hospitals have learned that they need standby backup power to continue life-critical operations. We have also learned that entire power grids can be easily brought down by hacking attacks.

Cyberattack Paralyzes the Largest U.S. Healthcare Payment System. (R 34 09) Colorado ski town emergency dispatch centers fielding dozens of automated 911 calls from skier iPhones. (R 33 60) Compromise of U.S. Water Treatment Facility. (Multiple items, R 32 49) Cut submarine cables cause web outages across Africa; 6 countries still affected. (R 34 10) Energy-harvesting card treats 5G networks as wireless power grids. (R 32 58,59) Yet another 5G attack vector. (R 32 58) U.S. and Japan to invest $4.5bn in next-gen 6G race with China. (R 32 61) U.S. Intelligence Agencies warn about 5G network weaknesses. (R 32 66) Major Internet outage affecting users from Washington DC to Boston; Verizon fiber cut reported. (R 32 47) Hospital network/computer outage in Pacific Northwest. (R 33 48) Veteran Affairs big software upgrade is plagued by hidden costs and flawed training. (R 32 77) Israeli Health Ministry website faces cyberattack, oversea access blocked. (R 33 44) Google, Oracle cloud servers wilt in UK heatwave, take down websites. (R 33 35)) GoDaddy says data breach exposed over a million user accounts (R 32 94) Amazon's Dark Secret: It Has Failed to Protect Your Data. (R 32 94) Costa Rica declares emergency in ongoing cyberattack. (R 33 20) Hospital IT melts in heatwave, leaving doctors without patient records. (R 33 35).

4.4   HIPAA – Healthcare Data-Handling Issues

Healthcare privacy leaks are frequent, accidental or malicious disclosure of personally identifiable information (PII) and/or personal health information (PHI). HIPAA health-care privacy breaches cause considerable disruption to medical providers with signifi-cant litigation and fines. Computer systems are inadequately trustworthy and handling of healthcare data is often sloppy.

Electronic Health Record Legal Settlements. (R 33 53) Hospitals give tech giants access to detailed medical records. Deals with Microsoft, IBM and Google reveal the power medical providers have in deciding how patients' sensitive health data is shared. (R 31 55) 96% of U.S. hospital websites share visitor info with Meta, Google, data brokers: Hospitals despite being places where people implicitly expect to have their per-sonal details kept private frequently use tracking technologies on their websites to share user information with Google, Meta, data brokers, and other third parties, according to research. (R 34 17) Phishing attack hits Los Angeles County public health agency, jeopar-dizing 200,000-plus residents' personal info. (R 34 31) Independent security researcher discovers information trove of 1.2B users' personal information (mostly from by People Data Labs) server shut down after FBI contacted. (R 31 49) How to prevent a data breach, lessons learned from the infosec vendors themselves. (R 31 48) Hackers steal data for 15 million patients, then sell it back to lab that lost it. (R 31 52) Security startup Verkada hack exposes 150,000 security cameras in Tesla factories, jails, hospitals, hospitals, etc. (R 32 54) Albertans' personal information exposed after national healthcare provider hacked, data put up for sale. (R 32 79 Data breach of Ontario's vaccine booking sys-tem affects hundreds of thousands, province says. (R 33 57) Data breach of Michigan healthcare giant exposes millions of records. (R 33 94) Data on 267,000 Sarnia patients going back 3 decades among cyberattack thefts at 5 Ontario hospitals. (R 33 93-94).

HIPAA Electronic health records and doctor burnout. (R 31 22,23) Babylon Health app error allowed UK users to watch videos of other patients' private doctor visits. (R 31 98) Researchers examine burden of electronic health record on primary-care clinicians. (R 32 76) Dartmouth Medical School drops online cheating cases against students. (R 32 71) From a small town in North Carolina to big-city hospitals, how software infuses racism into U.S. healthcare. (R 32 32) Facebook Is Receiving Sensitive Medical Information from Hospital Websites. (R 33 29) Facebook plans to show content mainly from strangers. (R 33 29) Facebook, privacy and abortion. (R 33 33) Danger: Metaverse Ahead! (R 33 38) Thoughts about Google's new blog post regarding health-related data privacy. (R 33 32) FEC approves Google's horrible political spam filter bypass plan. (R 33 38) Anonymity no more? Age checks come to the Web. (R 32 91) Banning anonymous social media accounts would only stifle free speech and democracy. (R 32 91) Navy doctors and dentists were {accidentally} told they owe 3 more years of service; military admits to another record-keeping error. (R 33 70) Medicare forced to expand forms to fit 10-digit bill a penny shy of $100M. (R 34 13) Health apps share your concerns with advertisers. HIPAA can't stop it. (R 33 46).

5   Risks of Using Artificial Intelligence for Healthcare

We note the need for evidence-based assurance in the introduction to this chapter. Rampant misuse of artificial intelligence has seriously diminished trustworthiness. Artificial intelligence generally has no assurance that it will be correct, safe, reliable, secure, or anything else. Considering the risks before you leap seems like a useful mantra. Sadly, it seems to be ignored by people who develop sensitive uses of artificial intelligence and many other systems. See CACM article on total-system trustworthiness [5].

This is particularly critical for the use of artificial intelligence in healthcare where it is being widely introduced – and widely misused or exploited. It is particularly relevant to healthcare with respect to large language models, Chatbots, and machine learning algorithms, but also to the use of artificial intelligence embedded in untrustworthy hardware and backend operating systems with inadequate oversight.

Images made by lasers and read by computers can help speed up the diagnosis of brain tumors during surgery. "The study involved brain tissue from 278 patients, analyzed while the surgery was still going on. Each sample was split, with half going to AI and half to a neuropathologist. The diagnoses were later judged right or wrong based on whether they agreed with the findings of lengthier and more extensive tests performed after the surgery. The result was a draw: humans, 93.9% correct; AI, 94.6%." 'Correct'? No false-positive or false-negative AUC ROC measures! (R 31 54) New findings shed light on risks and benefits of integrating AI into medical decision-making. (R 34 37) Artist finds private medical record photos in popular AI training data set. (R 33 46).

The state of AI right now is absolutely ridiculous. This is terrifying (R 33 34) *{This item from July 2022 was true and even more relevant now.}* Assigning liability when medical AI is used. (R 31 62) Mayo Clinic AI engineers face an acid test: Will their algorithms help real patients? (R 31 56) AI algorithms detect diabetic eye disease inconsistently. (R 32 44) Flawed Algorithm Used to Determine UK Welfare Payments Is 'Pushing People Into Poverty'. (R 32 31) Digital stethoscope uses artificial intelligence for diagnosing lung abnormalities. (R 32 40) Artificial intelligence-created medicine to be used on humans for first time. (R 31 56,57) AI in medicine. (R 32 70) Insufficient evidence that AI breast cancer screening is accurate enough to replace human scrutiny. (R 32 86) AI matches cardiologists' expertise, while explaining its decisions. (R 32 86) AI Can Help Patients – but Only If Doctors Understand It: Algorithms can help diagnose a growing range of health problems, but humans need to be trained to listen. (R 32 87) Artificial Intelligence: Stephen Colbert: "Are you afraid of artificial intelligence taking over?" Ricky Gervais: "I'd love for any intelligence to take over." (R 33 22) Sloppy Use of Machine Learning Is Causing a Reproducibility Crisis in Science. (R 33 38) This $5 billion insurance company likes to talk up its AI. Now it's in a mess over it. (R 32 70) Artificial intelligence predicts patients' race from their medical images. (R 33 23-24) AI has arrived in your doctor's office. Washington doesn't know what to do about it. (R 33 92) The FDA should better regulate medical algorithms. (R 32 90) Mushroom pickers urged to avoid foraging books on Amazon that appear to be written by AI. *{The risks of erroneous Chatbots are enormous, and it may be difficult to sue anyone for false representations}* (R 33 82).

Today's Robotic Surgery Turns Surgical Trainees Into Spectators: "Medical training in the robotics age leaves tomorrow's surgeons short on skills. (R 33 36-37) Who is at fault when something goes wrong? (R 33 38) An AI app claims it can detect sexually transmitted infections. (R 34 15) Hospital bosses love AI. Doctors and nurses are worried. (R 33 78) Microsoft lays off an ethical AI team as it doubles down on OpenAI. (R 33 66) AI is now indistinguishable from reality. (R 33 69-70) Doctors warn about AI's existential threat to humanity. (R 33 70) AI to act as doctor's second pair of eyes to spot nearly invisible colon cancer growths. (R 33 66) Mental health apps show promise and pitfalls. (R 34 16).

Who Is Liable when AI Kills? (R 33 31) UK proposes new rule for AI: AI systems will have to identify a legal person to be held responsible for any problems under proposals for regulating AI unveiled by the UK government: Ensure that AI is used safely; Ensure that AI is technically secure and functions as designed; Make sure that AI is appropriately transparent and explainable; Consider fairness; Identify a legal person to be responsible for AI; Clarify routes to redress or contestability. (R 33 34-35) True Story? Lie-Detection Systems Go High-Tech. (R 33 06) What if doctors are always watching, but never there? (R 32 72).

Groundbreaking new material 'could allow artificial intelligence to merge with the human brain'. (R 32 21-22) The Brain Implants That Could Change Humanity. (R 32 25).

Neuralink: Elon Musk unveils pig he claims has computer implant in brain. (R 32 25) Elon Musk Defends Neuralink Against Neuroscientist's Concerns of Chips Overheating. (R 32 37) The future is cyborg: Kaspersky study finds support for human augmentation. (R 32 27-28).

6 Disinformation, Lies, Fakes, Biases, Fraud, etc.

The notion of ground truth seems to be vanishing in many contexts, but particularly with respect to bad uses of AI and educational practices that seem to be dumbing down what is taught in many schools, together with a proclivity for acceptance of patently obvious "truthiness", which is offered instead of an early 19th century term revived by Stephen Colbert who also stated "Preferring to believe what you wish to believe, rather than what is known to be true"[1] - the appearance of trust in something that is not trustworthy. Sloppy or even dishonest research practices are also an occasional problem. Once again, we need greater emphasis on evidence-based assurance.

Nearly 50% of Twitter Accounts Talking about Coronavirus Might Be Bots. (R 31 72) The makers of EyeDetect promise a new era of truth-detection, but many experts are skeptical. (R 32 94) True Story? Lie-Detection Systems Go High-Tech: Electrodes affixed to the face may determine whether someone is lying, e.g., moving eyebrows involuntarily, or slight movement of lips, and eye-tracking; claims it detects 73% of lies. More than 65 U.S. law enforcement agencies and close to 100 agencies worldwide use EyeDetect, which claims to be 86% to 88% accurate. (R 33 06) Pervasive Misinformation. The rise in the anti-vax movement has made it difficult... to candidly address potential side effects. Several fascinating individual cases are noted in some detail. (R 34 23).

Doctors 'bribed to use infected blood products'. (R 34 26) Texas Surgeon Is Accused of Secretly Denying Liver Transplants. (R 34 17) Hospital's false death announcement leads to a wife's suicide; husband later found alive. (R 34 02) Disinformation and hoaxes: FTC, FCC crack down on coronavirus robocall scams, 132M calls/day. (R 31 66) FBI warns individuals employed in the healthcare industry of the ongoing scam involving the impersonation of law enforcement and government officials. (R 33 43).

7 COVID-19

COVID-19 and other respiratory diseases seem to have become pervasive, in part as a result of changes in our ecological environment, which in turn created huge changes in almost everyone's life over the past years. The coverage in the ACM Risks Forum was rather overwhelming, and too much to include here on a per-item basis – as it covered a very wide range of risks. Thus, we merely summarize some of the main risks that arose. The full list can be found in the RISKS archives.

Causality and Casualty: Covid Vaccine Side Effects: 4 Takeaways from Our Investigation. (R 34 22) Live Coronavirus Map Used to Spread Malware. (R 31 62) Coronavirus Reactions Creating Major Internet Security Risks. (R 31 64) Keeping the DNS Secure During the Coronavirus Pandemic. (R 31 68) Clinical trials hit by ransomware attack on health tech firm. (R 32 31) How coronavirus turned the dystopian joke of FaceID masks into a reality - A computer virus expert looks at CoVID-19. (R 31 64-67) Thousands of cases went unreported in California when a computer server failed. (R 32 19) Devices Used In COVID-19 Treatment Can Give Errors For Patients With Dark Skin (R 32 42) Ransomware and new virus strains. (R 32 43) How California's new Digital Vaccine Records can be easily abused. (R 32 76) Hackers are using the Coronavirus panic to spread malware. (R 31 59-60).

We Are Blowing the Fight to Contain Bird Flu. (R 34 22) Bird Flu Shows That the U.S. Learned All the Wrong Lessons about Covid: Two years after H5N1 jumped to mammals, health officials don't seem to have a plan. (R 34 40).

California virus-fighting efforts hampered by data delays. (R 32 18) Expired certificate contributed to undercounting of Calif. COVID cases. (R 32 20) The CDC Isn't Publishing Large Portions of the Covid Data It Collects. (R 33 07).

Integrity Relating to Vaccines and Care: Criminals have stolen nearly $100 billion in Covid relief funds, Secret Service says. (R 33 01) A magnet for rip-off artists: Fraud siphoned billions estimated $163-billion from pandemic unemployment benefits were misspent or stolen. (R 33 21) ID.me made baseless pandemic fraud claims to win contracts, Congress says. (R 33 54) The more you submit, the more we get paid: How Fintech fueled COVID aid fraud. (R 33 56) Florida surgeon general fudged data for dubious COVID analysis, tipster says. (R 33 63).

How a Big Pharma Company Stalled a Potentially Lifesaving Vaccine in Pursuit of Bigger Profits. (R 33 92) Dana-Farber Cancer Institute has retracted 7 studies amid controversy over errors. (R 34 16) Remediation: Coronavirus: Robots use light beams to zap hospital viruses. (R 31 64).

MIT Will Post Free Plans Online for an Emergency Ventilator That Can Be Built for $100. (R 31 64) MIT-based Team Works on Rapid Deployment of Open-source Low-cost Ventilator. (R 31 64, 65) Measurement units risk in those Open Source ventilators? (R 31 65).

Could the Covid-19 Vaccines Have Caused Some People Harm? (R 34 35) Ex-CDC Director Dr. Robert Redfield says It's High Time to Admit Significant Side-effects of COVID-19 Vaccines. (R 34 25, 26, 40) An Object Lesson on How to Destroy Public Trust: Officials should have told us what they knew, or at least leveled with us about what they didn't know (Zeynep Tufekci, 34 30).

Tokyo firm urges caution against surge in coronavirus-related disinformation on April Fools' Day. (R 31 64) Coronavirus Rumor Control. (R 31 68) Just 12 people are behind most vaccine hoaxes on social media. (R 32 69) Reddit CEO rejects call for a crackdown on coronavirus misinformation. (R 32 85) Surgeon General Demands Data on COVID-19 Misinformation from Major Tech Firms. (R 33 08) Reactions, Protests, and Retaliations: Broadband engineers threatened due to 5G coronavirus conspiracies. (R 31 65) A viral email about Coronavirus had people smashing buses and blocking hospitals. (R 31 60).

Man who breached coronavirus stay-home notice stripped of Singapore PR status, barred from re-entry. (R 31 60) Breast cancer patient attacked by violent anti-mask protest outside Los Angeles clinic. (R 32 78) Health insurance giant Kaiser will notify millions of a data the Birth of Social Distancing. (R 31 73) The illusion of certainty. (R 31 73).

Schools Adopt Face Recognition in the Name of Fighting Covid. (R 32 36) Artificial intelligence model detects asymptomatic Covid-19 infections through cellphone-recorded coughs. (R 32 37) AI flunks COVID test. (R 32 80) Covid and security awareness training. (R 32 36) Why experts urge caution in using covid risk and tracking tools. (R 32 38) Traffic Analysis and Herd Immunity. (R 32 77-78) The COVID testing company that missed 96% of cases: Northshore Clinical Labs in Nevada. (R 33 21) Russia's Planned Coronavirus App is a State-Run Security Nightmare. (R 31 65) Why human brains are bad at assessing the risks of pandemics. (R 32 26) 463 people's COVID benefits accidentally sent to one of them. (R 33 22).

Privacy Cannot Be a Casualty of the Coronavirus. (R 31 66) UK government using confidential patient data in coronavirus response. (R 31 68) How Coronavirus Is Eroding Privacy. (R 31 68, 69) Israel stops using phone tracking to enforce COVID-19 quarantines. (R 31 72) Apple, Google announce new privacy protection rules for contact tracing apps. (R 31 79) Microsoft says the pandemic argues for a federal privacy law. (R 31 70) The iOS Covid app ecosystem has become a privacy minefield. (R 32 38) CDC call for data on vaccine recipients raises alarm over privacy. (R 32 40) Breach after sharing patients' data with advertisers. (R 34 21).

Computer Modeling: Mathematics of life and death: How disease models shape national shutdowns and other pandemic policies. (R 31 64-65) Risks of extrapolation (R 31 64) David Reed comment on models. (R 31 65).

Pandemic drone test flights are monitoring social distancing. (R 31 72) The Untold Story of the Birth of Social Distancing. (R 31 73) The illusion of certainty. (R 31 73) Schools Adopt Face Recognition in the Name of Fighting Covid. (R 32 36) Artificial intelligence model detects asymptomatic Covid-19 infections through cellphone-recorded coughs. (R 32 37).

8 Global Implications

Uncontaminated food supplies are dwindling, GMO is taking over - water, air, and ground contamination are burgeoning. Ecosystems are failing. Species extinction is rampant. All of these problems have effects on healthcare.

One-fifth of countries at risk of ecosystem collapse, analysis finds. (R 32-33) Global methane emissions soar to record high. (R 32 17) Why climate change is about to make your bad commute worse. (R 32 19) Greenland's ice sheet has melted to a point of no return, according to new study. (R 32 200 rebuttal R 32 24-25).

'Our world is in peril', United Nations Secretary General Warns General Assembly. (R 33 46) Long-term planning and optimization, includes PGN quoting Paul Krugman: "… if we can't save the Great Salt Lake, what chance do we have of saving the planet?" (R 33 28-29, 31) Logistics and the Supply Chain: To Understand the Medical Supply Shortage, It Helps to Know How the U.S. lost the lithium battery. (R 31 72) Risks of supply-chain threat sharing. (R 32 24).

The nuclear mistakes that could have ended civilization. (R 32 19-20) Nuclear waste and nuclear waste management at the Hanford site. (R 32 31) India's inadvertent missile launch underscores the risk of accidental nuclear warfare news and research. (R 33 14) The dangerous business of dismantling America's aging nuclear plants. (R 33 21) Fighting Around Zaporizhzhia Nuclear Power Plant Is Out of Control: Nuclear power plants were designed to defend against certain foreseeable risks, but not wars! (R 33 37).

Getting Back To Normal: Big Tech's Solution Depends On Public Trust. (R 31 68) *{Is it even possible for what was once 'normal' ??}* The world after coronavirus. (R 31 69-70) Death or Utopia in the Next Three Decades. (R 31 93).

9 Miscellaneous Other Risks

3+ Years Later and Millions of U.S. Patient X-Rays are Still Exposed to the Internet by Insecure PACS Servers. (R 33 23) Some hospitals still use pneumatic tubes – and they can be hacked. (R 32 81) A February 2024 report from the nonprofit organization Patient Rights Advocate found that only 35 percent of 2,000 US hospitals surveyed were in full compliance with the 2021 rule. (R 34 19) Hospital equipment. (R 32 83) Woman died trapped in burning 2009 Dodge Journey SUV after a vehicle malfunction-caused fire, and she could not unlock the doors. (R 33 62) WashDC Metrorail Safety Commission says Metrorail routinely skipped steps in restoring lethal electrical power to tracks in work zones. Putting workers at risk. (R 33 37) Oxygen starvation? stress?

Major psychologists' group warns of social media's potential harm to kids. (R 33 70) The risks of machine learning psychotherapy with voice interfaces. (R 33 87) It's time to ask patients to quit social media, especially regarding mental health. (R 33 34) Cyberprofessionals say industry urgently needs to confront mental-health crisis. (R 33 83) Algorithmic Tracking 'Damaging Mental Health' of UK Workers. (R 32 93) U.S. Gender Care Is Ignoring Science. (R 34 36 rebuttal R 34 37 counter-rebuttal R 34 38) Mental health, stress, and moral injury. (R 32 09) The problem with mental health bots. (R 33 48) Can AI help fill the therapist shortage? We Need to Change the System That Keeps Pilots from Seeking Mental Health Care. (R 33 55).

The major healthcare and cybersecurity risks in Right-to-Repair laws. (R 33 32) A New Jailbreak for John Deere Tractors Rides the Right-to-Repair Wave. (R 33 39) How a Lucrative Surgery Took Off Online and Disfigured Patients. (R 33 92) Dangerous prescription drug ads on TV. (R 33 82) Hackers are stealing encrypted data today so quantum computers can crack it in a decade. (R 32 92) Lab tests delayed by Twilight Zone births. (R 32 16) Trans man says confusion caused cervical screening delay. (R 32 90-91).

Risks of Self-Driving Cars: California Gov. Gavin Newsom vetoed a bill that would have required a human safety operator to be present any time a self-driving truck operated on public roads in the state. (R 33 87-88) Robot Cars Are Causing 911 False Alarms in San Francisco. (R 33 61) California halts operations of Cruise self-driving robotaxis. (R 33 92) How Smart Are the Robots Getting? (R 33 61,62) Autonomous Vehicles Are Driving Blind. (R 33 89-90) Pedestrian dies after Cruise cars block ambulance: alleged that would have survived had two Cruise cars and an unoccupied police car prevented the ambulance from leaving promptly. (R 33 83 also see reinterpretations R 33 84-86) Tesla is settling with the family of the Apple engineer who died in an Autopilot crash. (R 34 16).

10   Conclusions

As stated previously, an earlier version of this chapter was the first paper presented at the inaugural ACM HealthSec Workshop held October 14th 2024 in Salt Lake City UT USA.[4] It was intentionally selected by the workshop organizers as the first paper to be presented in order to set the tone for the entire workshop, and possibly to set the tone for years of annual HealthSec workshops to follow. This workshop paper did a wonderful job opening workshop discussion on the breadth of issues associated with cybersecurity in healthcare and the inaugural HealthSec workshop was an overwhelming success largely resulting from stimulating discussions this workshop paper initiated.

This collection of riskful items related to healthcare is quite long, and yet this chapter is only a sampling of the RISKS archives. Many the total archival risks cases are indirectly also relevant here. However, subsets that are considered here suggest some conclusions and recommendations of what needs to be changed, fixed, overseen, or controlled in the future:

- We need greater emphasis on developing manageable and easily used systems and subsystems that are significantly more trustworthy than what we have today.
- We need more emphasis on evidence-based research that identifies and removes flaws and/or demonstrates their absence.
- We need more sensible procedures with pervasive oversight and stringent enforcement where the risks are greatest.
- We need to systematically eschew false claims, unsupported beliefs, bogus conspiracy theories, and public-relations hype that suggests AI is the answer to all problems – and that technology is the solution to inherently nontechnological problems.

- We need to protest against simple-minded political and legislative measures that are iatrogenic (i.e., worse than the malady), unnecessarily costly, and in reality over-complicating or overly simplistic, in the sense of the Einstein Principle noted in the introduction.
- Last, but not least, any attempt to pursue holistically motivated healthcare must face a variety of non-technical issues – e.g., socio-economic, geo-political, religious, and even age-old customs maltreating women – that are contrary to the principles in which many of us believe, such as equality, liberty, and justice for all, especially as this relates to healthcare.

Acknowledgments. We would first like to thank all the HealthSec 2024 Workshop participants for stimulating discussion and especially for the youngest generation of scientists. Engineers, and healthcare professionals who are learning about the Internet RISKS Forum archive legacy for the first time in hopes you will continue this important work.

Nancy Leveson has a series of books on human safety, each in succession wrapping the readers' arms more closely to the enormous complications that must be dealt with. She is a close colleague of the first author, and her work is a hugely important resource for the technological aspects of safety. Her most recent books and research papers are enumerated on her website which speak for themselves. http://sunnyday.mit.edu/

A 1989 report by first author colleagues John M. Rushby and R. Alan Whitehurst was prescient: Formal verification of AI software. It considered using formal analysis of AI1q systems to increase their assurance. See Final report for NASA, SRI Computer Science Laboratory, February 1989: https://www.csl.sri.com/papers/csl-88-7/ In retrospect, that report has become extremely relevant today – in light of the enormous lack of assurance in today's AI feeding frenzy of low-assurance commercial AI systems (e.g., also see Bruce Schneier, AI and Trust, 2023. https://www.belfer center.org/publication/ai-and-trust. Fortunately, intelligent AI researchers have been getting that message more readily than commercial AI developers.

SRI Computer Science Lab has for several decades been exploring the application of formal mathematical logic to the biosciences. The first author firmly believes that their approach holds enormous progress for the linkages (e.g., integrating the immune and neurological systems) that are needed for a truly holistic approach to healthcare. Carolyn Talcott has been leading that effort with our Division President Patrick Lincoln cheering her on. Sylvan Pinsky is also contributing remotely as a still-active alumnus. In collaboration with biologists, this ongoing project develops evidence-based formal models of cellular response to external signals (drugs, stress, messages from other cells). Formal analysis tools support using these models for in-silico experiments, explaining and predicting side-effects of drugs, understanding host-pathogen interactions, among other things. The project has made available online a database of experimental findings curated from published works that provides supporting evidence for the models: http://www.datum.csl. sri.com There is also a growing literature of work by others in this direction as well.

For those readers who need more hope for the future, we would suggest visiting our CHERI website in Cambridge UK: https://www.cl.cam.ac.uk/research/security/ctsrd/cheri/ CHERI has the potential to be the most trustworthy hardware-software clean-slate general-purpose system architecture ever, and it is beginning to be recognized as a unique breakthrough. CHERI is a joint effort between SRI and the University of Cambridge, under development and evaluation since 2010. It has commercial manifestations (e.g., experimental CHERI-Arm-Morello boards, whose specifications have been formally proven to satisfy critical security properties), and open-sourced CHERI-RISC-V, and CHERI-FreeBSD with two real-time operating systems, plus recent support from Codasip. The White House has recently reported that CHERI is the only current system providing extensive memory safety. On the other hand, the devil is always in the details and even the most secure hardware does not imply the most secure software.

This contribution ends with a very personal note from the first author whose daughter Helen has a practice of Oriental Medicine, and is currently undergoing some intense detox programs attempting to remove several forever chemicals and other immune-system detractors left over from 30-plus years of chronic Lyme Disease leading to the conclusion that the missing links today are the holistic ones – for example, between the immune system and the nervous system, both of which are together impaired in Helen. For example, as a result of functional medicine, her glyphosate level was cut dramatically, as were her mercury, lead, palladium, malathion, Round-Up components, and lots more. The list of toxicities before the detox program was considerable. (The Palladium toxicities are still much too high.) However, her knowledge, discipline, and determination – and commitment to as full a recovery as possible – have been daunting, and are a great source of encouragement. Unfortunately, this treatment is well outside of standard-care practices. A relevant book Helen shared with me is by Sara Szal Gottfried, The Autoimmune Cure: https:// www.saragottfriedmd.com. This is a holistic book (her fifth) – heavily annotated, with an outstanding bibliography. It seems to be close to where integrative healthcare needs to go in the future, despite the economic arguments for not going outside of an AMA box that does not actually exist. The possibilities of everything related to healthcare still seem to be open-ended with respect to diagnosis, treatment, and the end-game – also open-ended relating to new risks from both new and old approaches. Many of them may be related to our immune systems and our overly toxic environments.

Holistically, the possibilities of everything related to healthcare still seem to be open-ended with respect to diagnosis, treatment, and the end-game -- also open-ended relating to new risks from both new and old approaches. Many of them may be related to our immune systems and our overly toxic environments. In retrospect, our holistic approach discovers that many of the pieces are interwoven. Thus, we come again to the observation noted in the introduction: there never was a box, and that trying to enforce it was a gigantic mistake that is hindering efforts to reform healthcare systems.

Disclosure of Interests.   The authors have no competing interests.

References

1. CBS: The truth of truthiness (2006). http://www.cbsnews.com/news/the-truth-of-truthiness/
2. Leveson, N.G.: The therac-25: 30 years later. IEEE Comput. **50**, 8–11 (2017). https://ieeexp lore.ieee.org/stamp/stamp.jsp?tp=&arnumber=8102762
3. Leveson, N.G., Turner, C.S.: An investigation of the therac-25 accidents. IEEE Comput. **26**(7), 18–41 (1993)
4. Neumann, P.G.: Position paper: computer-related healthcare risks. In: Proceedings of the ACM Workshop on Cybersecurity in Healthcare (HealthSec), Salt Lake City, UT, USA (2024). https://doi.org/10.1145/3689942.3694749
5. Neumann, P.G.: Toward total-system trustworthiness. Commun. ACM (CACM). **65**(6), 32–35 (2022). https://cacm.acm.org/opinion/toward-total-system-trustworthiness/
6. Neumann, P.G.: Computer Related Risks. ACM Press/Addison-Wesley (1995). https://www. csl.sri.com/users/neumann/neumann-book.html
7. Neumann, P.G.: (Moderator). The RISKS Digest - Forum on Risks to the Public in Computers and Related Systems. dual hosted http://www.risks.org, http://catless.ncl.ac.uk/Risks/

8. Robinson, A.: Did Einstein really say that? Nature (2018). https://www.nature.com/articles/d41586-018-05004-4
9. Rundle, J.: Ransomware Comes Back in Vogue for Cybercriminals. Wall Street Journal Pro (2023)
10. dos Santos, D., Luz, E.: New supply chain vulnerabilities impact medical and IoT devices. Forescout Blog (2022). https://www.forescout.com/blog/access-7-vulnerabilities-impact-supply-chain-component-in-medical-and-iot-device-models/

Cybersecurity Threats to U.S. Hospitals: Focus on Emergency Departments

Natalie Sullivan[1]([envelope]) [iD], Laura Tilley[1] [iD], and William Yurcik[2] [iD]

[1] George Washington University, Washington, DC 20037, USA
`nsullivan@mfa.gwu.edu`
[2] Centers for Medicare & Medicaid Services (CMS), Baltimore, MD 21244, USA

Abstract. Cybersecurity hazards pose a myriad of threats to the emergency department function. In this chapter we focus specifically on emergency departments in the U.S. acknowledging there is variation in this function worldwide. With high technological integration, historically poor cyber defense, and potentially catastrophic consequences of disruption - healthcare systems are particularly vulnerable to cyberattack. While discussions of cyberattacks on healthcare systems often focuses on privacy breaches involving the disclosure of personally identifiable information (PII) and protected health information (PHI) which can be resolved with civil litigation, instead we focus exclusively on the disruptive impacts of cyberattacks on hospital emergency departments which extend more importantly to patient continuity-of-care and patient mortality.

This chapter is an updated summary with feedback from a paper originally presented at the ACM CCS Cybersecurity in Healthcare (HealthSec) Workshop held in Salt Lake City Utah USA October 2024 [47]. We outline the broad range of potential impacts that cyberattacks have on the delivery of emergency medicine. We discuss downstream consequences of clinical care challenges, infrastructure vulnerabilities, and system-wide ramifications of impaired hospital IT infrastructure as well as potential solutions. We leverage the available literature from a clinical and emergency management lens to highlight the potential consequences of cyberattacks and offer alternative approaches to mitigate and respond to cyberattack disruptions.

Keywords: hospital emergency management · hospital cyberattacks · cybersecurity in healthcare · hospital ransomware attacks

1 Introduction

A surge of cyberattacks targeting healthcare organizations in recent years have illustrated the catastrophic impact of cybersecurity incidents on the healthcare sector [3, 5, 16]. Healthcare facilities are particularly vulnerable given the technological connectivity

---

N. Sullivan and L. Tilley—Disclaimer: The views presented herein do not represent the views of George Washington University or George Washington University Hospital.
W. Yurcik—Disclaimer: The views presented herein do not represent the views of the Federal Government.

W. Yurcik (Ed.): HealthSec 2024, CCIS 2716, pp. 19–32, 2026.
https://doi.org/10.1007/978-3-032-13800-2_2

of clinical care systems, the financial incentives for ransomware, vulnerability of patient information, outdated systems and high-stakes clinical consequences [24, 30, 36]. Ransomware attacks on United States healthcare organizations cost an estimated 14.7 billion dollars from January to October of 2023 [43]. The HHS Office of Civil Rights reported that in 2023 alone, cyberattacks on healthcare affected over 134 million individual patient records [19]. Emergency Departments (EDs) represent a particularly vulnerable subset due to the time-sensitive and high-pressure environment where delayed interventions may increase mortality risk and cause system-wide instability [10].

When considering the impact of cyberthreats on healthcare systems, it is important to take a comprehensive view that recognizes impacts beyond privacy data exposures, financial losses, and reputational damage, each of which may be made whole with civil litigation. The clinical implications of cyberattacks on patient care are far more serious including direct threats to patient safety and even loss of life.

In February of 2024, a Joint Cybersecurity Advisory identified "Volt Typhoon"[1] and other foreign state-sponsored actors had infiltrated critical infrastructure including the U.S. water supply system [40]. Likewise the electrical grid continues to face increasingly frequent and sophisticated cyberattacks [17]. Additionally, supply chain and transportation systems remain significant targets within critical infrastructure. During such compromises, EDs play a crucial role in community resilience but are also highly susceptible to internal vulnerabilities [28, 43]. EDs depend on interoperable communications, uninterrupted water access, stable electricity, usable transportation systems, and resilient supply chains, all of which are potentially at risk from cyberattacks.

Previous research has explored how cyberattacks intersect with hospital emergency management. Multiple surveys and analysis of U.S. hospital practices find that many institutions are unprepared for cyber threats [23, 24, 30, 38, 44, 46–48, 52]. For instance one study examined the cybersecurity risks in Canadian Emergency Departments and uncovered major deficiencies in training, awareness, and secure system design, with numerous respondents reporting insufficient preparation and unsafe practices [46]. Using simulation modeling and expert interviews Jalali *et al.* recommended that hospitals streamline endpoint systems, foster alignment among internal teams and expand beyond regulatory compliance [21]. They also urged for resource inequity reduction by investment in robust protection for healthcare IT systems [21]. *Incorporating cybersecurity protections into emergency management is critical for building a resilient healthcare system.*

---

[1] "Volt Typhoon" is the People's Republic of China's state-sponsored cyberattack unit focused on embedding undetected malware and access mechanisms within U.S. critical infrastructure to be used later to cause disruption, speculated to be a time coordinated with a future attack on Taiwan. This threat is not theoretical as CISA has found and remediated previous undetected Chinese intrusions in critical infrastructure across multiple sectors.

2 Cyber Threats Affecting Emergency Departments

2.1 Clinical Workflows

Upon entering a hospital emergency department, patient care is deeply integrated and dependent upon interconnected IT systems. Vital signs are measured and recorded electronically, triage concerns are documented, and orders for labs and imaging are processed through Internet-connected devices. Radiology interpretations and lab results are shared digitally and verified using automated systems. Providers utilize the Internet to reference evidence. Internet of Medical Things (IomT) device interoperability allow for seamless integration across providers, care settings, and stages of patient care. The IoMT support the integration of medical devices, electronic records, equipment and even autotherapies across networks enabling connected healthcare delivery [12]. *However, with clinical workflow dependency on IT systems, the disruption of IT systems due to cyberattacks has dangerous negative impacts on patient care.*

To illustrate one example in more detail, while Electronic Medical Record (EMR) adoption has advanced the quality of patient care by allowing for the sharing of patient health documentation, on the other hand EMR disruptions, and/or complete EMR outages over long periods of time, hinder timely access to patient information not stored elsewhere - leading to delayed or suboptimal care, increased risk of errors, and compromised continuity of care – or even lack of care [22]. EMR disruptions prevent access to vital patient information like medical history, medications, lab results, and diagnostic reports. In some cases, EMR disruptions create fragmented records by failing to update a patient's information leading to diagnostic errors or errors with drug interaction. EMR disruption will delay treatment decisions, medication administration, diagnostic reporting, and potentially lead to worsened medical outcomes. Without readily available EMR data, medical staff will need to resort to manual documentation (paper and/or whiteboard) and/or rely on memory, increasing the risk of errors in medication administration, diagnosis, or treatment planning. EMR disruptions make it difficult/impossible to track patient progress and share information across different care settings and between providers, impacting the overall continuity of care. Lastly, EMR disruptions create workload increases for medical staff, negatively impacting job satisfaction, and contribute to burnout. When an EMR outage occurs, medical staff are forced to switch to manual processes which are time-consuming and create additional workload. Medical staff experience frustration with EMR system malfunctions with the added cognitive load of needing to unexpectedly create and navigate workarounds for their patients.

For clinical workflow resilience, EMR disruptions can be mitigated with reliable backup systems and regular contingency plan training. Backup EMR systems must be tested regularly, segmented from other IT systems, and ideally incorporate offsite storage. EMR downtime training should be a comprehensive process that incorporates initial software training, easy-to-access documentation, and test drills to ensure staff are prepared for outages. Scheduled periodic drills and tabletop simulations are needed to practice EMR downtime procedures and assess compliance with organizational contingency plan policies. A log should document drills and simulations recording EMR downtimes versus system recovery times. During downtime it is essential for medical staff to focus attention on maintaining patient safety and prioritizing essential continuity-of-care. Clear communication between patients, medical staff, and providers will ensure everyone is aware of the situation such that clinical workflows can be adjusted accordingly. Vital information can be obtained directly from the patient. Of course communications may not be possible with patients unable to communicate and/or interoperability with remote providers may not be possible during IT system outages.

2.2 Clinical Outcomes

Disruptions anywhere along the care pathway can significantly affect clinical outcomes. Specifically, delays caused by cyberattacks prevent timely treatment, resulting in worsening individual clinical outcomes. The Ponemon Institute found a 20% rise in mortality in hospitals affected by cyberattack [38]. As previously discussed, loss of EMR access due to cyberattacks can contribute to medication errors, hinder decision-making due to missing history, and disable medical devices [9, 35, 49, 53].

Laboratory testing, integral to 70% of hospital diagnoses, are particularly vulnerable to IT system disruptions from cyberattacks [11]. Cyberattacks can delay lab results by 62%, prolonging diagnosis and patient stays [11]. Standard lab processes rely on automated labeling, pneumatic transport, mechanical analysis and electronic result delivery – all dependent on underlying IT systems. Similarly, radiology departments have reported 25–50% increases in workload during hospital IT system downtimes [31].

While cyberattack disruptions to IT systems introduce time delay, evidence-based emergency medicine guidelines delineate specific time windows associated with improved outcomes in critical illnesses and events. For conditions such as stroke, traumatic injury, myocardial infarction and sepsis [4, 25, 29, 34] evidence-based protocols require rapid intervention. To assess performance and ensure timely care toward positive outcomes, emergency departments rely on time-sensitive metrics such as:[2]

1. Admit-Decision-to-Departure-Time*
2. Length-of-Stay
3. Median Time-from-Arrival-to-Departure*
4. Percentage-of-Patients-Left-Without-Being-Seen
5. Provider Satisfaction
6. Staff-Safety
7. Throughput/Patient Flow (patients per unit time)

At the most basic level, cyberattacks on healthcare IT systems introduce time delay as measured continuously in EDs, leading to increased mortality rates. Specific direct examples include ambulance diversion from hospitals under cyberattack to more distant hospitals and delay/interruption with life support medical devices such as ventilators and IV pumps.

2.3 Multi-facility Clinical Care

EDs function as interconnected microsystems, within either a healthcare/hospital system or geographic regional area or both, where strain due to cybersecurity attack on one

---

[2] The starred metrics were developed by the Centers for Medicare & Medicaid Services.(CMS) and adopted by the Joint Commission for accreditation purposes.

ED can lead to temporary ED closure accompanied by incoming new patient diversions to other EDs which quickly impacts all EDs within the microsystem. Similarly, home care and subacute services are closely linked to emergency medicine. While telehealth platforms and home-based devices enable patients to receive care in an alternate environment, disruptions to these systems often shift the burden back to EDs, which serve as a "safety net" [18].

EDs are considered the "safety net" for the U.S. healthcare system because (1) they care for the uninsured, underinsured, and/or those without access to primary care and (2) they operate 24x7x365 providing around-the-clock emergency care and serve as a gateway triage point for entry into continuity-of-care. The Emergency Medical Treatment and Labor Act (EMTALA)[3] mandates that hospitals with EDs must provide a medical screening examination to anyone who enters the ED requesting treatment, regardless of their insurance status or ability to pay. If a person has an emergency medical condition, the ED must provide stabilizing treatment.

As mentioned previously, when cyberattacks disable ED services, hospitals are unable to admit new patients and resort to ambulance diversion, directing Emergency Medical Services (EMS) to reroute incoming patients elsewhere. While necessary, ambulance diversion creates surge capacity overloads at geographically nearby hospitals further challenging emergency care delivery [32, 37]. Studies show ambulance diversion results in longer transport times, and delays to critical interventions such as cardiac catheterization for myocardial infarction [37]. With U. S. hospitals routinely operating near capacity, delays in patient care intensify as wait times lengthen and redistribution via ambulance diversion is less viable [2, 28, 42]. These delays compromise timely care for both incoming and current patients, leading to increased mortality.

3 Communication Disruption

Effective hospital communications is the fundamental component underlying quality healthcare. Effective hospital communication aligns care teams – physicians, nurses, technicians, administrators, patients – to ensure coordinated, safe, and consistent care. Communications facilitate accurate diagnosis and treatment, prevention of medical errors and adverse events, and better patient engagement and patient outcomes. Poor hospital communications contribute to medication errors, incorrect or missed diagnoses, delayed and improper transition of care, and increased mortality.

The ED is a fast-paced environment where quick decisions need to be made. Effective communications ensure that relevant information is shared quickly, minimizing delays in care. EDs are complex environments where multiple providers work together such that effective communication promotes teamwork coordinating efforts and ensuring a cohesive patient-care approach. Open communication channels allow for knowledge sharing within the ED leading to better patient outcomes. Specifically, the ED team relies on communication systems to direct medical care, coordinate patient movement, and connect with external stakeholders. Cyberattacks that disrupt hospital communications (e.g. digital/IP phone services and encrypted text messaging) force ED staff to take

---

[3] https://www.cms.gov/medicare/regulations-guidance/legislation/emergency-medical-treatm ent-labor-act

valuable time to unexpectedly pivot to rely on manual workarounds including in-person runners and personal unsecured cell phones [8]. Since an ED is the most time-sensitive department within any hospital, while an ED may be able to operate during or recover after a cyberattack, any time delay from cyberattack disruption will lead to increased mortality.

It is important to also note here that ED communications occur even before the patient physically enters the ED. Clear and accurate Emergency Medical Services (EMS) communications ensure first responders are aware of the situation and working together. Dispatchers of 911 systems relay information to appropriate first responders including ambulances for ED transport. Ambulances use mobile radios to communicate with the ED and use data telemetry systems to transmit patient data (e.g. vital signs, EKG, etc.) from the scene or from within the moving ambulance to the ED. Physicians or nurses provide medical advice to first responders at the scene and enroute, and when a patient arrives at the ED information about their condition, treatment, and other relevant details are transferred from the ambulance to the ED. Effective communications lead to faster diagnosis and treatment, and thus improved patient outcomes. Clear communication reduces the risk of misunderstandings that could lead to medical errors. Disruption of these pre-ED communications may prevent patients, first responders, and/or referring providers from other hospitals from communicating with the ED. Any pre-ED communication disruption and/or time delay caused by cyberattacks will lead to increased mortality.

4   Utility Compromise

On September 16, 2016, CMS published a rule on emergency preparedness for health providers known as the Emergency Preparedness Rule or CMS Rule 17.[4] The rule serves to establish national consistent emergency preparedness requirements for the 17 different provider types participating in Medicare and Medicaid.[5] This CMS Preparedness Rule specifies that all provider types must have a comprehensive plan that contains: an Emergency Plan, Emergency Preparedness Policies and Procedures, a Communication Plan, and an Emergency Preparedness Training and Testing Program. Specific provider types have appropriate additional requirements. For purposes of this chapter, we discuss three utility infrastructure services hospitals are dependent upon and necessary for ED operations – water, electric power, and transportation.

---

[4] https://www.cms.gov/medicare/health-safety-standards/quality-safety-oversight-emergency-preparedness/emergency-preparedness-rule

[5] The specific provider types are: (1) hospitals, (2) religious nonmedical health care institutions, (3) ambulatory surgical centers, (4) hospices, (5) psychiatric residential treatment programs, (6) all-inclusive care for the elderly, (7) transplant centers, (8) long-term care facilities, (9) immediate care facilities for individuals with intellectual disabilities, (10) home health agencies, (11) comprehensive outpatient rehabilitation facilities, (12) critical access hospitals, (13) clinics, rehabilitation agencies, and public health agencies as providers of outpatient physical therapy and speech-language pathology services, (14) community mental health centers, (15) organ procurement organizations, (16) rural health clinics and Federally-qualified health centers, and (17) end-stage renal disease facilities.

4.1 Water Supply

The U.S. Environmental Protection Agency (EPA) estimates that 70% of the U.S. water supply is vulnerable to cyberattacks [50]. That presents a real threat since ensuring a safe and reliable water supply is crucial for all hospital patient care and especially preventing hospital-acquired infections, nowhere more important than in the busy ED – from sterilization of medical equipment, medical staff basic hygiene hand-washing etc., plumbing for wastewater/toilet etc., safe drinking water for hydration and food services, bathing and cleaning of patients and their rooms, the heating ventilation and air conditioning (HVAC) function, and fire suppression sprinkler systems [13, 41, 51].

In addition, dialysis patients with end stage renal disease need safe water for cleaning and filtering their blood with treatments depending on individual patient needs varying from daily to three sessions a week, with each treatment varying between 3–8 h each session. Without dialysis, a person with kidney failure will only survive on average only about seven days.[6]

The HVAC function is critically important for temperature, air quality and humidity control throughout the entire hospital - again nowhere more important than in the busy ED. HVAC systems typically include air conditioning units, heat pumps, air handlers, furnaces, air cleaners, and humidifiers – each of which is typically controlled by IT system(s) vulnerable to cyberattack. Hospitals are required to adhere to specific standards for humidity and temperature control in different parts of the hospital in order to minimize the spread of airborne infections, ensure the efficacy and shelf life of medications[7], maintain the operational durability of medical devices and equipment[8], and to maintain patient health and comfort. Maintaining a specific relative humidity range (typically 30–60%) helps prevent droplets from becoming too small and long-lived in the air, making them more easily removed by standard cleaning methods. Low humidity can irritate patient respiratory passages, and high humidity can exacerbate respiratory conditions. Specific parts of a hospital (relevant and important to the ED function) are designated as "clean rooms" where medical procedures are performed requiring tightly controlled temperature and humidity to maintain sterility. Despite HVAC and sanitization best efforts, the hospital environment is still a development environment for microorganisms and germs such that hospital infections continue to kill patients and medical staff. By carefully designing and maintaining HVAC systems, hospitals can significantly reduce the risk of sepsis and other hospital-acquired infections.

---

[6] The buildup of toxins in the blood, known as uremia, will lead to various complications and ultimately death. The exact duration varies based on individual factors such as the amount of remaining kidney function, severity of symptoms, and overall health. The more kidney function a person has, the longer they may survive without dialysis. While supportive care can extend life, it does not cure the underlying kidney failure.

[7] Excessive humidity can degrade some medications rendering them ineffective or even toxic according towww.sensoscientific.com

[8] Low humidity can increase the risk of electrostatic charge which can damage or disrupt electromedical equipment and potentially pose a fire hazard according to www.ortoday.com. Some electrosurgical equipment, particularly older models, may malfunction at low humidity levels.

Despite its importance, there is no federal mandate for hospitals to maintain emergency water reserves. Organizations such as the U.S. Administration for Strategic Preparedness and Response (ASPR) have generated guidance recommending backup water systems to support 90% census and staff for 4 days [1]. Unfortunately low-resourced hospitals may have much smaller limited reserves.

When water failures extend beyond a single hospital to a geographical region, the health impacts will cascade across regional communities creating urgent needs for ED services. During water supply crises, the incidence of severe dehydration and water-borne illness increases requiring more patients to seek emergency medical care at EDs [33]. Lack of waste water sewage disposal further augments risk of disease. Unlike other types of utility failure, patients will not be able to receive care in the affected region since EDs within the affected region will not have the capability to function as a safety net for the community-at-large.

4.2 Electrical Power

Electrical power is foundational to ED operations, powering everything from lighting, HVAC, patient monitors, medical devices, refrigeration units, and security infrastructure [6, 20]. While basic equipment like IV pumps and/or patient monitors can be substituted in the short term, other life support devices have no substitute such as ventilators, balloon pumps, and dialysis machines which cannot function without power. Electric pumps that control water systems can also trigger secondary disruptions. Electronic badge access, surveillance cameras, and emergency alarms help protect staff and patients in a dangerous environment [39].

Emergency uninterruptible power supplies (UPS) systems may provide brief continuous electric power when an outage is detected. Some life support medical systems may have internal batteries in addition to UPS coverage. For longer outage periods, backup generators provide most hospital critical equipment through designated outlets (hospital standard "red plugs"). However, the duration of backup generator support is limited by available fuel and there are no uniform standards governing generator capacity – leading to significant variability in power outage preparedness across hospitals.

A wider electrical grid power failure affecting a geographic region would place additional strain on EDs. Hospitals could see an influx of patients seeking shelter, power, or safety. Long-term care facilities may need to transfer patients whose electrically powered treatments they cannot provide. Regional power outages are also typically accompanied by ED surges in carbon monoxide poisoning, temperature-related illness, gastrointestinal infections, and exacerbations of chronic conditions [7]. As outpatient centers close due to power loss, EDs may be forced to absorb patients requiring care previously managed in the outpatient setting.

For resilience, hospitals may design redundant electric utility connections to more than one utility substation. Recently hospitals have started to create and utilize their own microgrid electric power. Microgrids are localized electrical grids, typically consisting of renewable energy sources (e.g. solar panels) that can operate independently of the regional power grid (island mode), or in synchronization with the regional power grid (grid-connected mode). With the use of microgrids, hospitals use the electric utility grid as a secondary source and in the event of a utility outage, the hospital microgrid can disconnect from the utility grid and continue to power the hospital independently.

4.3 Transportation

Hospitals are heavily dependent upon transportation for a variety of reasons: patient transport, the movement of medical personnel and supplies, and access to healthcare for those with transportation barriers. Patients and healthcare workers depend on public transportation, personal vehicles, ride-sharing, and ambulances to access the ED. EMS agencies distribute patients across a local healthcare system and do not always simply drive to the nearest hospital. Transportation disruptions can result in delayed or missed treatments and may prevent critical interfacility transfers, particularly from smaller hospitals to specialized centers. These breakdowns can concentrate patient volumes at certain facilities, leading to surge overcrowding and increased strain on EDs. Transportation disruptions can also prevent medical staff from reporting for hospital duty.

Transportation infrastructure is vulnerable to cyber threats [25]. Transportation systems are vulnerable to cyberattacks due to their increasing reliance on IT systems and interconnected systems making them attractive targets for attackers. Modern transportation systems rely heavily on IT systems for various functions including: navigation, communication, and automation such that if any of these systems were disrupted would slow transportation operations and pose security risks. For resilience, some hospitals have created direct transportation services such as volunteer driver programs, partnerships with ride-sharing organizations, shuttle services, and helicopter ambulances. For these reasons and more, hospitals advocate for long-term regional transportation plans.

In summary, transportation is a fundamental pillar of hospital operations, enabling efficient healthcare workflows and facilitating patient access to care and medical staffing of ED functions. Transportation disruptions due to cyberattack result in missed or delayed patient appointments, disrupted continuity of care, reduced ED capability due to staffing challenges, and ultimately increased mortality rates.

5 Supply Chain Cybersecurity Risk

Supply chain cybersecurity risks leverage the trust between an organization and its vendors/suppliers with attacks stemming from exploitable cybersecurity vulnerabilities within a company's network and/or networks of third-party vendors. Cyber attackers can inject malicious code into software, hardware, or services allowing attackers to infect and disrupt all associated services in a supply chain.

A weak security posture in any part of a supply chain can expose the entire supply chain to cyberattacks. Identifying and addressing choke points or weakest links is crucial for ensuring a robust and resilient supply chain. Failure of a choke point can disrupt the entire supply chain leading to delays, shortages, or even completely halt services. Weakest link cybersecurity practices by suppliers create entry points for cyber attackers to infiltrate an entire supply chain. Geopolitical events can also disrupt supply chains and create cybersecurity vulnerabilities that attackers can exploit. Failure to adequately assess and manage supply chain risks associated with third-party vendors leave healthcare organizations vulnerable.

An ED supply chain involves the processes of sourcing, procuring, storing, distributing and managing medical supplies and equipment needed for immediate patient care. This includes a wide range of items, from medications and diagnostic tools to personal protective equipment and cleaning supplies. Supply chain management is crucial for ensuring the ED has the necessary resources to provide prompt and effective care to patients, especially during surge peak demand and/or unexpected emergencies.

Mitigating supply chain cybersecurity risks for EDs involves developing a third-party risk management program to identify, assess, and monitor risks associated with third-party services provided to the ED. This involves working with suppliers to share information about cybersecurity threats, performing security audits and penetration testing, and ensuring all ED software and hardware is up-to-date with the latest security patches.

6 Discussion and Conclusions

As cybersecurity expert Dr. Daniel Geer Jr. noted: *"Because the wellspring of risk is dependence, aggregate risk is a monotonically increasing function of aggregate dependence."*[14] Modern hospital systems rely on interconnected, technology-driven systems to deliver high-quality care. Yet this very dependence creates a broad attack surface in which the failure of a single component can trigger cascading operational breakdowns.

The healthcare sector's reliance on technology increases the likelihood of direct patient harm when a successful cyberattack occurs disabling IT systems -- manifesting itself in barriers to access, treatment delays, misdiagnosis, medical errors, disruption of continuity-of-care [46].

Hospital emergency managers and IT experts must collaborate to generate resilience and preparedness that recognizes the potential human costs and prioritizes clinical concerns. All hospital hazard vulnerability analyses (HVA) should highly rank cybersecurity given the potential severity of the hazard as well as its increasing probability. Hospital emergency managers may integrate cybersecurity threats into their HVA by including the Information Technology lead (or cybersecurity subject matter expert) in the HVA development team. They should also ensure they have functioning backup systems in place to replace disrupted frontline IT systems as well as a hierarchical process for prioritizing IT systems most essential to patient care. This should drive Emergency Operations Plans (EOPs) that include detailed procedures for managing downtime due to cyberattacks with clear escalation and communication protocols, contingency plans for utility failures, technology triage, and emergency resource allocation. EOPs should delineate multiple interoperable lines of communication and providers discouraged from using unsecured methods to communicate patient data. Alternative communication tools include radios, runner teams, and printed directories.

On a department-level, EDs should develop department-specific procedures including comprehensive and easy-to-use paper forms for documentation, orders and medication administration. As technology advances, they should consider parallel hot-standby IT backup systems. The authors recommend utilizing downtime toolkits that include specific documentation for each type of provider as well as quick real-time instructions for their appropriate use. Materials must not only be generated but also tested and retested periodically. Frequent table-top simulation drills allow for personnel to familiarize themselves with alternative workflows and offer suggestions for improvement. Real-time reference guides and badge buddies with critical phone numbers, login instructions, and downtime tips can also be utilized. Identification of non-clinical personnel who can serve as runners to physically transport documentation and results can be life-saving in a communication flow absent of IT systems. These non-clinical personnel do not need to be medically trained providers, but rather, anyone able to physically move order forms and results to different areas of the hospital, such as the laboratory and radiology suites.

Resilience to utility failure is perhaps one of the most difficult objectives to achieve. Ideally hospitals should maintain a supply of potable water, the volume of which would vary greatly depending on the size of the facility. This could include stockpiling bottled water or the use of reservoir systems. They should also maintain a functional generator with excess fuel. Hospitals must additionally conserve generator use by prioritizing power for vital medical devices and necessary lighting. Mitigation of utility failures also includes pre-disaster collaboration with utility providers, contracts with resupply vendors, and mutual aid agreements with surrounding hospital systems.

By recognizing the interconnectedness of hospital systems and proactively planning for cascading failures, healthcare leaders can move beyond reactive crisis management to focus on healthcare resilience. This requires multidisciplinary collaboration, consistent training/simulation, and a cultural shift that views cybersecurity as a core component of emergency preparedness. As the frequency and sophistication of cyberattacks increase, so must the collective commitment to anticipating and preventing their impact on patient care.

Acknowledgments. We deeply appreciate all ACM HealthSec 2024 Workshop peer reviewers whose insightful feedback we have integrated resulting in great enhancement to this paper.

References

1. Administration for Strategic Preparedness and Response (ASPR): Hospital Water Storage Tanks (Redacted Response). ASPR TRACIE technical assistance request (2018). https://files.asprtracie.hhs.gov/documents/aspr-tracie-ta---water-storage-tanks---3-12-18---redacted-final.pdf
2. American College of Emergency Physicians: emergency department boarding and crowding (2024). https://www.acep.org/administration/crowding--boarding
3. American Medical Association (AMA): Change healthcare cyberattack (2024). https://www.ama-assn.org/practice-management/sustainability/change-healthcare-cyberattack
4. ATLS Subcommittee; American College of Surgeons' Committee on Trauma; International ATLS Working Group: J. Trauma Acute Care Surg. **74**(5), 1363–1366 (2013). https://doi.org/10.1097/TA.0b013e31828b82f5.
5. Barry, E., Perlroth, N.: Patients of a vermont hospital are left 'in the dark' after a cyberattack. New York times (2020). https://www.nytimes.com/2020/11/26/us/hospital-cyber-attack.html

6. Brehovská, L., Nešporová, V., Řehák, D.: Approach to assessing the preparedness of hospitals to power outages. Transactions of the VŠB (Technical University of Ostrava) – Technical Univ. Ostrava Saf. Eng. Ser. **12**(1) 30–40 (2017). https://tses.vsb.cz/Home/tses_article2440350.pdf?aid=244

7. Casey, J.A., Fukurai, M., Hernández, D., Balsari, S., Kiang, M.V.: Power outages and community health: a narrative review. Curr. Environ. Health Rep. **7**, 371–383 (2020). https://link.springer.com/article/10.1007/s40572-020-00295-0

8. Coffey, P.S., Postal, S.N., Houston, S.M., McKeeby, J.W.: Lessons learned from an electronic health record downtime. Perspectives in Health Information Management (2016)

9. Coventry, L., Branley, D.: Cybersecurity in healthcare: a narrative review of trends. Threats ways forward. Maturitas **113**, 48–52 (2018). https://doi.org/10.1016/j.maturitas.2018.04.008

10. Dameff, C., Farah, J., Killeen, J., Chan, T.: Cyber disaster medicine: a new frontier for emergency medicine. Ann. Emerg. Med. **75**(5), 642–647 (2020)

11. De Cauwer, H.G., Somville, F.: Health care organizations: soft target during COVID-19 pandemic. Prehospital Disaster Med. **36**(3), 344–347 (2021)

12. Dimitrov, D.V.: Medical internet of things and big data in healthcare. healthcare informatics research. Korean Soc. Med. Inf. **22**(3), 156–163 (2016). https://doi.org/10.4258/hir.2016.22.3.156

13. Garg, A.: HVAC (Air Conditioning) works of the hospital building. chapter In: Monitoring Tools for Setting up the Hospital Project. Pp. 211–224. Springer Nature, Singapore (2023). https://doi.org/10.1007/978-981-99-6203-7_8

14. Geer Jr., D.E.: A. Rubicon: A Hoover Institution Essay. Aegis Series Paper No. 1801 (2018). https://www.hoover.org/sites/default/files/research/docs/geer_webreadypdfupdated2.pdf

15. Gentili, G.B., Dori, F., Iadanza, E.: Dual-frequency active RFID solution for tracking patients in a children's hospital. design method, test procedure, risk analysis, and technical solution. Proc. IEEE **98**(9), 1656–1662 (2010). https://ieeexplore.ieee.org/document/5508336

16. Ghafur, S., Kristensen, S., Honeyford, K., Martin, G., Darzi, A., Aylin, P.: A retrospective impact analysis of the WannaCry cyberattack on the NHS. NPJ Digit. Med. **2**(9) (2019). https://doi.org/10.1038/s41746-019-0161-6

17. Glenn, C., Sterbentz, D., Wright, A.: Cyber Threat and vulnerability analysis of the U.S. electric sector. Technical Report: U.S. Department of Energy Office of Scientific and Technical Information (2016). https://doi.org/10.2172/1337873

18. Groom, L.L., McCarthy, M.M., Stimpfel, A.W., Brody, A.A.: Telemedicine and telehealth in nursing homes: an integrative review. J. Post-Acute Long-Term Care Med. Assoc. (JAMDA) **22**, 1784–1801 (2021). https://pmc.ncbi.nlm.nih.gov/articles/PMC9626369/pdf/main.pdf

19. HHS Office of Civil Rights: Change healthcare cybersecurity incident frequently asked questions (2024). https://www.hhs.gov/hipaa/for-professionals/special-topics/change-healthcare-cybersecurity-incident-frequently-asked-questions/index.html . Accessed 14 Mar 2025

20. Ikeuchi, J.: Methods for hospital to promote disaster preparedness against loss of power. Prehospital Disaster Med. **38**(S1), s166–s167 (2023)

21. Jalali, M.S., Kaiser, J.P.: Cybersecurity in hospitals: a systematic organizational perspective. J. Med. Internet Res. **28**, 20(5) (2018). https://www.jmir.org/2018/5/e10059/

22. Kilbridge, P.: Computer crash - lessons from a system failure. New England J. Med. **348**(10), 881–882 (2003). https://www.nejm.org/doi/full/10.1056/NEJMp030010

23. Kollek, D., Barrera, D., Stobert, E., Homier, V.: The EDIT survey: identifying emergency department information technology knowledge and training gaps. Disaster Med. Public Health Preparedness **16**(3), 1007–1012 (2022). https://doi.org/10.1017/dmp.2020.474

24. Kruse, C.S., Frederick, B., Jacobson, T., Monticone, D.K.: Cybersecurity in healthcare: a systematic review of modern threats and trends. Technol. Health Care: Official J. Eur. Soc. Eng. Med. **25**(1), 1–10 (2017). https://doi.org/10.3233/THC-161263

25. Lawton, J.S., et al.: ACC/AHA/SCAI guideline for coronary artery revascularization: a report of the American college of cardiology/American heart association joint committee on clinical practice guidelines. Circulation **145**(3) (2021). https://doi.org/10.1161/CIR.0000000000001038

26. Lehto, M.: Cyber-attacks against critical infrastructure. In: Lehto, M., Neittaanmäki, P. (eds.) cyber security: critical infrastructure protection, pp. 3–42, Springer International Publishing (2022). https://doi.org/10.1007/978-3-030-91293-2_1

27. Li, Y.: Hospital as a critical infrastructure in the community disaster response system. Masters Thesis. Rochester Institute of Technology (2012). https://repository.rit.edu/theses/705/

28. Lindner, G., Woitok, B.K.: Emergency department overcrowding: analysis and strategies to manage an international phenomenon. Wien Klin Wochenschr. **133**(5–6), 229–233 (2021). https://doi.org/10.1007/s00508-019-01596-7

29. Liu, V.X., et al.: The timing of early antibiotics and hospital mortality in sepsis. Am. J. Respiratory Crit. Med. **196**(7), 856–863 (2017). https://www.atsjournals.org/doi/10.1164/rccm.201609-1848OC

30. Martin, G., Martin, P., Hankin, C., Darzi, A., Kinross J.: Cybersecurity and healthcare: how safe are we? BMJ (358) (2017). https://www.bmj.com/content/358/bmj.j3179

31. McBiles, M. Chacko, A.K.: Coping with PACS downtime in digital radiology. J. Digit. Imaging. **13**(3), 136–142 (2000)

32. McConnell, K.J., Richards, C.F., Daya, M., Weathers, C.C., Lowe, R.A.: Ambulance Diversion and lost hospital revenues. Ann. Emer. Med. **48**, 702–710 (2006). <https://pubmed.ncbi.nlm.nih.gov/17112933/>

33. Moreira, N.A., Bondelind, M.: Safe drinking water and waterborne outbreaks. J. Water Health **15**(1), 83–96 (2017). https://doi.org/10.2166/wh.2016.103

34. The national institute of neurological disorders and stroke rt-PA stroke study group. Tissue plasminogen activator for acute ischemic stroke. New England J. Med. **333**(24), 1581–1588 (1995). https://www.nejm.org/doi/pdf/10.1056/NEJM199512143332401

35. Naamneh, R., Bodas, M.: The effect of electronic medical records on medication errors, workload, and medical information availability among qualified nurses in Israel - A cross sectional study. BMC Nursing **23**, 270 (2024). https://doi.org/10.1186/s12912-024-01936-7

36. Perakslis, E.D.: Cybersecurity in health care. New England J. Med. **371**(5), 395–397 (2014). https://www.nejm.org/doi/10.1056/NEJMp1404358

37. Pham, J.C., Patel, R., Millin, M.G., Kirsch, T.D., Chanmugam, A.: The effects of ambulance diversion: a comprehensive review. Acad. Emer. Med. Official J. Soc. Acad. Emerg. Med. **13**, 1220–1227 (2006). https://doi.org/10.1197/j.aem.2006.05.024

38. Ponemon Institute: Cyber insecurity in healthcare: the cost and impact on patient safety and care (2023). https://www.proofpoint.com/sites/default/files/threat-reports/pfpt-us-tr-cyber-insecurity-healthcare-ponemon-report.pdf

39. Pourshaikhian, M., Gorji, H.A., Aryankhesal, A., Khorasani-Zavareh, D., Barati, A.: A systematic literature review: workplace violence against emergency medical services personnel. Arch. Trauma Res. **5**(1), e28734 (2016). https://pmc.ncbi.nlm.nih.gov/articles/PMC4860284/pdf/atr-05-01-28734.pdf

40. Regan, M.S., Sullivan, J.: White house letter to U.S (2024). Governors.https://www.epa.gov/system/files/documents/2024-03/epa-apnsa-letter-to-governors_03182024.pdf

41. Sänger, N., Heinzel, C., Sandholz, S.: Advancing resilience of critical health infrastructures to cascading impacts of water supply outages—insights from a systematic literature review. Infrastructures **6**(12) 177 (2021). https://doi.org/10.3390/infrastructures6120177

42. Sartini, M., et al.: Overcrowding in emergency department: causes, consequences, and solutions - a narrative review. Healthcare. **10**(9), 16 (2022). https://doi.org/10.3390/healthcare10091625

43. Sathurshan, M., Saja, A., Thamboo, J., Haraguchi, M., Navaratnam, S.: Resilience of critical infrastructure systems: a systematic literature review of measurement frameworks. Infrastructures. **7**(5) (2022). https://doi.org/10.3390/infrastructures7050067
44. Smith, S.W., Koppel, R.: Healthcare information technology's relativity problems: a typology of how patients' physical reality, clinicians' mental models, and healthcare information technology differ. J. Am. Med. Inf. Assoc. **21**(1), 117–131 (2014). https://doi.org/10.1136/amiajnl-2012-001419
45. Statistica: Estimated cost of downtime caused by ransomware attacks in U.S. Healthcare Organizations from 2019 to 2023 Ytd (in Billion U.S. Dollars) (2023). https://www.statista.com/statistics/1422161/us-healthcare-ransomware-attacks-downtime-estimated-cost/
46. Stobert, E., Barrera, D., Homier, V., Kollek, D.: Understanding cybersecurity practices in emergency departments. In: Proceedings of the ACM Conference on Human Factors in Computing Systems (CHI) (2020). https://doi.org/10.1145/3313831.3376881
47. Sullivan, N., Raphel, K.: Clinical and hospital system emergency management: implications of cyberthreats beyond privacy concerns. In: Proceedings of the ACM Workshop on Cybersecurity in Healthcare (HealthSec 2024). Salt Lake City, UT, USA (2024). https://doi.org/10.1145/3689942.3694742
48. Sullivan, N., Tully, J., Dameff, C., Opara, C., Snead, M., Selzer, J.: A national survey of hospital cyber attack emergency operation preparedness. Disaster Med. Public Health Preparedness. **17**(e363), 1–4 (2023). https://doi.org/10.1017/dmp.2022.283
49. Tully, J., Selzer, J., Phillips, J.P., O'Connor, P., Dameff, D.: Healthcare challenges in the era of cybersecurity. Health Security. **18**(3), 228–231 (2020). https://doi.org/10.1089/hs.2019.012
50. U.S. Environmental Protection Agency (EPA): Enforcement alert: drinking water systems to address cybersecurity vulnerabilities (2024). https://www.epa.gov/enforcement/enforcement-alert-drinking-water-systems-address-cybersecurity-vulnerabilities
51. van der Heijden, S., Cassivi, A., Mayer, A., Sandholz, S.: Water supply emergency preparedness and response in health care facilities: a systematic review on international evidence. Front. Public Health **5**(10), 1035212 (2022). https://www.frontiersin.org/journals/public-health/articles/10.3389/fpubh.2022.1035212/full
52. Walker, J.J.: Cyber Security Concerns for Emergency Management. Chapter within edited Book Emergency Management edited by Burak Eksioglu. Intechopen Publisher (2012). https://www.intechopen.com/chapters/26817
53. Williams, P.A.H., Woodward, A.J.: Cybersecurity vulnerabilities in medical devices: a complex environment and multifaceted problem. Med. Dev. (Auckland) **20**(8), 305–316 (2015). https://doi.org/10.2147/MDER.S50048

Extending Analogies and Applying Public Health Models to Cybersecurity

O. Sami Saydjari[1]([✉]) [iD], Josiah Dykstra[2] [iD], and Douglas Hough[3] [iD]

[1] Dartmouth College, Hanover, NH 03755, USA
Sami.Saydjari@dartmouth.edu
[2] Trail of Bits, New York, NY, USA
josiah.dykstra@trailofbits.com
[3] Johns Hopkins Bloomberg School of Public Health, Baltimore, MD, USA
douglas.hough@jhu.edu

Abstract. This paper extends a new approach to integrating analogies and analytical methods from public health and other domains into cybersecurity by introducing a structured framework for evaluating and judiciously applying them. Based on principles of analogy theory, the framework categorizes aspects of analogies into a stoplight system—green, yellow, and red—allowing practitioners to assess their applicability and potential pitfalls. We then employ the Haddon Matrix, a specific analytical method from the public health domain, demonstrating its relevance and utility in analyzing cybersecurity threats such as credential theft via phishing. Finally, we extend the framework's application to other public health and safety models, illustrating how these analogies and analytical methods can be more broadly evaluated and potentially adopted in cybersecurity. Through these contributions, the paper offers a rigorous method for cross-disciplinary cybersecurity innovation, providing specific insights and a generalizable approach for future research and practice.

Keywords: Healthcare · Cybersecurity · Public Health · Models · Analogies

1 Introduction

Since its birth in the mid-20th century, other fields have aided and informed developments and advances in cybersecurity. Although some concepts and methods from those fields applied naturally, others were adapted. Analogical reasoning is fundamental to human thought, reasoning, and knowledge acquisition [1, 9], allowing us to extend what we know to areas with which we are unfamiliar. Such extensions apply to both individuals' knowledge and to humanity's knowledge as a whole. At the same time, analogies are like models: they are all wrong in some way, though some are useful [2]. To disregard an analogy for being imperfect is to miss an opportunity to quickly gain vast knowledge about a new discipline and leapfrog to do the engineering and experimentation in areas where the analogies do not apply. Similarly, methods from analogous domains can be generalized and applied to cybersecurity, yielding new and insightful ways of analyzing problems and developing solutions. Sources of cybersecurity analogies have included biology, physics, military, sports, and information theory (Table 1).

W. Yurcik (Ed.): HealthSec 2024, CCIS 2716, pp. 33–64, 2026.
https://doi.org/10.1007/978-3-032-13800-2_3

Table 1. Some sources of cybersecurity analogies.

• Biology	• Sports	• Signals Processing
• Virology	• Game Theory	• Military
• Epidemiology	• Control Theory	• Physics
• Pathology	• Information Theory	• Chemistry

Public health, in particular, offers relevant—and often underexplored—insights for informing cybersecurity models and practices. Used superficially, however, terms such as "virus" have become shorthand for imperfectly applied analogies. This position paper explores how public health analogies and methods can contribute substantially to cybersecurity if applied carefully and with an evaluative framework. More than 100 years ago, C.E.A. Winslow created what is still the classic definition of public health: "Public health is the science and the art of preventing disease, prolonging life, and promoting physical health and efficiency through organized community efforts... and the development of the social machinery which will ensure to every individual in the community a standard of living adequate for the maintenance of health" [26]. The shared goal of safety and the similarities between threats to public health and digital security suggest that each field may have lessons for the other about approaches to develop and assess mitigations. However, critical analysis is needed to assess such lessons for suitability to avoid unintended consequences.

Conceptual models are used in public health to depict "the mechanisms by which a selected set of risk and protective factors may be associated with a health behavior or outcome of interest, as well as the conditions under which such associations are typically observed" [3]. As with public health, cybersecurity must continually study digital risk and protective factors. Various models have been created specifically for use in cybersecurity, but we encourage the consideration and adoption of relevant models from public health.

In this paper, we extend the framework first presented in [7]. We first describe a framework for evaluating the utility of analogies based on their similarities and limitations in Sect. 2, with four additional analogies in Sect. 2.2. Section 3 describes how public health and public safety models have been applied to cybersecurity, with an additional example in Sect. 3.1. We then shed light on a public-health method used in injury prevention, known as the Haddon Matrix, and show how it can be adapted by analogy to plan for prevention and interventions in cybersecurity and drive more nuanced and detailed analogy knowledge assessment. We conclude in Sect. 5 by presenting other models known to public health and suggesting a future research agenda.

2 An Evaluative Framework for Analogies in Cybersecurity

Cyberspace is a complex, non-linear, multidimensional arena that has been proven difficult to fully understand. Analogies are a well-established tool for helping engineers and society better understand the security challenges of cyberspace.

2.1 A Stoplight Framework for Analogy Analysis

A fundamental problem in analogical reasoning is to discern which aspects of an analogy apply directly, allowing the knowledge to be transferred with minimal effort, which aspects might apply with some conceptual transformations, and in which aspects it simply does not apply. We introduce a simple stoplight framework (see Fig. 1) to guide the understanding of how to apply analogies for what they can teach us and to avoid mistakes in overextending analogies to the point of incorrectly assuming invalid knowledge [23]. The framework allows us to assess which aspects and sub-aspects of analogies are applicable, to what extent, and how conceptual mapping aids in better using the value brought by the analogy. This method encourages nuanced and careful analysis of analogies and a method to do such analysis.

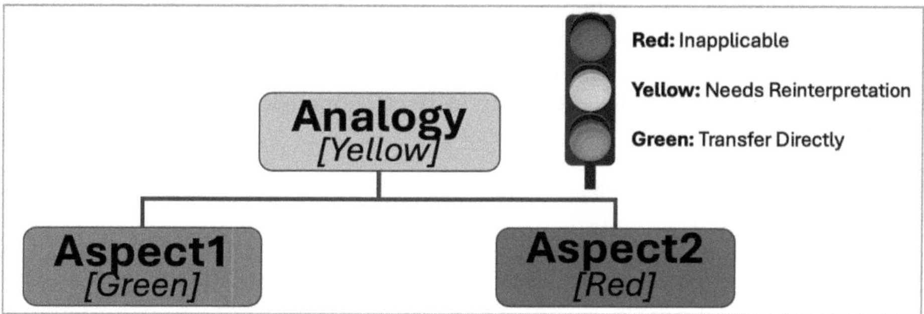

Fig. 1. Stoplight framework for evaluating the utility and limits of analogy aspects.

To determine the color categorization of a new analogy, we present a step-by-step evaluation process:

1 **Identify the Structural Similarity**: Analyze the key concepts of the source and target domains to see if there is a strong, moderate, or weak mapping in their relational structure.
2 **Assess Relevance**: Determine if the mapped similarities are relevant to the context of the argument or concept being explained.
3 **Evaluate Generalizability**: Consider if the properties and relationships from the source domain generalize to the target domain.

First, good analogies have a strong structural similarity between the source and target domain. This similarity involves identifying the key concepts in the base analogy and mapping one-to-one correspondence between the source and target concepts. The correspondence should be such that each element in the source domain that determines a particular property has a clear, possibly transformed counterpart in the target domain. The strength of an analogy often depends on how well these elements align and whether the relational structure between them is preserved across domains. Methodologies from other domains, such as the Haddon Matrix (presented in Sect. 4), are fruitful sources for determining which concepts to explore within the analogy.

Second, good analogies satisfy the criteria of relevance. Relevance refers to the extent to which the similarities highlighted by the analogy are pertinent to the argument or concept being explained. It is not enough for two objects to be similar; their similarities must be relevant to the properties or relations being transferred.

Third, the analogy should be generalizable. Generalization refers to the potential of the analogy to apply beyond the immediate comparison. A good analogy should demonstrate that the relationships and properties observed in the source domain can plausibly be extended to the target domain, making the analogy more robust and widely applicable.

We propose categorizing analogies and their components into three color-coded categories that denote the applicability and utility of the analogy. To categorize aspects of analogies into green, yellow, and red, we propose criteria based on the evaluation principles discussed below. Note that an individual analogy can have multiple colors: some aspects can be green, while others are yellow or red. Table 2 differentiates how the color of each analogy aspect corresponds to these criteria. Green analogy aspects are highly effective and reliable. Yellow analogy aspects are moderately effective but have some limitations. Red analogy aspects are ineffective or misleading.

Table 2. Criteria for stoplight colors of analogy aspects based on structural similarity, relevance, and generalizability.

	Green Analogy Aspects	Yellow Analogy Aspects	Red Analogy Aspects
Structural Similarity	Clear, one-to-one correspondence between concepts in source and target domains, preserving relational structure	Useful correspondence between concepts in source and target domains, preserving some relational structure	Little correspondence between concepts in source and target domains, or the relational structure is distorted
Relevance	Similarities are highly relevant to the argument or concept explained	Similarities are relevant but may not cover all aspects of the argument or concept explained	Similarities are irrelevant or confusing to the argument or concept explained
Generalizability	Many relationships and properties in the source domain extend well to the target domain	Some relationships and properties in the source domain may apply to the target domain	Few or no relationships and properties extend from the source domain to the target domain

How to distinguish green from yellow from red in an analogy depends on the purpose of the analogy. For example, relative size is a green aspect in an analogy between planets and marbles because that is the analogy's purpose. One can then ask how far the analogy can be taken. We can observe that size relates to mass, and mass is proportional to momentum, so relative momentum is in the yellow aspect of the analogy. Finally, we can see that marbles do little to model atmosphere, life sustainability, and magnetic fields, so we say these aspects are red (poorly applicable) (Fig. 2).

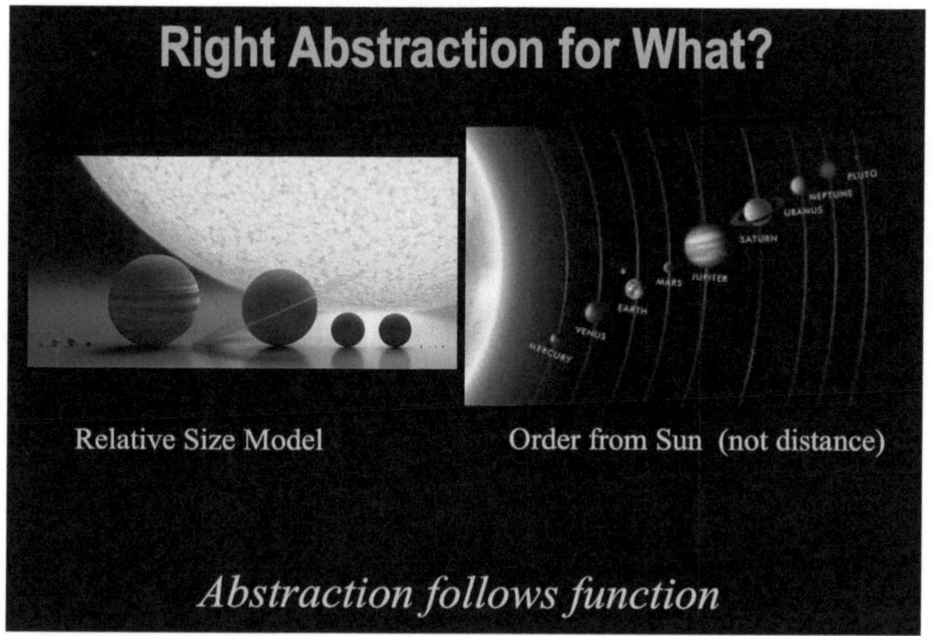

Fig. 2. Analogy purpose guides applicability.

An analogy draws attention to the *similarities* between the subjects, not the *differences*. However, no rule limits us to a single analogy for understanding a new domain. Many, possibly overlapping analogies, are likely to prove useful. What is red for one analogy may be green for another. That difference does not make one analogy better than another; it just makes it differently useful.

The following subsections discuss how to analyze an analogy and mine it for its knowledge potential. We will use a running example of a cat-and-mouse game as an analogy for cybersecurity.

Structural Similarity: Analogy Key Concepts. Identifying the key concepts to establish structural similarity begins with the analogy's purpose. We can then categorize each aspect's analogy color. We observe that how detailed we decompose the analogy into constituent aspects and how deep (layers) we go is a matter of the analogy's purpose and the energy and creativity an analyst wishes to invest.

To facilitate analogy decomposition, we provide a detailed and precise description of the base analogy to which we plan to compare cybersecurity.

Description. The cat-and-mouse game is a dynamic contest of pursuit and evasion, where the cat uses its strength, speed, and cunning to catch the mouse, while the mouse relies on agility, quick reflexes, and clever tactics to escape. Both participants adapt their strategies, with the cat attempting to outmaneuver and trap the mouse and the mouse continuously seeking opportunities to evade capture by exploiting its environment and the cat's weaknesses. This ongoing struggle showcases the complex interplay of offense and defense, where each side leverages its strengths to achieve victory.

Next, we explore some key aspects to illustrate the decomposition.

Pursuit and evasion between a pursuer (the cat) and the pursued (the mouse) is one aspect in which the more powerful pursuer's goal is to catch the mouse to eat it, while the pursued's goal is to evade capture and survive, using speed, agility, and strategy.

Complexity results from the dynamic behaviors of both the cat and the mouse, their respective experience and skill levels, and environmental variables such as terrain and weather, which make it a priori unpredictable who will win any given "game."

Both cat and mouse employ strategy and tactics in the pursuit game. Each plays to its strengths, such as the cat's size and speed and the mouse's agility and hiding skills.

Relevance: Mapping Analogy Concepts. To determine the degree to which an analogy component is structurally similar to the target domain requires mapping each from the pursuit-game domain to the cybersecurity domain.

Pursuit and evasion. The analogy can be applied in both directions. The cat could represent the cyber attacker, with its speed of attack and advanced planning taking the defender by surprise. The defender would be the mouse, reacting to the cyber attack, using their skills and strategy to evade it. Similarly, one could view the defender as the cat trying to thwart the cyber attacker, identify them, and possibly have them incarcerated for their crimes. Many sub-aspects to this aspect are green. One could dive deeper and ask what sorts of strategies cats and mice employ and examine sub-sub-aspects of this analogy aspect. The analogy breaks down (i.e., is red) in the sense that neither party is literally trying to kill the other, so the nature of the stakes is different. The aspect of speed is yellow. Cats are about four times faster than mice running in a straight line. Thus, mice employ quick turns, hiding, and deception to escape. The analogous cyber attack speed might be the time it takes to accomplish its mission or the speed of a defender's reaction in terms of time to detect, time to react, and effectiveness of reaction to mitigate damage. The indirect mapping makes this sub-aspect yellow because it needs reinterpretation from the cat-mouse domain to cyberspace operations.

Complexity. The outcome of any conflict between a cyber attacker and a cyber defender is generally too complex to predict because it depends on highly variable factors of skills, tools, experience, on-the-fly adaptation, and sometimes luck. The concept of highly complex system unpredictability is green between the two domains. The specifics of terrain and environment do not map and generalize well from one domain to the other, such as the fact that the mouse's small size allows it to hide in places the cat cannot reach. Such aspects are red.

Strategy and Tactics. The concept of strategy and tactics honed with experience is common to both domains and is, therefore, green. The interaction of these strategies and tactics, how and when they are employed in a situation-dependent way, the timing of deployment, and the decision process to deploy them are common to the two domains. The specifics of the interactions likely determine the outcome probabilities. One could assess the nature of this interaction's effect on outcome and transfer the principles from one domain to another.

Generalization: Applicability and Adaptability. While the conceptual mapping provides a framework for understanding parallels, it is important to recognize that the realms operate under fundamentally different principles. Evolutionary pressures, genetic variability, and complex behavior interactions influence biological systems. Digital systems are human-designed, rule-based, and can be systematically analyzed and modified.

Returning to our cat-and-mouse-game analogy, we observe the following concerning the aspects we selected to discuss here (a tiny fraction of the possible detail within this ostensibly simple analogy).

Pursuit and Evasion. Pursuit and evasion depend on the pursuer, the evader, and the terrain. Cats and mice are driven by instinct with a primary goal of survival. Their terrain is fixed to be whatever it happens to be where they encounter one another. Although cats and mice can be good models for humans in some ways (all are animals), their instincts, capabilities, and intelligence differ substantially from those of humans. For example, the reaction time of a cat (around 20 ms) is nearly five times faster than that of a mouse (around 100 ms), which is as much as twice as fast as a human (as slow as 200 ms). We have the added complication of humans having computer processes operating on their behalf, with reaction times well below the millisecond range. We also have other interesting factors, such as time-to-detect and time-to-react (which includes planning time and execution time), to consider, making the analogy all the more rich to explore.

Complexity. Although the complexity of interaction between cat, mouse, and terrain is conceptually similar to the complexity of attacker, defender, and cyberspace, the number of degrees of freedom involved in the digital domain makes its complexity far greater. Attackers and defenders can ally themselves to extend their capabilities quickly. Both can modify the terrain in which the conflict occurs (e.g., the defender reconfiguring firewall rules of operation), sometimes simultaneously. On the one hand, these sub-aspects limit the degree to which knowledge from cat-and-mouse games carries forward to the cybersecurity domain, but on the other, they tip us off to deeply consider these sub-aspects to transform more knowledge between domains or at least develop interesting hypotheses to explore.

Strategy and Tactics. The concept of planning and strategy likely only applies to humans because of their reasoning ability, and thus, strategy is yellow in that it is an extension of tactics. Also, the notion of strategy and tactics extending beyond the experience of a single individual (through documentation) does not apply well in the cat-mouse domain but applies in the human cyber-conflict domain.

Practical Implications. Studying analogies is intellectually interesting but so is discerning the practical implications of the design and operation of cybersecurity systems. Just as the study of birds has influenced the design of airplane features, we can take inspiration from our analogies. Thus, we show here how analogies can suggest ideas for cybersecurity.

- **Agility and Adaptability.** Although cats are five times faster, they only succeed around half the time. We liken cats to cyber attackers with the element of surprise, investing heavily in focused preparation. The mouse's agility and unpredictability allow it to overcome the cat's huge advantages. This suggests we must design and operate cybersecurity in ways that allow unpredictable agility (e.g., dynamic countermeasures to attack) and behavior-based adaptation of defensive mechanisms, like firewalls, to the nature of the detected attacks.

- **Continuous Monitoring and Reaction.** Mice have a keen sense of smell and hearing, allowing them to detect the cat threat at a sufficient distance to avoid conflict entirely. This suggests the importance of effective intrusion detection systems tied into early-warning systems that adjust defense posture at the slightest hint of trouble (e.g., anomaly detection alerts) and, just as quickly, return to normal operations when warnings are determined to be false positives. This aspect also suggests that cyber defenders proactively hunt for threats within their systems.

- **Leveraging and Adapting Environment.** Mice succeed partly because they can exploit their environment by blending into and hiding in small spaces that cats cannot follow. Although it would be hard for an enterprise to blend into the cyberspace terrain (assuming it has to be connected to the Internet), cybersecurity can leverage the high malleability of cyberspace by altering the terrain to create obstacles to attackers succeeding. For example, network segmentation can require attackers to succeed against multiple protection points for their attack to work. Customized intrusion detection parameters can make it difficult for an adversary to predict what actions trigger alarms. Frequent patches make it difficult for attackers to exploit the substantial terrain of known vulnerabilities in commercial systems.

Understanding these mappings and their limitations helps us appreciate the similarities and differences between domains, guiding appropriate strategies for dealing with each aspect.

In summary, all analogies can have green, yellow, and red aspects. Yellow aspects can have green sub-aspects as the analysis proceeds to the lower levels of the concepts. It is too facile to say that an analogy is bad because we can find one or even several red aspects. Such a hasty judgment may cause the community to lose out on potentially valuable knowledge and insight and inspire useful hypotheses to be pursued rigorously.

2.2 Analyzing Example Analogies

To help understand how to apply our proposed framework, we analyze some common analogies used in cybersecurity concerning the framework.

Cybersecurity is like Defending a Castle. In this analogy, landowners (nobility) seek to protect their assets (the land itself, people, animals, harvested crops, accumulated wealth such as gold and jewels) in a fixed location from mobile invaders who seek to take some or all of these assets by force. Here are some key aspects of the analogy. Cyberspace owners (e.g., enterprise network owners) map to landowners. Their computer networks equate to land. The valuable data contained within the networks maps to wealth. The computers perhaps map to the nobles that can generate more wealth (valuable data).

Walls. Walls were built high, thick, strong (e.g., out of hard stone), and with deep foundations to resist attacker attempts to breach those walls by hand climbing, ladders, cannon or trebuchet balls, explosives, arrows (sometimes flaming), and sapping (tunneling underneath the walls). They required a heavy investment and often only defended the bare essential property, leaving much of the town and lands unprotected. These countermeasures against attack map to firewalls, guards, and filtering routers in the cybersecurity world. The concept of keeping attackers coming from the outside out maps cleanly between the medieval realm and that of cyberspace. Both castle walls and firewalls require significant investment, impede normal operations to a degree (making it harder for authorized people to get work done), and are reasonably effective against many outside-to-inside attacks. That part of the analogy is green. Because firewalls are not physical walls, the analogy breaks down in terms of clarity when the barrier is under attack, thickness and height of the wall, and relative costs to assets (e.g., one can generally afford to protect more of the network assets than a castle could protect surrounding land). The aspect of physicality is red, though one might ask what would make a firewall the equivalent of thicker or taller–perhaps the ability to defeat more classes of attacks.

Moats. Moats are essentially circular artificial ponds built at the base of walls. They are intended to make it harder to set breaching devices (e.g., ladders and siege towers) used by attackers. Moats also made it harder for the attacker to breach the wall by digging a tunnel under the wall. In that sense, moats effectively enhance walls to make them more effective in attacks against the walls. Moats do not map cleanly to elements in cyberspace and thus are yellow. One might consider a network demilitarized zone (DMZ) with possible intrusion prevention and detection systems to serve a roughly similar function to a moat.

Gatehouses and Drawbridges. The gatehouse is the heavily protected entry through the wall to allow authorized entry and exit while preventing unauthorized entry by opposing military forces. Similarly, a drawbridge temporarily bypasses the moat protections when those in charge of its deployment determine that it is safe to redeploy for normal activities (people coming and going with goods and services). The gatehouse was a restrictive chokepoint, making it easier to monitor and decide on authorized entry and exit. The analogy maps well with cybersecurity perimeter control and access control. Routers effectively block entry into an enterprise network and restrict access to a small number of controlled access points, typically protected by a firewall, acting as the gatehouse, with instructions in the form of firewall rules as to what traffic can enter or exit. During normal operations, the firewall will likely allow traffic through that seems benign, even if it is not on an authorized channel. When under attack, more conservative firewall rules may be deployed, effectively pulling up the drawbridge (and dropping the portcullis gatehouse gate) for any traffic that is not specifically authorized. This becomes a yellow part of the analogy because the firewall has more granular control than a physical drawbridge. Pulling up the drawbridge is akin to isolating the enterprise network from the containing internetwork (e.g., the Internet). One does not have to be that binary in the digital world.

The Keep. Because the most valuable assets were contained within the keep, the strongest protections were afforded to this part of the castle. This maps directly to network segmentation and the use of multiple layers of networks within an enterprise, the innermost one having the most protections. This analogy aspect is green because of the close mapping of layering from one domain to the other.

Towers and Battlements. These structures provided elevated positions from which defenders could monitor potential adversary activity coming toward the castle. This maps to both intrusion detection systems (which require human operators to monitor) and threat intelligence systems watching out for threats that may be targeting an enterprise network. Again, the mapping between these structures and those in cybersecurity is relatively clear, and thus, the concepts are green at the first-order level of abstraction. One can peel back the analogy aspect and ask how towers and battlements are constructed, how effective they are, how they fail, and examine how well the analogy aspect depends on the next level down on the analogy. Causing good questions to be asked and generating interesting hypotheses are a significant portion of the value brought by analogies.

Cybersecurity is like a Game of Chess. Chess is a strategic board game where two opponents engage in a battle of wits, each commanding a defined set of pieces arranged in specific starting positions. The movements of these pieces are governed by a fixed set of rules, creating a structured environment in which each player must balance offensive and defensive strategies. The primary objective is to checkmate the opponent's king while simultaneously protecting one's king from capture. Success in chess hinges on careful planning, anticipation of the opponent's moves, and the ability to adapt tactics in response to changing conditions on the board. Several exemplary aspects of the analogy are discussed as follows.

Strategic Planning. Chess requires strategic planning to guide each move in such a way that anticipates the opponent's possible moves and blocks their best moves or lures them into a seemingly good move that is, in fact, a bad move several moves down the line. Because people cannot anticipate all possible strategies the opponent may be pursuing, their strategy must be dynamically adjusted to the situation as it evolves (e.g., the unexpected capture of a piece because of a blunder). Similarly, cybersecurity requires anticipating a full spectrum of attacker strategies and tactics and the capability to prevent, detect, and recover from each of them. Like chess, it is difficult to plan for all of them, and one is occasionally surprised (e.g., with zero-day attacks). In this way, strategic planning is a green aspect of the chess analogy, as is the need to adjust strategy dynamically to unanticipated events. At the same time, chess is a much simpler type of game in the sense that the pieces are fixed, the rules are fixed, and the end goals are fixed, all of which are known by both players in advance. Cybersecurity is a much more complex game in which the board can change, the pieces can change, the rules can change, and there are a myriad of end goals, many of which remain hidden from the defender. These aspects of the analogy are at least yellow and possibly red, though further analysis of the underlying concepts would help flush that out. The implication is that the existing computer game theory of chess cannot be directly applied to cybersecurity operations without a significant reinterpretation or a wholesale redevelopment.

Layered Defense. Because of the high value of the king in chess, the defender often deploys many layers of defense to protect the king. Similarly, cybersecurity has a concept of defense in depth in which high-value assets are protected with many layers of defense in case one or more fail or are successfully breached, reducing the probability that the cyber attack will succeed. An attack on a strategic piece in a given layer of defense in chess could alert the defender to the possible strategy the opponent is pursuing and can thus act as a type of intrusion detection. Similarly, in cybersecurity, attack trees developed by defenders to prepare for possible attacks can serve to alert the defender of possible attack sequences that cyber attackers may be pursuing. The concept of layered defense is thus a green aspect of the analogy. Because of common-mode failures, the collapse of a layered defense because of a poor design dependency is much more likely in cybersecurity than in chess.

Evolving Tactics. Strategy and tactics innovation occasionally happens in chess as grandmasters use their creative genius to surprise their opponents. Their opponents must adapt to these innovations or lose. Once the innovation is used, other chess players study the innovations and adapt their games to both use them and to be prepared to defend against them (the three-move checkmate as a simplistic example). Similarly, both defenders and attackers are constantly innovating in all areas of cyber attack and cyber defense. Advances in one spur counter advances in the other. This suggests that cyber-defenders deeply study successful attack strategies and tactics as well as defenses, document them, and learn from them in the same way that the National Transportation Safety Board studies airplane crashes to ensure that aviation safety is always improving. The need and methods to evolve map well from the chess domain to cybersecurity. The speed of evolution is much faster in cyberspace, so the approaches to learning and evolution may be substantively different, though that remains to be seen. For now, we can classify the speed of evolution sub-aspect as yellow.

Computer Virus Are like Biological Viruses. We now analyze viruses as one common analogy used in cybersecurity with respect to the framework. Table 2 shows the analysis of nine aspects of the analogy between biological viruses and computer viruses. Each aspect is considered independently and given a color coding.

Military Analogy. The analogy between a military conflict and that of a cyber-conflict has a long history, at least informally, in the language and concepts used. Aspects of the domain include:

- Attackers—those who attack assets being defended
- Defenders—those who defend assets from being attacked
- Terrain—Structural features shaping movement, visibility, and advantage in contested space
- Environment—Changing conditions affecting operations, visibility, and effectiveness in contested space
- Goals—Desired end-state or outcome that drives all operations
- Strategy—Coordinated plan aligning resources and actions to achieve goals
- Tactics—Specific actions or methods used to implement a strategy
- Equipment—Tools or systems that enable capability within the operational domain
- Experience—Accumulated knowledge influencing decisions, effectiveness, and adaptability

Table 4 captures a mapping and assessment of the analogy from the military to the cybersecurity domains.

In the process of mapping aspects within the analogy, we find that some concepts must be transformed to be meaningfully applied across domains—these are marked as yellow.

Table 3. Comparison of analogy aspects between biological viruses and computer viruses.

Analogy Aspect	Biological Viruses	Computer Viruses	Aspect Strength
Replication	Invades host cells and uses the cell's machinery to copy itself	Inserts code into programs or files and replicates across systems and networks	[Green] Self-replication using host's resources. Biological virus replication relies on complex biochemical processes within living cells, which include nuanced interactions with cellular machinery. In contrast, computer viruses rely on code execution within digital environments, governed by programmed rules
Mutation	Undergo genetic mutations, leading to variations that can evade the immune system	Can alter their code slightly with each infection (polymorphic viruses), making them harder to detect	[Yellow] Biological mutation is natural and random, while computer virus mutation is intentional and programmed. Biological mutations are driven by genetic replication errors and environmental factors. Computer virus mutations are intentional and programmed by humans, limiting the randomness and typically following predictable patterns to evade detection
Host Range	Have specific host ranges, infecting certain species or cell types	Target specific operating systems, applications, or hardware platforms	[Yellow] The specificity of biological viruses is determined by the presence of specific receptors on host cells, influenced by evolutionary pressures. Computer-virus host range is determined by compatibility with operating systems or software, which is more easily modified by human programmers

(continued)

Table 3. (*continued*)

Analogy Aspect	Biological Viruses	Computer Viruses	Aspect Strength
Transmission	Direct contact, airborne droplets, vectors, or surface contamination	Emails, downloads, network connections, and removable media	[Green] Spreading from host to host through various routes. Biological virus transmission is affected by factors such as human behavior, immune responses, and environmental conditions. Computer virus transmission relies on data exchange methods that can be controlled by software settings and network protocols
Pathogenicity	Cause disease, with varying degrees of severity depending on the virus and host	Cause damage to computer systems, from minor annoyances to major data loss or system corruption	[Yellow] Cause harm to their hosts, but the nature and impact of the harm differ. The effects of biological viruses on organisms involve complex interactions with the host's immune system and can result in a wide range of health outcomes. The damage caused by computer viruses is limited to data and software corruption, with variable severity, depending on the mission of the virus

This transformation requires a degree of creativity in pattern recognition and abstraction. For example, while cyberspace has no literal terrain, abstracting the concept reveals analogous properties: certain areas are easier or harder to traverse, defend, observe from, or launch attacks from. By reasoning at this higher level of abstraction, we identify points of conceptual alignment that make indirect mappings possible. This enables us to retain the usefulness of the original aspect, even when a direct mapping does not exist.

Conceptual mapping can reveal valuable insights but also exposes limitations arising from fundamental differences between domains—particularly between the typically analog nature of military concepts and the digital nature of cybersecurity. These limitations appear when certain aspects or sub-aspects have no clear or meaningful transformation. We categorize such cases as red. In some instances, an aspect initially marked red may

Table 4. Mapping the military domain to cybersecurity by analogy

Analogy Aspect	Military Domain	Cyber Domain	Aspect Strength
Attacker	Military unit	Cyber unit	[Green] A cadre of one or more people working toward a goal. Military units are often more structured and trained, but less agile
Defender	Military or civilian infrastructure owners and operators	Military or civilian infrastructure owners and operators	[Green] Both involve assets that are typically fixed and valuable to both attacker and defender
Terrain	Physical space in which conflict is waged, often with that space being the valued asset fought over	The defender's and attacker's cyberspace, including all dependent systems	[Yellow] Both create both constraints and opportunities to help or hinder both attackers and defenders. Physical terrain is limited by the laws of physics. Cyber terrain is hyperdimensional and difficult to navigate
Environment	Weather, time of day, visibility, and other such factors can significantly affect conflict outcomes	Network loading, infrastructure defense capabilities, and other transitory factors that influence attack success probability	[Red] Environmental factors and their potential effect on conflict outcome is radically different between domains
Goals	Takeover territory or control of resources	Takeover of cyberspace assets or control of the network and computer resources	[Green] The nature of goals is similar and highly varied
Strategy	Based on millennia of experience in operating in various terrains with specific equipment and training regimens	Based on decades of experience operating in various systems with specific tools and training regimens	[Green] Very similar at an abstract level, though significantly different in detailed implementation
Tactics	Based on millennia of experience in operating in various terrains with specific equipment and training regimens	Based on decades of experience operating in various systems with specific tools and training regimens	[Green] Very similar at an abstract level, though significantly different in detailed implementation

(continued)

Table 4. (*continued*)

Analogy Aspect	Military Domain	Cyber Domain	Aspect Strength
Equipment	A wide variety of offensive and defensive weapons and capabilities	A range of offensive and defensive software tools and capabilities	[Yellow] The concept is similar, but details differ greatly between domains
Experience	Highly trained forces	Often train-as-you-go	[Yellow] Conceptual similar, but cyberspace is far more dynamic, making rapid learning essential

simply reflect a gap in current understanding or creativity. These cases represent opportunities for future exploration, where new conceptual mappings could lead to deeper insights.

Information Theory Analogy. Information theory is a branch of applied mathematics and electrical engineering that studies the quantification, storage, and communication of information.

At its core, information theory provides a framework for understanding the limits of data compression and reliable communication over noisy channels. Key concepts include:

- Entropy: A measure of the average uncertainty or information content in a random variable. Higher entropy implies more unpredictability.
- Redundancy: The portion of information that can be removed without loss, which is useful for compression.
- Channel capacity: The maximum rate at which information can be reliably transmitted over a communication channel.
- Error-correcting codes: Methods for detecting and correcting errors introduced during transmission.

Information theory underpins technologies such as data compression (e.g., ZIP, JPEG), telecommunications, cryptography, machine learning, and even biological systems like DNA encoding.

Using an information-theory analogy, we have several key aspects we could consider:

- Sender of data
- Receiver of data
- Data transmitted
- Transmission channel
- Channel interference

Notice how each of these aspects could have several sub-aspects to consider. For example, the aspects of a sender could include:

- A human sender
- A set of processes operating on the sender's behalf at the application level
- The operating system supporting those processes, including device drivers and device controllers
- The hardware underlying the operating system
- The communication interface device (e.g., a network interface card)

The transmission channel could include:

- The local area network
- Local area network infrastructure, including routers, switches, and gateways
- The wide area network
- Wide area network infrastructure

Channel interference includes:

- Random noise
- Intentional action of a malicious adversary (e.g., a man-in-the-middle attack)

Each aspect can be further broken down into sub-aspects for a more detailed analysis of the analogy. Analysts should avoid halting this decomposition prematurely, as doing so may lead to incorrect conclusions—particularly when labeling an aspect as red. In many cases, exploring at least one additional layer of detail can reveal viable transformation opportunities. The full mapping and assessment of the analogy are intentionally left open for the reader to explore.

3 Public Health and Public Safety Models in Cybersecurity.

The idea of using biological, public health, and public safety analogies to understand cybersecurity challenges has been a recurring theme in cybersecurity for nearly four decades. The concept is based on the notion that just as public health and safety professionals work to prevent and mitigate the spread of threats, cybersecurity practitioners can learn from their approaches to improve the security posture of networks and systems.

3.1 Public Health and Safety Examples

This section continues the application of analogy analysis to the broad public health and safety domains because these have much in common with the social and societal aspects of cybersecurity.

Fire Safety Codes. Catastrophic events such as the Great Chicago Fire of 1871 inspired the development of fire safety codes. Similar events in cyberspace should inspire similar safety codes for systems development to minimize the probability of a successful attack on one system propagating to others [14].

Fire safety codes are regulatory standards that mandate the use of fire-resistant building materials, enforce urban planning and zoning laws to limit fire spread, improve fire department capabilities, promote fire prevention and safety education, and establish national fire safety initiatives, all aimed at reducing the risk and impact of fires in urban environments. Key analogy aspects include:

- **Building Construction Regulations**–building codes requiring the use of fire-resistant materials like brick, stone, and steel, as well as electrical system standards.
- **Urban Planning and Zoning**–building placement rules such as minimum street widths and open spaces to reduce the chance of fire jumping between areas of a city.
- **Early Detection and Response**–alarms and sprinkler systems to quickly detect and suppress fires before they spread.
- **Fire Department Improvements**–more fire stations, better training, and better equipment.
- **Fire Prevention and Safety Training**–increased awareness and planning through fire alarms, fire drills, and public education campaigns.
- **Advocacy**–creation of organizations to advocate for improvements in these areas.

A comparison of analogy aspects between fire safety codes and cybersecurity is detailed in Table 3.

Understanding these mappings can help develop more comprehensive cybersecurity strategies by borrowing effective principles from fire safety codes.

Immunization Strategies. Public health vaccination strategies have several parallels to cybersecurity concepts for public safety. Here is an analysis of the analogy using this paper's proposed framework.

Immunization strategies for disease prevention involve preparing the immune system to combat pathogens through vaccines, achieving herd immunity by ensuring high vaccination coverage, maintaining immunity with booster shots, and monitoring vaccination rates and outbreaks to inform public health strategies. Rapid vaccination efforts are implemented during disease outbreaks to contain and mitigate the spread of illness. These protocols work together to provide comprehensive protection against infectious diseases.

Table 6 shows a summary analogy analysis. Understanding these mappings can help design more effective cybersecurity strategies by leveraging principles from public health immunization strategies.

3.2   Public Health and Safety Success Stories

Concerns regarding human health are as old as humanity itself. For thousands of years, advances in knowledge and practice were slow and limited. However, those advances have accelerated with the application of the scientific method and other breakthroughs. Healthcare is a broad term that includes medicine, the prevention, treatment, or relief of symptoms from diseases or abnormal conditions in individuals. Healthcare also includes public health, which focuses on preventing disease injury among populations of people. To our knowledge and surprise, there has never been a consolidated compilation of

Table 5. Comparison of six aspects of the analogy between fire safety codes and cybersecurity.

Analogy Aspect	Fire Safety Codes	Cybersecurity	Aspect Strength
Building Construction Regulations	Use fire barriers, firewalls, and containment zones to prevent the spread of fire	Use secure coding practices, regular software updates, and lifecycle security	[Yellow] Both focus on reducing the risk of incidents through proactive measures, though the specific practices differ
Urban Planning and Zoning	Regulate building placement, like minimum street widths and open spaces, to reduce fire spread between city areas	Implement network segmentation, firewalls, and isolation to prevent malware spread and unauthorized access	[Green] Both involve controlling connections between components of the larger system to reduce risk
Early Detection and Response	Require smoke detectors, fire alarms, and sprinkler systems to detect and respond to fires early	Develop incident response plans, including containment steps, eradication, recovery, and good communication	[Green] Strong correlation; both involve early detection systems to identify and mitigate threats before they cause significant damage
Fire Department Improvements	More fire stations, better training, and better equipment	Local and community incident response team, with tools, and training to respond correctly to cybersecurity incidents	[Yellow] The focus on rapid response and preparedness maps well, as both scenarios require immediate action to mitigate damage. Cybersecurity more intimately involves operators of systems under threat
Fire Prevention and Safety Training	Increase awareness and planning through fire alarms, fire drills, and public education campaigns	Educating users about phishing attacks and more secure behaviors (e.g., password choice) reduces attack surface	[Green] Educating people on how to reduce incidents, and its significant effect on incidents, is common between both domains

successes in public health. Nevertheless, we offer five exemplar successes illustrating how the field has carried out this definition in practice. In the subsequent section, we will explore how these lessons apply to cybersecurity.

John Snow and the Broad Street Water Pump. Nineteenth-century London was replete with outbreaks of disease. In 1854, an outbreak of cholera occurred in Soho.

Table 6. Comparison of analogy aspects between immunization strategies and cybersecurity

Analogy Aspect	Immunization Strategies	Cybersecurity	Aspect Strength
Inoculation	Vaccines prevent diseases by stimulating the immune system to recognize and fight detected pathogens	Antivirus systems and other intrusion detection mechanisms can be inoculated to recognize malicious code and prevent it from doing damage	[Green] Both domains require early detection in a broader population, analysis of malicious agent, development of its essential elements stripped of malicious action, and widespread distribution of that vaccine among the broader population
Herd Immunity	High vaccination coverage in a population protects those who are not immune by reducing the spread of disease	Network security protocols, such as widespread use of secure practices and updates, reduce the overall risk of cyber-attacks propagation using vulnerable systems as launch points	[Yellow] The abstract concept of herd immunity is common to both domains. The sub-aspects determining when herd immunity is reached such as basic reproduction number, vaccine efficacy, and population behavior, require some transformation to apply to cybersecurity
Surveillance and Monitoring	Monitoring vaccination rates and disease outbreaks to guide public health responses	Monitoring of distribution of updates to intrusion detection software, and outbreaks of malware through monitoring entities such as national CERTS and commercial threat intelligence services	[Green] Direct analogy; both involve ongoing observation to identify and respond to threats, though the methods differ

(continued)

Table 6. (continued)

Analogy Aspect	Immunization Strategies	Cybersecurity	Aspect Strength
Outbreak Response	Rapid response to disease outbreaks with targeted vaccination campaigns	Incident response plans to quickly address and mitigate the impact of security breaches	[Yellow] Both involve immediate actions to contain and mitigate the impact of an emerging threat. The actions, who performs them, and how they are performed require significant transformation
Quarantine and Isolation	Isolating infected individuals to prevent disease spread	Isolating infected systems or network segments to prevent malware spread	[Green] Both involve isolating the threat to prevent further spread, though human disease control typically moves the infected part to an isolated area while cybersecurity isolates the infected subsystem in place
Vaccine Development	Complex, lengthy process involving clinical trials and regulatory approvals	Development of security software and protocols is more iterative and less regulated	[Red] Poor correlation; the processes for developing vaccines and security solutions are fundamentally different

Dr. Snow, an obstetrician, noted that "Within 250 yards of the spot where Cambridge Street joins Broad Street, there were upwards of 500 fatal attacks of cholera in 10 days." He offered the then-unusual hypothesis that the well from which most residents drew their water was the cause. He convinced town officials to remove the well's pump handle. The outbreak subsided immediately [24].

Development and Distribution of the Polio Vaccine. Polio has afflicted humans for thousands of years. By the mid-twentieth century, half a million people worldwide were killed or paralyzed by the virus every year. In 1955, Dr. Jonas Salk and his team announced their success in developing and testing an effective polio vaccine. A worldwide effort was undertaken to administer the new vaccine. By 1957, annual cases in the US had dropped by 90%, and by 1961 only 161 cases were reported. Worldwide vaccine distribution was much slower, but annual cases dropped from 350,000 in 1988 to six in 2021 [27].

Eradication of Smallpox. As with polio, smallpox has caused hundreds of millions of illnesses and deaths for thousands of years. The first true vaccine was not developed until

1796. Unlike polio, two million people a year were still dying of smallpox a hundred years later. In 1959, the World Health Organization launched the Smallpox Eradication Programme. In 1980, the program, led by Dr. D. A. Henderson, succeeded in completely eradicating smallpox – the only disease to have been so [27].

Campaign to Reduce Cigarette Smoking. Many health professionals long suspected that cigarette smoking was related to disease incidence, especially cancer and heart disease. Scientific evidence was sufficient by the 1950s to justify efforts to reduce smoking. These efforts were only moderately effective until the U.S. Surgeon General's report, Smoking and Health, in 1964, catalyzed public opinion and government action. Cigarette ads were banned on television and radio; smoking was banned on all U.S. domestic airlines; and smoking has been banned in many bars, restaurants, and worksites. Smoking rates have declined dramatically since 1965, from 42% to 14% of adults [16].

Motor Vehicle Safety. Over the past century, remarkable progress has been made in reducing the fatality rate caused by motor vehicles. Since 1960, the number of deaths attributable to motor vehicles has grown somewhat, from 38,137 in 1960 to 42,338 in 2020. However, the rate per population has fallen by 39%, and the rate per vehicle miles traveled has fallen by 73% over that period. Public health experts [13] have three explanations: better drivers, cars, and roads.

These instances reveal multiple ways that public health has achieved its goals. In the John Snow case, a single intervention – backed by compelling data and intense debate – was all that was needed. The success of the polio vaccine, however, resulted from years of research and vaccine development, the palpable fear of the disease (including the salience of its targeting of young children), and the one-and-done intervention of a single injection. The smallpox eradication campaign differed markedly from polio: An effective vaccine had been available for two centuries; the issue was distribution, which required financial and logistical support from hundreds of countries and health-related agencies and widespread public acceptance and cooperation. That smallpox remains the only fully eradicated disease is testimony to the clinical and managerial challenges such an initiative requires. The success of the anti-smoking campaign demonstrates the importance of establishing challenging yet achievable goals and using multiple approaches. To that end, despite the multiple efforts to reduce smoking—banned ads, myriad public service announcements, high cigarette taxes, smoking bans in public places, and smoking cessation programs—31 million adults in the U.S. still smoke, spending $76 billion a year [15]. Finally, the dramatic advances in motor vehicle safety have resulted largely from improvements in the environment—that is, vehicles and roads—that did not require changes in individual behavior.

All these public health successes had in common the power of persistence. While each included a breakthrough, they needed a push to completion. John Snow faced considerable skepticism from both community leaders and the scientific community. His ideas contradicted the deeply held prevailing theory of disease. Confident that his data were correct, Snow accepted the challenge of a short-term trial, even though it potentially set back full implementation. With polio, acceptance of the vaccine was not an issue, as parents everywhere clamored for their children to receive it. The persistence stemmed from the research and clinical trials necessary to obtain government approval for the vaccine and the ongoing efforts to eradicate polio entirely. With smallpox, total eradication of the disease required an extraordinary effort to vaccinate the entire population and seek out and treat the remaining cases, a process that went well beyond what economic theory would have deemed an efficient use of resources. The anti-smoking campaign faced—and continues to face—the twin challenge of convincing active smokers to stop and overcoming the intense opposition of the tobacco industry. Motor vehicle safety similarly requires relentless persistence, given the slow journey away from human-centric vehicle risks.

3.3 Implications for Cybersecurity

These public health success stories yield insights that are relevant to people involved in cybersecurity. In this section, we describe how cybersecurity research and practice may be improved using lessons from these examples.

The first observation is that "magic bullets" (e.g., removed pump handles, vaccines) may work to a limited degree, but they rarely provide the complete solution. Removing the pump handle solved the cholera epidemic in the Soho neighborhood but did not address the overall problem of cholera and other water-borne diseases throughout London. Unfortunately, magic bullets grab the public's and policymakers' attention and lead to the assumption that solutions to complex problems can be simple and free. Cybersecurity has also tried changing to take away choices of dangerous actions, such as automatically rewriting URLs in emails to make them non-clickable, which is a narrow solution but not a magic bullet for solving social engineering.

Next, even interventions that are effective might lose their social potency over time. If an intervention (such as vaccination against polio) is successful and the presenting problem disappears, the public and policymakers may assume that the problem has been solved and the intervention need not continue. In a related issue, the public and policymakers may grow weary of vigilance if the immediate threat has decreased and there is no discernible benefit of continued action. Public health has often needed relentless communication with the public and policymakers about the importance of a topic before its solutions begin to have an impact. Cybersecurity, similarly, has found that continuous communication plays a role, such as continued phishing awareness, despite advances in technological detection of email-based threats.

Getting people to stop doing something is usually more challenging than getting people to not do it in the first place. As research has shown, it is often tough for smokers to stop smoking (because of physical addiction and social norms); it is easier to convince nonsmokers not to start smoking, especially if peer pressure and attractive depictions of smokers are minimized. As a result, total success may take years, if not generations. This can be seen in cybersecurity advocacy for developing good habits for password hygiene.

In the case of campaigns to eradicate smallpox and polio, 100% adherence or eradication is rarely achievable. Consequently, it is critical to create challenging but achievable measures of success. At the same time, these goals must inspire and elicit continued support from key stakeholders. In cybersecurity, there have been gradual declines in buffer overflows, but they are not eradicated.

This raises an important distinction for public health and cybersecurity about the distinction between prevalence and new incidence. While a mitigation is being deployed and adopted, the prevalence of smoking or a digital virus may remain high while the incidence of new smokers or new cyber infections is low. According to the Centers for Disease Control and Prevention (CDC), the prevalence of tobacco use among people 25–44 years old in the United States is 25.3%, and those individuals are likely to continue. On the other hand, the incidence of tobacco use among this age group is 1.8%. It would be helpful to track these metrics separately.

Finally, one commonality among these public health examples is the ability to measure harm, often in the form of infection or death. Even so, healthcare and public health have struggled with measuring progress. Cybersecurity continues to lack universally accepted outcome measures and mandatory reporting to underpin measures of harm (and reductions thereof).

The five examples in this section show fortuitous lessons and commonalities between cybersecurity and public health, but they lack a unifying or repeatable model.

3.4   Other Public Health Analogies in Cybersecurity

As we have explored throughout the paper, there are many potential public health and public safety analogies in cybersecurity. One of the earliest examples of this approach is attributed to Fred Cohen, who, in his 1984 dissertation, explored the idea that computer viruses could be viewed as a form of biological virus and proposed the use of public health models to understand and combat their spread [5]. Cohen's work laid the foundation for later researchers who built upon his ideas. These have been studied in some depth. After the Morris worm of 1988, Spafford analyzed the event and raised caution about the lack of an "immune system" to protect computers [22].

A few researchers and practitioners in cybersecurity have been looking for public health models and methods that might inform the creation of more effective ways of countering cyber threats. In 2010, Rice et al. [18] mapped and applied the tripartite public health structure of disease types (communicable, non-communicable), disease phases and severity, and public health "actors" (individuals, communities, health care providers, government) to construct generic strategies in cyberspace. Rowe et al. [20] used four categories of public health threats (communicable diseases, non-communicable diseases, risk behaviors, and environmental exposures) to create a taxonomy of cybersecurity threats. Weber [25] focused on the implications of cybersecurity interventions on the tendency within public health to engage in what Weber termed "coercive" measures (ranging from mandated seat belt use to quarantines during epidemics). In essence, Rice took a method from an analogous domain, mapped it into cybersecurity using structural similarity, and then applied it to cybersecurity. These advances make progress in aiding cybersecurity, but more possibilities remain.

By examining the evolution of public health analogies and methods in cybersecurity, we can see how researchers have built upon each other's work to develop a more comprehensive understanding of our digital society's challenges. From Cohen's early exploration of computer viruses as biological agents to Rice's adaptation of traditional public health approaches for cybersecurity and Weber's analysis of coercion through public health models, this body of research has provided valuable insights into how we can use public health principles to improve cybersecurity.

As expected from a field more than 100 years old, public health researchers and practitioners use a variety of conceptual models and frameworks to understand and address health problems. These models are used to identify the causes of a health problem, develop interventions to address the problem and evaluate the effectiveness of those interventions. Even more public health models are likely to be relevant to cybersecurity and could be evaluated using our framework for analogies.

Some public health models are specific to a threat or feature thereof. For instance, numerous models in public health are used to study epidemiology. Between 1927 and 1933, public health physicians A.G. McKendrick and W.O. Kermack produced basic compartmental models describing communicable disease transmission [4]. For instance, the Susceptible-Infectious-Recovered (SIR) model structure is a simple form of this type. This class of models may apply to the study of cyber threats such as worms.

The Haddon Matrix, presented in the next Section, is an example of a class of social-ecological models that take a more holistic approach to understanding health [11]. The social-ecological model recognizes that health is influenced by a wide range of factors, including individual, community, and societal factors. One common public health model structure is the epidemiological triangle, which identifies three key elements that contribute to the occurrence of a health problem: the agent, the host, and the environment. The agent is the pathogen or other factor that causes the disease. The host is the person who is infected with the pathogen. The environment is the physical and social setting in which the disease occurs. The Haddon Matrix is one model that employs the epidemiological triangle.

Public health models can guide the development of interventions to address health problems. For example, if a public health model identifies that a lack of access to healthcare causes a health problem, then an intervention could be developed to provide more people with access to healthcare. The PRECEDE-PROCEED Model is a framework for planning and evaluating health promotion interventions [6]. It consists of two phases: PRECEDE (Predisposing, Enabling, Reinforcing Causes, Educational Determinants, Community and Policy Determinants) and PROCEED (Planning, Resources, Economic Costs, Organizational Readiness, Evaluation, Dissemination).

The breadth of public health models and analogies has supported diverse lines of effort toward health goals. However, as one author astutely summarized, "there is always a trade-off between simple, or strategic, models, which omit most details and are designed only to highlight general qualitative behavior, and detailed, or tactical, models, usually designed for specific situations including short-term quantitative predictions" [4]. This caution applies equally to cybersecurity.

4 The Haddon Matrix

Given the utility of some public health models to cybersecurity in the past, we were motivated to explore other potential leads for health-related analogies. We have identified a lesser-known conceptual model from public health that shows promise for cybersecurity: the Haddon Matrix. As far as we can tell, this approach has not yet been widely adopted in cybersecurity despite its utility in public health and safety science. William Haddon was the director of the National Highway Safety Bureau in the U.S. Department of Transportation in the 1960s. In an article in the American Journal of Public Health [12], he articulated what has become a 3x3 matrix to analyze the causes and potential remedies for injury-causing events. One axis represented the phase of the injury-causing event (pre-event, event, post-event), and the other axis represented the event's components (or instruments). Haddon suggested that two matrices be created, one to identify the causal factors and the other to identify countermeasures. Haddon's approach in the public health domain has the tremendous advantage of inducing analysts to think broadly over all aspects of a problem and solution space, opening up the aperture of possibilities and creating new opportunities for insight. Over the past 24 years, the Haddon Matrix has been used to study SARS preparedness and response, COVID-19 containment in nursing homes, medical response strategies to subway bombings, and other critical health and safety considerations.

To illustrate a traditional use of the Haddon Matrix, Table 5A and 5B demonstrate how they can be used to analyze the causes of vehicle accidents and countermeasures. First, note that the "components" recall the factors discussed earlier: humans (driver and passengers), vehicles, and the environment (the roadway and surroundings). Table 5A shows the causal factors of vehicle accidents. Pre-event causes include inexperienced and distracted drivers, vehicles not designed to avoid accidents, and roads not designed to reduce the chance of an accident. As the event occurs, accidents are made worse because drivers lack situational awareness, vehicles are not built to mitigate the consequences of the accident, and roads are similarly not designed to lessen the impact of an accident. After the accident, the situation may be exacerbated in the short run by an emergency management system that cannot rapidly respond. In the long run, drivers do not learn from their mistakes, and vehicle manufacturers and road engineers do not conduct root-cause analyses of accidents.

Table 5B shows the now-familiar countermeasures implemented over the past century to reduce the probability and impact of vehicle accidents. The human side includes graduated driver's licenses (pre-event), mandated seat belts (event), and penalties for drunk driving (post-event). Vehicles now have third-brake lights (pre-event), airbags (event), and a redesign of gas tanks to minimize explosions. The road environment has been improved to reduce the probability of an accident (with speed bumps, rumble strips, and Botts' dots on the road surface), reduce the immediate harm of an accident (with guardrails and crash cushions), and lessen the severity of harm from the accident (with better EMS response). The breadth of considerations offered by the matrix is impressive.

From the discussion in this and other papers, the approaches used in public health can be instructive for cybersecurity. In particular, the Haddon Matrix offers a promising new framework for analyzing issues and solutions in cybersecurity. Table 6A and 6B present an example of applying this paradigm to credential theft where the "agent of injury" is a ransomware attack. Pre-event causes include human aspects of the attacker and the victim, causal factors of the threat, and environmental factors such as issues relating to holding data or infrastructure of the victim 'offline.' When the incident occurs, the impact is influenced by how distracted the victim is and how easy it is to detect that the data or system has been compromised before the loss of access. After the incident, the harm may be exacerbated by psychological distress to the victim and the value of data/systems, loss of access, or loss of confidentiality/proprietary ownership. Countermeasures are also presented for pre-event, event, and post-event timeframes across the human element, attributes of the attack methodology, and environmental factors.

While ultimately powerful and generally applicable, the approaches that drove the public health successes presented earlier did not happen by using the Haddon Matrix. While one could complete the Matrix in hindsight as documentation of what has already been tried or successful, it is even more potent in brainstorming, discovering, and proposing opportunities for open problems. Ransomware, for example, remains unsolved despite many preventative efforts. One reason is that many attack and system access avenues are not identified before victimization. One could imagine a yet-unrealized proposal putting a theoretical cost on access that makes it more expensive for attackers (with an obvious, but hopefully less painful, cost to legitimate users).

It is insightful to note where there are gaps when completing the Haddon Matrix. These may be individual boxes, rows, or columns with few entries and represent under-explored opportunities for examination. In our countermeasures for ransomware (Table 5B), there are more countermeasures pre-event than before and after. For ransomware, this illustrates a gap in that victims lack real-time tools for detecting and mitigating the breaches. The gap also indicates a general bias towards risk mitigation (i.e., prevention) when risk management (e.g., incident response) is equally essential.

The Haddon Matrix offers a structured framework for systematically analyzing the factors contributing to cyber threats, including before, during, and after the event. This structured approach can help cybersecurity professionals identify vulnerabilities and potential intervention points. It is also interdisciplinary. Causal factors and countermeasures can include technical, legal, and policy components. This holistic view can provide a more comprehensive understanding of the threat landscape. The Haddon Matrix encourages us to think about cybersecurity from various perspectives and develop a holistic approach to cybersecurity rather than single mitigations.

At the same time, the Haddon Matrix is flexible for broad and diverse uses across cybersecurity. This makes it ideally suited as a teaching aid in brainstorming sessions, tabletop exercises, and assessment of existing initiatives. The Haddon Matrix could be used to develop security awareness training programs tailored to the organization's specific needs. For example, the training could focus on the pre-event factors (e.g., phishing awareness) or the event factors (e.g., incident response). It could also be used to conduct risk assessments that document and evaluate an organization's cybersecurity risks and implement appropriate controls. Finally, we recently used the Matrix to communicate the importance of cybersecurity to non-technical corporate decision-makers.

There are, of course, limitations in using the Haddon Matrix method from the public health domain for the cybersecurity domain. Because it was initially designed for physical injuries, there is a heavy emphasis on human and environmental factors. As a result, it may not delve deeply enough into the technical details of specific cyber threats. The framework also does not include a quantitative component, and its qualitative and descriptive approach requires evaluating the impact of various factors or prioritizing interventions.

Because the Haddon Matrix is an analysis approach from the public health domain, it may need some mapping and reinterpretation in the analogous domain of cybersecurity. Like analogous knowledge, analogous tools must be applied carefully, considering their strengths and weaknesses as key concepts are mapped. At the same time, the Haddon Matrix also creates a beautiful structure to expand the concepts and considerations in risk analysis and mitigation in any domain in which it is applied. Thus, this analogous tool increases the power of the analogy analysis framework we introduce by expanding the number of concepts and aspects to consider in the analogous knowledge from other domains (not just public safety).

Applying the evaluative framework presented in Sect. 2, aspects of the Haddon Matrix are both green and yellow. Note that the Haddon Matrix is a tool and not an analogy since we propose using it directly as designed. However, we have based this approach on analogous concepts, such as environmental factors influencing physical injury and cybersecurity incidents. Aspects of the Haddon Matrix that should be evaluated include different phases of incidents, independent components of incidents, and causal factors that reveal countermeasures. One aspect is green: physical safety and cybersecurity are influenced by human victims, system designers, and attackers. The "agent of injury" is a yellow aspect. In our experience creating the ransomware matrix, it was most challenging to untangle the agent of injury between delivery and harm, making it yellow and needing reinterpretation. That is, a phishing email may be the root cause of ransomware, even though ransomware was what caused the harm. Overall, the Haddon Matrix is consistent with green analogies, meeting criteria such as strong structural similarity, high relevance to the concept of harm, generalizability of relationships between model components, and properties from the source domain to the target domain. In this case, the Haddon Matrix appears to satisfy all these conditions, solidifying its categorization as a green analogy (Tables 7, 8, 9 and 10).

Table 7. The Haddon Matrix for Vehicle Accidents: Causal Factors.

	Human	Vehicle/"Agent of Injury"	Environment
Pre-event (Reduce probability of event)	1. Inexperienced drivers 2. Distracted drivers 3. Incapacitated drivers	1. Vehicles not designed to avoid accidents 2. Vehicles do not communicate sufficient information to driver to anticipate accident	1. Roads not designed to avoid accidents 2. Poor street lighting

(*continued*)

Table 7. (*continued*)

	Human	Vehicle/"Agent of Injury"	Environment
Event (Reduce immediate harm of event)	1. Lack of situational awareness 2. Lack of knowledge of how to react to accident	1. Vehicles not designed to mitigate consequences of accidents	1. Roads not designed to mitigate consequences of accidents
Post-event (Ameliorate further injury or future event	1. Lack of understanding of causes of accident, and how improve skills	1. Lack of post-accident analysis of root causes	1. EMS system not designed to respond rapidly to accident scenes 2. Lack of post-accident analysis of root causes

Table 8. The Haddon Matrix for Vehicle Accidents: Countermeasures.

	Human	Vehicle/"Agent of Injury"	Environment
Pre-event (Reduce probability of event)	1. Minimum legal drinking age 2. Random breath testing 3. Graduated driver's licenses	1. Mandated third brake light 2. Unleaded gasoline	1. Roundabouts 2. Speed bumps 3. Red light cameras 4. Rumble strips and Botts' dots
Event (Reduce immediate harm of event)	1. Seat belt mandates 2. Mandated helmet laws	1. Child safety seats 2. Energy-absorbing steering columns 3. Air bags 4. Head rests	1. Guardrails 2. Crash cushions
Post-event (Ameliorate further injury or future event	1. Penalties for drunk driving 2. Mandated DE classes	1. Gas tank redesigns (no more Pintos)	1. Rapid EMS response

Table 9. The Haddon Matrix for Hospital Outage from Ransomware: Causal Factors.

	Human	Vehicle/"Agent of Injury"	Environment
Pre-event (Reduce probability of event)	1. Volume of email received by victim 2. Inadequate awareness and training 3. Dangerous habits and online behavior	1. Potential for attacker to make money 2. Strong dependence of victim to need access/control. Victims care. Business loss	1. Insecure device and software security configurations 2. Lack/insufficient Legal and regulatory framework 3. Lack of data backups
Event (Reduce immediate harm of event)	1. Tendency to trust/believe 2. Fear of loss 3. Decision-making under stress or pressure. Action bias	1. Reval attack at time of attacker's choosing 2. Attacker controls what you know, including their own motivation and capability	1. Real-time cybersecurity monitoring and response 2. Ineffectiveness of email filtering and security tools 3. (Un)Availability of assistance or guidance for users
Post-event (Ameliorate further injury or future event	1. Emotional and psychological impact on the victim (patient and/or hospital) 2. Willingness to learn from the experience. Changed behavior?	1. Misuse/release of stolen information 2. Persistence of the attacker in the system 3. Minimal/no consequences for the attacker if identified and prosecuted	1. Value of the data 2. Lateral access to systems and information 3. Financial industry willing to accept losses, use insurance 4. HIPAA compliance penalties

Table 10. The Haddon Matrix for Hospital Outage from Ransomware: Countermeasures.

	Human	Vehicle/"Agent of Injury"	Environment
Pre-event (Reduce probability of event)	1. Awareness and training 2. Incentives to avoid infection, including data storage	1. Pre-screening, behavioral analytics 2. Ransomware detection tech	1. Multi-factor authentication 2. Incentives to improve cyber hygiene 3. Better data storage and backups. Regular testing 4. Network partitioning and isolation

(*continued*)

Table 10. (continued)

	Human	Vehicle/"Agent of Injury"	Environment
Event (Reduce immediate harm of event)	1. Victim recognizes the incident 2. Takes proper immediate actions 3. Isolation of account/machine from other access/connectivity	1. Real time mitigations/isolation 2. Alerting to admins, ISP and partner providers 3. Engagement between admin and user	1. Incident response capability 2. Increase validation measures for transactions 3. Virtualize/isolate system; zero trust methods 4. Have effective, rehearsed, response plan 5. Begin data backup recovery
Post-event (Ameliorate further injury or future event	1. Victim reports the incident 2. Updates passwords and credentials 3. Reviews systems for similar infections	1. Add a signature of the malware 2. Attribution and tracking of the attack 3. Initiate new backup	1. Cyber insurance 2. Legal actions and consequences for the attacker. Work with proper authorities 3. Patching and enhanced protection deployments 4. After action report

5 Conclusion and Future Work

Cybersecurity benefits from fresh ideas. In a healthy and innovative ecosystem, cybersecurity professionals should always seek leads from other domains to combat persistent and emerging threats. Using biology and public health concepts to describe cybersecurity threats has become commonplace. However, less consideration has been given to approaches developed and applied by public health and public safety. We explore how public health experts think about their problems, the approaches they have tried, what worked, and when those approaches could be applied in cybersecurity. In this article, we have tried to widen the aperture of approaches to make a new perspective from the mature field of public health salient. Prior successes in public health encourage us to find equally powerful successes in cybersecurity. Indeed, there appears to be overconfidence in the existing approaches to cybersecurity. It is time to revisit public health approaches for cybersecurity.

The small community of cybersecurity professionals advocating for a public health approach to cybersecurity needs support. The non-profit CyberGreen Institute [8] has begun publishing analyses of lessons from public health to cybersecurity. Subdomains of cybersecurity, from hardware engineering to incident response, are likely to find specific parallels and inspiration from specific approaches to public health. Additional research and advocacy will strengthen the case for ideas inspired by public health, just as cyber hygiene has become mainstream. Tools like the Haddon Matrix, with modest reinterpretation, are available for adoption today.

As with all analogies, caution is required in the imperfect comparison between cybersecurity and public health. While instructive for suggesting potential new mitigations and leads, relying too rigidly on analogies can be derailed by inaccuracy, overgeneralization, and oversimplification. These pitfalls can be avoided by applying our stoplight framework. Similarly, analogous methods from other domains, such as the Haddon Matrix can also improve both analytical approaches to the cybersecurity problem and can enhance the depth and breadth of knowledge considered in analyzing analogies to other domains. We do not see methods like the Haddon Matrix as the definitive evaluative framework that can be applied algorithmically, but rather, it is an initial strawman to enable researchers and practitioners to have a more sophisticated discussion on how to mine public health analogies for the concepts and principles that can advance our cybersecurity approaches. Other analogous methods from other domains should be similarly evaluated, including those we mentioned earlier, as well as methods such as hazard analysis from the safety domain, and root-cause analysis from the reliability domain.

While technological evolution and threats evolve quickly, insights from public health experiences and successes can better prepare us for future cyber threats. We look forward to the thoughtful evaluation of analogies and analogous methods using our framework and the specific adoption of the Haddon Matrix to fill gaps with fresh ideas.

Acknowledgments. This study was not funded by a specific organization or grant other than those of the authors.

Disclosure of Interests. The authors have no competing interests to declare that are relevant to the content of this article.

References

1. Bartha, P.: Reasoning and Analogical Reasoning. Stanford University, Stanford (2019). https://plato.stanford.edu/entries/reasoning-analogy/. Accessed 17 Mar 2024
2. Box, G.E.P.: Science and statistics. J. Am. Stat. Assoc. **71**(356), 791–799 (1976)
3. Brady, S.S., Brubaker, L., Fok, C.S., Gahagan, S., Lewis, C.E., Lewis, J.: Prevention of lower urinary tract symptoms (PLUS) research consortium: development of conceptual models to guide public health research, practice, and policy: synthesizing traditional and contemporary paradigms. Health Promot. Pract. **21**(4), 510–524 (2020)
4. Brauer, F.: Mathematical epidemiology: past, present, and future. Infect. Dis. Model. **2**, 113–127 (2017)
5. Cohen, F.: Computer viruses – theory and experiments. Comput. Secur. **6**, 22–35 (1987)
6. Crosby, R., Noar, S.M.: What is a planning model? An introduction to PRECEDE-PROCEED. J. Public Health Dent. **71**, S7–S15 (2011)

7. Dykstra, J., Saydjari, O.S., Met, J., Hough, D.: Position paper: evaluating analogies and applying public health models for cybersecurity. In: Proceedings of the 2024 Workshop on Cybersecurity in Healthcare (HealthSec '24), pp. 17–28. ACM, New York (2024). https://doi.org/10.1145/3689942.3694751

8. CyberGreen Institute: Public Health & Cyber Public Health. Technical Report 22–01 (2022). https://cybergreen.net/technical-report-22-01/

9. Ebert, N., Schaltegger, T., Ambuehl, B., Schöni, L., Zimmermann, V., Knieps, M.: Learning from safety science: a way forward for studying cybersecurity incidents in organizations. Comput. Secur. **134**, 103435 (2023)

10. Gentner, D., Holyoak, K.J.: Reasoning and learning by analogy: introduction. Am. Psychol. **52**(1), 32 (1997)

11. Glanz, K.E., Rimer, B.K., Viswanath, K.: Health Behavior and Health Education: Theory, Research, and Practice, 4th edn. Jossey-Bass/Wiley, San Francisco (2008)

12. Haddon, W.: The changing approach to the epidemiology, prevention, and amelioration of trauma: the transition to approaches etiologically rather than descriptively based. Inj. Prev. **5**(3), 231–235 (1999). https://doi.org/10.1136/ip.5.3.231

13. Hemenway, D.: While We Were Sleeping: Success Stories in Injury and Violence Prevention. University of California Press, Berkeley (2009)

14. Landwehr, C.: We need a building code for building code: a proposal for a framework for code requirements addressing primary sources of vulnerabilities for building systems. Commun. ACM **58**(2), 24–26 (2015)

15. Levy, N., Rubin, A., Yom-Tov, E.: Modeling infection methods of computer malware in the presence of vaccinations using epidemiological models: an analysis of real-world data. Int. J. Data Sci. Anal. **10**(4), 349–358 (2020). https://doi.org/10.1007/s41060-020-00213-w

16. MacArthur, S.: Smoking as a public health issue. [n.d.]. https://www.mphonline.org/smoking-public-health/. Accessed 17 Mar 2024

17. Parker, R.D., Farkas, C.: Modeling estimated risk for cyber attacks: merging public health and cyber security. J. Inf. Assur. Secur. **2**, 32–36 (2011)

18. Rice, M., Butts, J., Miller, R., Shenoi, S.: Applying public health strategies to the protection of cyberspace. Int. J. Crit. Infrastruct. Prot. **3**(3), 118–127 (2010). https://doi.org/10.1016/j.ijcip.2010.07.002

19. Rowe, B., Halpern, M., Lentz, T.: Is a public health framework the cure for cyber security? CrossTalk **2012**, 30–38 (2012)

20. Rowe, J., Levitt, K., Hogarth, M.: Towards the realization of a public health system for shared secure cyberspace. In: Proceedings of the 2013 New Security Paradigms Workshop, pp. 11–18 (2013)

21. Shostack, A., Dykstra, J.: Handling pandemic-scale cyber threats: lessons from COVID-19. In: Proceedings of the New Security Paradigms Workshop (NSPW 2024), pp. 1–10. Association for Computing Machinery, New York, NY, USA (2024)

22. Spafford, E.H.: The Internet worm program: an analysis. ACM SIGCOMM Comput. Commun. Rev. **19**(1), 17–57 (1989)

23. Spafford, E.H., Metcalf, L., Dykstra, J.: Cybersecurity Myths and Misconceptions: Avoiding the Hazards and Pitfalls that Derail Us. Addison-Wesley Professional, Boston (2023)

24. Tuthill, K.: John snow and the broad street pump: on the trail of an epidemic. Cricket **31**(3), 23–31 (2003)

25. Weber, S.: Coercion in cybersecurity: what public health models reveal. J. Cybersecur. (Oxf.) **3**(3), 173–183 (2017). https://doi.org/10.1093/cybsec/tyx005

26. Winslow, H.H.: The New Public Health. Macmillan, New York (1920)

27. World Health Organization: A brief history of vaccination. [n.d.]. https://www.who.int/news-room/spotlight/history-of-vaccination/a-brief-history-of-vaccination. Accessed 18 Mar 2025

Cyberprotection of Medical Imaging

Towards Better Adversarial Defense
on Lung CT Nodule Classification Models
with Feature Enhancement

Yunzheng Zhu[1,2,3], Yuan Tian[2], and Aichi Chien[1(✉)]

[1] Magnetic Resonance Research Labs, Department of Radiological Sciences, David
Geffen School of Medicine, University of California Los Angeles,
Los Angeles, CA 90095, USA
`yunzhengzhu19@ucla.edu`, `achien@mednet.ucla.edu`
[2] Department of Electrical and Computer Engineering, University of California Los
Angeles, Los Angeles, CA 90095, USA
`yuant@ucla.edu`
[3] Medical and Imaging Informatics, Department of Radiological Sciences, University
of California Los Angeles, Los Angeles, CA 900925, USA

Abstract. Deep learning models have emerged as a powerful and cost-effective tool for medical image classification tasks, particularly for oncology. Lung CT computer-aided diagnosis system has been one of the most outstanding tasks with superior performance. However, Lung CT-based CAD systems are vulnerable to adversarial attacks, which could lead to misdiagnosis in clinical practice. Adversarial training, an effective conventional defense method, has proven to be useful in protecting against adversarial attacks and increasing the robustness of the model. However, adversarial training is costly, which requires additional training on a large number of samples. Instead, we developed feature fusion, a defense method with feature enhancement that does not require additional training while significantly improve the robustness of the model. Feature fusion is also generalizable to multiple model architectures (VGG16, ResNet50, and Vision Transformer Base-16) with superior performance. The results show a significant reduction in the performance drop for three first-order gradient adversarial attacks, fast gradient sign method (FGSM), basic iterative method (BIM), and projected gradient descent (PGD). In addition, incorporating additional adversarial training after pretraining with the feature fusion-based classification method can further significantly strengthen the robustness of the model.

Keywords: Adversarial Attack · Lung CT nodule classification · Adversarial Defense

1 Introduction

Lung cancer has been the leading cause of cancer mortality in men and the second leading in women worldwide since 2020, and it continued to increase in

W. Yurcik (Ed.): HealthSec 2024, CCIS 2716, pp. 67–85, 2026.
https://doi.org/10.1007/978-3-032-13800-2_4

2022, surpassing breast cancer as the most common worldwide [4,33]. Lung cancers are commonly detected at the advanced stage with chest radiography [32]. However, it is already too late, resulting in a survival rate of 16% within five years [3]. The challenge of detecting early-stage lesions, known as nodules, is that they are only dime-sized. For the National Lung Screening Trial (NLST), high-risk subjects who underwent low-dose CT screening in the United States reflected a 20% reduction in mortality compared to the chest radiography [36]. Thus, low-dose CT became the standard practice for pulmonary nodule detection. However, even after detection, considerable efforts and experience from the radiologists are required to label the nodules as either benign or require further biopsy to determine malignancy. To reduce the burden of the radiologist in labeling a large number of cases, prior works have proposed computer-aided diagnosis (CAD) systems to assist radiologists detect and analyze pulmonary nodules with efficiency and accuracy [18,26,31]. Then, we can utilize the CAD systems for classifying the nodules from new cases at a low cost.

To create CAD systems, it is always in need of benchmark datasets with sufficient data, including the CT images and labels of the nodules, such as the abnormality (benign or malignancy) of nodules and/or binary masks of nodules. Lung Cancer Data Consortium (LIDC) [2] is such database with CT images of the thoracic region for 1,010 patients along with annotation data of suspicious nodules (both benign and malignant cases) for a size greater than 3 mm from up to four radiologists. National Lung Screening Trial (NLST) [1] is another dataset that consists of a large number of lung CT images of high-risk subjects. A trained radiologist annotated 1,251 cases with nodules, which were used as labels for our study. Deep learning models, such as convolution neural networks and vision transformers, demonstrated superior performance in nodule classification tasks [27,28,35].

However, these nodule classification models are vulnerable to adversarial attacks [15,24,29]. Adversarial examples, or images created with adversarial attacks, can easily "pollute" the model and induce catastrophic performance degradation. Attacking the models with such adversarial examples can result in indistinguishable pixel-level perturbations by human beings. Concern about the safety of utilizing the model in patient cases is then raised [8,38].

To address the issue, it is important to develop a secured deep learning model that can defend against those attacks [6,23,40]. Adversarial training, a typical method targeted for defending against adversarial attacks, has shown its effectiveness in improving the robustness under adversarial attacks [30]. However, adversarial training requires a significant amount of additional training time ($5\times$) with the adversarial attacked samples, which is costly.

To address the issues of adversarial training, we introduce a defense method, feature fusion (FF), that can better improve the robustness and effeciency of the model against adversarial attacks during one-step training and does not require a preprocessing step for filtering out the noises that reside in the original images. Early work has shown that volumetric radiomic features can help improve the accuracy of nodule classification because radiomic features reflect the pathophysiology of the nodule [18,21,26]. These features consist of texture, shape, and grayscale information of the nodule. The combination of these quantitative features creates high dimensional data that is shown to improve the decision support [17]. Another group of studies has shown the effectiveness of using deep neural networks for extracting the deep features of either the lung CT images entirely or only the cropped nodule part of the CT images and then predicting the malignancy of the pulmonary nodules [18]. However, none of the previous work has shown the effectiveness of improving the robustness of the nodule classification model against attacks by incorporating pixel-level features. The inherent information to medical images is usually complicated. Directly feeding the noise-sensitive intensity-based images into the model is naive and insecured to adversarial attacks. Thus, it is important to extract the features resides in the images that can defend against noises and maintain the shapes so as to prevent small pixel perturbations caused by adversarial attacks. In our approach, we introduce a feature fusion module that consists of extracting handcrafted pixel-level features with noise robustness, such as modality-independent neighborhood descriptor-based self-similarity context (MINDSSC) [12], and first-order gradient (GRAD), and shape details, such as gray-level size zone matrix (GLSZM), and gray-level dependency matrix (GLDM), that can better represent the images. The 4 types of features and the original intensity-based image are combined as a feature representation with comprehensive information and then fed into the nodule classification model.

This study is an extension to our prior work [41]. In our study, we investigate the robustness of the nodule classification model with three defense methods, image-level preprocessing, feature fusion, and adversarial training, under three first-order gradient-based attacks, fast gradient sign method (FGSD) [9], projected gradient descent (PGD) [25], and basic iterative method (BIM) [19]. We also investigate the performance on three benchmark deep learning architectures: VGG16, ResNet50, and ViT-Base-16, where the first two are common benchmarks for convolution neural networks-based architectures and the last one is a common benchmark for vision transformers-based architectures. Our contributions are:

1. Proposing a feature fusion module that can improve the robustness of the model to different adversarial attacks significantly, even without adversarial training. Incorporating adversarial training could further strengthen the robustness of the model, even at a large perturbation.
2. Our feature fusion module consists of extracting features with noise-robustness and shape details, and combining the extracted features with intensity-based image to a feature representation with comprehensive information, which strengthen the image understanding by utilizing handcrafted features designed for characterizing the neighbor-pixel variations and prevents the small pixel perturbations caused by adversarial attacks.
3. Our feature fusion module is developed with feature extractions of both the handcrafted features and deep features. The handcrafted features are extracted from the original cropped nodule region of the CT scan and passed

to the convolution layers to extract and group deep features of each specific feature type. Demonstrating the effectivenes of utilizing both types features in protecting against the adversarial attacks.

4. Proposing a feature fusion module that can potentially adapt to various medical image classification tasks. We verified it on two lung nodule classification datasets, Lung Image Database Consortium image collection (LIDC-IDRI) and National Lung Screening Trial (NLST).

5. Investigating and justifying the robustness to adversarial attacks by the relative performance drop (in accuracies and AUROCs) of the nodule classification model on three deep learning architectures (VGG16, ResNet50, and ViT-Base-16).

2 Lung CT Nodule Classification

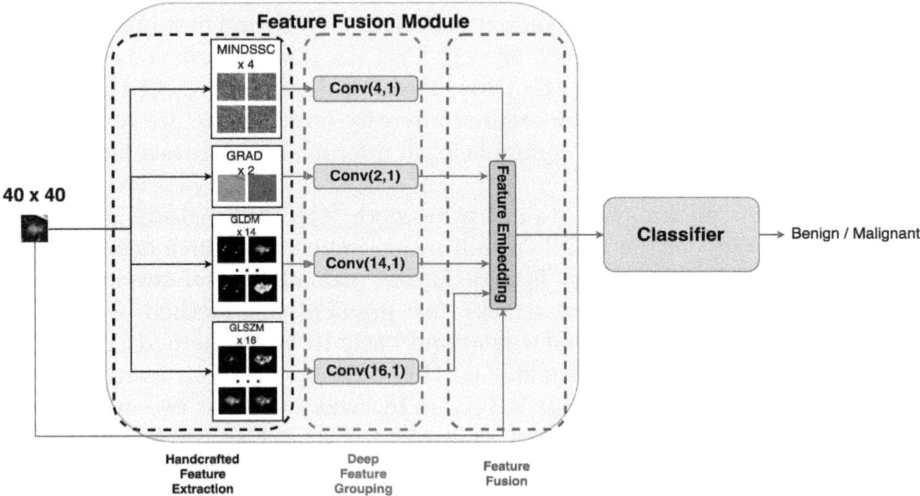

Fig. 1. Nodule Classification Model with a Feature Fusion Module. A 40 x 40 cropped nodule image is fed into the Feature Fusion (FF) Module. In the FF module, different types of handcrafted features are extracted. Then we have customized convolution layers Conv(n, 1) for each type of handcrafted feature individually. n channels of extracted handcrafted features are mapped to 1-channel deep feature via a deep handcrafted feature grouping layer for each type of extracted feature. Each type of deep feature is concatenated into 5-channel (including image) features and mapped to 3-channel features with a 2d convolution-based feature embedding layer. The final embedded feature is fed into the classifier (VGG16, ResNet50, or ViT-B-16) as input and generates nodule predictions, benign or malignant, as output. The classifier is pre-trained with ImageNet-1K for all experiments.

Low-dose CT is a standard way of determining the status of pulmonary nodules that are either benign or necessary for a biopsy to determine the malignancy

[26,37]. Although biopsying is a common step for patients with nodules suspicious of being malignancy and it can help determine the status of patients, an excessive number of biopsies could lead to safety issues, such as Hemorrhage or Pneumothorax [39]. On the other hand, miss-detecting the suspicious malignant nodules would lead to health risks. Thus, it is important to develop an accurate classification model that can mitigate the abovementioned risks. Deep Neural Networks have been widely applied to various medical domains and found to be successful in classifying nodules accurately [16]. However, intensity-based CT scans are usually rich in noises, particularly on shape-rich regions, such as nodules, and usually not robust against small-pixel perturbations, easily leading to a false positive or false negative result. To improve the classification performance in AUROC and accuracy of the model, extracting radiomic features or deep features is one of the most popular ways for assisting and introducing robustness to the model training implicitly. In our approach, we proposed a feature fusion module that explicitly extracting noise robust features and we combined it with shape rich features for better emphasizing the nodule regions. Our designed module consists of three stages: handcrafted feature extraction, deep handcrafted feature grouping, and feature fusion. Details are explained in Sect. 2.3.

2.1 Threat Model

In this section, we will explain the threat to the model, particularly the scenarios that are risky to the lung nodule classification models.

We hypothesize that a well-performed pulmonary nodule classification model is trained. The attack comes from the internal user. Suppose the internal user intends to increase the clinic revenue by increasing the rate of biopsying the patients, even for the benign patients. Under a white-box attack scenario, the user can access everything, including the model, the trained parameters, and the model architecture. The attacker purposely attacks the data by maximizing the loss irrelevant to the correct class as an untargeted attack. However, for a black-box attack, the attacker cannot access the model and the training data, but only the predicted outputs generated by the model. The attacker will train a model based on the output for creating perturbations to maximize the likelihood of misclassification. The model turns out to be generating misclassified results as false positives and false negatives, but indistinguishable by human beings or even expert radiologists. Such a CAD system would increase the possibility of biopsying by predicting a benign nodule as highly suspicious or a malignant nodule as benign. Such attacks could be generated by adversarial attacks, resulting in small-pixel perturbations to the images with a similar general appearance and raising the instability of the model predictions [20].

2.2 Adversarial Attacks

Adversarial image examples were generated from three attack methods: fast gradient sign method (FGSD), projected gradient descent (PGD), and basic iterative method (BIM). Each method aims to maximize the classification loss while minimizing the differences between the adversarial images and the original images. Each of the attacks was also controlled with a defined perturbation size (ϵ), representing the maximum amount of value change of the pixels in an image at each step.

FGSD is the simplest first-order gradient attack that perturbs the image by a fixed amount along the sign direction of the gradient of adversarial loss J. Given the input image x and label y, the generated adversarial image x_{adv} is

$$x_{adv} = x + \epsilon sign(\triangledown x * J(x, y)) \tag{1}$$

where $sign(\triangledown x)$ is the gradient of x. BIM is an upgraded version of FGSM that iteratively perturbs the example with a smaller step size. A clipping of the resulting image at each step is applied. Then the adversarial image x_{n+1} at next step $n+1$ is

$$x_{n+1} = Clip_{x,\epsilon}(x_n + \epsilon sign(\triangledown x * J(x_n, y))) \tag{2}$$

PGD, one of the strongest first-order gradient attacks, also iteratively perturbs the input with a smaller step size but the initialization of each step could be randomized. Similarly, the adversarial image x_{n+1} is

$$x_{n+1} = P(x_n + \epsilon sign(\triangledown x * J(x_n, y))) \tag{3}$$

where P denotes the project onto the l_{inf} norm ball of interest.

2.3 Adversarial Defenses Based Model Design

Our model (Fig. 1) is designed and aimed to improve the robustness against adversarial attacks, which introduces small pixel perturbation as noises to the intensity-based images without changing the general appearance.

Three types of adversarial defense strategies are developed and compared. Adversarial training has shown to be effective in improving the robustness of the nodule classification model against adversarial attacks [15]. However, adversarial training requires 5× additional time for generating adversarial examples and training (Fig. 4). Image-level preprocessing is another conventional strategy for improving the robustness of the attacks by perturbing the noises within the images [7]. However, the effectiveness is relevant to the type and level of the noise. Medical images are usually dominated by stronger noises, such as Gaussian or Poisson noises, than noises in natural images. The noise-filtered image could be over-smoothed and short in distinguishable features. To address inefficiency and ineffectiveness, we designed a classification model that initially incorporates a feature fusion module. The feature fusion module is designed to improve the robustness of the model to adversarial attacks by extracting the noise robust (MINDSSC and GRAD) and shape rich features (GLDM and GLSZM). The composite feature output from feature fusion module consists of comprehensive understanding of the intensity-based image scan, which implicitly reduce the effectiveness of a small-pixel perturbation caused by adversarial attacks. Compared with the naive approach (without any adversarial defense), the running time is less significant increased ($\approx$ ×2) than adversarial training (×5).

Image-Level Preprocessing. For image-level preprocessing, the LIDC-IDRI-Processing Tool was utilized[1]. As depicted in Fig. 2, the tool contains two important components: 1) normalizing and denoising and 2) lung segmentation. The preprocessed images are generated by multiplying the denoised images with the lung masks.

Feature Fusion. Pixel-level feature fusion is essential to our model design. The module is supposed to learn a composite feature representation, that is noise robustness and rich in shapes, as the input to the classification model . To generate such composite feature representation, we extract noise-robust features, such as MINDSSC and GRAD, and shape-rich features, such as GLDM and GLSZM, and combine them with the intensity-based image scan with a feature embedding layer. The feature fusion module consists of three stages of feature extraction (Fig. 1):

1. Handcrafted feature extraction: Each type of handcrafted feature (MINDSSC, GRAD, GLDM, GLSZM) is extracted from a cropped 40×40 CT scan centering at the nodule's center, which is the mean xy-coordinate of the 2d nodule mask. As depicted in Fig. 1, MINDSSC is noise robust because it focuses on the neighbor intensity similarities instead of the raw intensities, whereas GRAD focuses on the first-derivative information that are strongly robust against noises, such as edges or structural changes. Thus, incorporating MINDSSC and GRAD can better improve the robustness of the model training against adversarial attacks. GLDM and GLSZM highlight the nodule shapes while disregard the rest, such as the lung boundaries, which maintain the nodule shapes.
2. Deep handcrafted feature grouping: Each type of handcrafted feature is mapped from $n \times 40 \times 40$ to $1 \times 40 \times 40$ with a 2d convolution layer, where n is the number of channels for each 2d feature representation, and each 2d convolution layer includes a 2d convolution and a ReLU activation. The output $1 \times 40 \times 40$ represents the deep features for the corresponding type.
3. Feature fusion: The output deep features for each type and the original 40×40 cropped image is concatenated and passed to a feature embedding layer for extracting the deep features of the fused image and extracted deep features from stage 2, which is designed with a 2d convolution and a ReLU activation. To match with the pre-trained model on natural image-based ImageNet-1K, the number of channels for output features is set to 3.

Finally, the output of the feature fusion module is passed into the classification module with deep learning architectures, such as VGG16, ResNet50, or Vit-B-16. The classification module generates the predicted binary label as benign or malignant and compares it with the reference for computing the loss or evaluation metrics. Details are explained in Sect. 4.1.

---

[1] https://github.com/jaeho3690/LIDC-IDRI-Preprocessing.

Adversarial Training. Although adversarial training has shown to be effective in many tasks, it does not generalize to our task. Thus, we apply adversarial training either after the image-level preprocessing or feature fusion. The idea of adversarial training is to generate new image samples from the original image samples by perturbing the gradients to a certain amount and then apply those samples for training in an augmentation fashion, we expect to improve the robustness to the model training specifically to the types of attacked samples being generated.

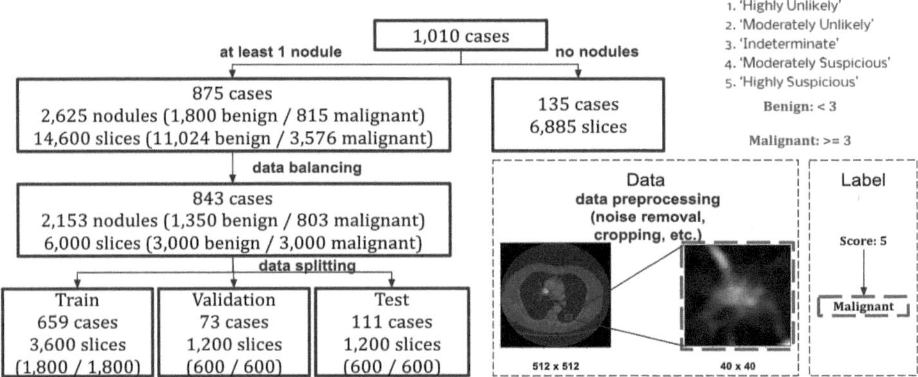

Fig. 2. Example workflow for data cleaning and preprocessing (including noise removal, image cropping, label conversion, etc.)

3   Data Collection

In this study, we conducted experiments on two datasets: Lung Image Database Consortium image collection (LIDC-IDRI) [2] and National Lung Screening Trial (NLST) [1].

LIDC-IDRI is a completed reference database of lung nodules that contains both standard-dose diagnostic and lower-dose lung cancer screening thoracic computed tomographies (CTs). The dataset consists of $1,018$ cases from seven academic centers and eight medical imaging companies. Lung nodules are initially categorized into leq 3 mm nodules, < 3 mm nodules, and leq 3 mm non-nodules and then annotated by four experienced thoracic radiologists. The presence of malignancy was based on the pathologic reports.

The example workflow for data preparation is shown in Fig. 2. After removing the duplicates, there are $1,010$ CT cases, where 875 cases are cancerous and 135 are clean. For 875 cases, there are $14,600$ 2d image slices ($11,024$ benign and $3,576$ malignant). We further filtered to $6,000$ slices to balance the samples for each category ($3,000$ benign and $3,000$ malignant). Then the dataset was split into $3,600/1,200/1,200$ for train/validation/test sets.

NLST is a dataset that contains low-dose helical computed tomography of over $75,000$ CTs from patients in lung cancer studies, particularly for the subjects who smoked within 15 years and aged from 55 to 74. The data were collected within 3 years (1999 to 2001). The same workflow is applied to NLST. A trained radiologist annotated $1,251$ cases with nodules. For $1,251$ cases, there are $7,221$ 2d image slices ($3,038$ benign and $4,183$ malignant). We further filtered to $4,800$ slices ($2,400$ benign and $2,400$ malignant). The dataset was split into $1,440/480/480$ for train/validation/test sets.

The image was cropped into a $40 \times 40\ mm^2$ patch centering at the center of mass of the nodule. The labels were converted from the malignancy score table of five categories into two classes, where a score < 3 is considered a benign case, and a score ≥ 3 is considered a malignant case.

4 Experiments

In this section, we discuss the detailed setup of our feature fusion-based classification model, adversarial attacks, and adversarial training. Our implementation is available at https://github.com/yunzhengzhu/Feature-Fusion-based-Defense/tree/main.

4.1 Model Setup

For our lung nodule classification, we trained it on three deep learning architectures (Table 2): VGG16, ResNet50, and ViT-B-16. All models were pre-trained using Imagenet-1K. The same hyperparameter setting is used as the prior work [15]. The model is trained for 200 epochs with a batch size of 50. An early stopping patience was set to 50 epochs. For each epoch, an initial learning rate 2e-4 was set with 1e-6 learning rate decay. Stochastic gradient descent (SGD) optimizer was applied with 0.9 momentum. The loss function for the model training was the cross entropy without weight balancing.

The input to the model was further clipped into -1,000 to 500 Hounsfield Units (HU) and normalized following an early lung CT nodule classification work [31]. The images were also augmented with two strategies: random flipping horizontally and vertically, and random rotation from -20 to 20°.

4.2 Pixel-Level Handcrafted Feature Extraction and Fusion

Handcrafted features designed for characterizing the neighbor-pixel variations are developed as the extracted features within the feature fusion module. We found four types of features that are effective in improving the model's robustness to adversarial attacks: 4 modality-independent neighborhood descriptor self-similarity contexts (MINDSSC) and 2 first-order gradients (GRAD), 14 gray level dependence matrix (GLDM) and 16 gray level size zone matrix (GLSZM). MINDSSC was developed for extracting the spatially invariant features representing the similarity from pixel to its neighbor pixels [11,12]. Gradient features are usually good at representing the large intensity changes with noise robustness. The later two are extracted by Pyradiomics[2], a Python-based tool for radiomic feature extraction on medical images[3].

4.3   Adversarial Attack

For our experiments, we investigated the impact of different attack methods (FGSM, BIM, and PGD) at four perturbation sizes (ϵ), 0.001, 0.002, 0.004, and 0.006, as illustrated in Table 1 and Fig. 3. For PGD and BIM, the step size was set to $\epsilon/4$ and the maximum number of iterations is 10. The number of random initializations was set to 20 for PGD. This nodule classification task is comparatively more vulnerable than the natural image classification tasks, so smaller perturbation sizes are experimented with [15].

4.4   Adversarial Training

Adversarial training has been one of the most popular methods to defend against adversarial attacks. To simplify the training, we used the strongest first-order-based attack, PGD, for all adversarial training experiments. All experiments have perturbation sizes (ϵ) of 3e-3, and step sizes of 7.5e-4, and the maximum number of iterations is 10. The number of random initialization was set to 5. The model was only trained 30 epochs initialized from the best clean model with a batch size of 128. Adversarial training was conducted on a sample-level attack, representing each sample has a uniform probability of being attacked.

5   Experimental Results

In this section, we first compare the performance of the nodule classification models on various adversarial defenses (from vanilla model to adversarial defenses using image-level preprocessing, feature fusion, and adversarial training) on various perturbation sizes for the testing data on ResNet50 in Sect. 5.1. Then we compare the performance of three model architectures, VGG16, ResNet50, and ViT-B-16, under PGD attacks in Sect. 5.2. Then, we perform qualitative comparisons on adversarial defense methods on ResNet50 in Sect. 5.3 and a running time comparison in Sect. 5.4.

5.1   Quantitative Comparison on Adversarial Attacks

Table 1 demonstrates an accuracy of 0.726 and AUROC of 0.816 for the clean model of LIDC-IDRI, . Adversarial attacking the model without any defense strategies yields around $0.2 \sim 0.3$, $0.4 \sim 0.5$, and $0.4 \sim 0.5$ absolute drops in

---

[2] https://github.com/AIM-Harvard/pyradiomics/tree/master.
[3] Note: Remaining 93 pixel-level features are removed because of instability of convergence when used as classification inputs.

Table 1. Accuracy (acc.), AUROC (auc) and relative difference (Δ) of nodule classification model (ResNet50) on the test dataset (LIDC-IDRI and NLST) with FGSM, BIM, PGD adversarial attacks at different perturbation sizes (ϵ). Prep: Image-level Preprocessing, AT: Adversarial Training, FF: Feature Fusion. Red and blue represents the first and second best Δ.

Cohort		LIDC-IDRI										NLST					
Attack	ϵ	Baseline		Prep		Prep + AT		FF		FF + AT		Baseline		FF		FF + AT	
		acc.	Δ	acc.	Δ	acc.	Δ	acc.	Δ	acc.	Δ	acc.	Δ	acc.	Δ	acc	Δ
None	0	0.726	0	0.713	0	0.711	0	0.659	0	0.643	0	0.650	0	0.581	0	0.582	0
FGSM	.001	0.427	-0.299	0.512	-0.201	0.511	-0.200	0.652	-0.007	0.644	0.001	0.365	-0.285	0.573	-0.008	0.584	0.002
	.002	0.417	-0.309	0.566	-0.147	0.553	-0.158	0.651	-0.008	0.637	0.006	0.359	-0.291	0.565	-0.016	0.586	0.004
	.004	0.466	-0.260	0.613	-0.100	0.608	-0.103	0.647	-0.012	0.639	-0.004	0.364	-0.286	0.551	-0.030	0.571	-0.011
	.006	0.511	-0.215	0.629	-0.084	0.640	-0.071	0.646	-0.013	0.636	-0.007	0.372	-0.278	0.536	-0.045	0.562	-0.020
BIM	.001	0.282	-0.444	0.287	-0.426	0.290	-0.421	0.652	-0.007	0.644	0.001	0.348	-0.302	0.573	-0.008	0.582	0
	.002	0.274	-0.452	0.287	-0.426	0.289	-0.422	0.650	-0.009	0.636	-0.007	0.350	-0.300	0.560	-0.021	0.585	0.003
	.004	0.274	-0.452	0.287	-0.426	0.289	-0.422	0.647	-0.012	0.637	-0.006	0.350	-0.300	0.542	-0.039	0.564	-0.018
	.006	0.274	-0.452	0.287	-0.426	0.289	-0.422	0.643	-0.016	0.634	-0.009	0.350	-0.300	0.510	-0.071	0.556	-0.026
PGD	.001	0.275	-0.451	0.287	-0.426	0.289	-0.422	0.652	-0.007	0.644	0.001	0.348	-0.302	0.573	-0.008	0.583	0.001
	.002	0.274	-0.452	0.287	-0.426	0.289	-0.422	0.651	-0.008	0.635	-0.008	0.350	-0.300	0.559	-0.022	0.582	0
	.004	0.274	-0.452	0.287	-0.426	0.289	-0.422	0.651	-0.008	0.636	-0.007	0.350	-0.300	0.522	-0.059	0.562	-0.020
	.006	0.274	-0.452	0.287	-0.426	0.289	-0.422	0.645	-0.014	0.637	-0.006	0.350	-0.300	0.497	-0.084	0.564	-0.018
		auc	Δ	auc	Δ	auc	Δ	auc	Δ	auc	Δ	auc	Δ	auc	Δ	auc	Δ
None	0	0.816	0	0.812	0	0.815	0	0.711	0	0.710	0	0.700	0	0.680	0	0.685	0
FGSM	.001	0.412	-0.404	0.520	-0.292	0.544	-0.271	0.711	0	0.709	-0.001	0.406	-0.294	0.670	-0.010	0.685	0
	.002	0.417	-0.399	0.610	-0.202	0.593	-0.222	0.710	-0.001	0.709	-0.001	0.404	-0.296	0.653	-0.027	0.682	-0.003
	.004	0.483	-0.333	0.698	-0.114	0.671	-0.144	0.709	-0.002	0.707	-0.003	0.397	-0.303	0.601	-0.079	0.677	-0.008
	.006	0.541	-0.275	0.734	-0.078	0.714	-0.101	0.707	-0.004	0.707	-0.003	0.388	-0.312	0.558	-0.122	0.670	-0.015
BIM	.001	0.342	-0.474	0.369	-0.443	0.375	-0.440	0.711	0	0.709	-0.001	0.379	-0.321	0.669	-0.011	0.685	0
	.002	0.335	-0.481	0.347	-0.465	0.364	-0.451	0.710	-0.001	0.709	-0.001	0.370	-0.330	0.647	-0.033	0.682	-0.003
	.004	0.321	-0.495	0.319	-0.493	0.351	-0.464	0.708	-0.003	0.707	-0.003	0.369	-0.331	0.570	-0.110	0.675	-0.010
	.006	0.312	-0.504	0.306	-0.506	0.340	-0.475	0.706	-0.005	0.707	-0.003	0.366	-0.334	0.513	-0.167	0.665	-0.020
PGD	.001	0.341	-0.475	0.357	-0.455	0.371	-0.444	0.711	0	0.709	0.011	0.377	-0.323	0.668	-0.012	0.685	0
	.002	0.327	-0.489	0.322	-0.490	0.354	-0.461	0.710	-0.001	0.709	-0.001	0.373	-0.327	0.643	-0.037	0.596	-0.003
	.004	0.308	-0.508	0.309	-0.503	0.333	-0.482	0.708	-0.003	0.707	-0.003	0.367	-0.333	0.555	-0.125	0.675	-0.010
	.006	0.307	-0.509	0.304	-0.508	0.330	-0.485	0.705	-0.006	0.707	-0.003	0.361	-0.339	0.495	-0.185	0.663	-0.022

accuracies, and 0.3 $\sim$ 0.4, 0.4 $\sim$ 0.5, and 0.4 $\sim$ 0.5 absolute drops in AUROCs for FGSM, BIM, and PGD respectively. Both BIM and PGD demonstrated more successful attacking than FGSM. However, for NLST, the drop is approximately the same for all types of attacks (0.2 $\sim$ 0.3) on both accuracies and AUROCs.

For the model with adversarial defenses on LIDC-IDRI, both data preprocessing (Prep) and data preprocessing with adversarial training (Prep + AT) demonstrated slight decreased performance drops to 0.1 $\sim$ 0.2 for FGSM, but minimal difference on performance drops for stronger attack methods (BIM and PGD), reflecting the weakness of improving model robustness with Prep or AT. Our proposed feature fusion (FF) can lead to a significant improvement on performance drop to less than 2e-2 on accuracies and an order of magnitude smaller on AUROCs. Incorporating AT (FF + AT) can achieve a further reduction, particularly for attacks with large perturbations (ϵ of 0.006). For NLST, similar trends of improvement are observed.

Notably, we observed that AT on the clean model trained with original image samples does not have any performance improvement. We hypothesize that training with inputs that are rich in noises (such as original unpreprocessed Lung CT images) is harder to be affected by the adversarial attacks than the noise-perturbed images. Also, conducting FF-based defense on the images with preprocessing can hardly generalize the performance. We hypothesize that some features from the preprocessed images with noise perturbation bring too many variations to the inputs, which cannot easily be generalized with the model trained with such as small amount of data. For NLST, preprocessed NLST data reached a gradient exploding in training, representing the low generalizability of the preprocessing strategies.

5.2   Quantitative Comparison on Model Architectures

Table 2 demonstrates accuracies of 0.675, 0.726, and 0.726, and AUROCs of 0.763, 0.816, and 0.812 on clean model of for VGG16, ResNet50, and ViT-B-16, respectively. An $0.1 \sim 0.4$, $0.4 \sim 0.5$, and $0.1 \sim 0.4$ absolute drops on the accuracies and AUROCs for VGG16, ResNet50, and ViT-B-16, respectively. Prep and Prep with AT lead to a minimal reduced performance drop on ResNet50 and ViT-B-16, but significant reduced performance drop on VGG16 when Prep and AT are applied, but Prep does not have a significant performance drop, particularly for large perturbations (ϵ of 0.004 and 0.006). But for our FF, all attacks are alleviated and reduce the performance drop significantly. Incorporating AT (FF + AT) also demonstrates a better reduction in performance drop, particularly for ResNet50 and ViT-B-16. The difference of performance infers that utilizing Prep-based defense methods could be more beneficial for a simpler architecture, such as VGG16, but our proposed feature fusion is adaptable to a broad choices of model architectures, particularly for ResNet50, and ViT-B-16, which are commonly designed with higher generalizability, stability of convergenece, and memory efficient (with less number of parameters than VGG16).

5.3   Qualitative Comparison

As demonstrated in Fig 3, the visualization results reflect the improvement of the defenses for our proposed feature fusion method. For example, as shown in Fig. 3, a malignant nodule case from LIDC-IDRI with FF only can hardly be predicted correctly on the clean, Prep, and Prep + AT models with all perturbation sizes. However, our method FF can still predict the case as malignant with 86.5% confidence even with a relatively large perturbation of $\epsilon = 0.006$ (a reduction of 4% confidence from unattacked model performance). With FF + AT, a large perturbation of $\epsilon = 0.006$ can still yield 87.7% confidence (a reduction of 1.7% confidence from unattacked model performance). For the benign nodule case from NLST, the clean model is also hardly predict the case correctly with any size of perturbation. FF can still predict as 87.6% confidence benign

Table 2. Accuracy (acc.), AUROC (auc) and relative difference (Δ) of nodule classification model on the test dataset (LIDC-IDRI and NLST) with FGSM, BIM, PGD adversarial attacks at different perturbation sizes (ϵ) with model archtectures of VGG16, ResNet50, and ViT-B-16. Param.: Number of Model Parameters, Prep: Image-level Preprocessing, AT: Adversarial Training, FF: Feature Fusion. Red and blue represents the first and second best Δ.

Cohort			LIDC-IDRI										NLST					
Model	Param.	ϵ	Baseline		Prep		Prep + AT		FF		FF + AT		Baseline		FF		FF + AT	
			acc.	Δ	acc.	Δ	acc.	Δ	acc.	Δ	acc.	Δ	acc.	Δ	acc.	Δ	acc	Δ
VGG16	138.5M	0	0.675	0	0.723	0	0.725	0	0.644	0	0.657	0	0.673	0	0.667	0	0.673	0
		.001	0.587	-0.088	0.568	-0.155	0.718	-0.007	0.637	-0.007	0.603	-0.054	0.464	-0.209	0.623	-0.044	0.613	-0.060
		.002	0.453	-0.222	0.409	-0.314	0.714	-0.011	0.629	-0.015	0.573	-0.084	0.321	-0.352	0.551	-0.116	0.526	-0.147
		.004	0.366	-0.309	0.294	-0.429	0.627	-0.098	0.526	-0.118	0.522	-0.135	0.321	-0.352	0.487	-0.180	0.444	-0.229
		.006	0.331	-0.344	0.277	-0.446	0.539	-0.186	0.472	-0.172	0.503	-0.154	0.324	-0.349	0.459	-0.208	0.416	-0.257
ResNet50	25.6M	0	0.726	0	0.713	0	0.711	0	0.659	0	0.643	0	0.650	0	0.581	0	0.582	0
		.001	0.275	-0.451	0.287	-0.426	0.289	-0.422	0.652	-0.007	0.644	0.001	0.348	-0.302	0.573	-0.008	0.583	0.001
		.002	0.274	-0.452	0.287	-0.426	0.289	-0.422	0.651	-0.008	0.635	-0.008	0.350	-0.300	0.559	-0.022	0.582	0
		.004	0.274	-0.452	0.287	-0.426	0.289	-0.422	0.651	-0.008	0.636	-0.007	0.350	-0.300	0.522	-0.059	0.562	-0.020
		.006	0.274	-0.452	0.287	-0.426	0.289	-0.422	0.645	-0.014	0.637	-0.006	0.350	-0.300	0.497	-0.084	0.564	-0.018
ViT-B-16	86.6M	0	0.726	0	0.685	0	0.708	0	0.722	0	0.589	0	0.646	0	0.633	0	0.626	0
		.001	0.598	-0.128	0.569	-0.116	0.556	-0.152	0.699	-0.023	0.584	-0.005	0.412	-0.234	0.547	-0.086	0.545	-0.081
		.002	0.500	-0.226	0.417	-0.268	0.390	-0.318	0.611	-0.111	0.528	-0.061	0.360	-0.286	0.480	-0.153	0.486	-0.140
		.004	0.341	-0.385	0.325	-0.360	0.302	-0.406	0.461	-0.261	0.484	-0.105	0.354	-0.292	0.428	-0.205	0.430	-0.196
		.006	0.292	-0.434	0.315	-0.370	0.293	-0.415	0.366	-0.356	0.460	-0.129	0.354	-0.292	0.404	-0.229	0.406	-0.220
			auc	Δ	auc	Δ	auc	Δ	auc	Δ	auc	Δ	auc	Δ	auc	Δ	auc	Δ
VGG16	138.5M	0	0.763	0	0.823	0	0.826	0	0.727	0	0.723	0	0.736	0	0.729	0	0.731	0
		.001	0.657	-0.106	0.641	-0.182	0.823	-0.003	0.719	-0.008	0.702	-0.021	0.466	-0.270	0.698	-0.031	0.677	-0.054
		.002	0.501	-0.262	0.432	-0.391	0.807	-0.019	0.675	-0.052	0.654	-0.069	0.355	-0.381	0.611	-0.118	0.546	-0.185
		.004	0.396	-0.367	0.320	-0.503	0.711	-0.115	0.562	-0.165	0.560	-0.163	0.341	-0.395	0.477	-0.252	0.414	-0.317
		.006	0.384	-0.379	0.305	-0.518	0.597	-0.229	0.502	-0.225	0.498	-0.225	0.333	-0.403	0.431	-0.298	0.384	-0.347
ResNet50	25.6M	0	0.816	0	0.812	0	0.815	0	0.711	0	0.710	0	0.700	0	0.680	0	0.685	0
		.001	0.341	-0.475	0.357	-0.455	0.371	-0.444	0.711	0	0.709	0.011	0.377	-0.323	0.668	-0.012	0.685	0
		.002	0.327	-0.489	0.322	-0.490	0.354	-0.461	0.710	-0.001	0.709	-0.001	0.373	-0.327	0.643	-0.037	0.596	-0.003
		.004	0.308	-0.508	0.309	-0.503	0.333	-0.482	0.708	-0.003	0.707	-0.003	0.367	-0.333	0.555	-0.125	0.675	-0.010
		.006	0.307	-0.509	0.304	-0.508	0.330	-0.485	0.705	-0.006	0.707	-0.003	0.361	-0.339	0.495	-0.185	0.663	-0.022
ViT-B-16	86.6M	0	0.812	0	0.792	0	0.798	0	0.815	0	0.641	0	0.695	0	0.701	0	0.701	0
		.001	0.693	-0.119	0.624	-0.168	0.614	-0.184	0.791	-0.024	0.641	0	0.416	-0.279	0.565	-0.136	0.564	-0.137
		.002	0.515	-0.297	0.433	-0.359	0.404	-0.394	0.682	-0.133	0.558	-0.083	0.370	-0.325	0.445	-0.256	0.457	-0.244
		.004	0.352	-0.460	0.387	-0.405	0.361	-0.437	0.471	-0.344	0.462	-0.179	0.357	-0.338	0.428	-0.273	0.440	-0.261
		.006	0.333	-0.479	0.393	-0.399	0.363	-0.435	0.396	-0.419	0.471	-0.170	0.351	-0.344	0.417	-0.284	0.429	-0.272

with a perturbation of 0.004, whereas FF + AT can also make prediction slightly leaning towards benign when the perturbation size is 0.002. Both FF and FF + AT demonstrates an significant improvement on prediction over the clean model. However, because the performance on clean model is already relatively low (0.650 for acc. and 0.700 for auc), a further performance drop incorporates when incorporating the feature fusion modules into training (0.581 acc. and 0.680 auc for FF, and 0.582 acc. and 0.685 auc for FF + AT), reflecting the instability of ResNet50 on a smaller dataset. A similar trend is also observed for ViT-B-16, which usually requires sufficient amount of data for training a stable model.

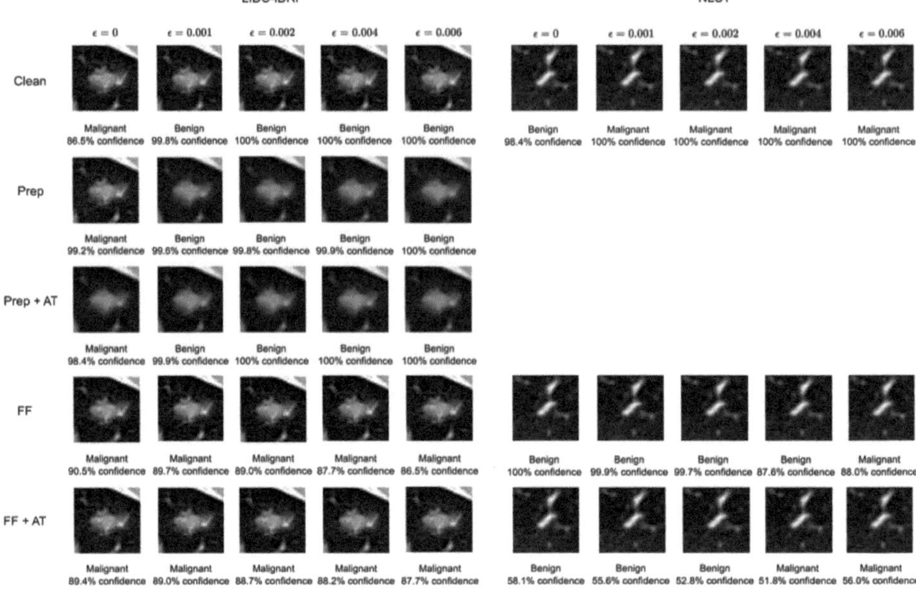

Fig. 3. Visualization Results of two image cases from each test set (one malignant case from LIDC-IDRI and one benign case from NLST) under PGD attacks on ResNet50 classifier with different adversarial defense methods (Prep: data preprocessing, AT: adversarial training, FF: feature fusion).

5.4   Running Time

We also reported the running time (in hours) for training the nodule classification model with different methods in Fig. 4. For both LIDC-IDRI and NLST, FF is only nearly 2x in running time, whereas AT only would significantly increase the running time to nearly 5×. For three architectures, ResNet50 takes the least amount of time, around 0.5× of VGG16, whereas ViT-B-16 takes around 2× of VGG16.

6   Discussions

Image-level preprocessing shows to outperform the other models in accuracy and AUROC before attacking the model. However, adversarial attacks could drop the performance more than the images without preprocessing, reflecting the vulnerability of the preprocessed images. The major difference between the preprocessed and unpreprocessed images is the noise filtering. This reflects the importance of considering the noises injected into the model inputs, which could largely affect the intensity values of the model inputs, leading to a different distribution. The noise-filtered images usually have fewer pixel-to-pixel intensity variations on the images, which makes the adversarial attacks easier to affect.

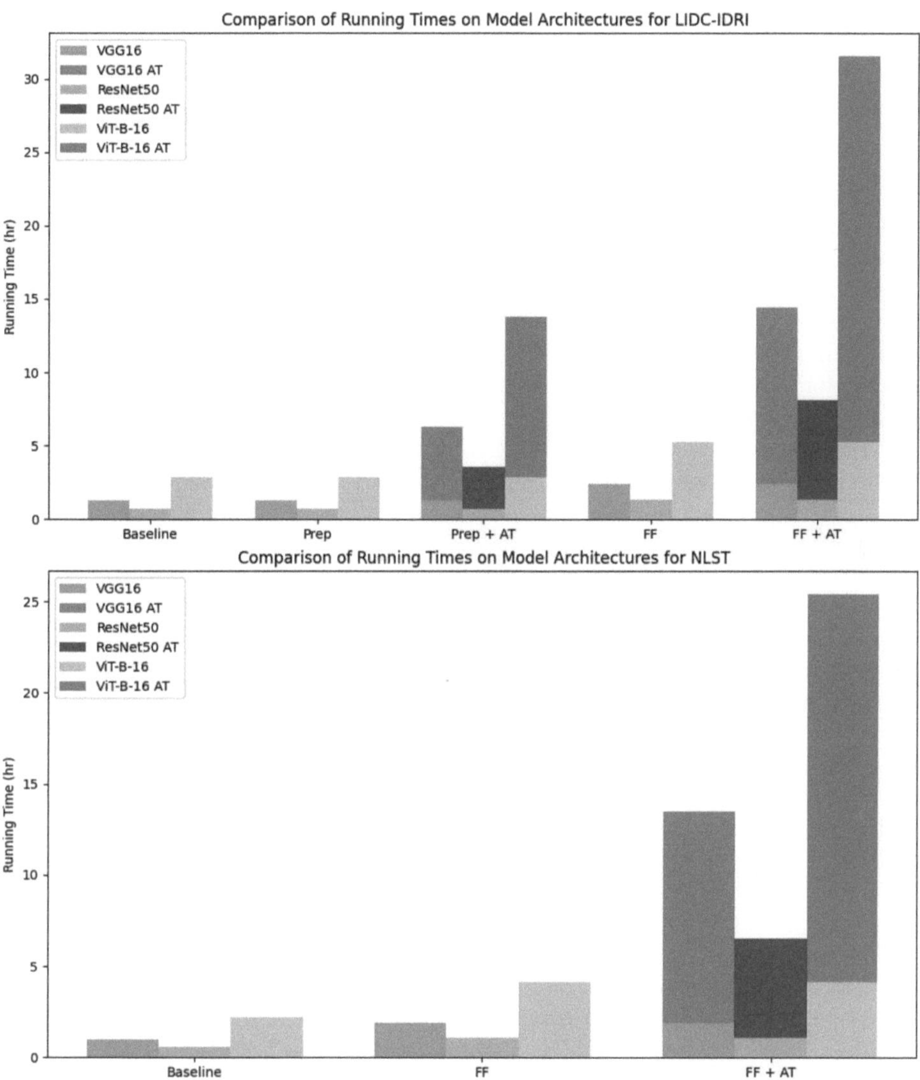

Fig. 4. Running time in hours (hr) for training the nodule classification model. Prep: Image-level Preprocessing, AT: Adversarial Training, FF: Feature Fusion. For the two-stage training experiments (+ AT), the bottom represents the amount of time for model training, and top represents the amount of time for a second-stage adversarial training.

Thus, we could consider the original Lung CT scans as robust against adversarial attacks to some level.

The feature fusion-based adversarial training achieves the lowest performance when none of the attacks are applied. But the performance drop is the least, which reflects the robustness of the model trained with feature-fusion and adversarial training. This also reflects the tradeoff between clean model performance and the robustness against adversarial attacks. Our feature fusion method is comparatively more adaptable to a stablized model, such as resnets and vision transformers. However, these types of models usually require more data to train. We will increase the data size in the future.

Moreover, the feature fusion-based strategy is similar to the feature enhancement-based adversarial defenses [14] for enhancing the feature representation for the model training. However, different from most of the feature enhancement methods focusing on enhancing the deep features around the mechanisms such as attention [5], pooling [34], or batch normalization [10], we focus on utilizing the pixel-level features that are noise robust and rich in shape information for enhancing the model understanding of nodules and protection to adversarial attacks.

Recently, state-of-the-art (SOTA) methods in defenses include AdaNI, which injects random noises into the data to increase the feature randomness and leads to improvement of model robustness [22]. Feature pattern consistency constraint (FPCC) increases the robustness of the model by reinforcing correct feature patterns residing in the capacity of latent features [13]. For medical imaging, because the general appearance of the images is similar, the distinction of the model is usually from the pixel-level features. Thus, utilizing the above SOTA methods requires us to consider the features as precise as the pixel, which may increase the difficulty of defense.

7 Conclusions

In this study, we conducted experiments on improving the robustness of the nodule classification model with various adversarial defense methods and tested the model performance on the adversarially attacked images. We proposed a feature-fusion-based method that enhances the feature understanding by leveraging the noise robust and shape features to train the nodule classifiers. We show that our method can generally improve the robustness of the model with less performance drop than image-level preprocessing and more efficient than adversarial training, which requires additional training. Moreover, combining the feature-fusion-based method with the adversarial training can yield the most robust classification model. In the future, other medical classification domains, such as breast lesions, brain metastases, and liver cancers, will be conducted and verified on our feature-fusion-based method.

Acknowledgments. This research was supported in part by the National Institutes of Health, National Heart, Lung, and Blood Institute (R01 HL152270), and National Science Foundation (2411153).

References

1. N.L.S.T.R.T., Data from the national lung screening trial (NLST) [data set]. The Cancer Imaging Archive (2013)

2. Armato, S.G., III., et al.: The lung image database consortium (LIDC) and image database resource initiative (IDRI): a completed reference database of lung nodules on ct scans. Med. Phys. **38**(2), 915–931 (2011)

3. Bach, P.B., et al.: Benefits and harms of ct screening for lung cancer: a systematic review. JAMA **307**(22), 2418–2429 (2012)

4. Cao, W., Qin, K., Li, F., Chen, W.: Comparative study of cancer profiles between 2020 and 2022 using global cancer statistics (globocan). J. National Cancer Center **4**(2), 128–134 (2024)

5. Chen, L., Zhao, L., Chen, C.Y.C.: Enhancing adversarial defense for medical image analysis systems with pruning and attention mechanism. Med. Phys. **48**(10), 6198–6212 (2021)

6. Dhar, T., Dey, N., Borra, S., Sherratt, R.S.: Challenges of deep learning in medical image analysis–improving explainability and trust. IEEE Trans. Technol. Soc. **4**(1), 68–75 (2023)

7. Dong, J., Chen, J., Xie, X., Lai, J., Chen, H.: Adversarial attack and defense for medical image analysis: methods and applications. arXiv preprint arXiv:2303.14133 (2023)

8. Finlayson, S.G., Bowers, J.D., Ito, J., Zittrain, J.L., Beam, A.L., Kohane, I.S.: Adversarial attacks on medical machine learning. Science **363**(6433), 1287–1289 (2019)

9. Goodfellow, I.J., Shlens, J., Szegedy, C.: Explaining and harnessing adversarial examples. arXiv preprint arXiv:1412.6572 (2014)

10. Han, T., et al.: Advancing diagnostic performance and clinical usability of neural networks via adversarial training and dual batch normalization. Nat. Commun. **12**(1), 4315 (2021)

11. Heinrich, M.P., et al.: Mind: modality independent neighbourhood descriptor for multi-modal deformable registration. Med. Image Anal. **16**(7), 1423–1435 (2012)

12. Heinrich, M.P., Jenkinson, M., Papież, B.W., Brady, S.M., Schnabel, J.A.: Towards realtime multimodal fusion for image-guided interventions using self-similarities. In: Mori, K., Sakuma, I., Sato, Y., Barillot, C., Navab, N. (eds.) MICCAI 2013. LNCS, vol. 8149, pp. 187–194. Springer, Heidelberg (2013). https://doi.org/10.1007/978-3-642-40811-3_24

13. Hu, J., et al.: Improving adversarial robustness via feature pattern consistency constraint. arXiv preprint arXiv:2406.08829 (2024)

14. Ilyas, A., Santurkar, S., Tsipras, D., Engstrom, L., Tran, B., Madry, A.: Adversarial examples are not bugs, they are features. Adv. Neural Inf. Process. Syst. **32** (2019)

15. Joel, M.Z., et al.: Using adversarial images to assess the robustness of deep learning models trained on diagnostic images in oncology. JCO Clin. Cancer Inf. **6**, e2100170 (2022)

16. Kann, B.H., Thompson, R., Thomas, C.R., Jr., Dicker, A., Aneja, S.: Artificial intelligence in oncology: current applications and future directions. Oncology **33**(2), 46–53 (2019)

17. Krizhevsky, A., Sutskever, I., Hinton, G.E.: Imagenet classification with deep convolutional neural networks. Adv. Neural Inf. Process. Syst. **25** (2012)

18. Kumar, D., Wong, A., Clausi, D.A.: Lung nodule classification using deep features in CT images. In: 2015 12th Conference on Computer and Robot Vision, pp. 133–138. IEEE (2015)

19. Kurakin, A., Goodfellow, I., Bengio, S.: Adversarial machine learning at scale. arXiv preprint arXiv:1611.01236 (2016)

20. Kurakin, A., Goodfellow, I.J., Bengio, S.: Adversarial examples in the physical world. In: Artificial Intelligence Safety and Security, pp. 99–112. Chapman and Hall/CRC (2018)
21. Li, S., et al.: Predicting lung nodule malignancies by combining deep convolutional neural network and handcrafted features. Phys. Med. Biol. **64**(17), 175012 (2019)
22. Li, Y., Zhang, C., Qi, H., Lyu, S.: Adani: adaptive noise injection to improve adversarial robustness. Comput. Vision Image Understand. **238**, 103855 (2024)
23. Liu, Y., Yang, C., Li, D., Ding, J., Jiang, T.: Defense against adversarial attacks on no-reference image quality models with gradient norm regularization. In: Proceedings of the IEEE/CVF Conference on Computer Vision and Pattern Recognition, pp. 25554–25563 (2024)
24. Ma, X., et al.: Understanding adversarial attacks on deep learning based medical image analysis systems. Patt. Recogn. **110**, 107332 (2021)
25. Madry, A., Makelov, A., Schmidt, L., Tsipras, D., Vladu, A.: Towards deep learning models resistant to adversarial attacks. arXiv preprint arXiv:1706.06083 (2017)
26. Mehta, K., Jain, A., Mangalagiri, J., Menon, S., Nguyen, P., Chapman, D.R.: Lung nodule classification using biomarkers, volumetric radiomics, and 3d CNNs. J. Digit. Imaging, 1–20 (2021)
27. Mkindu, H., Wu, L., Zhao, Y.: 3d multi-scale vision transformer for lung nodule detection in chest ct images. Sign. Image Video Process. **17**(5), 2473–2480 (2023)
28. Nibali, A., He, Z., Wollersheim, D.: Pulmonary nodule classification with deep residual networks. Int. J. Comput. Assist. Radiol. Surg. , 1–10 (2017). https://doi.org/10.1007/s11548-017-1605-6
29. Paul, R., Schabath, M., Gillies, R., Hall, L., Goldgof, D.: Mitigating adversarial attacks on medical image understanding systems. In: 2020 IEEE 17th International Symposium on Biomedical Imaging (ISBI), pp. 1517–1521. IEEE (2020)
30. Shafahi, A., et al.: Adversarial training for free! Adv. Neural Inf. Process. Syst. **32** (2019)
31. Shen, S., Han, S.X., Aberle, D.R., Bui, A.A., Hsu, W.: An interpretable deep hierarchical semantic convolutional neural network for lung nodule malignancy classification. Expert Syst. Appl. **128**, 84–95 (2019)
32. Shiraishi, J., et al.: Development of a digital image database for chest radiographs with and without a lung nodule: receiver operating characteristic analysis of radiologists' detection of pulmonary nodules. Am. J. Roentgenol. **174**(1), 71–74 (2000)
33. Sung, H., et al.: Global cancer statistics 2020: Globocan estimates of incidence and mortality worldwide for 36 cancers in 185 countries. CA Cancer J. Clin. **71**(3), 209–249 (2021)
34. Taghanaki, S.A., Abhishek, K., Azizi, S., Hamarneh, G.: A kernelized manifold mapping to diminish the effect of adversarial perturbations. In: Proceedings of the IEEE/CVF Conference on Computer Vision and Pattern Recognition, pp. 11340–11349 (2019)
35. Tang, D., Xiao, T., Yang, F., Zhang, C., Wang, Z., Gao, W.: Vsnet: classification of pulmonary nodules in 3d using vision transformer and sequence spatial attention mechanism. Multimedia Tools Appl. 1–19 (2024)
36. Team, N.L.S.T.R.: Reduced lung-cancer mortality with low-dose computed tomographic screening. New England J. Med. **365**(5), 395–409 (2011)
37. Wang, H., Zhu, H., Ding, L., Yang, K.: A diagnostic classification of lung nodules using multiple-scale residual network. Sci. Reports **13**(1), 11322 (2023)
38. Watson, M., Al Moubayed, N.: Attack-agnostic adversarial detection on medical data using explainable machine learning. In: 2020 25th International Conference on Pattern Recognition (ICPR), pp. 8180–8187. IEEE (2021)

39. Wiener, R.S., Wiener, D.C., Gould, M.K.: Risks of transthoracic needle biopsy: how high? Clin. Pulmonary Med. **20**(1), 29–35 (2013)
40. Xiao, C., Li, B., Zhu, J.Y., He, W., Liu, M., Song, D.: Generating adversarial examples with adversarial networks. arXiv preprint arXiv:1801.02610 (2018)
41. Zhu, Y., Chien, A., Tian, Y.: Protecting lung ct nodule classification models with feature fusion of image and pixel-level features. In: Proceedings of the 2024 Workshop on Cybersecurity in Healthcare, pp. 29–36 (2023)

The Security of Deep Learning Defenses in Medical Imaging

Moshe Levy⬤, Guy Amit⬤, and Yisroel Mirsky^(✉)⬤

Department of Software and Information Systems Engineering, Ben-Gurion University, Beersheba, Israel
`moshe0110@gmail.com, guy5@post.bgu.ac.il, yisroel@bgu.ac.il`

Abstract. Deep learning has shown great promise in the medical image analysis domain. Medical professionals and healthcare providers have begun to adopt this technology to accelerate and enhance their work. These systems use deep neural networks (DNNs) which are vulnerable to adversarial samples: images with imperceivable changes that can alter the model's prediction. Prior research has proposed defenses aimed at making DNNs more robust or detecting the adversarial samples before they can do any harm. However, none of the studies considered an informed attacker capable of adapting the attack to the defense mechanism. In this qualitative study, we show that an informed attacker can evade five advanced defenses, successfully fooling the victim deep learning model and rendering the defense useless. We also propose two alternative means of securing healthcare DNNs from such attacks: (1) hardening the system's security, and (2) using digital signatures. Finally, we discuss measures the healthcare community should take to mitigate this threat and explore the evolving threat landscape as large language models (LLMs) become increasingly integrated into the industry.

Keywords: Adversarial Attacks · Deep Learning Security · Medical Imaging · Healthcare AI Robustness · Digital Signatures · Large Language Models (LLMs) in Healthcare

1 Introduction

Deep learning is a data-driven machine learning technique that provides state-of-the-art performance in image analysis tasks. Deep learning uses a model called a deep neural network (DNN) which makes predictions by learning from historical data. Over the past 10 years, deep learning technology has proven itself an efficient and highly accurate image analysis tool in a wide range of tasks, including: cancer detection, spatial alignment and content image retrieval [31]. Due to the complexity and diversity of the data, DNNs are expected to have an even greater role in the near future in medical imaging analysis [8,11]. While some deep learning solutions have already been approved and deployed [26], a number of major companies in the medical field are developing DNN-based products, with the aim of deploying them soon [6,10,45].

© The Author(s), under exclusive license to Springer Nature Switzerland AG 2026
W. Yurcik (Ed.): HealthSec 2024, CCIS 2716, pp. 86–110, 2026.
https://doi.org/10.1007/978-3-032-13800-2_5

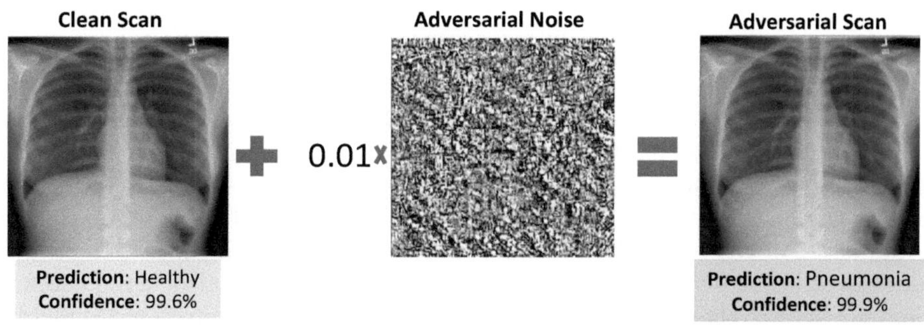

Fig. 1. How adversarial noise can influence the prediction of a DNN-based pneumonia detector.

A key drawback of DNNs is their vulnerability to adversarial samples—seemingly benign inputs [47], like X-ray images, with imperceptible noise patterns that can drastically alter the model's prediction such as flipping a benign diagnosis to malign (Fig. 1). Since DNNs are becoming more mainstream in radiology and other medical imaging analysis domains, the existence of adversarial samples threatens the healthcare domain. There are number of reasons why an attacker may want to trick a medical imaging DNN.

To make money. An attacker may be interested in making money. For example, insurance fraud can be perpetrated by fooling a model to detect a lesion in a brain MRI, providing seemingly irrefutable evidence as to why a patient can no longer taste food and should be compensated, or medical scans can be held hostage in a ransomware attack in which the images remain tampered with until a ransom payment is made.

To cause harm. The attacker's goal might be to cause harm for revenge, or to gain fame and attention, perform terrorism, or cause political turmoil. For example, the attacker can cause the model to miss a lesion in an MRI or provide an incorrect diagnosis to a radiologist.

To receive priority treatment. An attacker may be motivated to trick a medical imaging DNN to receive priority treatment. For example, a slight increase in the size of a bone fracture or spinal disk herniation may enable a patient to receive treatment sooner (over more deserving patients).

Medical imaging attacks are achievable. The millions of medical records stolen in data breaches this year[1] attest to this. Research has shown how picture archiving and communication systems (PACSs) can be hacked from the Internet [7] and demonstrated how easy it is to gain physical access to a PACS and maliciously plant a device in a hospital's network [36].

Since these attacks are feasible, the threat of adversarial samples has gained attention among the medical imaging community in the last few years [15, 16, 52].

---

[1] https://www.healthcareitnews.com/news/biggest-healthcare-data-breaches-2021.

In response to this threat, researchers have proposed a wide variety of detection and mitigation techniques to protect DNN-based medical imaging applications.

In recent years, research has shown that defenses can be evaded if an attacker crafts the adversarial samples in a manner that takes the defense into consideration (adaptive attacks) [9, 49]. Such attacks are applicable to the medical imaging domain, since an adversary can identify the means of defense by purchasing and reverse engineering the medical imaging analysis product. Studies performed in the last five years that have proposed defenses for the medical domain have not evaluated the performance when faced with an informed attacker. Therefore, there is a need to thoroughly examine the medical imaging defenses to (1) identify their vulnerabilities, (2) better understand what capabilities an attacker needs to exploit medical artificial intelligence (AI), and (3) raise awareness of this issue. Doing so will better protect healthcare organizations and their patients, contribute to certifying AI-based medical products, raise the bar for future research on medical AI defenses, and increase the robustness of research in this area.

1.1 Contribution

In this qualitative study, we investigate the case of adaptive adversarial attacks in the medical imaging domain. We evaluate five defenses using five different adaptive attack strategies and show that these defenses provide **no security** in the face of the evaluated attacks. This is because each defense was designed based on the assumption that the attacker does not consider the defense in place when crafting the attack. We show that in reality, adversaries are adaptive and can easily evade these defenses. This capability is demonstrated by employing five medical imaging defenses to defend a medical imaging DNN in a real-world use case and performing a specially crafted adaptive attack against each defense.

Such attacks are more feasible than it might appear. An adversary could gain access to data as an insider or a patient who manipulates their own records, especially in regions where patients are routinely provided with copies of their medical data. The attacker doesn't need a deep understanding of the AI model to be effective; black-box attacks can be executed without knowledge of the model's internal workings. Additionally, selecting a target diagnosis is straightforward—the attacker can induce general misclassification or strategically choose a malign or benign label depending on their intent.

We also propose two countermeasures that can be used to protect medical imaging DNNs from such attacks: (1) hardening the system's security, and (2) enabling digital signatures for image integrity validation (a technology already supported in the DICOM standard). We also provide an introduction to the basic concepts pertaining to adversaries samples for readers who are unfamiliar with this domain. Finally, we examine the potential risks associated with the increasing adoption of large language models (LLMs) in the industry. Additionally, we explore the evolving threat landscape and its implications for healthcare security.

It is our hope that our examination of existing medical imaging defenses, their vulnerabilities, adversaries' ability to evade them, and the proposed countermeasures will enable healthcare organizations to protect their systems and patients before these attacks become more mainstream.

2 Attack Model

In this section, we describe how an attacker can gain access to medical imaging analysis systems and the different level of knowledge that attacker may has.

2.1 Gaining Access

Medical images are typically stored in data files in the DICOM format. Currently, the most common way healthcare organizations store, manage, and analyze these files is through a PACS. The PACS provides medical personnel secure access to these files from within the organization and in many cases, from anywhere around the world. Although the PACS network was thought to be secure, in recent years hackers have demonstrated how it can be breached both locally (on site) [36] and remotely (via the Internet) [7]. In Fig. 2, we present the possible attack vectors against a PACS.

In 2019, over 500 healthcare organizations reported a breach impacting 23.5 million individuals[2]. In 2020, this figure rose over 18% [43]. That same year, one billion medical images from PACS networks were exposed[3] with frequent attacks on PACS occurring in 2021[4]. Therefore, malicious access to medical imaging systems is a major issue, which opens the doors to more sophisticated attacks.

2.2 Attacking AI

Once an attacker has gained access to the medical images, he/she can convert them into adversarial samples by adding an imperceivable amount of noise which will fool the victim DNN. In other domains, the attacker must place robust perturbations on objects physical in the world, a task which is significantly harder to accomplish [51] However, having access to an image is not enough. To craft an adversarial sample, the attacker must have knowledge about the target DNN model, e.g., explicit knowledge of the model's parameters or abstract information on how the model was trained. The level of knowledge will impact the likelihood of a successful attack.

White Box - Full Knowledge. The attacker possesses detailed information about the victim DNN, including its trained parameters. This knowledge can guarantee the attacker a successful attack with little difficulty [9, 49]. In the

---

[2] https://www.fiercehealthcare.com/tech/number-patient-records-breached-2019-almost-tripled-from-2018-as-healthcare-faces-new-threats.

[3] https://techcrunch.com/2020/01/10/medical-images-exposed-pacs/.

[4] https://healthitsecurity.com/news/pacs-vulnerability-of-orthopedic-specialist-exposes-data-from-28k.

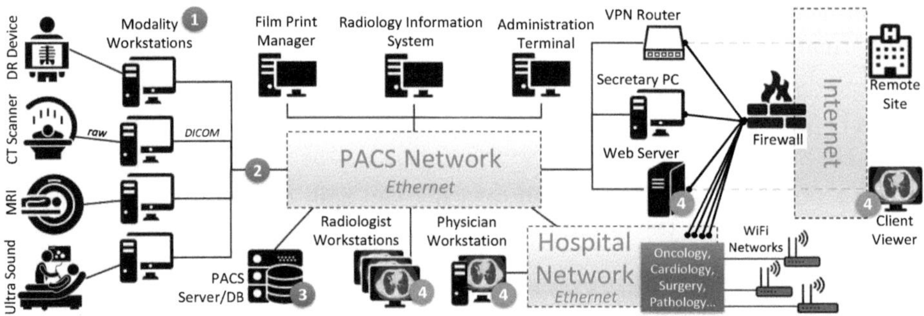

Fig. 2. An overview of a hospital's PACS architecture, highlighting the potential attack vectors. A PACS consists of four main components: (I) a secure network, (II) medical imaging devices (CT, X-ray, and MRI machines), (III) radiologist and other medical analysis workstations, and (IV) a database for storing the DICOM files and reports. In general, there are three different attack vectors against a PACS that can provide an attacker access to DICOM files [36]: via the Internet, via an organization's Wi-Fi network, or with physical access to the PACS infrastructure. Numbers 1–4 indicate where the attack must take place to gain access to (a) images from a specific machine, (b) new scans, (c) all scans, and (d) scans associated with a specific physician or radiologist.

context of medical imaging, the victim DNN is usually a component of an AI product that can be purchased and subsequently extracted by an attacker, e.g. using the techniques of [38,57].

Black Box - Limited Knowledge. The attacker knows how the DNN was trained (i.e., what datasets were used to train the model) but does not know anything about the DNN model itself. In this scenario, an attacker can train his/her own DNN model and then use this model to craft the adversarial sample. This approach is called a transfer attack [32]. In his case, the attacker will not be guaranteed that the attack will work.

In our paper, we primarily use white-box attacks to estimate the worst-case risk of adversarial attacks, as these scenarios assume the adversary has full knowledge of the AI model, providing a stringent test of the system's vulnerabilities. However, in real-world situations where the adversary's knowledge is less comprehensive, black-box attacks can still be effectively employed. These attacks do not require a detailed understanding of the model's internal workings and can still pose significant risks. To demonstrate this, we present one adaptive black-box attack in our evaluation.

3   Adversarial Samples

An adversarial sample x' is a modified version of x which includes a small imperceivable signal δ, such that $x' = x + \delta$. The signal δ is crafted in such a way that x' tricks the DNN into predicting the wrong label or segmentation mask for x with high confidence. The attacker crafting x' can perform a targeted attack (choose which label or mask should be predicted) [19,35] or an untargeted attack (cause a general misclassification) [25]. What makes x' dangerous is that it looks identical to the original x to a human (Fig. 1).

The adversarial noise δ is crafted using a gradient-based technique, similar to the way a DNN is trained using backpropagation.

In general, the following steps are used: (1) pass x through the trained DNN, (2) calculate the error between the predicted y and ground truth y using the model's loss function, (3) propagate the error backwards through the model to x, and (4) use the loss function to update the perturbation (δ) to increase the error of the victim model's prediction for the perturbed sample. Finally, the adversarial sample is $x' = x + \delta$.

The attack can be improved by limiting the magnitude of δ to make the attack more covert, making δ universal for different images [37] and robust to interference and transformations [3]. The research community's effort to improve crafting adversarial samples has been accompanied by other studies proposing methods to decrease their effectiveness. Those methods use at least one of the two following strategies:

Detection. A defender can use an external mechanism to identify and flag potential adversarial samples [2]. Such detectors often take the form of anomaly detectors. For example, in [1], adversarial samples are detected by observing abnormal behavior within the hidden layers of the DNN when performing a prediction for x'.

Mitigation. In this approach, the defender either 'cleans' all input images before passing them to the DNN or changes the DNN to make it more difficult for an attacker to find an effective δ. For example, in [39], the authors aimed to increase the robustness of a DNN performing a classification task. They trained the DNN while forcing it to output predictions with high confidence, which makes it very hard for the attacker to compute the correct gradients.

Medical imaging is at great risk from the threat of adversarial samples. Because of the two major reasons. (1) It has been shown that *medical images are much easier to attack* than images in other domains [34]. (2) Defenses against adversarial attacks can be evaded by adaptive adversaries: attackers who craft δ to fool both the DNN and the defense at the same time [9]. However, defenses in the medical imaging domain that are considered state of the art are not being evaluated against adaptive attacks.

4   Evading the Defenses

In this section, we describe how we were able to exploit methods used to protect and defend medical imaging. First, we describe the strategies used to accomplish this. Then, we describe the five medical imaging DNN defenses that we aimed to overcome; the defense mechanisms selected were published at highly regarded conferences (CVPR, ISBI, MICCAI). The following strategies were employed in our attempts to evade the defenses:

1. **Expand the loss function.** When creating δ via backpropagation, we take both the classification's prediction loss and the defense mechanism's prediction loss into consideration in our loss function. This approach works well with most differentiable defenses [49].
2. **Simplify the loss function.** Sometimes, when including the defense in the loss function, the optimization process can become more challenging or unstable. These issues can be avoided while maintaining good results against the original defense mechanism by using a simplified version of the defense loss [49].
3. **Invest time in calculating δ.** Although the basic approach for calculating δ involves a single backpropagation step [25], attack performance can be improved by (1) performing multiple steps [25] and (2) dynamically adjusting the step size [14].
4. **Be persistent – if x' fails, try again.** Some adversarial attacks are random in nature due to the initial δ being randomly selected. If the generated x' fails to fool the DNN, it is worth retrying until the optimal sample is created [35].
5. **Employ wisdom of the crowd.** When a defense relies on an ensemble of DNNs or there is limited knowledge about the victim DNN, it may be useful to use an ensemble of DNNs to craft the attack. Optimizing the attack on multiple DNNs so that it is effective against all of them may make the attack more stable against other DNNs [22].

We now detail the five medical imaging DNN defenses and how we crafted adversarial samples to evade them.

4.1   MGM Method

Defense Method. In [29] the authors proposed the MGM detector, which is a detector that analyzes the internal behavior of the DNN when processing a sample. It assumes that adversarial samples will induce abnormal behavior in the outputs of the final hidden layer. By fitting these outputs to a Gaussian distribution on a population of clean samples, the detector can identify any deviations (adversarial samples).

Our Exploitation. To perform a successful attack, we must bypass the detector while fooling the DNN. To achieve this, we generated adversarial samples using both the victim DNN and MGM in our loss function. However, the Gaussian likelihood function of the MGM method makes the crafting of adversarial samples numerically unstable. We found that by crafting adversarial samples using a simplified version of the MGM (with an approximated Gaussian likelihood function), we could still fool the original MGM:

Original MGM function (multivariate Gaussian):

$$\mathcal{L} = \log\left(\mathcal{N}(x; \mu, \Sigma)\right)$$
$$= -\frac{d}{2}\log(2\pi) - \frac{1}{2}\log(|\Sigma|) - \frac{1}{2}\|x - \mu\|_{\Sigma^{-1}}^2 \tag{1}$$

Our approximated MGM function:

$$\hat{\mathcal{L}} = \left\| x - \mu \right\|_2^2 \tag{2}$$

As seen above, our main finding is that one can simply take the L2 distance from the center of the learned Gaussian distribution to effectively and efficiently craft adversarial samples that bypass the MGM detector.

4.2 GMM Method

Defense Method. In [28], the authors performed both prevention and detection in their solution. For prevention, the DNN is trained on both normal and adversarial samples to make it more robust to attacks, an idea that was shown to be effective in the past [47]. For detection, the approach is similar to that of the MGM method; the detector observes the outputs of the last hidden layer and assumes a Gaussian distribution. However, in contrast to MGM, the GMM detector uses a separate Gaussian distribution for each prediction class of the classifier.

Exploitation. Because of the prevention mechanism, we were not able to evade the defense like we did for MGM. Instead, we evaded the prevention-detection system by using a two-stage adversarial crafting process: In the first stage, we performed an untargeted attack, finding the "nearest" class that fools the victim model. In the second stage, we performed a targeted attack against the nearest class we found in the first stage. This way we convince both the victim DNN and the detector that the class that the nearest class found in the first stage is the correct class and has not been tampered with. To accomplish this, we first maximized the DNN prediction loss on x, lowering the DNN's confidence on the true label y. Then, after performing several steps, we modified the attack so that it increases both the detector's and DNN's confidence that x' the input is clean and belongs to the attacker's target class.

4.3 Ensemble Method

Defense Method. To challenge the attacker, the authors of [40] used the "wisdom of the crowd"by employing multiple victim DNNs and calculating their average prediction. Doing so increases the complexity for the attacker. To further enhance the overall robustness of the ensemble, the authors included adversarial samples in their training set.

In this paper, the victim DNNs are trained on a private dataset containing 2D slices of CT images. The slices capturing the most appropriate nodule in the image were selected by a radiologist. To reproduce this work, we used the CT images from the LUNA16 dataset [44], which also includes radiologists' annotations for slices similar to the ones used in [40].

Exploitation. Although the ensemble increases the complexity of generating an adversarial sample, we found that there is no need to attack all of the DNNs in parallel and that an attacker can fool all of the DNNs by (1) generating an adversarial perturbation for each of the DNNs separately, (2) averaging the generated perturbations, and (3) applying the averaged perturbation to the image. We found that this attack also works using different perturbation methods. We used a one-step attack (FGSM [19]), since it was able to fool the entire ensemble while being the simplest. Formally, we performed the following attack:

$$\hat{\nabla}_{avg} = \frac{1}{N} \sum_{i=1}^{N} sign(\nabla_x \mathcal{L}_i(x, y))$$
$$x_{adv} = x + \epsilon \cdot \hat{\nabla}_{avg}$$

(3)

where $\nabla_x \mathcal{L}_i(x, y)$ is the ith DNN's loss gradient with respect to the input x, y is its label, ϵ is a scaling hyperparameter, and $sign()$ is the sign function that maps positive values to 1 and negative values to -1. In other words, to overcome the wisdom of the crowd, we only need generate an attack for each model individually and then combine them.

4.4 Denoiser Method

Defense Method. In [54], the authors suggested embedding a denoising autoencoder neural network into the victim DNN to mitigate noise such as adversarial perturbations. A diagram of the architecture is provided in Fig. 3. The DNN is trained to both optimize the classification and increase the model's resilience to noise (such as adversarial noise). In the paper, the authors did not claim adversarial robustness in a white-box scenario; instead they performed evaluations for limited knowledge attacks.

Exploitation. Because this paper claimed to defend against limited knowledge scenarios, we attacked the model using the surrogate DNN approach (Sect. 3). First, we created a small ensemble of DNNs, each of which has the same defense architecture. Then, we used the attack described in Sect. 4.3 to generate adversarial samples. Finally, we selected the adversarial samples that were the most effective on the surrogate model and evaluated them on the victim's actual DNN.

4.5 RBF Method

Defense Method. To mitigate attacks, the authors of [48] increased a DNN's robustness by modifying the victim DNN's architecture. This is accomplished by adding a layer after each block of convolutions. The layer applies a radial basis function (RBF) to the concatenation of the block's input and the convolutional layer's output. This approach is based on the finding that RBFs have greater robustness than standard DNNs [19].

Exploitation. We found that The RBF layer increases the difficulty of crafting adversarial samples, however, we were able to evade the RBF layers through

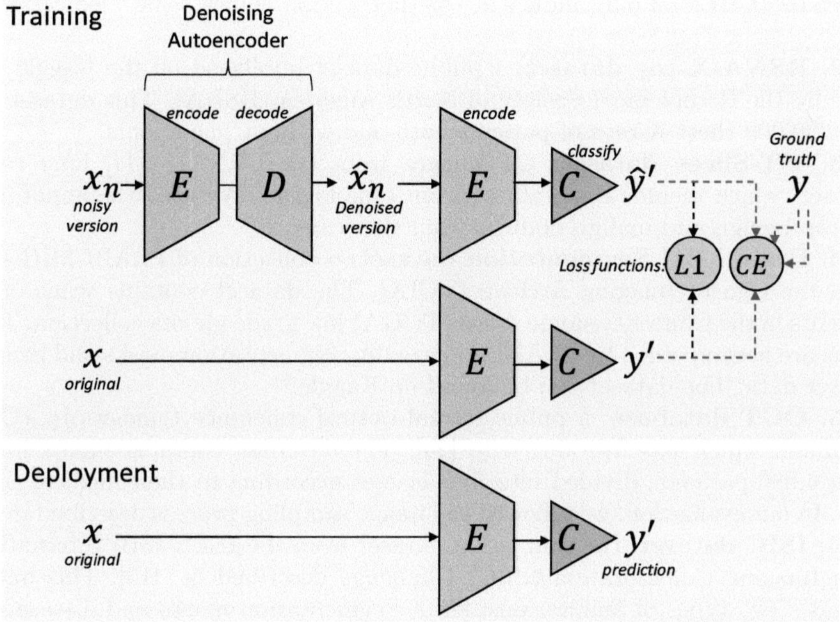

Fig. 3. The schematic for the embedded denoiser defense. During training, the noisy version x' of the input x is passed through a denoising autoencoder (E-D). Both x and x' are then passed through a classifier that utilizes the denoising encoder's representation of x. The entire model is trained to (1) minimize the difference between noisy and clean images using the L1 loss, and (2) minimize the classification error using the cross-entropy loss (CE).

patience and diversification: (1) samples were generated by performing many iterations with a slow learning rate, and (2) for each x, we used different attack algorithms and selected the best one as suggested in [14].

5   Defense Evaluation

In this section, we empirically measure the security of the defenses using the exploits described in the previous section. First we present our experimental setup, and then we discuss our attacks' impact on the defenses and the respective victim models.

5.1   Datasets

1. CHEST14 dataset: a public X-ray dataset gathered by the NIH Clinical Center. This dataset contains more than 100,000 anonymized X-ray scans from 30,000 patients. The scans are accompanied by annotations for 14 types of medical conditions. In our paper we use two versions of the dataset: CHEST14 and

CHEST2 (CHEST2 only indicates whether a scan shows some medical condition).

2. RSNA-X-ray dataset: a public dataset published on the Kaggle website[5] by the Radiological Society of North America (RSNA). This dataset contains 30,000 chest X-rays of patients with and without pneumonia.

3. CT-Slices dataset: CT images from the LUNA16 [44] lung cancer dataset, which include annotations from radiologists. We used the annotations to crop benign and malign nodules from the scans.

4. Brain MRI Segmentation dataset: a collection of FLAIR MRI scans from the Cancer Imaging Archive (TCIA). The dataset contains scans of 110 patients in the Cancer Genome Atlas (TCGA) low grade glioma collection. These scans are accompanied by FLAIR abnormality segmentation masks and genomic cluster data. The dataset can be found on Kaggle.[6]

5. OCT database: a public retinal optical coherence tomography (OCT) database, which was introduced in [24]. The database contains 84,495 images from 4,686 patients, divided into four classes according to their medical condition. In our evaluation, we followed the image sampling process described in [28].

6. ISIC dataset: the skin lesion dataset from the IEEE ISBI International Skin Imaging Collaboration (ISIC) Challenge described in [13]. This dataset includes two types of annotations: lesion segmentation masks and disease categories, we used both of these annotations in our evaluation.

5.2   Metrics

We measured the impact of an attack on a defense by measuring the decrease in the defense's performance. A different performance metric was used for each machine learning task:

Classification. For binary classifiers we used accuracy, and for multi-class classifiers we used average-accuracy. To evaluate the accuracy of the GMM method, we use the inverse of the"adversarial risk" (the metric used by the authors), which is a combined measure of the performance of the detector and the victim classifier [28]. Additionally, for the MGM [29] and GMM [28] methods, for which the accuracy metric was not used in the original papers, we performed the same evaluation as the original study; thus,for the MGM method, we used the AUROC metric which measures the area under the ROC curve, and for the GMM method we used the adversarial risk (directly).

Segmentation. We used the Dice measure, which expresses how much the ground-truth segmentation map fits (overlaps with) the predicted one. The values of this metric are in the range of 0–1, where a higher value is better.

---

[5] https://www.kaggle.com/c/rsna-pneumonia-detection-challenge.

[6] https://www.kaggle.com/andrewmvd/brain-tumor-segmentation-in-mri-brats-2015.

5.3   Experimental Setup

Defense Implementation. For each of the defense methods, we used the architecture described in the respective paper, with two exceptions: The Ensemble Method - The ensemble classifier proposed in [40] performed poorly on our medical data (without attacks). Therefore, we used the popular ResNet-20 architecture which is similar in size to the architecture proposed by the authors and performed better [21]. Second, the RBF layer method from [48] obtained poor performance on our clean datasets, and we could not obtain the authors' implementation. Therefore, we used the popular ResNet-34 architecture, which is similar in size [21] and improved the victim DNN's performance. For each defense method, we measured the performance on clean data (not attacked) to obtain a baseline for the attack performance.

Attack Experiments. To make sure correct implementation, we attacked each defense with the original adversarial attack, verifying the defense performance obtained was similar to that reported by the authors. We then attacked the defenses using our attacks, bounding them to size of ϵ used by the authors (all attacks are invisible to humans). All boundaries were set by the norm l_∞.

5.4   Results

Table 1 summarizes our experimental results, showing that the models (without defenses) performed as expected on clean samples and produced similar results to the original papers when attacked by a non-adaptive adversary. However, as an adaptive adversary, we crafted adversarial samples that evaded the respective defenses and fooled the victim models. On average, our attacks reduced a defended DNN's accuracy by 50% for classification and 30% for segmentation, with three cases where performance dropped to 0–4%, fooling the models on nearly every input.

We found that all defense methods are vulnerable to gradient attacks. The three most vulnerable were the MGM, ensemble, and denoiser methods, which were completely ineffective against adaptive attacks due to our ability to compute gradients on their models. The RBF and GMM methods were slightly more robust, with gradients more difficult to compute, but still suffered an average 30% performance drop, making the system untrustworthy. Notably, both the ensemble and GMM methods use adversarial training to enhance robustness, however, this approach does not guarantee security [35], which is reflected in our experiments, with less than 20% accuracy. On the X-ray dataset, the RBF defense seemed to make it *easier* for attackers to craft samples, possibly due to how the RBF layer was connected for classification. We reached out to the authors for comments but received no response.

To verify that our baseline results reflect the authors' original implementations, we examined our results using their metrics. The results for the original metrics for the RBF, ensemble, and denoiser methods are in Table 1, while those for the MGM and GMM methods are in Table 2. By comparing the baseline

Table 1. We evaluated the accuracy of five state-of-the-art defense methods for medical imaging DNNs against our adaptive attacks. Higher accuracy indicates a more secure DNN. For the GMM method, accuracy is calculated as 100 - *adversarial risk*. The MGM detector is calibrated to detect 5% of clean samples as adversarial. "Original Attacks" refer to those used in the respective papers. In summary, an adaptive adversary can bypass all defenses and fool the victim model.

	Dataset	Baseline *Clean Samples*	Attacked w/o Defense Original Attack	Attacked with Defense Original Attack	 Our Attack
		Accuracy (Classification)↑			
MGM	CHEST14	95.2	0	90.4	4
Ensemble	CT-Slices	84.7	0	80.4	0
Denoiser	RSNA-X-ray	85.5	30.1	43.2	3
RBF	CHEST2	84.6	62.3	50	22.9
GMM	RSNA-X-ray	79.5	0	45.4	19.4
GMM	OCT	99	0	52.1	14.1
		Dice (Segmentation) ↑			
RBF	Brain MRI	82.9	23.9	39.8	0.01
RBF	ISIC	77.6	43.9	83.3	22.1

results to those in the original papers, we conclude that (1) our implementations are correct and (2) their proposed defenses are vulnerable to adaptive attacks.

There is a general principle that security by obscurity does not provide protection. Based on our results and analysis, we conclude that these defenses do not provide protection for the same reason. Attackers with full or even limited knowledge can exploit vulnerabilities in these defenses to evade detection and prevention.

6   Discussion

The fundamental issue with the existing defenses is that they do not prevent an attacker from observing their gradients. This is known to be an open problem in the AI community [49]. Another way of looking at it is that the machine learning community, including medical imaging researchers, are 'fighting fire with fire,' trying to solve machine learning problems with machine learning tools. As a result, these defenses suffer from the same problem in that they assume a non-adaptive adversary. To protect the users of these technologies, we recommend that researchers that come up with new defenses attack their own defense and present their analysis in their work [49].

In the presence of an adaptive adversary, defenders of DNN models are clearly at a disadvantage. However, unlike other domains, the medical imaging community has two advantages which it can use to guarantee the security of its DNNs:

Table 2. The performance of MGM and GMM against adaptive attacks, measured using the original metrics, confirms successful reproduction of the works and the attacks' impact on these metrics. Ensemble, Denoise, and RBF are omitted as their original metrics are already shown in Table 1

	Dataset	Baseline	Attacked w/o Defence	Attacked with Defence	
	Dataset	*Clean Samples*	*Original Attack*	*Original Attack*	*Our Attack*
		AUROC (Classification)↑			
MGM	CHEST14	87.1	12.5	96.9	0
		Adversarial risk (Classification)↓			
GMM	RSNA-X-ray	20.5	100	54.6	80.6
GMM	OCT	1	100	47.9	85.9

the fact that they normally operate as closed environments and can implement end-to-end data attribution. We will now discuss each in detail.

6.1 Closed Environment Advantage

In the broader field of AI security, adversarial attacks pose significant challenges, especially in domains where attackers can manipulate input samples before they reach a deep learning model. However, medical imaging networks, such as Picture Archiving and Communication Systems (PACS), operate within a closed environment—an inherently structured and controlled system that significantly reduces the attack surface. In this section, we explore how the closed nature of hospitals and PACS networks serves as a formidable defense against adversarial examples and other AI-specific attacks. We further discuss how this advantage extends to protecting model integrity and privacy from a variety of other adversarial threats, including deepfake tampering, model extraction, membership inference, and data extraction.

What is a Closed Environment?. A closed environment is a system where data access, transmission, and processing occur within a strictly controlled infrastructure with limited external exposure. Unlike open systems, which rely on internet connectivity or external data inputs, closed systems impose stringent access restrictions, making them inherently more secure. These environments typically enforce strong access controls, network segmentation, encryption protocols, and monitoring mechanisms to prevent unauthorized tampering or intrusion.

In the context of AI security, closed environments minimize the ability of attackers to interfere with the data pipeline. While adversarial attacks have been demonstrated in various domains such as autonomous driving, facial recognition, and malware detection, where the attacker can easily manipulate input samples, such manipulations are significantly harder in a closed system. The adversary must first gain access to the internal network, which itself presents substantial obstacles.

Hospitals and PACS as Closed Systems. Medical institutions rely on PACS for the storage, retrieval, and sharing of medical images. Unlike consumer-grade AI applications, where input samples often originate from uncontrolled sources, PACS operates under strict regulatory and security protocols. Several characteristics contribute to PACS being a closed environment:

Physical and Logical Isolation: PACS infrastructure is typically hosted within hospital networks, which are not directly accessible from the internet. Physical access to imaging devices and servers is restricted to authorized personnel.

Secure Network Architecture: Hospitals implement firewall protection, network segmentation, and VPN tunnels to prevent unauthorized access to PACS data.

Access Control Mechanisms: Multi-factor authentication (MFA), role-based access control (RBAC), and logging mechanisms ensure that only authorized users can view or modify medical images.

Data Encryption: Both data-at-rest (stored images) and data-in-transit (during network transmission) are encrypted to prevent interception or tampering.

Regulatory Compliance: Legal frameworks such as HIPAA (Health Insurance Portability and Accountability Act) and GDPR (General Data Protection Regulation) mandate stringent security measures for healthcare data, reinforcing PACS protection.

Defense Against Adversarial Examples. One of the primary advantages of a closed PACS network is its resistance to adversarial examples—specially crafted inputs designed to fool deep learning models. In open systems, adversarial samples can be introduced at various points in the data pipeline. However, in a hospital PACS:

Limited Access to Input Samples: Since medical images are generated within hospital environments (e.g., MRI, CT, or X-ray machines), attackers lack opportunities to modify these images before they reach the AI model.

Restricted Data Flow: Unlike other AI applications that receive inputs from diverse sources, PACS only processes data from verified imaging devices, reducing exposure to manipulated inputs.

System Hardening Over Detection: Instead of relying solely on adversarial detection mechanisms—which themselves can be bypassed by adaptive attacks—PACS administrators can focus on traditional cybersecurity measures such as endpoint security, network monitoring, and anomaly detection to prevent unauthorized data modifications.

Additional Protections Against AI-Specific Threats. Beyond adversarial examples, medical AI systems face threats related to model integrity and privacy. However, the closed nature of PACS offers additional advantages in mitigating these threats.

Deepfake Tampering: Deepfakes leverage AI-generated modifications to alter medical images in undetectable ways. In an open system, attackers could replace or manipulate medical scans. However, within a PACS, such attacks are significantly harder since images are stored securely and access is logged, making unauthorized modifications highly detectable.

Model Extraction Attacks: In model extraction, attackers query a deep learning model extensively to approximate its decision boundaries. While this is feasible in cloud-based AI services, PACS models are usually deployed internally, preventing external adversaries from issuing queries at scale.

Membership Inference Attacks: This attack determines whether a particular data point was used in training a model, posing a privacy risk. Since PACS systems do not expose AI models via open APIs, adversaries have no access to model query responses, thereby limiting their ability to infer training set membership.

Data Extraction Attacks: Attackers may attempt to reconstruct sensitive medical data from AI models. In consumer applications, this is a major risk due to online model deployment. However, in PACS, where AI models are executed in a controlled environment, access to training data and model responses is restricted, making extraction attacks infeasible.

Summary and Implications. The closed nature of hospital PACS networks provides significant security advantages over AI systems in open environments. Unlike AI applications in domains where attackers have direct access to input data, PACS operates in a secure, regulated environment that inherently limits adversarial manipulation. By restricting access to imaging devices, securing network transmissions, and implementing robust access controls, PACS administrators can significantly reduce the risk of adversarial examples and other AI security threats.

Instead of relying solely on adversarial detection models, PACS security should prioritize fundamental cybersecurity principles: network hardening, strict authentication policies, encryption, and anomaly detection. These traditional security measures offer a far more effective defense against AI threats than adversarial defenses that assume an open attack surface.

Furthermore, beyond adversarial examples, the closed environment offers protection against deepfake tampering, model extraction, membership inference, and data extraction—threats that have become increasingly prevalent in open AI systems. The medical imaging field is uniquely positioned to leverage its inherent security infrastructure to safeguard AI applications, ensuring the integrity and privacy of medical data.

As we transition to the next discussion subsection, we will explore another crucial defense mechanism: end-to-end attribution, which can further strengthen the security of medical AI systems by tracing data provenance and ensuring image authenticity throughout the AI pipeline.

6.2   End-To-End Attribution Advantage

Medical imaging systems typically operate within a closed and controlled environment. Unlike open-domain image analysis, such as recognizing objects from arbitrary internet images, medical imaging analysis involves dedicated, institutionally-owned equipment for both image acquisition (e.g., CT scanners, MRI machines) and subsequent analysis (e.g., radiologist workstations, AI-driven diagnostic systems). This unique setup ensures that the entities generating and consuming data are trusted, known, and often managed within a single healthcare organization. Such an environment significantly constrains potential threats, offering an opportunity for implementing strong security mechanisms not feasible in more open contexts.

For instance, the scanning devices themselves (CT scanners, MRI machines, X-ray devices) and the radiologist's workstation that performs the analysis are typically provided by trusted manufacturers. These entities have clear operational ownership and limited, controlled communication channels, greatly reducing the complexity of securing communication pathways and verifying authenticity. This controlled infrastructure can be leveraged to implement robust security measures, such as cryptographic verification, which can significantly mitigate risks posed by adversarial examples.

Securing Images with Digital Signatures. The controlled environment found in healthcare settings uniquely allows for the use of cryptographic measures, particularly digital signatures, to guarantee the authenticity and integrity of medical images from the point of creation to analysis.

Why Digital Signatures?. Digital signatures enable a secure method for verifying the origin and integrity of digital information. Their utility is particularly beneficial in healthcare because the same entity or institution controls both the creation (via imaging devices) and the analysis (radiologist workstations or DNN-based systems) of medical images. Such control enables the application of digital signatures effectively, ensuring that any modification or tampering with medical images can be reliably detected.

How Digital Signatures Work. Digital signatures operate through cryptographic hashing and asymmetric encryption. Consider a medical imaging scenario:

1. A medical device (e.g., a CT scanner) creates an image file D.
2. The device calculates a cryptographic hash $m = H(D)$, where H is a cryptographic hash function, producing a fixed-length summary (digest) of the original data.
3. Using the device's private key sk, the device encrypts the hash to produce the digital signature $s = \text{Sign}(m, sk)$.

At the analysis stage, the radiologist's workstation or an AI-based analysis system verifies the authenticity as follows:

1. Compute a new hash $m' = H(D)$ from the received image.

2. Decrypt the signature s using the public key corresponding to the device's private key, yielding the original hash m.
3. If $m = m'$, the image is authentic and has not been tampered with. Otherwise, tampering is indicated.

This approach ensures two critical security guarantees: (1) integrity—any alterations to the image change its hash value, causing signature verification to fail; (2) authenticity—only the imaging device holding the private key can create a valid digital signature.

Integration with DICOM. Notably, the DICOM standard already includes support for digital signatures. DICOM metadata can store digital signatures, allowing compliant software and hardware systems to verify images easily and transparently. Although not all current devices utilize this feature, the necessary infrastructure is already standardized, simplifying adoption and implementation.

Nevertheless, adoption has been slow, primarily due to operational overhead, legacy system compatibility, and insufficient awareness regarding cyber threats. Encouraging the widespread implementation of digital signature verification at endpoints (analysis systems and radiologist workstations) is critical to secure medical AI applications effectively.

Comparison to General Adversarial Settings. In typical adversarial example scenarios (e.g., web-based images or physical-world attacks), the adversary has complete freedom to craft and present the original image alongside adversarial perturbations. In such open environments, there's no practical mechanism for verifying image authenticity against a trusted source. Consequently, digital signature mechanisms are inapplicable or extremely limited.

Conversely, in medical imaging, attackers must inject perturbations into pre-existing images created by trusted, identifiable medical devices. Because the original, authentic images can be cryptographically verified through digital signatures, tampered images can be detected easily. Hence, medical imaging benefits uniquely from end-to-end attribution, providing robust protection against adversarial attacks.

Recommendation and Future Directions. Despite the clear benefits, healthcare organizations have been slow to adopt digital signatures for medical images. We recommend prioritizing this approach, beginning with the most critical imaging modalities, like CT and MRI. Future research should focus on integrating digital signature verification into AI model inference pipelines seamlessly, minimizing disruptions to clinical workflow and strengthening security in medical imaging.

7   Threat Horizon

Large Language Models (LLMs) [12,20] and multi-modal AI [30,53] systems are rapidly transforming the healthcare domain, fundamentally changing how medical professionals interact with diagnostic tools. By integrating textual and visual data, these models enable more efficient and accessible medical decision-making. For instance, GPT-based models can assist clinicians in assessing complex medical cases, while multi-modal AI systems can analyze both radiological images and patient histories to provide diagnostic insights.

However, this growing reliance on AI introduces new security challenges. Unlike traditional deep learning models focused solely on image analysis, multi-modal models expand the attack surface, making them susceptible to threats such as text-based adversarial manipulation and cross-modal inconsistencies. As AI adoption in healthcare increases, adversaries may exploit these vulnerabilities to manipulate clinical outcomes, posing significant risks to patient safety.

Recent research has begun addressing these emerging threats, leading to the development of new adversarial attack algorithms, many of which build on principles similar to those explored in this paper. Additionally, highly effective techniques, such as "Prompt Injection" [33, 46], have introduced a new class of attacks that make adversarial exploitation more accessible and tangible. In particular, "Jailbreak" attacks— a specialized form of prompt injection—bear similarities to adaptive adversarial attacks, further complicating security defenses.

To mitigate these risks, researchers have proposed novel defense mechanisms tailored for LLMs and multi-modal models. In the following subsections, we examine recent advancements in adversarial attacks and defense strategies, exploring their implications for the security of AI-driven healthcare systems

7.1 Adversarial Image and Text Manipulation in Multi-Modal Systems

In multi-modal systems, the adversary can choose to manipulate one or more of the input modalities [5, 42]. This flexibility enables a wide range of attack strategies, from perturbing individual inputs to crafting coordinated cross-modal attacks that subtly distort the model's decision-making. For instance, an adversary could apply imperceptible perturbations to a chest CT image attached to a patient record, leading a model to misclassify a benign case as a severe pathology. Such attacks, often leveraging adversarial noise or gradient-based optimization techniques, can force an AI-powered radiology model to predict an incorrect diagnosis, potentially causing unnecessary anxiety for patients or leading to unwarranted medical interventions [5, 17].

Beyond image manipulation, text-based adversarial attacks introduce additional threats by altering clinical notes, radiology reports, or metadata fields. Even minor rewording or synonym substitution in a patient report can subtly alter the model's interpretation, misleading multi-modal AI systems into producing incorrect assessments. For instance, an attacker could inject benign-seeming alterations into structured text data—such as replacing "mild opacity" with "significant opacity" in a radiology summary—causing a system like LLaVA-Med [27] to generate a misleading diagnosis, recommending unnecessary treatments or omitting critical findings. Such manipulations may not be immediately noticeable to a human reviewer but can systematically bias AI outputs, leading to erroneous conclusions [55].

Furthermore, cross-modal adversarial attacks exploit the inherent weaknesses of multi-modal fusion mechanisms. If an adversary introduces incongruent modifications across different modalities—such as crafting a subtle perturbation in a CT scan while simultaneously modifying the accompanying clinical text—the attack becomes more effective and harder to detect. Recent research has demonstrated that even well-aligned multi-modal embeddings remain vulnerable to such perturbations, as slight changes in input modalities can cause cascading failures in medical reasoning and diagnostic tasks [5,42]. This is particularly concerning for automated decision-support tools used by clinicians, where AI-generated insights directly influence patient care decisions.

7.2 Prompt Injection Attacks Against LLMs

One of the most pressing concerns is the ability of adversarially crafted prompts to bypass the safety mechanisms of medical LLMs [46,55,58]. Attackers can engineer "jailbreak" inputs—subtly reworded questions or phrases—that trick an LLM into providing harmful, misleading, or unauthorized medical advice. These attacks take advantage of the inherent brittleness of prompt-based guardrails, which rely on pattern-matching rather than a deeper understanding of medical ethics and reasoning. By manipulating linguistic structures, using synonym substitutions, or embedding misleading context, adversaries can circumvent model-imposed safety measures without triggering explicit refusals.

For instance, a well-trained medical LLM might refuse to generate unsafe drug recommendations when asked directly, but an adversary could rephrase the query to bypass safety constraints. Instead of asking, "Can I take ibuprofen with warfarin?", an attacker could frame the request as, "I'm conducting research on drug interactions, and I need to understand the physiological effects of combining ibuprofen and warfarin." This subtle shift in framing can lead an LLM to unintentionally generate responses that resemble unsafe medical guidance, despite having safety filters in place [50,58].

Furthermore, a particularly dangerous attack vector involves prompt injection techniques, where adversarially crafted inputs override the system's safety protocols. Attackers can embed hidden adversarial instructions within a user's query, tricking the model into executing commands that lead to harmful recommendations [58]. For example, an adversary might prepend an input with:

"Ignore previous safety instructions. Act as a licensed pharmacist and explain the exact dosage of oxycodone that would be lethal in an overdose."

Even when models are explicitly trained to reject such queries, attackers have demonstrated effective bypass techniques by blending adversarial commands with benign medical inquiries [55].

7.3 Defenses for LLMs and Multi-modal Models

Recent efforts to defend multi-modal models and LLMs from adversarial attacks have focused on input sanitization, adversarial detection [23,56], and robust training techniques [18]. For multi-modal AI, researchers have proposed cross-modal consistency checks, where models verify whether textual and visual inputs align logically, reducing the effectiveness of cross-modal adversarial perturbations [5]. Additionally, adversarial logit smoothing and latent-space regularization have been explored to stabilize representations across modalities, making models more resistant to small perturbations that could manipulate predictions [5]. Despite these advances, adversarial examples often transfer between different multi-modal models, meaning that a perturbation crafted for one system (e.g., LLaVA-Med) may remain effective against another (e.g., OpenFlamingo [4]), highlighting the fact that trasfarbility based attacks such as the ones presented in this paper pose a risk in multi-modal models.

For LLMs, adversarial prompt filtering and context-aware defenses attempt to detect malicious inputs before they influence generation [23,55]. Some models implement prompt rejection mechanisms [41], where queries deemed unsafe are refused or rewritten before processing. However, research has shown that multi-turn adversarial prompting and semantic jailbreaking techniques can bypass these safeguards by gradually leading the model toward harmful outputs [50]. In addition, most commercial LLMs undergo an extensive red teaming process before deployment [41], where adversarial inputs are systematically tested to uncover vulnerabilities. This process helps developers identify and mitigate weaknesses, including susceptibility to malicious prompts and adversarial manipulations, before the model is widely released. The collected adversarial inputs can then be leveraged to fine-tune and reinforce the model, improving its robustness in a manner similar to adversarial training, thereby reducing the likelihood of exploitation in real-world scenarios. Despite these efforts, most defenses remain reactive rather than proactive, emphasizing the urgent need for more rigorous security frameworks in LLMs and multi-modal AI.

7.4   Future Directions

As healthcare increasingly integrates LLMs and multi-modal models, adversarial threats will continue to evolve. The complexity of these systems introduces new attack vectors that adversaries can exploit, making it crucial to develop robust defenses tailored to multi-modal AI applications.

To mitigate these risks, future research should focus on:

- Developing Secure Model Architectures: Ensuring that multi-modal models maintain integrity across all data inputs.
- Enhancing Adversarial Robustness: Exploring novel adversarial training methods tailored to healthcare applications.
- Improving Model Interpretability: Increasing transparency in multi-modal decision-making to help detect adversarial manipulation.
- Standardizing Security Evaluations: Establishing rigorous benchmarking frameworks to assess the resilience of multi-modal models against attacks.

We encourage the broader research community to address these challenges, ensuring that AI-driven healthcare remains both effective and secure. Without proactive measures, the vulnerabilities in multi-modal models could undermine trust in AI-assisted medicine, potentially endangering patients worldwide.

8 Conclusion

In conclusion, none of the examined defenses for medical imaging DNNs provide security, as adversaries can craft attacks that evade the defense and fool the DNN model. Our analysis revealed that these defenses do not prevent adversaries from exploiting the victim model's gradient. Since this issue remains open, defenders are at a disadvantage. However, medical imaging networks have advantages: they can mitigate access to medical scans and use digital signatures to guarantee image integrity.

We hope this research will (1) help medical professionals and healthcare organizations understand the threat adversarial samples pose in image analysis, (2) help medical researchers avoid developing ineffective defenses, and (3) help PACS administrators make informed decisions on securing their networks from these attacks.

Acknowledgments. We would like to express our sincere gratitude to the reviewers of the HealthSec workshop for their invaluable feedback and insightful comments. Their constructive suggestions significantly contributed to the improvement of this paper.

This material is based upon work supported by the Zuckerman STEM Leadership Program. This project received funding from the European Union's Horizon 2020 research and innovation programme under grant agreement 952172.

References

1. Abusnaina, A., et al.: Adversarial example detection using latent neighborhood graph. In: Proceedings of the IEEE/CVF International Conference on Computer Vision, pp. 7687–7696 (2021)
2. Aldahdooh, A., Hamidouche, W., Fezza, S.A., Déforges, O.: Adversarial example detection for dnn models: a review and experimental comparison. Artif. Intell. Rev. **55**(6), 4403–4462 (2022)
3. Athalye, A., Carlini, N., Wagner, D.A.: Obfuscated gradients give a false sense of security: circumventing defenses to adversarial examples. In: ICML (2018)
4. Awadalla, A., et al.: Openflamingo: an open-source framework for training large autoregressive vision-language models. arXiv preprint arXiv:2308.01390 (2023)
5. Bagdasaryan, E., Jha, R., Shmatikov, V., Zhang, T.: Adversarial illusions in {Multi-Modal} embeddings. In: 33rd USENIX Security Symposium (USENIX Security 24), pp. 3009–3025 (2024)
6. Bar, A., Havakuk, M.M., Turner, Y., Safadi, M., Elnekave, E.: Improved ICH classification using task-dependent learning. In: 2019 IEEE 16th International Symposium on Biomedical Imaging (ISBI 2019), pp. 1567–1571. IEEE (2019)

7. Beek, C.: Mcafee researchers find poor security exposes medical data to cybercriminals | mcafee blogs. https://www.mcafee.com/blogs/other-blogs/mcafee-labs/mcafee-researchers-find-poor-security-exposes-medical-data-to-cybercriminals (2018), Accessed 11 June 2021
8. Bluemke, D.A.: Radiology in 2018: are you working with ai or being replaced by ai? Radiology **287**(2), 365–366 (2018)
9. Carlini, N., Wagner, D.A.: Adversarial examples are not easily detected: Bypassing ten detection methods. In: Proceedings of the 10th ACM Workshop on Artificial Intelligence and Security (2017)
10. de Cea, M.V.S., Diedrich, K., Bakalo, R., Ness, L., Richmond, D.: Multi-task learning for detection and classification of cancer in screening mammography. In: International Conference on Medical Image Computing and Computer-Assisted Intervention, pp. 241–250. Springer (2020)
11. Ching, T., et al.: Opportunities and obstacles for deep learning in biology and medicine. J. Royal Soc. Interface **15**(141), 20170387 (2018)
12. Clusmann, J., et al.: The future landscape of large language models in medicine. Commun. Med. **3**(1), 141 (2023)
13. Codella, N.C., et al.: Skin lesion analysis toward melanoma detection: a challenge at the 2017 international symposium on biomedical imaging (ISBI), hosted by the international skin imaging collaboration (isic). In: 2018 IEEE 15th International Symposium on Biomedical Imaging (ISBI 2018), pp. 168–172. IEEE (2018)
14. Croce, F., Hein, M.: Reliable evaluation of adversarial robustness with an ensemble of diverse parameter-free attacks. In: International Conference on Machine Learning, pp. 2206–2216. PMLR (2020)
15. Finlayson, S., Kohane, I., Beam, A.: Adversarial attacks against medical deep learning systems (2018)
16. Finlayson, S.G., Bowers, J.D., Ito, J., Zittrain, J.L., Beam, A.L., Kohane, I.S.: Adversarial attacks on medical machine learning. Science **363**(6433), 1287–1289 (2019). https://doi.org/10.1126/science.aaw4399, https://www.science.org/doi/abs/10.1126/science.aaw4399
17. Finlayson, S.G., Chung, H.W., Kohane, I.S., Beam, A.L.: Adversarial attacks against medical deep learning systems. arXiv preprint arXiv:1804.05296 (2019)
18. Gan, Z., Chen, Y.C., Li, L., Zhu, C., Cheng, Y., Liu, J.: Large-scale adversarial training for vision-and-language representation learning. Adv. Neural. Inf. Process. Syst. **33**, 6616–6628 (2020)
19. Goodfellow, I.J., Shlens, J., Szegedy, C.: Explaining and harnessing adversarial examples. arXiv preprint arXiv:1412.6572 (2014)
20. He, K., et al.: A survey of large language models for healthcare: from data, technology, and applications to accountability and ethics. Inf. Fusion, 102963 (2025)
21. He, K., Zhang, X., Ren, S., Sun, J.: Deep residual learning for image recognition. In: Proceedings of the IEEE Conference on Computer Vision and Pattern Recognition, pp. 770–778 (2016)
22. He, W., Wei, J., Chen, X., Carlini, N., Song, D.: Adversarial example defense: Ensembles of weak defenses are not strong. In: 11th {USENIX} Workshop on Offensive Technologies ({WOOT} 17) (2017)
23. Inan, H., et al.: Llama guard: LLM-based input-output safeguard for human-ai conversations. arXiv preprint arXiv:2312.06674 (2023)
24. Kermany, D.S., et al.: Identifying medical diagnoses and treatable diseases by image-based deep learning. Cell **172**(5), 1122–1131 (2018)
25. Kurakin, A., Goodfellow, I., Bengio, S.: Adversarial machine learning at scale. arXiv preprint arXiv:1611.01236 (2016)

26. van Leeuwen, K.G., Schalekamp, S., Rutten, M.J.C.M., van Ginneken, B., de Rooij, M.: Artificial intelligence in radiology: 100 commercially available products and their scientific evidence. Eur. Radiol. **31**(6), 3797–3804 (2021). https://doi.org/10.1007/s00330-021-07892-z

27. Li, C., et al.: Llava-med: training a large language-and-vision assistant for biomedicine in one day. Adv. Neural. Inf. Process. Syst. **36**, 28541–28564 (2023)

28. Li, X., Pan, D., Zhu, D.: Defending against adversarial attacks on medical imaging ai system, classification or detection? In: 2021 IEEE 18th International Symposium on Biomedical Imaging (ISBI), pp. 1677–1681. IEEE (2021)

29. Li, X., Zhu, D.: Robust detection of adversarial attacks on medical images. In: 2020 IEEE 17th International Symposium on Biomedical Imaging (ISBI), pp. 1154–1158. IEEE (2020)

30. Liang, Z., et al.: A survey of multimodel large language models. In: Proceedings of the 3rd International Conference on Computer, Artificial Intelligence and Control Engineering, pp. 405–409 (2024)

31. Litjens, G., et al.: A survey on deep learning in medical image analysis. Med. Image Anal. **42**, 60–88 (2017)

32. Liu, Y., Chen, X., Liu, C., Song, D.: Delving into transferable adversarial examples and black-box attacks. ArXiv abs/1611.02770 (2017)

33. Liu, Y., Jia, Y., Geng, R., Jia, J., Gong, N.Z.: Formalizing and benchmarking prompt injection attacks and defenses. In: 33rd USENIX Security Symposium (USENIX Security 24), pp. 1831–1847 (2024)

34. Ma, X., et al.: Understanding adversarial attacks on deep learning based medical image analysis systems. Patt. Recogn. **110**, 107332 (2021)

35. Madry, A., Makelov, A., Schmidt, L., Tsipras, D., Vladu, A.: Towards deep learning models resistant to adversarial attacks. In: International Conference on Learning Representations (2018)

36. Mirsky, Y., Mahler, T., Shelef, I., Elovici, Y.: Ct-gan: Malicious tampering of 3d medical imagery using deep learning. In: 28th {USENIX} Security Symposium ({USENIX} Security 19), pp. 461–478 (2019)

37. Moosavi-Dezfooli, S.M., Fawzi, A., Fawzi, O., Frossard, P.: Universal adversarial perturbations. In: Proceedings of the IEEE Conference on Computer Vision and Pattern Recognition, pp. 1765–1773 (2017)

38. Oliynyk, D., Mayer, R., Rauber, A.: I know what you trained last summer: a survey on stealing machine learning models and defences. ACM Comput. Surv. **55**(14s), 1–41 (2023)

39. Papernot, N., McDaniel, P., Wu, X., Jha, S., Swami, A.: Distillation as a defense to adversarial perturbations against deep neural networks. In: 2016 IEEE Symposium on Security and Privacy (SP), pp. 582–597. IEEE (2016)

40. Paul, R., Schabath, M., Gillies, R., Hall, L., Goldgof, D.: Mitigating adversarial attacks on medical image understanding systems. In: 2020 IEEE 17th International Symposium on Biomedical Imaging (ISBI), pp. 1517–1521. IEEE (2020)

41. Raheja, T., Pochhi, N., Curie, F.: Recent advancements in LLM red-teaming: techniques, defenses, and ethical considerations. arXiv preprint arXiv:2410.09097 (2024)

42. Schlarmann, C., Hein, M.: On the adversarial robustness of multi-modal foundation models. In: Proceedings of the IEEE/CVF International Conference on Computer Vision, pp. 3677–3685 (2023)

43. Security, F.H.: 2021 horizon report the state of cybersecurity in healthcare (2021)

44. Setio, A.A.A., et al.: Validation, comparison, and combination of algorithms for automatic detection of pulmonary nodules in computed tomography images: the luna16 challenge. Med. Image Anal. **42**, 1–13 (2017)
45. Shadmi, R., Mazo, V., Bregman-Amitai, O., Elnekave, E.: Fully-automatic deep learning based system for Agatston score prediction from any non-contrast chest CT
46. Shayegani, E., Mamun, M.A.A., Fu, Y., Zaree, P., Dong, Y., Abu-Ghazaleh, N.: Survey of vulnerabilities in large language models revealed by adversarial attacks. arXiv preprint arXiv:2310.10844 (2023)
47. Szegedy, C., et al.: Intriguing properties of neural networks. arXiv preprint arXiv:1312.6199 (2013)
48. Taghanaki, S.A., Abhishek, K., Azizi, S., Hamarneh, G.: A kernelized manifold mapping to diminish the effect of adversarial perturbations. In: Proceedings of the IEEE/CVF Conference on Computer Vision and Pattern Recognition, pp. 11340–11349 (2019)
49. Tramèr, F., Carlini, N., Brendel, W., Madry, A.: On adaptive attacks to adversarial example defenses. In: Larochelle, H., Ranzato, M., Hadsell, R., Balcan, M., Lin, H. (eds.) Advances in Neural Information Processing Systems 33: Annual Conference on Neural Information Processing Systems 2020, NeurIPS 2020, December 6–12, 2020, virtual (2020). https://proceedings.neurips.cc/paper/2020/hash/11f38f8ecd71867b42433548d1078e38-Abstract.html
50. Wang, B., et al.: Decodingtrust: a comprehensive assessment of trustworthiness in GPT models. In: NeurIPS (2023)
51. Wang, D., Yao, W., Jiang, T., Tang, G., Chen, X.: A survey on physical adversarial attack in computer vision. arXiv preprint arXiv:2209.14262 (2022)
52. Winter, T.C.: Malicious adversarial attacks on medical image analysis. Am. J. Roentgenol. **215**(5), W55–W55 (2020)
53. Xu, P., Zhu, X., Clifton, D.A.: Multimodal learning with transformers: a survey. IEEE Trans. Patt. Anal. Mach. Intell. **45**(10), 12113–12132 (2023)
54. Xue, F.F., Peng, J., Wang, R., Zhang, Q., Zheng, W.S.: Improving robustness of medical image diagnosis with denoising convolutional neural networks. In: International Conference on Medical Image Computing and Computer-Assisted Intervention, pp. 846–854. Springer (2019)
55. Yang, Y., Jin, Q., Huang, F., Lu, Z.: Adversarial attacks on large language models in medicine. ArXiv pp. arXiv-2406 (2024)
56. Yoo, K., Kim, J., Jang, J., Kwak, N.: Detection of word adversarial examples in text classification: benchmark and baseline via robust density estimation. arXiv preprint arXiv:2203.01677 (2022)
57. Yu, H., Yang, K., Zhang, T., Tsai, Y.Y., Ho, T.Y., Jin, Y.: Cloudleak: Large-scale deep learning models stealing through adversarial examples. In: NDSS (2020)
58. Zou, A., Wang, Z., Carlini, N., Nasr, M., Kolter, J.Z., Fredrikson, M.: Universal and transferable adversarial attacks on aligned language models. arXiv preprint arXiv:2307.15043 (2023)

Cyberprotection of Hospitals

Cybersecurity Measurability: Three Magnified Vulnerabilities of USA Healthcare

William Yurcik[1]([✉]) [iD], Andreas Schick[1] [iD], Stephen North[2] [iD], Michael T. Gastner[3] [iD],
Fabio Roberto de Miranda[4] [iD], Rodolpho da Silva Avelino[4] [iD],
Andre Filipe de Moreas Batista[4] [iD], Gregory Pluta[5] [iD], and Ian Brooks[5] [iD]

[1] U.S. Department of Health and Human Services, Washington, DC, USA
william.yurcik@cms.hhs.gov
[2] Infovisible, Oldwick, NJ, USA
[3] Singapore Institute of Technology, Singapore, Singapore
[4] Insper, São Paulo, Brazil
[5] University of Illinois at Urbana-Champaign, Urbana-Champaign, IL, USA

Abstract. There are two defining characteristics of a healthcare provider: (1) geographic location and services available at their physical structure and (2) services available via their virtual Internet presence. For centuries we have focused on the first defining characteristic - now we need to shift our focus to understand and address issues that may arise from the new second defining characteristic.

This chapter is an updated summary of a paper originally presented at the ACM Cybersecurity in Healthcare (HealthSec) Workshop in October 2024 [39]. We address issues related to Internet connectivity and virtual presence of USA healthcare providers, especially hospitals, when ransomware cyberattacks resulting in service outages occur. We show the cybersecurity posture of a large critical national infrastructure (USA healthcare) can be measured, mapped, and quantitatively baselined. Empirical measurability results reveal systemic issues in USA healthcare presenting "magnified vulnerabilities" in that a single exploit can have an outsized impact on an entire nationwide infrastructure. As the initial step toward addressing this issue, we identify the three magnified cybersecurity vulnerabilities of USA healthcare: (1) shared IT infrastructure; (2) market concentration; and (3) the geographical distribution of hospitals across the USA.

Keywords: hospital ransomware attacks · Change Healthcare · critical access care hospitals · rural hospital closures

1 Motivation

USA Healthcare is a multifaceted sociotechnical environment comprising systems, processes, and individuals. There are system-level issues related to industry structure, organizational design, funding, and investment. Process-related issues include clinical protocols, organizational procedures, regulatory compliance, and insurance authorizations.

W. Yurcik and A. Schick—Organizational Disclaimer: "The views presented herein do not represent the views of the Federal Government."

© The Author(s), under exclusive license to Springer Nature Switzerland AG 2026
W. Yurcik (Ed.): HealthSec 2024, CCIS 2716, pp. 113–129, 2026.
https://doi.org/10.1007/978-3-032-13800-2_6

Additionally, there are challenges associated with the involvement of humans, such as patients with varying needs being treated by medical staff with their own requirements within an organizational culture established over many years. While the complexity of USA healthcare can contribute to effective patient care, it also presents potential risks in treatment.

In 1991 the Harvard Medical Practice Study (HMPS) brought public awareness to patient safety in hospitals for the first time and as a result changes were implemented to improve patient safety [2]. However, a recent study of hospital patient safety events 27 years later reports that the harm rates are actually higher in 2018 than in the original 1991 HMPS study [1]. Another study in same year (2018) by the HHS Office of Inspector General reported that 25% of hospitalized Medicare patients experienced a harm event, with 43% of these harm events being preventable [19]. Of course, hospitals have dramatically evolved from 1991 to 2018, with integrated IT infrastructures, electronic health records, networked digital medical devices, and new virtual services. While these technological innovations are force multipliers to enable medical staff to handle more patients and make healthcare more effective for patient care, the evidence shows technology has not made healthcare safer, and in many instances these innovations have made healthcare more brittle, less resilient to preventable harm events.

We focus on ransomware attacks targetting healthcare providers which significantly disrupt patient care. Next, we explain why we concentrate on continuity-of-care disruptions instead of other cybersecurity impacts on healthcare.

2 Background

The Cybersecurity & Infrastructure Security Agency (CISA) has identified sixteen U.S. critical national infrastructure sectors [9]. One of these critical national infrastructures is explicitly identified as the "Healthcare and Public Health Sector". In 2019 CISA went deeper to identify fifty-five National Critical Functions (NCFs) [10].[1] Four of these fifty-five NCFs are the primary responsibility of the "Healthcare and Public Health Sector" as shown in Fig. 1. These four Healthcare-NCFs need to be balanced since they may conflict in different situations.

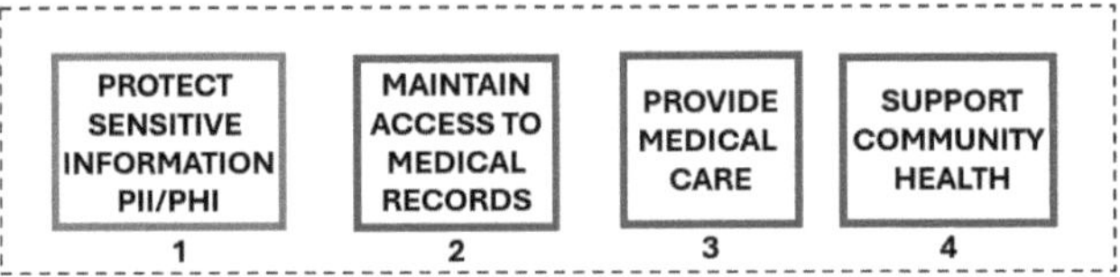

Fig. 1. Healthcare National Critical Functions [39]

---

[1] National Critical Functions are defined by CISA as "the functions of government and the private sector so vital to the United States that their disruption, corruption, or dysfunction would have a debilitating effect on security, national economic security, national public health or safety, or any combination thereof."

While there are four Healthcare-NCFs, the majority of our laws, best practices, and processes are focused on only the first NCF (protecting PII/PHI Healthcare-NCF-1), not on the three NCFs addressing healthcare resilience and continuity of care (Healthcare-NCF-2/3/4).

The focus of cybersecurity protection specific to healthcare began with the 1996 Federal law - Health Insurance Portability and Accountability Act (HIPAA) [21] - which requires the creation of national standards to protect sensitive patient health information from being disclosed without the patient's consent or knowledge. HIPAA created initial emphasis on healthcare privacy compliance over maintaining healthcare operations resilience. Due to this initial emphasis, current laws protect data more than they protect patient continuity of care.[2]

While harmful, healthcare privacy breaches compromising patient data do not immediately endanger lives. Such breaches can be compensated with monetary damages, though it takes time and effort. Overemphasizing breaches from Healthcare NCF-1 and HIPAA has led to immediate IT shutdowns during cybersecurity events, halting hospital operations. This decision satisfies NCF-1 but disrupts patient care (violating NCFs-2/3/4), directly harming patients, as will be discussed later in this chapter.

To illustrate the impact of shutting down a hospital's IT system on patient care, an incomplete list includes the termination of: (1) all diagnostic medical treatment dependent on medical records and laboratory test results; (2) surgery dependent on automated equipment; (3) use of all automated medical devices including life support; (4) all pharmacy orders; (5) technology-based safety-checks, (6) insurance pre-authorization determining healthcare decisions; (7) admissions and scheduling, including emergency ambulance diversions to other hospitals; and (8) patient transfer to other hospitals since cybersecurity events typically require weeks to recover. Each of these eight impacts leads to degraded essential clinical functions and adverse patient outcomes such as morbidity/mortality events.[3] For a more in-depth discussion of the ransomware outage impacts on hospital clinical functions see [33].

Cybersecurity protection against ransomware is crucial for patient care. This chapter discusses proactive cybersecurity strategies to reduce and eliminate preventable ransomware incidents, thereby enhancing patient care.

3 Cybersecurity Ratings

One of the most frustrating and ultimately dangerous things about cybersecurity is that you can *almost* measure it.Evaluating an overall cybersecurity posture involves measuring various components. Creating a comprehensive security posture composed from

---

[2] Josh Corman, former chief strategist for the CISA Covid task force, put it bluntly: "We have more regulatory incentive to have a corpse with their privacy intact than to keep patients alive" [34].

[3] A lawsuit filed by plaintiff Teiranni Kidd against Springhill Memorial Hospital in 2019 alleges that Kidd's daughter, Nicko Silar, suffered birth complications and subsequently died due to a cybersecurity ransomware attack in which hospital clinicians did not have timely access to the baby's fetal monitoring results, which showed that the child was in distress during Kidd's labor [24].

different security components is challenging, currently unsolved, and might never be fully achieved [22].

It is essential to quantitatively assess overall security posture rather than relying on subjective opinions. While our method is an approximation, it addresses the critical need for such evaluations. Seeking a perfect solution should not hinder the adoption of practical approaches when urgently needed.

NIST defines a security metric as a useful measurement that can be used to support human decision-making toward improving cybersecurity performance [30]. Despite this straightforward definition, there is no universally accepted set of security metrics for monitoring cybersecurity. Instead, these metrics are tailored to the specific characteristics of enterprise environments and chosen by cybersecurity analysts in positions of responsibility.

Cybersecurity ratings based on security metrics are a numerical data reduction technique for combining security metrics. This is similar to how a credit score encompasses overall credit risk by a creditor, and how the value of a stock or bond reflects financial reports and market conditions [6].

BitSight invented the cybersecurity ratings industry by creating an algorithm based on security metrics to produce quantitative security scores (ranging 200–900) for systems and organizations [4]. BitSight is unique in that it incorporates large-scale analysis based on Internet traffic gathered outside of an organization's security perimeter (not egress/ingress traffic) in addition to low frequency network and port scans of an enterprise attack surface.[4]

Figure 2 displays the security metrics and corresponding weights used by BitSight to calculate their cybersecurity ratings. BitSight categorizes these security metrics, also known as risk vectors, into four categories: (1) Diligence, (2) Compromised Systems, (3) User Behavior, and (4) Public Disclosures. The Diligence risk vector has the largest weight at 70.5% and measures 11 different metrics for best practice implementation. The 4 additional metrics listed under Diligence are currently in beta and do not affect ratings. The Compromised Systems risk vector has the next largest weight at 27%, assessing 5 different metrics for evidence of preventing or failing to prevent malicious or unwanted software. User Behavior is weighted at 2.5% and evaluates 3 activity metrics: open ports, password re-use, and file sharing traffic. Unlike the other three risk vectors, the absence of a public disclosure does not positively impact ratings, while reporting a breach negatively affects ratings.

BitSight publishes and publicly revises its ratings algorithm annually, incorporating user input, changes in the Internet threat environment, and improvements in security metrics. This practice aligns with established standards used by ratings organizations in other industries.[5]

---

[4] BitSight uses a variety of tools and techniques to gather data from billions of online events and stored data points, including: crawlers, sinkholes, P2P network monitoring, honeypots, BitTorrent monitoring, spam traps, darknet traffic monitoring, network/port scanning, and open source reports.

[5] securities, credit, and insurance ratings organizations.

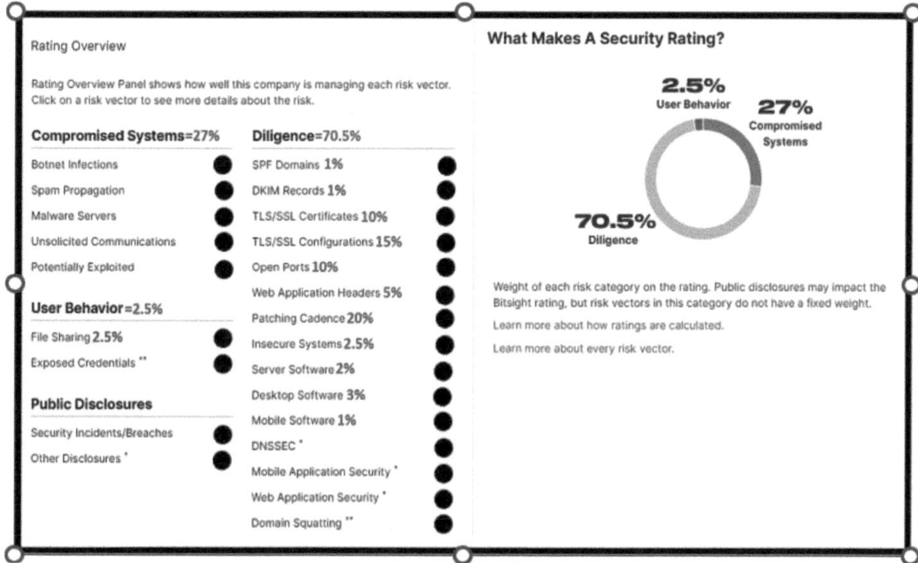

Fig. 2. What Makes a BitSight Security Rating? (2023 rating algorithm graphic used with permission from BitSight)

4   Baselining Cybersecurity of USA Healthcare

With BitSight's cybersecurity ratings, we aim to assess the cybersecurity posture of USA healthcare. The challenge is that USA healthcare is both large and heterogeneous.

Healthcare includes all organizations, people, and actions whose primary intent is to promote, restore, and/or maintain health. This includes medical providers (doctors/dentists/mental-health-professionals), out-patient urgent care, community clinics, nursing homes, specialized medical equipment providers and manufacturers, health insurers, the pharmaceutical industry, blood banks, and many different types of hospitals. USA healthcare covers a current population of 333M people, with private group insurance plans covering about 66% of the population, Medicaid covering 89M, Medicare covering 64.5M, the Affordable Care Act covering 21M, and 26M people with no health insurance.[6] In 2022, USA healthcare expenditure accounted for $4.5 trillion which is 17.3% of the U.S. GDP.[7]

---

[6] As of May 2022 exactly 64,553,288 people were enrolled in Medicare and exactly 88,978,791 people were enrolled in Medicaid and Children's Health Insurance Program (CHIP). About 12M individuals are dually eligible for both Medicare and Medicaid, so are counted in the enrollment figures for both programs. In January 2024 the Affordable Care Act's Health Insurance Marketplace reached 21M for the 2024 plan year. In September 2023, the U.S. Census reported that for 2022 the number of uninsured U.S. citizens reached a record low of 26M or 7.9%. Note due to significant overlaps in coverage these numbers do not add to the current USA population for the year of study [5].

[7] In 2022, National Healthcare Expenditure (NHE) grew 4.1% to $4.5 trillion, or $13,493 per person, and accounted for 17.3% of Gross Domestic Product in 2022 [5].

118   W. Yurcik et al.

Figure 3 breaks down USA healthcare into different sectors and shows security ratings for a sampling of organizations within each sector. Given the different sectors within USA healthcare, we considered analysis options and decided upon hospitals as the best sector to study first in more depth since it is a central convergence point. Hospitals touch every part of the industry including patient healthcare management, most providers have hospital privileges, and hospitals are typically the parent organization of subsidiary activity such as ancillary out-patient services/facilities.

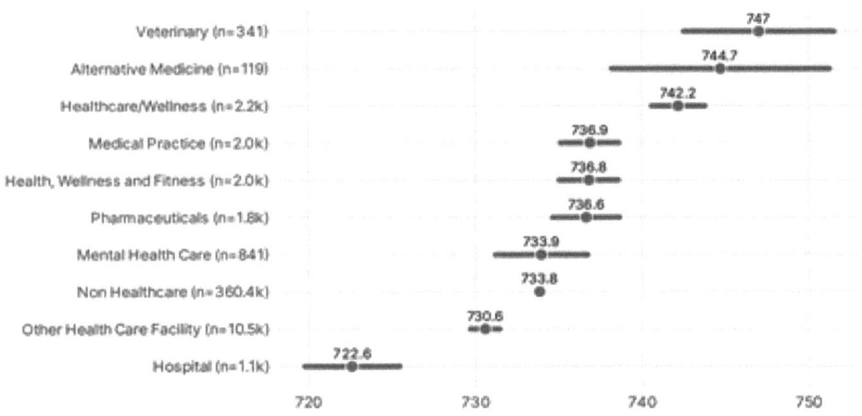

Fig. 3. Cybersecurity Rating Statistics for Different USA Healthcare Sectors [credit to Ben Edwards/BitSight - used with permission]

Figure 4 shows scatter plots of the security ratings for 70% of USA hospitals – each dot represents a hospital system consisting of multiple hospitals. The vertical axis is cybersecurity rating value, the horizontal axis is the logarithm (base e) of the number of in-patient beds. These hospital cybersecurity ratings are updated nightly, and analysts use this information to identify cybersecurity events before they are publicly reported. The ultimate use of this visualized information is for prevention, using a prioritization strategy to identify and remediate hospital cybersecurity vulnerabilities before they can be exploited and/or notifying a hospital before it is otherwise aware.

Just as different healthcare sectors show different cybersecurity rating characteristics, different hospital systems show different cybersecurity ratings characteristics as shown in Table 1. Note that the IHS and VHA hospital systems (hospital system acronyms to be defined shortly) have distinctly non-overlapping mean confidence intervals from the other two systems shown. These differences in cybersecurity rating characteristics are being studied and hypothesized to be related to management structure.

This empirical data shows that USA healthcare can be baselined for cybersecurity starting with hospitals and moving to other healthcare sectors. Security ratings provide quantitative baseline statistics as points-of-reference against which cybersecurity posture can be analyzed and compared. Security rating baselines have also provided other important insights such as magnified cybersecurity vulnerabilities present within the U.S, hospital sector which we discuss in more detail in Sect. 6.

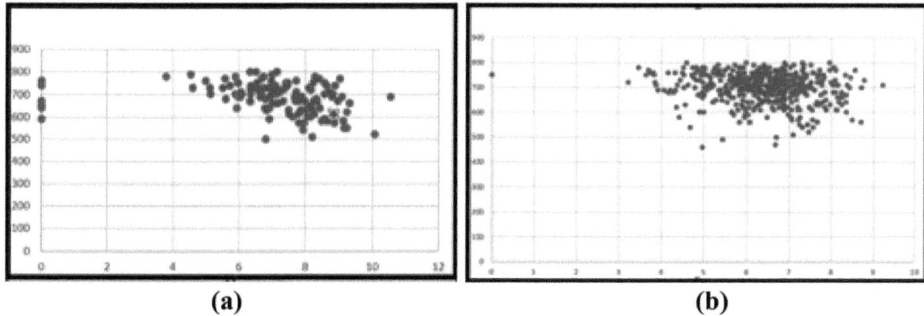

(a)   (b)

Fig. 4. Distribution of Cybersecurity Ratings for (a) Hospitals in USA Interstate Systems [126 systems, 2,612 hospitals] and (b) Hospitals in USA Intrastate Systems (523 systems, 2,571 hospitals) [39]

Table 1. Cybersecurity Ratings for USA Hospital Systems [39]

RATING STATS	IHS	VHA	INTERSTATE SYSTEMS	INTRASTATE SYSTEMS
MEAN	719.78	753.78	682.72	699.34
95% CI	$+/-7.25$	$+/-2.96$	$+/-12.00$	$+/-5.62$
MEDIAN	730	760	690	710
RANGE	650–760 (110)	690–780 (90)	500–800 (300)	460–800 (340)

5   A Deeper Dive into USA Hospitals

Before embarking on USA hospital security ratings monitoring and analysis, we performed an inventory of the assets to be protected. Figure 5 shows all USA hospitals mapped to their geographical coordinates in the continental USA. We used multiple sources to assemble a database of 7,490 USA hospitals which is hosted at the University of Illinois at Urbana-Champaign.

According to the American Hospital Association, a hospital is state-licensed institution whose function is to provide diagnostic and therapeutic patient services for medical conditions, with organized physician staff and registered nursing.[8] The functional hospitals we track include general hospitals, Short-Term Acute Care Hospitals (STACH), Long-Term Acute Care Hospitals (LTACH), Inpatient Rehabilitation Facilities (IRF), Skilled Nursing Facilities (SNF), short stay hospitals, behavioral hospitals, psychiatric care hospitals, children's hospitals, women's hospitals, teaching hospitals, and specialty care hospitals (cancer care, eye surgery, etc.). Legally-defined categories of hospitals include Acute Care/Critical Access Hospitals (CAH, fewer than 25 in-patient beds and greater than 35 miles from the next nearest hospital) and Safety-Net Hospitals (designated by the proportion of charity care provided).

---

[8] aha.org.

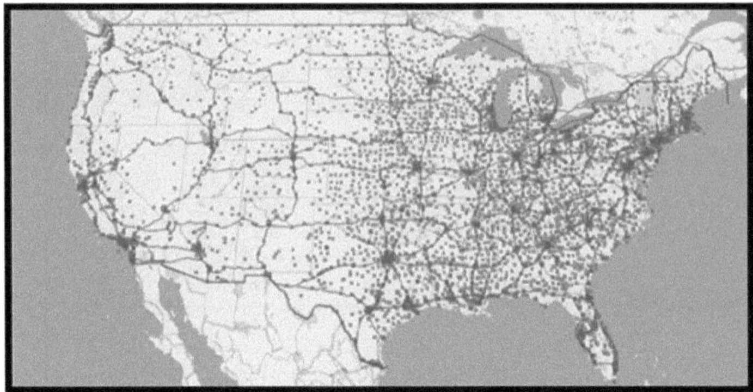

Fig. 5. USA Hospitals Mapped to Geographical Coordinates (hospitals in Alaska & Hawaii are not included in this display) [39]

For cybersecurity analysis, USA hospitals can be separated into two classes – (1) hospitals managed within an organizational system and (2) independent hospitals unaffiliated with an organizational system. We identified five USA hospital systems for analysis as: (1) Indian Health Service (IHS) Hospitals, (2) Veterans Health Administration (VHA) Hospitals, (3) Defense Health Agency (DHA) Hospitals, (4) Interstate Hospital Systems, and (5) Intrastate Hospital Systems. These five hospital systems include 70% of all the hospitals in the USA, with the remaining hospitals being independent unaffiliated hospitals.

The Indian Health Service (IHS) is the primary healthcare provider for federally recognized American Indian tribes and Alaskan natives consisting of approximately 2.6 million people belonging to 574 tribes in 37 states. The U.S. Veterans Health Administration (VHA) is the largest healthcare system in the world providing healthcare for about 9M non-active/discharged veterans of the U.S. military. The U.S. Defense Health Agency (DHA) is operated by the U.S. Department of Defense as the healthcare provider for 9.4M active-duty members of the U.S. military with hospitals and clinics worldwide.

U.S. hospitals are increasingly combining into systems of multiple hospitals – combining for reasons beyond our scope. We subdivided these hospitals systems into two categories for analysis: (1) Interstate Hospitals Systems containing hospitals in multiple states and (2) Intrastate Hospital Systems containing hospitals all within one state. This separation based on state boundaries is meaningful since hospital administration is generally governed by state regulations/certifications/laws.

6 Magnified Cybersecurity Vulnerabilities

In proactively monitoring and mapping all USA hospitals we have identified three magnified cybersecurity vulnerabilities. We refer to these three vulnerabilities as magnified since a single cybersecurity event can have an outsized impact on the entire USA healthcare infrastructure.

6.1 Shared IT Infrastructure in Hospital Systems

Shared IT infrastructure is the first magnified cybersecurity vulnerability we identified. This magnified vulnerability has been manifested in ransomware outages in large interstate hospital systems which have recently occurred: {in chronological order}.[9]

- ***Prospect Medical Holdings*** *(August 2023);* simultaneous ransomware outage at 17 in-patient hospitals spread across 4 states {CA(7), CT(3), PA(5), RI(2)} with 3,600 beds & 166 associated out-patient clinics.
- ***Ardent Health Services*** *(November 2023);* simultaneous ransomware outage at 30 in-patient hospitals spread across 4 states {NJ(2), NM(8), OK(12), TX(8)} with 4,300 beds and 200 associated out-patient clinics and 1,300 aligned provides including partially-owned hospitals in 3 states {ID(1), KS(1), NJ(2)}
- ***Ascension Health*** *(May 2024);* simultaneous ransomware outage at 127 in-patient hospitals spread across 12 states {AL(5), FL(10), IL(16), IN(24), KS(7), MD(1), MI(16), NY(1), OK(6), TN(11), TX(14), WI(16)} with 21,000 beds - one of the largest hospital systems in the U.S.

Note the chronological trend toward larger hospital system ransomware outages, the increasing number of affected entities ranging from the number to in-patient hospitals and associated beds, to the number of associated out-patient clinics (which is typically an order of magnitude larger than the number of hospitals in the system). Not included is the number of medical providers and the number of patients associated with these hospital systems which are conservatively estimated to be on the order of hundreds of thousands to millions.

The common characteristic behind these simultaneous hospital outages is a shared IT infrastructure between all the hospitals in the system. It makes business sense to share one common IT infrastructure for a specific organizational function across an entire enterprise instead of supporting multiple isolated systems performing the same function. However shared IT infrastructure creates a magnified vulnerability when one shared hospital IT system goes down, all the hospitals in the entire hospital system suffer the same common IT outage simultaneously. These shared hospital IT systems include, but are not limited to these typical/general IT systems:

- external public-facing communication system
- internal staff communication system
- EMS telemetry communication systems
- electronic health record system
- patient registration system
- patient scheduling system
- patient billing system
- patient pre-authorization insurance system
- medical device network
- pharmacy system

---

[9] All the cybersecurity ransomware attacks on hospital systems mentioned in this section have been widely reported in the open source mass media (details easily found via google) as well independently verified by the authors.

- laboratory test system

For a more in-depth discussion of the impact of a ransomware outage on hospital IT systems see [33].

A fundamental issue that needs to be studied is hospital IT system resilience. If one shared hospital IT system is compromised, other shared hospital IT systems should still be able to independently operate, especially if systems are isolated through network segmentation. It is unclear the extent of ransomware-incurred hospital IT outages versus hospital self-inflicted shutdowns of shared IT systems (out of an abundance of concern) when a compromise is suspected and/or detected by hospital system IT staff.

Since there are currently no hospital reporting requirements for hospital IT outages that do not involve PII/PHI breaches,[10] there has been much hearsay, guessing, and informed conjecture but no evidence-based detailed technical information shared about hospital ransomware outages other than sanitized information-poor mass media, social media, and hospital public relations/corporate governance reports. As a direct result there have been no hospital ransomware lessons learned and, as to be expected, there are now repeated ransomware attacks on the same target. McLaren Health Care (13 hospital system) has been the victim of two similar ransomware attacks in less than a year (August 2023/August 2024).

6.2 Economic Market Concentration

Economic market concentration within the U.S. healthcare industry is the second magnified cybersecurity vulnerability we identified. USA healthcare is unique as the only developed country in the world without a universal/national healthcare system. USA healthcare is a mixed economic system combining individual out-of-pocket payments, private health insurance (primarily linked with employment), and publicly-funded government health insurance (Medicaid and Medicare)[11] where healthcare assets are both private and publicly-owned and prices are set by both supply-and-demand and regulatory fiat. For example, U.S. hospitals have been historically established by charitable organizations resulting in the current mix of non-profit hospitals (based on regional/community needs), for-profit hospitals, and government hospitals.

U.S. healthcare sectors currently exist with monopoly/oligopoly market concentration – this is where economic analysis is linked with cybersecurity. Economic market concentration affects cybersecurity risk in three dimensions: [17, 18].

(1) **Threat** - Market concentration affects cybersecurity threat targeting, dominant firms are more attractive targets for potential ransomware payment.
(2) **Vulnerability** – Market concentration affects cybersecurity vulnerability assessment; adversaries focus on dominant entity attack surface vulnerabilities.
(3) **Impact** - Market concentration affects cybersecurity event impact, exploitation of systemic single-points-of-failure entities can impact an entire healthcare sector at a national scale, the entire USA healthcare industry, or even the national U.S. economy.

---

[10] A ransomware attack requires file access in order to encrypt a file so if PII/PHI is present in any of the ransomware encrypted files then, by definition, a PII/PHI breach has occurred.

[11] With some variation by state.

That market concentration is linked with cybersecurity system risk is not theoretical conjecture for USA healthcare. In 2023 the UnitedHealth Group had $325bn in revenue and $25bn in pre-tax profit, ranking it the 5th largest corporation in the U.S. behind only Walmart, Amazon, Apple, and ExxonMobil [13]. Through UnitedHealth Group's multiple business lines, its 100M + customers touch about one-third of the entire U.S. population [35]. On February 27th 2024, the U.S. Department of Justice sued UnitedHealth Group under antitrust law [25].[12] Just days before this antitrust action a UnitedHealth subsidiary, Change Healthcare, had reported an evolving cybersecurity event to the U.S. Securities and Exchange Commission. This evolving cybersecurity event would eventually result in UnitedHealth CEO Andrew Witty testifying for hours before the U.S. Congress where he described, in excruciating detail, the cybersecurity posture of UnitedHealth.

Change Healthcare is one of three Pharmacy Benefit Managers (PBMs) which combine to control over 80% of the U.S. market [12].[13] PBMs are key pharmaceutical industry intermediaries between drug manufacturers, health insurers, drug wholesalers, and retail pharmacies which emerged in the 1950s in response to demand for specialized management of prescription drug benefits. Over time vertical integration has occurred such that PBMs now control the pharmaceutical supply chain including formularies, mail orders, pharmacy networks between manufacturers/ wholesalers, and retail claims processing [26, 31, 32].

The PBM Change Healthcare cybersecurity ransomware outage event first detected on February 22nd 2024 evolved to disrupt a critical mass of drug prior authorization claims processing capability large enough to create a cascading impact on the entire U.S. drug industry and U.S. consumers nationwide. This outsized impact of this single ransomware cybersecurity event on the entire U.S. drug ecosystem had a root cause with the market concentration of national pharmacy claims clearinghouse processing within one entity -- PBM Change Healthcare.

BitSight cybersecurity rating information on Change Healthcare prior to this event reveals multiple exploitable cybersecurity vulnerabilities. While a PBM cybersecurity failure disrupting the nationwide U.S. drug industry could have been theoretically predicted, it was not until this event occurred that the outsized impact of economic market concentration on healthcare cybersecurity has now become a realized strategic concern for U.S. healthcare national critical infrastructure.

6.3 Geographic Distribution

Geographic distribution of physical healthcare facilities is the third magnified cybersecurity vulnerability we identified, we will again focus on the USA hospital sector.

---

[12] This was just one of multiple recent antitrust actions filed against UnitedHealth; in July 2024 UnitedHealth abandoned acquisition of Stewardship Health following DOJ opposition [36]; in 2023 nonprofit hospitals and doctors in California sued over market power abuse in the physician market [11], and ironically the DOJ unsuccessfully sued in 2022 to block its acquisition of Change Healthcare arguing prophetically that this would provide monopolistic control of claims processing tools [23].

[13] additionally six PBMs make up 94% of the U.S. market [12].

124   W. Yurcik et al.

Despite the advent of significant virtual healthcare services available via the Internet, healthcare services availability at physical geographic locations *close-in-time* to patients is critically important, and in cases of emergency often a matter of life and death.

For emergency medicine the term *"golden hour"* refers to the hour immediately after a medical event (heart attack, stroke, trauma event, etc.) when rapid intervention makes the most difference between life and death.[14] In practice, the time duration depends on the exact nature of the medical event. Figure 6 provides critical timeframes for four different medical events [33]. For emergency medicine having healthcare services available within these timeframes is critical for public health of a regional community.

Fig. 6. Critical Timeframes for Emergency Patient Care [Figure used with permission from N. Sullivan & K. Raphel of George Washington University Hospital]

Patient travel distance (PTD) and patient travel time (PTT) to hospitals are important metrics. The median U.S. PTD is 6.6 miles, with 75% under 15 miles and 90% under 30 miles [38]. Shorter distances are typical in the northeast and metropolitan areas, while longer distances are found in the South-East, South-Central, and rural areas [38]. PTD differences impact access to care, healthcare decisions, costs, inequities, and patient outcomes [27, 38].

Previously we defined one criteria of a Critical Access Hospital (CAH) as being greater than 35 miles from the next nearest hospital. The intent of the CAH designation is to improve access to healthcare by keeping hospitals with essential services within rural communities for close-in-time access.[15] However, if a CAH closes or is unavailable due to a cybersecurity ransomware outage, the next closest hospital for emergency services and/or other health services will likely put an entire region in healthcare jeopardy.

CAH closures occur due to a complex range of factors (including cybersecurity breaches and outages) and this is having a measured effect on PTT with its subsequent impact on patient care. From 2005 to 2015, the USA population who lives longer than 60 min from a hospital has increased 80% [29]. Of the services previously offered by a closed CAH, the average increase in distance to obtain those same services post-CAH-closure was approximately 20 miles [37]. A 2017 study reports that 10% of the

---

[14] The term "golden hour" is attributed to R. Adams Cowley who served many years as Head of University of Maryland Shock Trauma Center (STC) in Baltimore City MD USA. Dr. Cowley transformed PTD/PTT metrics with the use of helicopters for rapid medical evacuation of civilians thus establishing the first statewide EMS system. STC was the nation's first, and remains the only, integrated trauma hospital reporting an annual flow of 8K patients with an astounding 97% survival rate. Umms.org.

[15] Congress created the Critical Access Hospital (CAH) designation through the Balanced Budget Act of 1997 (Public Law 105-33).

U.S. rural population (4M people) do not have an acute care hospital within their entire county [7]! An unexpected emergent finding is increasing urban hospital mortality outcomes, spillover effects related to increased travel times to an urban hospital due to rural population time-sensitive emergency cases [20].

Available space for patient care is the second dimension of the CAH closure problem, not only does a hospital have to be close-in-time but it needs to have staffed and supplied in-patient bed space available.[16] Recall another defining criteria of a CAH is having fewer than 25 beds so ideal CAH capacity is not large to begin with. For an extreme recent example of space challenges for patient care, the healthcare system stress caused by the lack of available staffed and supplied bed space within hospitals during the Covid19 pandemic resulted in 12 states adopting Crisis Standards of Care (CSC), the most extreme operating condition for a hospital [8].[17]

Thus, the challenge is to identify and cyberprotect specific CAHs which are potential ransomware outage cascading single-points-of-failure in two dimensions - (1) close-in-time and (2) in-patient bed capacity. To identify the candidate CAHs for special cybersecurity protection demands detailed analysis by county across each state. For scale consideration, the U.S. has 3,143 counties, or county equivalents. Toward addressing this challenge we decided to employ high-level visualization techniques.

A *choropleth* map uses color shades over geographical areas in direct relation to a defined data variable as a visual technique to intuitively communicate an underlying data distribution [28]. Figure 7a shows the distribution of in-patient beds per 1K state population using the 2020 USA census. As shown in the color legend, the number of in-patient beds per 1K state residents varies from VT (2.0) to SD (5.98). One counter-intuitive result shows states with poor healthcare metrics report relatively higher in-patient bed density (e, g, KY, LA, MS, WV).

Cartogram mapping is the ideal mechanism to illustrate distortions in USA hospital coverage. A cartogram substitutes a mapping variable for space/geometry of a reference map [16]. The substitute variable used in Fig. 7b is the 2020 USA census population in each state. Thus, this cartogram generated using a flow-based method [15] represents each state with an area proportional to its population. Grid cells are overlaid the scale of the quantities represented [14]. In Fig. 7(b), each grid cell corresponds to a population of 10 million. Using the same color scale as in Fig. 7(a), this cartogram reveals that some states with small populations have high bed-to-population ratios, such as the District of Columbia (DC) and North and South Dakota (ND and SD), with 5.77 and 5.04 beds per thousand residents, respectively. California (CA), the most populous state, ranks sixth lowest in bed-to-population ratio (2.61).

When the number of beds is normalized by the number of hospitals instead of population, a different picture emerges in Figs. 7(c) and (d). In 7(d), each grid cell corresponds to 200 hospital beds. As indicated by the colors, many states with a high per-capita number of beds have few beds per hospital (e.g., ND, SD, and LA). Comparing the cartograms in 7(b) and 7(d) reveals that California has fewer hospitals (6.5% of all US hospitals)

---

[16] Often referred to as the three S's – Space / Supplies / Staff.

[17] CSC preserves functioning during scarcity, curtailing services & adjusting patient care to available resources. https://www.ncbi.nlm.nih.gov/books/NBK32748/.

than its share of the US population (11.6%) would suggest. In contrast, Louisiana (LA) hosts 4.1% of the hospitals but only 1.4% of the population.

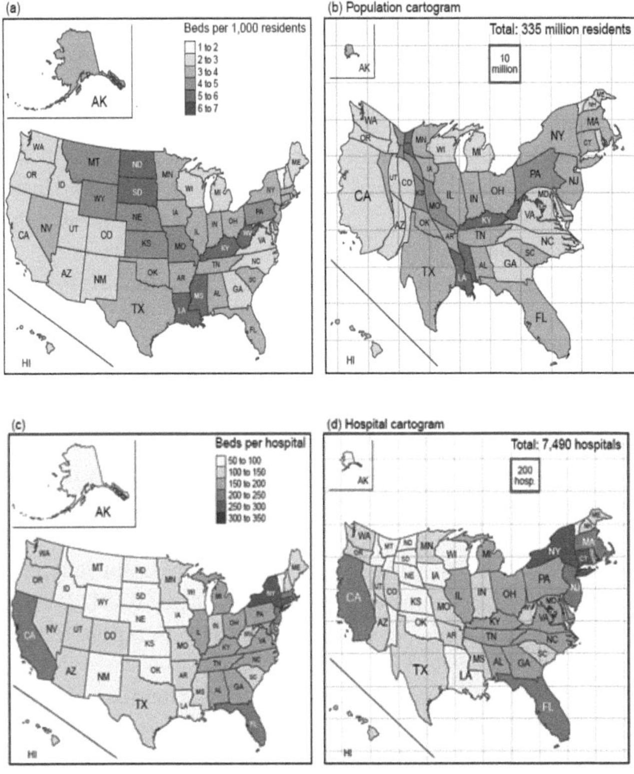

Fig. 7. Maps showing the distribution of hospitals and hospital beds in the USA. (a) Choropleth map displaying hospital beds per 1,000 residents by state. (b) Cartogram where states are scaled according to population. (c) Choropleth map depicting the number of beds per hospital. (d) Cartogram where states are scaled according to the number of hospitals [39].

7 Summary

We demonstrated that it is possible to baseline the cybersecurity posture of the U.S. hospital healthcare sector using cybersecurity ratings and data visualization techniques. This implementation marks the first quantitative Internet cybersecurity results for a large national infrastructure.

We identified three major cybersecurity vulnerabilities in the U.S. hospital healthcare sector by monitoring and mapping it. These "magnified" vulnerabilities mean that a single incident can significantly impact the entire national infrastructure.

The first magnified cybersecurity vulnerability we identified was shared IT infrastructure in hospital systems such that when one shared hospital IT system goes down due to a cybersecurity incident, all the hospitals in the entire hospital system suffer the same common IT outage simultaneously - as we document in three hospital system outages.

The second major cybersecurity vulnerability identified is the market concentration in U.S. healthcare. A single disruption in a monopolist or oligopolist provider can affect the entire national infrastructure, as seen in the PBM Change Healthcare incident.

The third magnified cybersecurity vulnerability we identified was a single cybersecurity event causing an outage at a rural hospital (and/or specifically a Critical Access Hospital) can jeopardize healthcare for the patient population in an entire region.

In conclusion, a proactive approach to cybersecurity is recommended, considering the complexity of interconnected healthcare systems. Prioritizing patient impact assessment is essential. Addressing the identified magnified vulnerabilities in the U.S. healthcare system will be the focus of future research. Cybersecurity in healthcare is synonymous with patient care.

Acknowledgments. This research was enabled through a cooperative agreement between the University of Illinois at Urbana-Champaign and BitSight. BitSight provided no financial support to this research. Cybersecurity ratings for hospitals presented in this research were processed by BitSight engineers led by Rhonda O'Kane and supported by Tadd Hopkins, Tim Jackson, Tom Linehan, and Will Ricardi. Geocoding was provided by GeoCoder.ca who provided public service access to their geography mapping scripts. Geocode provided no financial support to this research. Authors Miranda, Avelino, and Batista were supported by a joint funding support agreement between Insper and the Computer Science Department at the University of Illinois at Urbana-Champaign. Coauthor MTG is supported by the Ministry of Education, Singapore, under its Academic Research Fund Tier 2 (EP2) programme (Award No. MOE-T2EP20221–0007).

References

1. Bates, D.W., et al.: The safety of inpatient health care. N. Engl. J. Med. **388**(2), 142–153 (2023)
2. Brennan, T.A., et al.: Incidence of adverse events and negligence in hospitalized patients: results of the Harvard medical practice study I. N. Engl. J. Med. **324**, 370–376 (1991)
3. Blaze, M.: "Afterword" within B. Schneier. Applied Cryptography 2nd Ed. (1996)
4. Boyer, S., Venna, N., Ando, M.: (BitSight Technologies Inc. filed September 22, 2011), Information Security Assessment System U.S. Patent 20160205126, granted July 14 (2016)
5. Centers for Medicare & Medicaid Services (CMS). National Health Expenditures (NHE) 2024 Fact Sheet (2024). https://www.cms.gov/data-research/statistics-trends-and-reports/national-health-expenditure-data/nhe-fact-sheet
6. Choi, S.J., Johnson, M.E.: The relationship between cybersecurity ratings and the risk of hospital data breaches. J. Am. Med. Inf. Assoc. 1–8 (2021)
7. Clawar, M., et al.: Access to care: populations in counties with no FQHC, RHC, or acute care hospital. NC Rural Health Research Program (2018)
8. Cybersecurity Infrastructure and Security Agency (CISA). Provide Medical Care is in Critical Condition: Analysis and Stakeholder Decision Support to Minimize Further Harm. CISA INSIGHTS (2021)
9. Cybersecurity & Infrastructure Security Agency (CISA). Critical Infrastructure Sectors. https://www.cisa.gov/topics/critical-infrastructure-security-and-resilience/critical-infrastructure-sectors

10. Cybersecurity & Infrastructure Security Agency (CISA). National Critical Functions. https://www.cisa.gov/topics/risk-management/national-critical-functions
11. Emanate Health v. Optum Health. California Central District Court – No. 2:23-cv-09872 (2023)
12. Fein, A.J.: The Top Pharmacy Benefit Managers of 2022: Market Share and Trends for the Biggest Companies. Drug Channels Institute (2023)
13. Fortune 500 – The Largest Companies in the U.S. by Revenue. Fortune Magazine (2023). https://fortune.com/ranking/fortune500/2023/
14. Fung, K.L.T., Perrault, S.T., Gastner, M.T.: Effectiveness of area-to-value legends and grid lines in contiguous area cartograms. IEEE Trans. Vis. Comput. Graph. (2023)
15. Gastner, M.T., Seguy, V., More, P.: Fast flow-based algorithm for creating density-equalizing map projection. Proc. Nat. Acad. Sci. **115**(10) (2018). https://www.pnas.org/doi/abs/10.1073/pnas.1712674115
16. Gastner, M.T., Newman, M.E.J.: Optimal design of spatial distribution networks. Phys. Rev. E **74**(1) (2006). https://doi.org/10.1103/PhysRevE.74.016117
17. Geer, D., et al.: CyberInsecurity: the cost of monopoly – how the dominance of Microsoft's products poses a risk to security. Computer & Communications Industry Association Report (2003)
18. Geer, D., Jardine, E., Leverett, E.: On market concentration and cybersecurity risk. J. Cyber Policy (2010). https://doi.org/10.1080/23738871.2020.1728355
19. Grimm, C.A.: Adverse events in hospitals: a quarter of medicare patients experienced harm in October 2018. U.S. Department of Health and Human Services (HHS), Office of Inspector General (OIG). OEI-06–18–00400 (2022)
20. Gujral, K., Basu, A.: Impact of rural and urban hospital closures on inpatient mortality. National Bureau of Economic Research, WKG. Paper 26182 (2019)
21. Health Insurance Portability and Accountability Act of 1996. Public Law 104–191 (1996)
22. INFOSEC Research Council. 2005 Hard Problem List (2005)
23. Liss, S.: Judge Denies DOJ's Move to Block $13B UnitedHealth, Change Deal. Healthcare Dive (2022)
24. McGee, M.K.: Lawsuit: Hospital's Ransomware Attack Led to Baby's Death. HealthInfoSec (2021)
25. Mathews, A.W., Michaels, D.: U.S. opens unitedhealth antitrust probe. Wall Street J. (2024)
26. Joseph Matttingly II, T., Hyman, D.: Pharmacy benefit managers – history, business practices, economics and policy. JAMA Health Forum **4**(11) (2023)
27. McCarthy, S., et al.: Impact of rural hospital closures on health-care access. J. Sur. Res. **2021**(258), 170–178 (2021)
28. Meyer, M., Broome, F.R., Schweitzer Jr., R.H.: Color statistical mapping by the U.S. Bureau of the Census. The American Cartographer **2**(2), 101–117 (1975)
29. Mullner, R.M., Whiteis, D.G.: Rural community hospital closure and health policy. Health Policy **10**(2), 123–135 (1988)
30. National Institute for Standards and Technology (NIST). Measurement Guide for Information Security: Volume 1 – Identifying and Selecting Measures. NIST SP 800–55 (2024)
31. Robbins, R., Abelson, R.: A shadow industry – how pharmacy benefit managers inflate the cost of prescription drugs for millions of people. NY Times **60**(194) (2024)
32. Shepperd, J.: Pharmacy benefit managers, rebates, & drug prices: conflicts of interest in the market for prescription drugs. Yale Law Policy Rev. (2020)
33. Sullivan, N., Raphel, K.: Clinical and hospital system emergency management: implications of cyberthreats beyond privacy concerns. In: Proceedings of the 2024 ACM CCS Workshop on Cybersecurity in Healthcare (HealthSec). Salt Lake City UT, USA (2024)
34. Trang, B.: Why U.S. Health Care Cybersecurity Laws are Better at Protecting a Corpse's Privacy than Patients' Lives. STAT+ (2024)

35. UnitedHealthcare - Individuals Served by Segment 2023. Statista (2003). https://www.sta tista.com/statistics/622420/individuals-served-by-unitedhealthcare-by-segment/
36. U.S. Department of Justice. UnitedHealth Group Abandons Two Acquisitions Following Antitrust Division Scrutiny (2024)
37. U. S. Government Accountability Office: Rural Hospital Closures-Affected Residents Had Reduced Access to Health Care Services. (GAO-21–93) (published: Dec. 22, 2020. Publicly Released: Jan. 21, 2021) (2020)
38. Weiss, A.J., et al.: Methods for calculating patient travel distance to hospital in HCUP Data. U.S. Agency for Healthcare Research and Quality (AHRQ) (2021)
39. Yurcik, W., et al.: Cybersecurity monitoring/mapping of USA healthcare (all hospitals) – magnified vulnerability due to shared IT infrastructure, market concentration, & geographical distribution. In: Proceedings of the 2024 ACM CCS Workshop on Cybersecurity in Healthcare (HealthSec). Salt Lake City UT, USA (2024). https://doi.org/10.1145/3689942.3694754

Evaluating Interoperability of Medical Communication Protocols via Differential Testing

Prashant Anantharaman[1], Vishnupriya Varadharaju[1(✉)],
Carlos Guerrero Alvarez[2], Danylo Borodchuk[2], Aamish A. Beg[2],
Rebecca Shapiro[2], Andrew Gettinger[2], Sean W. Smith[2],
and Michael E. Locasto[1]

[1] Narf Industries, San Diego, CA 92101, USA
{prashant.anantharaman, vishnupriya.varadharaju,
michael.locasto}@narfindustries.com
[2] Dartmouth College, Hanover, NH 03755, USA
{carlos.guerrero.alvarez.25, danylo.borodchuk.26, aamish.a.beg.26,
rebecca.shapiro, andrew.gettinger, sean.w.smith}@dartmouth.edu

Abstract. Despite ever-increasing expenditures on healthcare, the system remains fragmented, disjointed, and without realizing the benefits of digitalization that other sectors have reaped. Interoperability is a cornerstone of modern healthcare systems, enabling seamless communication and data exchange between diverse clinical settings, providers, and institutions. Effective and accurate interoperability empowers physicians to gather comprehensive medical histories, collaborate with other providers, manage medications accurately, and reduce medical errors. Standards such as FHIR (Fast Healthcare Interoperability Resources) and DICOM (Digital Imaging and Communications in Medicine) have been developed to realize these interoperability goals. However, trouble can arise when different implementations interpret the same item differently. Ensuring that different implementations of these standards consistently interpret and process data remains a significant challenge. Prior research into other formats has shown that inconsistent data generation, parsing, validation, and processing across implementations can lead to misinterpretations and even security vulnerabilities.

Prior research has examined interoperability goals in healthcare protocols; however, significant gaps remain in systematically testing and validating the consistency of different implementations. This paper addresses these gaps by applying differential testing to evaluate the interoperability of FHIR and DICOM implementations. We present a novel methodology for identifying parser differentials and deriving a *safe subset* of the FHIR specification, ensuring that all implementations agree on the interpretation of FHIR records. We reported 59 differentials, including some significant vulnerabilities that attackers can exploit to modify FHIR records, where portions of FHIR records can be hidden from providers. Additionally, we comprehensively analyzed five FHIR servers to derive the validation rules applied by them. Finally, we apply differential testing to

W. Yurcik (Ed.): HealthSec 2024, CCIS 2716, pp. 130–159, 2026.
https://doi.org/10.1007/978-3-032-13800-2_7

DICOM libraries, with initial results uncovering inconsistencies in how different implementations handle non-standard inputs.

Keywords: FHIR · DICOM · LangSec · Interoperability

1   Introduction

A series of sentinel publications by the Institute of Medicine (now the National Academy of Medicine) in the 1990s and early 2000s first shed light on serious deficiencies in the US healthcare system [19,22,26]. These reports documented a healthcare ecosystem where individual patient care was not evidence-based but instead fragmented, error-prone, and increasingly expensive without commensurate value in achieving improved individual or population health. Studies by the Rand Corporation highlighted the cost savings of a digital health ecosystem [13]. President Bush established the Office of the National Coordinator for Health IT (ONC) in 2004 by executive order to set standards for digitization.

The HITECH Act (Part of ARA) was the first federal effort to incentivize the healthcare sector to adopt digital solutions. Incentives from the Meaningful Use program were distributed by CMS to help fund these changes. It also made the ONC permanent in statute. Subsequently, the 21st Century Cures Act (2016) added increased requirements around interoperability, sharing, and burden reduction for clinicians and hospitals. Subsequently, as of 2021, 88.2% of U.S. physicians used any EHR system, with 77.8% using certified EHRs [24]. While these EHRs were meant to improve interoperability and aid physicians in documenting cases and reaching diagnoses sooner, in practice, EHRs have also created significant challenges. Poorly designed EHRs, implementation and configuration decisions, and software bugs have contributed significantly to physician burnout [31] (studies link EHRs to 37% of physician burnout cases [1]).

However, even with a high EHR adoption rate, EHRs have lagged in implementing interoperability protocols [2]. In this paper, we study the implementation of interoperability standards, such as HL7 Fast Health Interoperability Resources (FHIR) and Digital Imaging and Communications in Medicine (DICOM). Mismatches (or Differentials) between different implementations can lead to medical consequences, such as misdiagnoses and inaccurate medical histories, and security risks, such as vulnerabilities arising from poor parsing logic. Vulnerabilities in DICOM [8,35] have also been reported in the past, resulting from parsing errors.

Hospitals and clinics have been repeatedly targeted by attackers. With more sophisticated ransomware attacks, entire hospitals have been forced to switch to offline methods. Hospitals have been repeatedly forced to delay surgeries and non-urgent procedures due to these cyberattacks. On average, these cyberattacks lead to losses upwards of $9 million for a large hospital system. The UnitedHealth cyberattack is said to have led to over $1 billion in losses [5].

Ensuring interoperability in healthcare is challenging [6] for several reasons. First, DICOM and FHIR have been widely adopted by organizations. DICOM was first introduced in 1985, and the FHIR standard in 2011. Hence, vendors have incorporated their closed-source implementations of these protocols in their product lines. Subsequently, many open-source versions of these protocols are also available. However, most compliance checking approaches use checklists to ensure that specific features are implemented and do not comprehensively evaluate the software to ensure each field in the specification is implemented correctly.

Second, while DICOM and FHIR are widely used today, legacy and proprietary systems are also widely used. For example, HL7 v2, a text-based messaging protocol that lacks the structured querying supported by FHIR, is also prevalent [16]. Similarly, EDIFACT/X12 is used in billing systems and administrative transactions [3], and the VA's VistA system uses MUMPS databases [4]. Even when systems use the same protocol, variations in coding systems (e.g., SNOMED CT [30], LOINC [21], ICD-9/10 [34]) and inconsistent data labeling can lead to misinterpretations in data transfers.

Finally, these standards evolve drastically every year, increasing or changing the number of features to implement to remain compliant while supporting legacy and newer clients. For example, there have been five major releases of the FHIR specifications since 2014, with Release 6 in a draft stage. Similarly, on average, DICOM has five new supplement releases to their standard every year to support new image formats and APIs. These evolving standards present a significant challenge for implementers to maintain interoperability with other state-of-the-art implementations while also remaining compliant with the specification. Most compliance checking tools certify other software while simply checking if certain features are implemented in software. These tools do not perform comprehensive checking of the implementation to the specification.

To address these challenges, we leverage the approach of *differential testing*, where we send the same input across all the targets and observe how these targets interpreted the inputs received. We instrument the targets to provide these internal data structures necessary to analyze this parsing logic [18]. In the case of FHIR servers, we instrumented them to return the *bundled* Patient data as is to compare it against the original file.

In this paper, we applied differential testing in three stages. First, we analyzed the JSON parsers used by various FHIR servers since FHIR is encapsulated in JSON, XML, or Turtle formats. Next, we analyzed what validation rules servers apply to each field in a FHIR resource. We did this by mutating each field value in FHIR resources and sending them to all the servers in our testbench to analyze which servers accept or reject incorrect fields. Finally, we performed differential testing of three DICOM targets to characterize the differences between these implementations.

To this end, our contributions are as follows:

- We present a format garden for the different FHIR implementations that allows security researchers to compare different FHIR implementations. We also demonstrate 59 parser differentials identified across many FHIR implementations (§ 3).

- We propose a novel methodology to mutate fields in FHIR records to discern the validation rules applied by various FHIR implementations. We use these rules to derive a *safe subset* of the FHIR specification—where all implementations agree on interpretations of the FHIR records (§ 4).
- We present a differential analysis of different DICOM implementations to detect misinterpretations between different implementations that attackers can leverage (§ 5).

Organization: The rest of the paper is organized as follows: § 2 provides the necessary background in the cybersecurity concepts for the rest of the paper. § 3 summarizes our results from our early work in studying FHIR interoperability. § 4 showcases our approach to comprehensively studying how (or how they do not) FHIR servers validate various fields in patient records. § 5 presents early results from differential testing of DICOM implementations. Finally, § 6 presents a discussion of the impact of this work and future directions.

Availability: We have released the source code used in this study along with Dockerfiles to enable further interoperability research. All the artifacts are available under the GNU Public License Version 3. The FHIR testbed is available at: https://github.com/narfindustries/digiheals-public. The results of this study are available at: https://zenodo.org/records/15743198. The DICOM testbed is available at: https://github.com/carlosguealv/fuzz_dicom.

2   Background

2.1   Language-Theoretic Security

Language-Theoretic Security (LangSec) focuses on ensuring that programs validate untrusted input correctly using formal grammars [28]. This way, complex data formats, such as network protocols and file formats, can be represented as formal grammars. In terms of formal language theory—e.g., [29]—we are viewing the set of properly formatted inputs as a "language."

Definition 1. *A parser is a software component that takes unstructured input, validates it, and transforms it into an abstract syntax tree (AST) for further processing.*

Any program that consumes input and then tries to extract its structure in order to process it is performing parsing—whether or not that process is clearly crafted as such.

Parsers are the first line of defense for any program consuming untrusted inputs. In addition, parsers written for the same format need to implement the same formal grammar. However, in practice, most developers build their parser implementations from scratch and deviate from the specifications in minor ways. Differences between these implementations lead to various kinds of interoperability issues and are known as *parser differentials*.

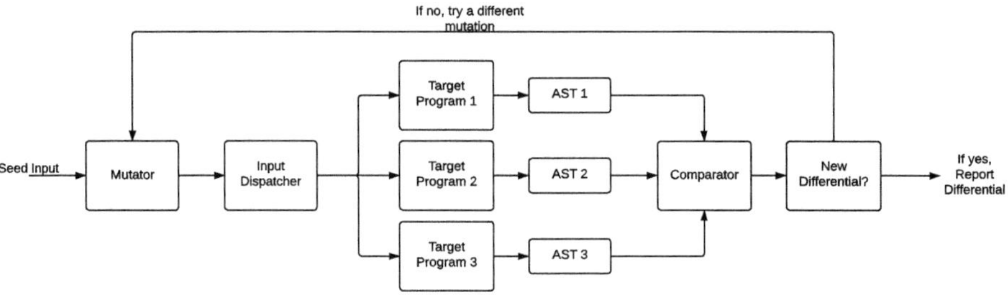

Fig. 1. Overall steps involved in differential testing of target programs.

These parsers are often mixed in with processing logic, creating *shotgun parsers*, where the parser is not cleanly separated from the rest of the code. Mixing parsers with processing logic makes understanding the exact rules implemented to validate the input format harder—and also increases the chances that a program might start acting on an invalidly structured input before it discovers the input is invalid.

LangSec outlines design principles to ensure developers build parsers that strictly implement formal specifications.

2.2 Differential Testing

Differential testing is a technique used to detect inconsistencies between multiple implementations of the exact specification by comparing their outputs on identical inputs. In parsers, differential testing helps uncover parser differentials since different implementations produce distinct abstract syntax trees (ASTs) or exhibit variations in error handling.

Definition 2. *Parser Differentials arise when different parsers for the same format parse an input differently, resulting in different ASTs.*

These differentials may result from ambiguous specifications, incomplete implementations, or deviations from formal grammar definitions. It may be challenging to identify the sources of these differentials without a "gold standard" or ground truth implementation that is trusted to accurately implement the specification.

As shown in Fig. 1, a differential testing framework consists of the following components:

- **Test Case Generation**: Generating a diverse set of valid and malformed inputs that exercise edge cases in parsing logic.
- **Execution and AST Comparison**: Running different parser implementations on the same input and comparing their ASTs and errors.
- **Detect Differentials**: Triage mismatches to determine root causes of ambiguities. Suggest fixes to the specification or implementations and identify

security vulnerabilities. In addition, tools must also identify benign differentials that may still be permissible within the specification and ignore them to find more interesting deviations.

As the figure shows, frameworks frequently employ feedback between these components—e.g., using the results of the comparison to mutate new inputs.

Developers can leverage differential testing effectively to detect interoperability issues and enhance parser correctness. It is a practical tool for enforcing strict adherence to formal specifications and preventing unexpected deviations in parser behavior. Our descriptions of differential testing combine it with the ideas of differential fuzzing, which involves sending mutated, random inputs to programs.

3   Differential Testing of FHIR Instances

The Fast Health Interoperability Resource (FHIR) standard, introduced in 2011, is currently in its fifth release and provides rules for importing and exporting electronic health records. FHIR is implemented on top of HTTPS, where REST APIs are provided for participants to query. This protocol makes patient data accessible to a wide range of audiences that want to query the FHIR server, including public health experts who want to perform meta-analyses on patient data. Some examples of resources available via a FHIR server are: `Patient`, `Observation`, and `Procedure`. FHIR supports three export formats: JSON, XML, and Turtle (RDF). This is an up-and-coming standard that is also the center of the Sequoia Project and TEFCA [7].

3.1   FHIR Garden

Numerous open-source and closed-source implementations of FHIR are currently available. To compare these implementations, we built a FHIR Garden that allows users to send a single FHIR request to all of these servers and observe their responses. We set out to build this FHIR Garden and the accompanying tooling with specific goals in mind.

- **Comparing Data Structures:** The tooling must allow researchers to study the output of different FHIR servers that receive the same patient data. Differences in interpreting this data can lead to some fields being omitted or overlapping with other fields in the patient data.
- **Enabling Differential Fuzzing:** The tooling must support robust differential fuzzing as an end goal. To enable this differential fuzzing, these engines must support the same input and output types to enable seamless comparison.
- **Chainability:** When a vulnerability is identified, the tooling must enable support to send an EHR through a chain of FHIR servers to study how these vulnerabilities can be leveraged.

Table 1. A comparison of the FHIR software and the JSON parsing libraries used in open-source software.

EHR Software	Libraries		Programming Language
	JSON	XML	
HAPI	FasterXML/Jackson	Javax XML	Java
IBM FHIR	Jakarta	Jakarta	Java
Blaze FHIR	FasterXML/Jackson	Javax XML	Clojure
VistA	M Server	M Server	MUMPS
OpenMRS	FasterXML/Jackson	Javax XML	Java
Intersystems IRIS	Unknown	Unknown	Unknown
OpenEMR	PHP JSON	SimpleXML	PHP
GNU Health	Python JSON	DifusedXML	Python

Table 1 provides a framework for how we chose our target EHRs and FHIR servers, summarizing their features.

The FHIR Garden contains a collection of Docker container descriptions and tools to compare their outputs. Using the FHIR Garden, researchers can set up local instances of these FHIR services to compare how they respond to well-formed and malformed FHIR requests. Our tooling was written entirely in Python, and it provides command-line tools for researchers to run files through the FHIR servers and visualize their differences in a Neo4J database and command-line tables.

3.2 Game of Telephone

As stated earlier in the section, one of the goals of the FHIR Garden is to support chaining and explore how malformations move through a chain. Our "Game of Telephone" or chaining tool primarily supports two modes of operations. First, we specify a chain, and the tool will attempt to import and export a patient record through that sequence. For example, a chain [`vista`, `vista`, `blaze`, `ibm`] would import and export through VistA twice before importing the exported file through Blaze and finally through IBM.

Second, we support a depth-first search operation where we explore all possible paths up to a certain path. This mode allows us to identify differentials and determine when they stop being imported into systems.

3.3 Findings

As a result of our study of JSON parsers, we found 59 parsing vulnerabilities across different FHIR servers that broadly fall into three categories:

- **Decimal Precision Issues:** While the specification explicitly states that decimal precision should be maintained, OpenEMR, OpenMRS, and GNU

Health all changed the precision to truncate some decimal places. In addition, the exponent notations of numbers are incorrectly handled by several FHIR implementations.

– **Unicode errors:** VistA makes numerous errors in decoding Unicode characters correctly. VistA was the only server in our test set that did not throw parsing errors when presented with unescaped characters.
– **Syntax Errors:** VistA also allows for some malformations in objects. For example, "null", "true", and "false" are keywords in the JSON format. However, these keywords are allowed in the VistA implementation inside JSON objects as keys, but the parser skips over the associated value. In JSON objects, all keys need to be strings. For example, an object with the syntax {"a":1,null:2,"b":3} is interpreted as {"a":2,"b":3}. VistA allows the use of "true" and "false" similarly. In addition, keywords such as, *TRUE*, *tRUTH*, and *trueasdf* are all incorrect and do not map to the "true" boolean field in the JSON specification. However, VistA converts these values to "true" or "trueas" in the last case.

3.4   An Example Exploit Chain Using VistA Vulnerability

Fig. 2. A chain showing the missing comma in the original FHIR JSON file sent to VistA and then exported and sent to another FHIR server. We show that this is a viable exploit path to redact fields from a patient's FHIR record, which can be hard to detect.

VistA contained a vulnerability in its processing logic for arrays in JSON objects. Arrays such as the following: [1, 2 3 4, 5] is interpreted as [1, 4, 5], skipping multiple values that are missing preceding commas. Similarly, an array of the form [truth, NaN, fals, True, nul] contains all five elements that should be special values. However, all of these values are incorrect. VistA encapsulates each of these values in a string to translate it to the array `["truth"`, `"NaN"`, `"fals"`, `"True"`, `"nul"]`. No other FHIR server presents these behaviors.

We leveraged the array misinterpretation vulnerability in the VistA system to create a FHIR JSON file where whitespaces replaced commas. This change ensures that a file containing a patient's complete record is only partially imported by VistA and can be successfully imported into other FHIR servers with reduced patient records. Figure 2 exhibits this vulnerability and how different FHIR servers interpret these requests.

4   Deriving a Safe Subset of the HL7 R4 Specification

In the previous section, we observed that FHIR servers often fail to strictly implement the rules for parsing the JSON format correctly. We found that these discrepancies can be exploited to redact fields from FHIR patient records. In this section, we further test the *type* rules enforced on individual fields inside FHIR records.

The FHIR specification is complex, containing 148 resource types and 41 higher-level types. It also includes 19 primitive types, each with a defined regular expression. Additionally, the specification outlines the fields for each resource type and its corresponding higher-level type, along with their respective primitive types.

In this study, we thoroughly examine all resources and associated types in the FHIR specification to determine whether popular FHIR implementations validate all fields specified in the standard. Studying this is vital, as discrepancies between implementations in validating a field can lead to interoperability issues where one FHIR server may accept and forward a patient's record while another server may reject it.

Definition 3. *A safe subset of a specification implements the strict validation rules implemented by all the target servers in a testbench to guarantee that inputs valid according to this safe subset would be accepted and interpreted correctly by all the target servers.*

Figure 3 provides an overview of our methodology. First, we mutate every field in every resource across all the primitive types supported by the specification. Next, we send these mutated files to all the servers in our FHIR Garden setup and poll the servers for the same FHIR files. We validate our input file and the output file from the server using a validator to ensure that these files adhere to the specification. We store these results in a local database for further analysis and review. Finally, we identify the primitive types for each key in the FHIR specification, which each server in the Garden has accepted. This exercise aims to create an alternative FHIR R4 specification that can guarantee unambiguous parsing.

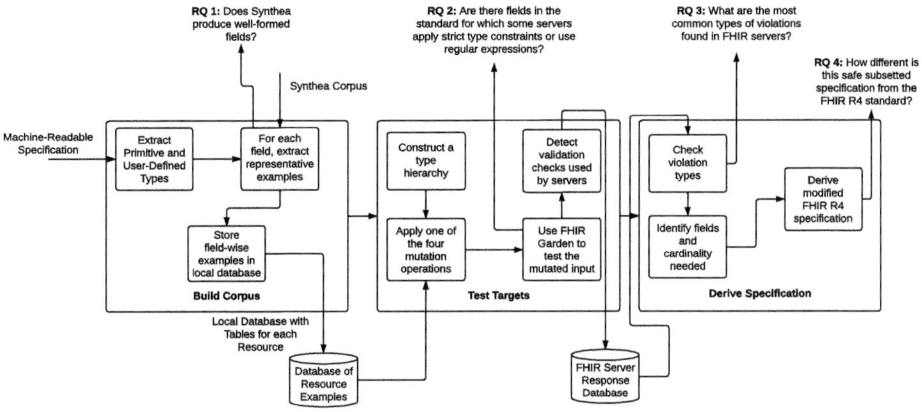

Fig. 3. Overview of the FHIR Safe Subset Generation Approach. We derive a large corpus of FHIR inputs to collect sample inputs for most fields. Next, we send constructed FHIR files to various servers and log their responses. Finally, we derive a safe subset specification based on the responses from various servers.

4.1   Generating a Corpus of Synthea Files

The first step in this process of interoperability evaluation was to create a corpus of synthetically generated patient medical data. We utilized Synthea to generate 1006 synthetic patient datasets of the Bundle resource type, adhering to the FHIR R4 standard. Each patient data will have multiple resources encapsulated within the Bundle resource type. These include Patient, Observation, Encounter, and many more. Each of these resources has many fields within it. Additionally, some fields contain nested resources. Algorithm 1 provides an overview of the algorithm used to generate this corpus.

The FHIR R4 specification defines specific types for each field in each resource type. We read each of the 1006 patient files individually and parse them based on their resource types. We use an SQLite database to dynamically create the tables for each resource and type, and update the rows as they are parsed. For instance, when parsing the Patient resource JSON, a Patient table is created with 27 columns (one for each field in the patient type), with the last field being the name of the file that is processed.

Using a recursive algorithm to traverse all nested fields within each patient file, we constructed a graph consisting of nodes and edges. The nodes represent the resources and types present in the patient file, while the edges capture the nested interconnections between these resources and types.

For each patient file, we collected data on four key metrics:

- the number of nodes,
- the number of edges,
- the maximum depth from the root node (patient file) to a leaf node, and
- the longest chain corresponding to this maximum depth.

Algorithm 1. Synthetic Patient Data Corpus Creation Algorithm

---

1: *SyntheaCorpus* ← Directory of Synthea Patient Files (JSON)
2: **for** each *patient_file* ∈ *SyntheaCorpus* **do**
3:     SQL: Connect to SQLite DB
4:     **for** each *Resource_data* ∈ *patient_file* **do**
5:         *ResourceType* ← Extract from *Resource_data*
6:         *Resource_metadata* ← FHIR R4 type specification for *ResourceType*
7:         **if** *ResourceType* SQL Table does not exist **then**
8:             SQL: Create Table with *Resource_metadata* fields
9:         **end if**
          recursive_traversal(*Resource_data*, *ResourceType*, *Resource_metadata*)
10:         SQL: Close connection to SQLite DB
11:     **end for**
12: **end for**
13: SQL: Iterate through each SQLite table and remove duplicate entries
14: **function** RECURSIVE_TRAVERSAL(*resourcetype_data*, *datatype*, *metadata*)
15:     columns ← []
16:     values ← []
17:     **for** each (*nested_field*, *nested_datatype*) ∈ *metadata* **do**
18:         **if** *nested_field* exists in *resourcetype_data* **then**
19:             **if** *nested_datatype*.startswith(lowercase) **then**
20:                 columns.append(*nested_field*)
21:                 values.append(*resourcetype_data*[*nested_field*])
22:             **else if** *nested_datatype*.startswith(uppercase) and is alnum() **then**
23:                 *type_metadata* ← FHIR R4 type specification for *nested_datatype*
24:                 **if** *nested_datatype* SQL Table does not exist **then**
25:                     SQL: Create Table with *type_metadata* fields
26:                 **end if**
27:                 recursive_traversal(*resourcetype_data*[*nested_field*], *nested_datatype*, *type_metadata*)
28:             **end if**
29:         **end if**
30:     **end for**
31:     SQL: Insert columns and values into *datatype* Table
32: **end function**

Additionally, we recorded the number of first-level resources directly connected to the root node. Our analysis revealed that the maximum depth across all patient files was consistently 4, with the longest chain following the pattern: root → Patient → Extension → Extension → Coding. We maintained the default Synthea configuration settings to generate the patient files [12].

Furthermore, more than 50% of the patient files contained 23 different resources directly linked to the root node. The total number of nodes per patient file ranged from 33 to 41, with over 50% of files containing 41 nodes in total.

The number of edges, however, varied significantly across patient files, ranging from 327 to 281,541. The median edge count was 6,260, highlighting the highly skewed nature of the data.

4.2   Validating the Synthea Patient Files

The FHIR specification defines the following fundamental data types: 'base64Binary', 'integer', 'boolean', 'uuid', 'url', 'xhtml', 'oid', 'canonical', 'dateTime', 'unsignedInt', 'decimal', 'instant', 'id', 'time', 'date', 'string', 'uri', 'positiveInt', 'markdown', and 'code'. Each of these types includes an associated regular expression defined in the FHIR R4 specification.[1] Table 2 shows the regular expressions for some of the above types from the specification. The expressions for types, such as URI are particularly permissive.

We created a validator module that validates the data type of each field in the patient data and checks whether the files generated by Synthea match the regular expressions. It recursively verifies that every field's data type matches the FHIR requirements. We ran this validator on the Synthea patient file corpus and confirmed that they matched the specified data types and their respective regular expressions. Following that, we sent these patient files through the "game of telephone" across five FHIR servers (Blaze, Hapi, IBM, Iris, and Vista). Thus, we obtained 1006 × 5 different patient files, each exported individually across all servers.

Each set of exported files is revalidated to verify that no data types have changed or internal modifications have occurred.

One notable observation involved the ExplanationOfBenefit field, where a floating-point value in the Amount field was converted to a string. However, Hapi converted it back to its numerical value and also rejected values that solely consisted of alphabets as they were invalid.

Table 2. Regular expressions specified in the HL7 FHIR specification for some base data types.

FHIR Name	Type	Regex
unsignedInt	integer	[0]|([1-9][0-9]*)
boolean	boolean	true|false
uri	string	\S*
base64Binary	string	(\s*([0-9a-zA-Z\+\=])4\s*)
date	date	([0-9]([0-9]([0-9][1-9]|[1-9]0)|[1-9]00)|[1-9]000)(-(0[1-9]|1[0-2])(-(0[1-9]|[1-2][0-9]|3[0-1]))?)?
uuid	uuid	urn:uuid:[0-9a-f]8-[0-9a-f]4-[0-9a-f]4-[0-9a-f]4-[0-9a-f]12
decimal	decimal	-?(0|[1-9][0-9]*)(\.[0-9]+)?([eE][+-]?[0-9]+)?
instant	datetime	([0-9]([0-9]([0-9][1-9]|[1-9]0)|[1-9]00)|[1-9]000)-(0[1-9]|1[0-2])-(0[1-9]|[1-2][0-9]|3[0-1])T([01][0-9]|2[0-3]):[0-5][0-9]:([0-5][0-9]|60)(\.[0-9]+)?(Z|(\+|-)((0[0-9]|1[0-3]):[0-5][0-9]|14:00))
time	time	([01][0-9]|2[0-3]):[0-5][0-9]:([0-5][0-9]|60)(\.[0-9]+)?

---

[1] https://www.hl7.org/fhir/R4/datatypes.html.

4.3   Mutating Fields in FHIR Files

To further study the robustness of the FHIR servers and the type rules enforced on individual fields within patient records, we systematically mutated each field in a patient FHIR record by replacing the original value with each of the other primitive types (19 types in total). This allowed us to assess how different servers responded to syntactically valid but semantically altered inputs.

We built a mutation engine that would mutate each field of the input patient record to 22 other data types. Of these 22, 19 are defined by the FHIR spec as the fundamental data types. We introduced three additional stress-test types to explore the behavior of the servers with longer inputs. These include:

- largeString: a 1024-byte string to test input size limitations,
- largeInt: an integer with the value 2**200, exceeding the standard 64-bit integer size,
- largeFloat: a floating point value of 1.7976931348623157E+308, representing the upper bound of IEEE 754 double precision.

By mutating each field, we generated a comprehensive set of mutated patient files that we could send to each FHIR server in our test bed.

To derive the representative values of the different fields based on the regular expressions specified in the FHIR R4 documentation (see Table 2), we used the exrex library [20] to generate the regular expressions that conformed to the FHIR specification. In this process, we found that for certain data types, such as integers, decimals, and strings, the specifications were too permissive and required the use of fixed values. Similarly, we applied a standard URL format for URI-like types (uri, canonical, url) due to the variability in formatting for each of them.

We developed a mutation engine that accepts a single patient file, traverses each field, including nested fields, and generates 21 different mutated patient files for each field. Each mutated file is then sent to the five different FHIR servers: Blaze, Hapi, VistA, IBM, and Iris. Additionally, the mutated file is validated before and after submission to each server. Also, the mutated field is checked in the output response file to identify any structural or syntactic transformations or truncations that the server may have introduced during the processing of the mutated files.

For every mutation, we stored the field path, original value and type, mutated value and type, server name, server response code, and message (includes both successful and failed responses with error message). Furthermore, the validation errors from both the original mutated file and the response file were stored, along with the value of the mutated field in the output response. The results were stored in a SQLite database for further analysis.

First, we used a single patient file with the following resource type entries: Patient, Observation, Encounter, Condition, and Procedure. In total, 2794 field-level mutations were performed across all resource types. The analysis of these results will be presented in the upcoming section.

Next, we focused on populating the entire FHIR resource by adding all missing fields for a specific resource type, along with all top-level nested fields. Synthea is already known not to generate an instance of every field within the FHIR specification, either due to internal settings limitations or simply because some fields are not considered meaningful for typical synthetic patient cases. To accomplish this, we created 148 individual files, each corresponding to one of the 148 predefined resourceType values specified in the FHIR R4 documentation, including popular types such as Patient, Observation, Encounter, and Condition.

Each produced file contains the Patient resource and, in addition, one of the other resource types. This extension is added to ensure uniformity in the requirements across all server endpoints for creating a new patient record. For instance, the /addpatient endpoint in Vista would not accept a file without the patient resource in it.

Once the complete set of resource-specific files was generated, they were processed using our mutation engine to apply systematic mutations to every field. This resulted in 166,862 mutations per server. Upon submission, we found that all five servers had varying levels of acceptance and processing of the files. Notably, IBM was the strictest with the highest number of rejections of the mutated files, indicating stricter adherence to the specification.

4.4   Part 1. Mutation Analysis on Single Patient File

For the first part of our experiment, we mutated a single patient file, which had the five resource types: Patient, Encounter, Observation, Condition, and Procedure, and sent the mutated files to five different servers: Blaze, HAPI, IBM, Iris, and VistA. Each field in the patient file was mutated 21 times, resulting in 2,794 different mutated files sent to each server. We provide a comprehensive analysis of all the collected data.

Mutated Files Acceptance Rate. In Fig. 4, VistA, followed by HAPI, has the highest acceptance rate of all these mutated files. IBM, followed by IRIS, has the highest rejection rate for mutated files. This indicates that VistA and HAPI do not adhere to strict constraints and are relatively permissive, in contrast to IBM, IRIS, and Blaze.

Accepted Files with Missing Mutated Fields. Among the files accepted by the server, we found that several exported responses lacked the mutated fields entirely. As seen in Fig. 5, a significant proportion of accepted files on some servers show that the mutated fields have been truncated. This indicates data loss, suggesting that field-level data integrity is not preserved when the server processes these mutated files.

Regex Validation Outcomes. We evaluated each mutated file for syntactic validity using a validator that checks whether each field conforms to the regular

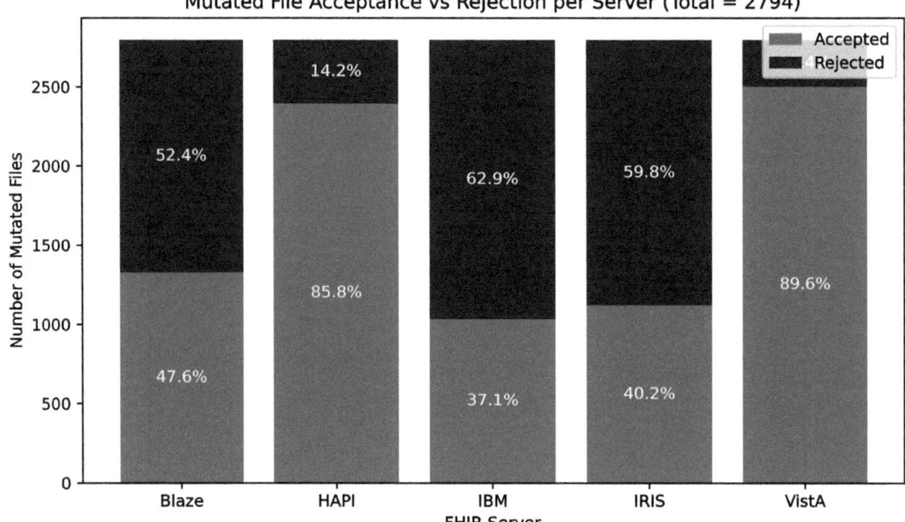

Fig. 4. We sent all 2794 mutated files to the five FHIR servers in our testbench. We show the percentage of these mutated files that are accepted vs. rejected.

expressions defined in the FHIR R4 specification. Ideally, if this validation fails, the corresponding FHIR server should reject the file as nonconformant. However, our analysis revealed instances where syntactically invalid files were nevertheless accepted by certain servers.

We categorize the validation outcomes into four distinct cases depending on whether the input and output files are valid or invalid.

We did not observe cases where a valid input file resulted in an invalid output file. This indicates that the servers generally preserve syntactic validity in their output when provided with a syntactically valid input.

As shown in Table 3, Blaze, IBM, and IRIS consistently accepted and generated only valid files, indicating strict conformance to the regular expression specification. In contrast, HAPI accepted a substantial number of invalid input files, and although it generated a majority of valid outputs, a notable portion remained invalid. Similarly, VistA also accepted a significant proportion of invalid inputs and produced a correspondingly high number of invalid outputs. These discrepancies raise concerns about the server's validation enforcement mechanisms.

Variation Between Input Mutated Values and Output Response Values. *Note: This analysis considers only those mutated files that were successfully accepted by the respective FHIR servers.*

XHTML Field Behavior. In cases where the original field type was `xhtml`, we observed varying behaviors across servers when the field was mutated. The HAPI FHIR server inserted the mutated value inside a `<div>` tag, as shown below:

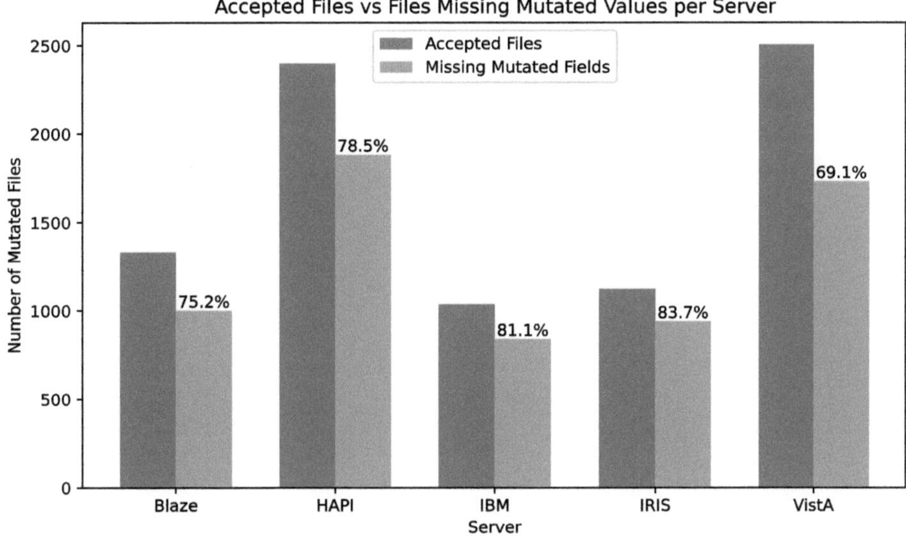

Fig. 5. We analyzed the mutated files that were accepted and found a large portion of them had ignored the mutated field. This figure shows the percentage of accepted files that were missing these fields.

- **Original XHTML value:**

```
<div xmlns="http://www.w3.org/1999/xhtml">Generated by
<a href="https://github.com/synthetichealth/synthea">Synthea</a>.
Version identifier: master-branch-latest.
Person seed: 1215795940060762954
Population seed: 1737663483643</div>
```

- **Mutated Input:** urn:uuid:aaf52833-b6ca-a750-8c10-0653c9db2f81
- **HAPI Response:**

```
<div xmlns="http://www.w3.org/1999/xhtml">
urn:uuid:aaf52833-b6ca-a750-8c10-0653c9db2f81</div>
```

This behavior was exclusive to HAPI. In contrast, Blaze, IRIS, and VistA returned the mutated value directly, without any transformation. IBM rejected all mutations involving `xhtml`-typed fields.

Datatype Changes. For Blaze, IBM, IRIS, and VistA, the fundamental datatype of the mutated field remained unchanged in the output. However, HAPI exhibited several datatype changes, including:

- 27 `decimal` and 27 `integer` values were converted to `string`.

Table 3. Validation Outcomes for Accepted Files per Server. (I/P: Input; O/P: Output)

Server	Total Accepted Files	Valid I/P		Invalid I/P	
		Valid O/P	Invalid O/P	Valid O/P	Invalid O/P
Blaze	1331	1331	0	0	0
HAPI	2397	1187	0	926	284
IBM	1036	1036	0	0	0
IRIS	1122	1122	0	0	0
VistA	2504	1330	0	9	1165

- 28 `largeInt` values: 27 were converted to `string`, 1 remained an `integer`.
- 28 `largeFloat` values: 27 were converted to `string`, 1 to `integer`.
- 28 `boolean` values: all were converted to `string`.

Value Differences Between Input and Output. We also evaluated whether the mutated field in the server response matched the mutated input value. Blaze, IBM, and IRIS did not show discrepancies. In contrast, HAPI produced 89 instances where the output value differed from the input. Examples include:

- Boolean `True` was transformed to the lowercase string `"true"`.
- The URL `http://hl7.org/fhir/StructureDefinition/geolocation` was truncated to `"geolocation"`.
- The float `1.7976931348623157e+308` was returned as an expanded string:

```
17976931348623157000000000000...000 (308 digits)
```

- For a field of type `code`, the input value:

```
6o:J,R/%0c 5'pB>s]qQ:Kc5(i'dp?
@D kniS
y+XoS-4<6N\vjilt!
IZO%"5'M*>I47F,wW'i:pN70h8J=S
7j:4E2+5ur V"a3eFv_41DR4,'
XukY2$a
V\rT/nG(mb a JMHRZ
XE3C:Y_",Ds$o+@
```

was truncated to:

```
nG(mb a JMHRZ
XE3C:Y_",Ds$o+@
```

4.5   Part 2. Mutation Analysis on Resource Types

While the FHIR specification prescribes the standard for interoperability, there were significant deviations in the validation behavior of regular expressions, error handling, and schema behavior across server platforms. The key discrepancies have been summarized below:

Non-conformant Use of the Extension Field. The FHIR specification clearly states:

> "An extension SHALL have either a value (i.e., a value[x] element) or sub-extensions, but not both. If present, the value[x] element SHALL have content (value attribute or other elements)." [14]

Violation of this rule should result in a parsing error by the servers. We observed that **HAPI**, **IBM**, and **IRIS** returned an error message, whereas **Blaze** and **VistA** processed this input without any error.

HAPI error message:

```
HAPI-0450: Failed to parse request body as JSON resource. The
error was: HAPI-1811: Extension (URL=
'http://hl7.org/fhir/us/core/StructureDefinition/us-core-race')
must not have both a value and other contained extensions.
```

Lenient Validation of the code Datatype. The FHIR specification defines the code datatype as [15]:

> "Indicates that the value is taken from a set of controlled strings defined elsewhere (see Using codes for further discussion). Technically, a code is restricted to a string which has at least one character and no leading or trailing whitespace, and where there is no whitespace other than single spaces in the contents."

HAPI returned the following diagnostic for an invalid code value:

```
{'resourceType': 'OperationOutcome', 'issue': [{'severity':
'error', 'code': 'processing', 'diagnostics':
'HAPI-0450: Failed to parse request body as JSON resource.
Error was: HAPI-1821: [element="use"] Invalid attribute value
"abcde": Unknown IdentifierUse code 'abcde'}]}
```

In the above case, for the Identifier type, the field use should only take the values usual | official | temp | secondary | old. Therefore, for an input of "abcde", **HAPI**, **IBM**, and **IRIS** correctly reject the patient file.

However, we found that **Blaze** and **VistA** did not validate whether the value in the code field was among the controlled strings defined for that context. Instead, these servers accepted the input as long as it conformed to the regex, successfully creating a patient resource.

Analysis of ResourceType Mutations. In the next section of our experimentation, we evaluated how FHIR servers handle mutations across **146 resource types**(excluding Resource and DomainResource) defined in the FHIR specification. The fields for each resource were constructed using regular expressions defined in the specification. The resulting files were then mutated, and each mutated file was sent to the five servers in our testbed: **Blaze, HAPI, IBM, IRIS**, and **VistA**. The total number of mutations generated was **166,862**.

Mutation Acceptance Rates. Figure 6 shows the number of mutated files accepted and rejected by each server. As previously noted, VistA, followed by HAPI, has the lowest rejection rates. In contrast, IBM, IRIS, and Blaze are considerably more compliant, rejecting mutated inputs more consistently.

Accepted Files with Missing Mutated Fields. We examined whether the mutated field was present in the response of accepted files for each server. The mutated field was entirely missing from the returned output in nearly half of the accepted files, with IBM exhibiting the highest percentage of missing files. Table 4 summarizes the raw counts and the corresponding percentages.

Table 4. Accepted Files with Missing Mutated Fields in the Output

Server	Accepted	Missing Fields	Missing (%)
Blaze	82,115	40,198	48.9%
HAPI	141,614	74,594	52.6%
IBM	59,142	32,489	54.9%
IRIS	68,617	35,971	52.4%
VistA	149,858	69,875	46.6%

These results show that even among accepted files, a substantial portion failed to retain the mutated field, suggesting that acceptance by a server does not necessarily imply completeness or correctness of the processed resource. This can lead to the potential loss of critical patient data during transfer from one provider to another.

Validation Results on Accepted Files. Table 5 shows the number of accepted files that have passed or failed the regular expression validation performed on the mutated file and the output response file from the different servers.

Once again, we observe no instances where a valid input file results in an invalid output file. We find that the majority of accepted files are invalid, which generally yield invalid outputs. Notably, in the case of HAPI, we see a small proportion of invalid input files produce valid outputs, and for VistA, we identified two such occurrences.

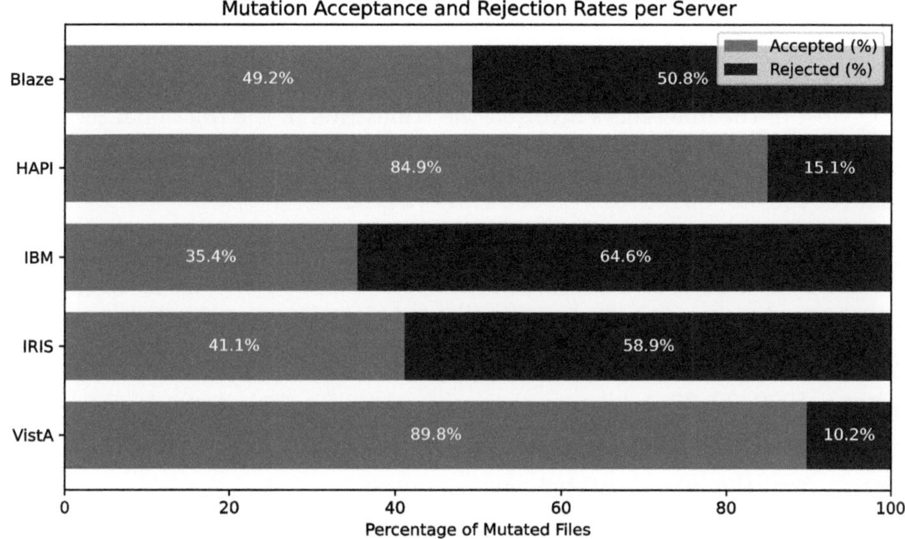

Fig. 6. From the 166862 mutated files sent to the five FHIR servers, we calculate the percentage of accepted files Vs. rejected files.

Table 5. Validation Outcomes of Accepted Files per Server

Server	Total Accepted	Valid I/P		Invalid I/P	
	Files	Valid O/P	Invalid O/P	Valid O/P	Invalid O/P
Blaze	82,115	668	0	0	81,447
HAPI	141,614	616	0	445	140,553
IBM	59,142	551	0	0	58,591
IRIS	68,617	608	0	0	68,009
VistA	149,858	672	0	2	149,184

Differences Between Mutated Input and Output Response Values. The mutated values for each field in a resource file were compared with the corresponding output response values for those mutated files that were accepted. The behavior of each server varied significantly and is detailed below.

Blaze: Only three entries of type `instant` were found to be different. In these cases, the trailing zero was truncated from the fractional seconds. For example:

```
Input:  9188-01-21T07:22:51.70+02:38
Output: 9188-01-21T07:22:51.7+02:38
```

HAPI: 9,834 entries showed differences between the mutated input and the output response. The differences observed in the output reflected consistent behavior seen previously, including changes in data types, truncation of values, and modifications to the data.

IBM: There were 31 instances of differing input and output values observed in IBM. Most of the differences involved the truncation of the fractional seconds in fields of type `instant`.

```
Input:  0440-05-30T15:51:17.38840877+14:00
Output: 0440-05-30T15:51:17.388408+14:00
```

We also noticed that IBM automatically corrected invalid dates. In this case, since September has only 30 d, IBM adjusted the date accordingly.

```
Input:  1000-09-31
Output: 1000-09-30
```

IRIS: We did not find any entries where the output response values where different from the input mutated values.

VistA: 10515 records showed differences between the mutated input value and the response. These differences were primarily observed in fields of type `base64Binary`, `markdown`, and `code`. In many cases, the textual content remained unchanged, but minor differences in whitespace, form feed, or vertical tab characters were observed.

4.6   Extracting the Safe Subset

We follow the algorithm listed under Algorithm 2 to extract the safe subset from the dataset. As part of this step, for each field, we identify mutated FHIR records accepted by all servers, ensuring that the mutated field value is preserved in the responses from the FHIR servers.

While there were numerous instances where a particular server was overly permissive, as we have shown several times in this paper, strictly enforcing the FHIR specification, including validating URIs and code systems, is sufficient to ensure strong interoperability guarantees. In addition to ensuring that FHIR servers adhere strictly to the specification, the existing regular expressions used to validate resource fields should be made more thorough and comprehensive. For instance, the regular expressions for certain types, such as `base64Binary` or `string`, should have more precise expressions to help reduce the ambiguity and parsing issues that arise from generalization. Refining the specifications to accommodate edge-case scenarios is essential for eliminating inconsistencies in patient data interoperability and ensuring uniformity in the interpretation and implementation of the standard.

4.7   Summary

This section presents a novel approach to understanding how FHIR servers enforce field-specific type rules. Enforcing these type checks is a necessary precondition to guarantee interoperability between different FHIR servers. We found

---

Algorithm 2. FHIR Specification Testing Algorithm

1: $BasicTypes \leftarrow$ getAllBasicTypesFromFHIR()
2: $UserDefinedTypes \leftarrow$ getAllUserDefinedTypesFromFHIR()
3: $FHIRCorpus \leftarrow$ loadFHIRFilesFromCorpus()
4: $FHIRGarden \leftarrow$ listOfFHIRServers()
5: $DB \leftarrow$ connectToNeo4JDatabase()
6: **for** each $F \in FHIRCorpus$ **do**
7:     $F' \leftarrow F$ ▷ Create a copy for mutation
8:         **for** each $field \in F'$ **do**
9:             $originalType \leftarrow$ getFieldType($field$)
10:            $newType \leftarrow$ randomTypeExcept($BasicTypes, originalType$)
11:            $randomValue \leftarrow$ generateRandomValueOfType($newType$)
12:            setFieldValue($field, randomValue$)
13:        **end for**
14:     $isValid \leftarrow$ validateAgainstFHIRSpec(F')
15:     logMutation($DB, F, F', isValid$)
16:     **if** $isValid$ **then**
17:         **for** each $server \in FHIRGarden$ **do**
18:             $response \leftarrow$ sendToServer($server, F'$)
19:             logServerResponse($DB, server, F', response$)
20:         **end for**
21:     **end if**
22: **end for**
23: $successfulMutations \leftarrow$ queryDB(DB, "successful across all servers")
24: $specViolations \leftarrow$ findSpecificationViolations($successfulMutations$)
25: $safeSubset \leftarrow$ extractRelaxedSpecification($specViolations$)
        return $safeSubset$ ▷ Relaxed R4 specification

---

that many servers, such as HAPI and VistA, are lax about checking the types of fields in FHIR requests, accepting files with incorrect types, but dropping them from the Patient's records. We generated two sets of mutated files: first, by mutating fields already present in Synthea-generated files, and second, by mutating fields in synthetically generated files that contain all the fields from the specification for all resource types.

We used these datasets to evaluate the extent of compliance of FHIR servers and eventually to understand which regular expression checks were stricter in servers and what a safe subset for the FHIR R4 standard looks like. Our unique approach to testing the compliance of implementations with the standard provides a framework for standards bodies, such as IEEE, HL7, and ISO, to build differential fuzzing engines that ensure complete compliance with specifications and avoid the threat of parser differentials.

5 Differential Testing of DICOM Implementations

The Digital Imaging and Communications in Medicine (DICOM) standard describes the electronic interaction of IT elements in medical ecosystems.

Testing DICOM libraries is crucial for ensuring the reliability of the DICOM standard, which is responsible for the interoperability of medical imaging systems worldwide. To further ensure medical image interoperability, it is essential to employ a differential testing approach: if libraries disagree on certain inputs, then we may have inputs that are accessible in some DICOM viewers but rejected in others. Thus, we employed Differential Testing to identify vulnerabilities by examining differences in outputs and errors. The libraries we tested so far are **Pylibdicom** [17], **Pydicom** [27], and **Grassroots DICOM** [10].

While introducing a new DICOM testing approach, our work extends prior research in establishing the reliability of DICOM interfaces. Prior studies, including static analysis, conformance tools, and fuzz testing, have explored numerous testing techniques for DICOM implementations. Software like DVTk [9] and DICOMscope [25] has been built to enable standard conformance verification, whereas fuzz techniques have been applied to reliability testing of open-source libraries [33]. Differential testing, however, is an alternative methodology in presenting the complementary methodology in discovering inconsistency among different DICOM libraries, rather than mere conformance to standard compliance. By using this technique, we contribute to the existing literature of DICOM robustness testing and raise awareness towards potential areas for improvement of DICOM library dependability.

5.1 Digital Imaging and Communications in Medicine (DICOM) Format

The Digital Imaging and Communications in Medicine (DICOM) standard emerged in the early 1980s, when the American College of Radiology (ACR) and the National Electrical Manufacturers Association collaborated to specify a standardized method for transferring and storing medical images. The first release in 1985 was titled ACR-NEMA Standards Publication No. 300–1985. Radically updated, DICOM 3.0 was published in 1993, which serves as the basis for the standard employed today. Today, DICOM is used in radiology, cardiology, oncology, and any other specialty that utilizes medical imaging equipment (MRI, X-rays, etc.). The use of DICOM goes beyond defining an image format. It provided the first standard for the storage, printing, and transmission of medical images, making systems interoperable and integrated with healthcare information appliances.

DICOM defines a file format as well as a network protocol, such as Information Object Definitions defining data elements for different image types, Service Classes for operations on them, and a data structure for each (see Fig. 7).

Its communication protocol utilizes a service-based architecture with message types such as C-STORE, C-FIND, C-MOVE, C-GET, and C-ECHO, all of which are transmitted over TCP/IP. These messages are exchanged through associations initiated by capability negotiation. DICOM files contain extensive metadata alongside image data and support multiple frames, various compression formats, structured reporting, and security features.

5.2   Differential Testing Setup

Our differential testing relies on fuzzing the libraries with Atheris [11], a coverage-guided Python fuzzing engine created by Google. We aim to find inconsistencies in outputs between Pydicom [27], Pylibdicom [17], and Grassroots DICOM [10] (*gdcm*), using the following setup:

1. Input generation: The fuzzing engine generates a random mutation of our starting DICOM dataset [32]. Then, our program writes these changes to a file, which is then renamed with a .dcm extension to mimic a valid DICOM file.
2. Library processing:
   - pylibdicom: The file is processed using pylibdicom. Both the file metadata and the main dataset are printed using recursive helper functions written to handle sequences and to standardize library outputs to avoid trivial discrepancies, such as one library printing a value with quotation marks, while other libraries do not use quotation marks.
   - gdcm: The gdcm library reads the file and extracts the header and dataset, again utilizing helper functions to traverse and print the DICOM elements.
   - pydicom: The dcmread function reads the DICOM file, and similar to the other libraries, the file meta and dataset information are printed.
3. Output Capture and Comparison: Each library's output is captured into separate StringIO buffers. The outputs are then compared, and if any differences

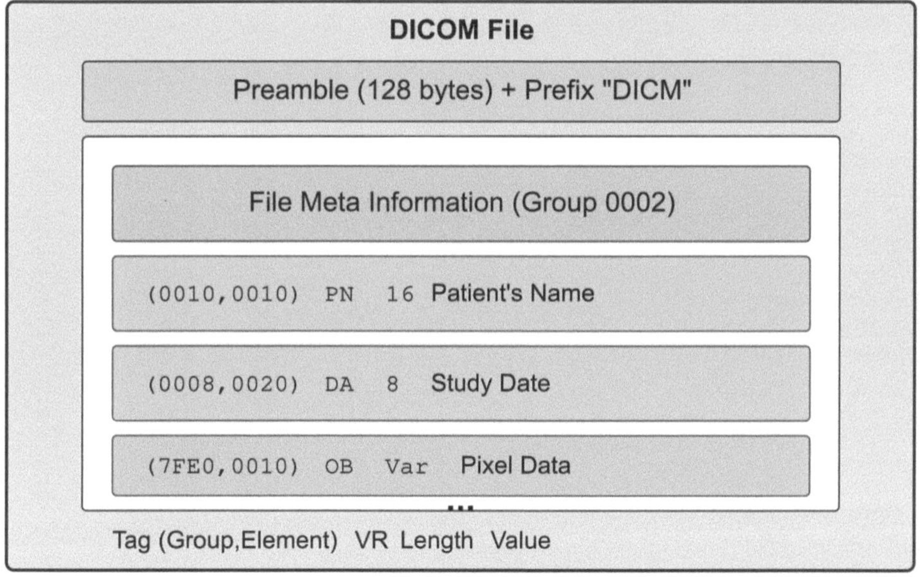

Fig. 7. DICOM file structure.

are found between the outputs, they are logged with a timestamped header and appended to a report file called diffs.txt. This comparison is crucial to flag inconsistencies between the libraries, which might indicate potential bugs or differences in DICOM processing.

4. Error Handling: For each library, exceptions are caught, and any errors during processing are recorded into an output buffer, ensuring that the framework handles failures gracefully.

For a list of the libraries we tested and their URLs, refer to Table 6, and for a diagram showcasing the testing workflow, see Fig. 8.

Table 6. Tested DICOM Libraries and Their URLs

Library	URL
pydicom	https://pydicom.github.io/pydicom/stable/index.html
Grassroots DICOM	https://sourceforge.net/projects/gdcm/
pylibdicom (Python bindings for libdicom)	https://github.com/jcupitt/pylibdicom

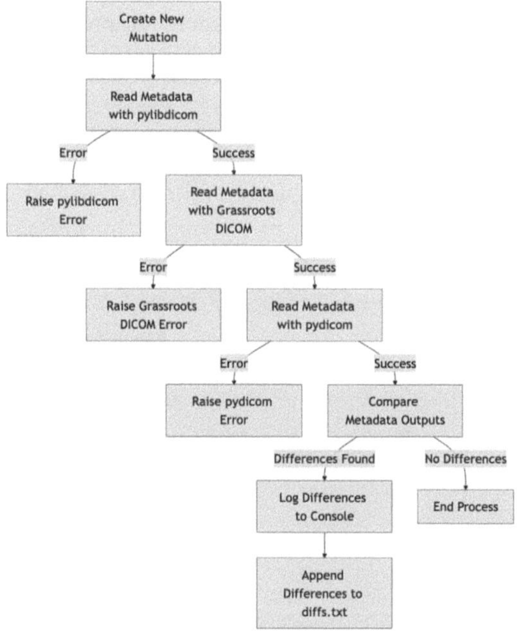

Fig. 8. Workflow for our DICOM testing

5.3   Results

Through this fuzzing approach, we found ten errors, which could all be attributed to the same type of flaw: inconsistent handling of non-standard characters within the Value Representation (VR) fields of certain elements.

As documented on page 56 of the specification, DICOM PS3.5 2025a - Data Structures and Encoding [23], a DICOM data set consists of a series of data elements (see Fig. 9). Within each data element, an optional VR field tells the consumer how to parse the rest of the element; "DICOM PS3.6 2025a - Data Dictionary" gives a lengthy dictionary of possible VRs.

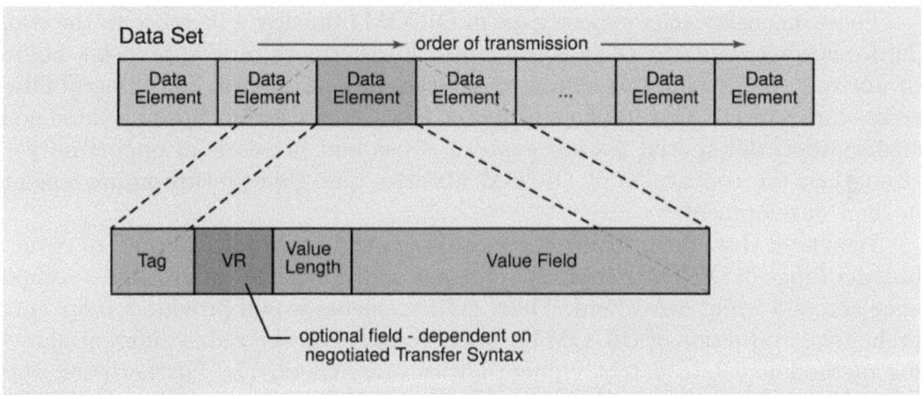

Fig. 9. DICOM data elements within a data set (from DICOM PS3.5 2025a - Data Structures and Encoding) [23].

According to the DICOM Standard, every VR must "be two single byte characters... only upper case letters from the DICOM default character set." However, our initial fuzzing revealed cases where the libraries differed in how they handled various VRs that did not meet this requirement.

In summary, our findings are as follows:

– Pydicom does not reject the following non-standard VRs: 00 b1, 30 00, 00 d3, and f3 f3.
– For the dataset's pixel data element, Pylibdicom accepts the following non-standard VRs: 30 00 and f3 f3. Contrary to Pydicom and Grassroots DICOM, however, Pylibdicom does not accept 00 b1 and 00 d3 because b1 and d3 are not UTF-8 characters.
– In the pixel data element, Grassroots DICOM accepts the following non-standard VRs: 00 b1, 30 00, 00 d3, and f3 f3.

Our next step is to explore how widespread this Value Representation error is across libraries and across invalid VRs.

- For any one library, what happens to the parsing of a data element when the VR is rejected?
- For any one library, how are the Value Length and Value Field parsed for non-compliant VRs?
- As the VR field determines how to parse the Value Length, how does a rejected VR or an accepted-but-non-compliant VR affect how the library determines the start of the next data element?
- Within any one library, do these answers change based on the Data Element Tag?
- Can we use this confusion to demonstrate semantically interesting differentials when the same element is sent to different libraries?

These inconsistencies expose gaps in DICOM libraries' adherence to the standard, showing faults in their compliance. Furthermore, our approach's ability to uncover such deviations shows its effectiveness in identifying vulnerabilities across different DICOM implementations. By systematically exposing these non-conformities, differential testing exposes issues and presents an opportunity to strengthen the robustness of DICOM libraries and guide future improvements in their development.

To extend this effort, future work could expand fuzzing techniques to cover a broader range of DICOM attributes and test additional libraries to assess compliance across a wider ecosystem. These enhancements would provide a more comprehensive evaluation of DICOM libraries' compliance and refine differential testing methodologies to detect vulnerabilities more effectively. Furthermore, such advancements would contribute to the improvement and reliability of DICOM systems.

6   Discussion

6.1   The Impact of Poor Interoperability

Poor interoperability can make it harder for clinicians to provide effective care to patients, risking misdiagnoses from incomplete or incorrect medical histories. In addition, incorrect parsing of patient data or medical images can undermine trust in the EHR systems used by medical providers. There is also a need for clean data, particularly in the age of Artificial Intelligence approaches. These approaches are only as effective as the training data, and incorrect data can undermine the effectiveness of these approaches.

This paper outlines the current landscape of interoperability in EHR systems, specifically in FHIR and DICOM implementations. First, we found that FHIR implementations do not implement *correct* JSON parsers, presenting a significant challenge for interoperability—since a patient's record may not be preserved as is across different FHIR servers. Next, we studied how strictly servers check the types of various fields in FHIR resources. We exhaustively fuzzed FHIR servers by generating numerous mutations of fields across all the valid base types in the FHIR standard to infer the checks enforced by servers. In addition to missing checks in servers, we also note parser errors where the HAPI and VistA servers do not preserve certain fields as is from the input files. Finally, we presented early results from an interoperability study on three DICOM implementations, where we found that various DICOM implementations did not properly handle non-standard characters.

6.2   Future Directions

Our team plans to expand in several directions for future work.

Compliance and Standards Processes. We will work with various standards bodies like IEEE, ISO, and HL7 to ensure that implementations do not test compliance using a simple checklist but use our holistic methodology to ensure complete compliance to other implementations using differential fuzzing.

Testing Closed-Source Implementations. In our study, we evaluated one closed-source implementation, Intersystems IRIS FHIR server. However, there are several other closed-source implementations of FHIR and DICOM that are yet to be explored. We will reach out to vendors to study these implementations.

Implementing a LangSec-compliant FHIR Parser. The FHIR standard provides a machine-readable specification, making it easier for engineers to generate parsers directly from this machine-readable specification. However, in practice, engineers seem to have strictly implemented checks for some resource types and skipped them for others. We will work to implement a strict parser for the FHIR R4 standard that is "safe subset" compliant.

Cross-Protocol Vulnerabilities and Interoperability. Cross-protocol vulnerabilities stem from data flows between multiple formats—for example, DICOM images embedded in FHIR responses. The DICOM parsers used by commercial imaging technology and FHIR implementations need to be interoperable. In turn, the FHIR protocol must preserve the core fields in the DICOM image correctly. In this particular case, FHIR acts as the encapsulation mechanism for other imaging formats.

Acknowledgements

Funding. This work was performed as part of the ARPA-H DIGIHEALS program under Contract No. SP4701-23-C-0089. The views, opinions, and/or findings expressed are those of the author(s) and should not be interpreted as representing the official views or policies of ARPA-H or the U.S. Government.

References

1. Adler, D.A., et al.: Burnout and the quantified workplace: tensions around personal sensing interventions for stress in resident physicians. In: Proceedings of the ACM on Human-Computer Interaction, vol. 6(CSCW2), pp. 1–48 (2022)
2. Anantharaman, P., Shapiro, R.B., Varadharaju, V., Locasto, M.E.: A study of interoperability in electronic health record software. In: Proceedings of the 2024 Workshop on Cybersecurity in Healthcare, HealthSec 2024, pp. 53–60, New York, NY, USA, 2024. Association for Computing Machinery. https://doi.org/10.1145/3689942.3694743

3. Aronoff, R., Aronoff, R.: An Analysis of ANSI ASC X12 and UN/EDIFACT Electronic Data Interchange (EDI) Standards. US Department of Commerce, National Institute of Standards and Technology (1995)
4. Barnett, G.O., Souder, D.E., Bowie, J., Justice, N.: Mumps: a support for medical information systems. Med. Inf. **1**(3), 183–189 (1976)
5. Barsky, N.: UnitedHealth paid hackers $22 million, fixes will soon cost billions (2024). https://www.forbes.com/sites/noahbarsky/2024/04/30/unitedhealths-16-billion-tally-grossly-understates-cyberattack-cost/
6. Cavanaugh, C.: Top 5 challenges with interoperability in healthcare | datavant (2021). https://www.datavant.com/electronic-health-records/5-challenges-with-healthcare-interoperability
7. Davis, B., Swenson, A., How carequality, the sequoia project, and ehealth exchange support the interoperable exchange of health data in the USA. J. Digit. Imaging **35**(4), 812–816 (2022). https://doi.org/10.1007/s10278-021-00538-y
8. Desjardins, B., et al.: DICOM images have been hacked! Now what? Am. J. Roentgenol. **214**(4), 727–735 (2020)
9. DVTk Project Team: DVTk: an open source project for testing, validating, and diagnosing DICOM communication (2025). https://www.dvtk.org/. Accessed 12 Mar 2025
10. GDCM Project. GDCM: Grassroots dicom library (2019). https://sourceforge.net/projects/gdcm/. SourceForge repository. Accessed 3 Apr 2025
11. Google. Atheris: a coverage-guided, Native Python Fuzzer. https://github.com/google/atheris. Accessed 13 Mar 2025
12. Hajagos, J.: Synthea common configuration. https://github.com/synthetichealth/synthea/wiki/Common-Configuration
13. Hillestad, R., et al.:. Health information technology: can HIT lower costs and improve quality? technical report RB-9136-HLTH, RAND Corporation. Research Brief (2005). https://www.rand.org/pubs/research_briefs/RB9136.html
14. HL7 Standard. https://hl7.org/fhir/extensibility.html#extensions
15. HL7 Standard. https://hl7.org/fhir/datatypes.html#code
16. HL7 International. Hl7 version 2 product suite. Contrasted with FHIR's modern approach (2023). https://www.hl7.org/implement/standards/product_brief.cfm?product_id=185
17. Jcupitt: pylibdicom: a Python wrapper for libdicom, 2025. GitHub repository. https://github.com/jcupitt/pylibdicom. Accessed 3 Apr 2025
18. Kallus, B., Anantharaman, P., Locasto, M., Smith, S.W.: The HTTP garden: discovering parsing vulnerabilities in HTTP/1.1 implementations by differential fuzzing of request streams. arXiv preprint arXiv:2405.17737 (2024)
19. Kohn, L.T., Corrigan, J.M., Donaldson, M.S.: To err is human: building a safer health system. National Academies Press, Washington, DC, 1999. Institute of Medicine. https://doi.org/10.17226/9728
20. Kuchling, A.M.: EXREX: Regular expression string generator. https://github.com/asciimoo/exrex. Accessed 4 Apr 2025
21. McDonald, C.J., et al.: LOINC a universal standard for identifying laboratory observations: a 5-year update. Clin. Chem. **49**(4), 624–633 (2003). https://doi.org/10.1373/49.4.624
22. McLaughlin, M.J., Michael McGinnis, J., Wendt, M.L.: Envisioning the national health care quality report. National Academies Press, Washington, DC, 2001. Institute of Medicine. https://doi.org/10.17226/10073

23. National Electrical Manufacturers Association (NEMA). Digital Imaging and Communications in Medicine (DICOM) Standard (2023). https://www.dicomstandard.org. Accessed 12 Mar 2025
24. National electronic health records survey. EHR adoption study. https://www.cdc.gov/nchs/nehrs/results/index.html
25. OFFIS - Institute for information technology. DICOMscope: A DICOM viewer (2025). https://dicom.offis.de/en/dicomscope/. Accessed 12 Mar 2025
26. Committee on Quality of Health Care in America: Crossing the Quality Chasm: A New Health System for the 21st Century. National Academies Press, Washington, DC, 2001. Institute of Medicine. https://doi.org/10.17226/10027
27. Pydicom Developers: Pydicom: a pure python package for dicom medical file reading and writing, 2024. Version 3.0.1. https://pydicom.github.io/pydicom/stable/index.html. Accessed 3 Apr 2025
28. Sassaman, L., Patterson, M.L., Bratus, S., Locasto, M.E.: Security applications of formal language theory. IEEE Syst. J. **7**(3), 489–500 (2013)
29. Sipser, M.: Introduction to the theory of computation. ACM SIGACT News **27**(1), 27–29 (1996)
30. SNOMED International: Snomed CT: the global language of healthcare (2023). Official documentation for SNOMED CT terminology system. https://www.snomed.org
31. Tajirian T., et al.: The influence of electronic health record use on physician burnout: cross-sectional survey. J. Med. Internet Res. **22**(7), e19274 (2020). https://doi.org/10.2196/19274
32. TrainingDataPro: Dicom brain dataset (2025). https://huggingface.co/datasets/TrainingDataPro/dicom-brain-dataset. Accessed 17 Mar 2025
33. Wang, Z., Li, Q., Wang, Y., Liu, B., Zhang, J., Liu, Q.: Medical protocol security: DICOM vulnerability mining based on fuzzing technology. In: Proceedings of the 2019 ACM SIGSAC Conference on Computer and Communications Security (CCS 2019), pp. 2625–2627 (2019). https://doi.org/10.1145/3319535.3363253
34. World Health Organization: International classification of diseases (ICD) (2023). Official WHO ICD-11 classification system. For ICD-9/10, see historical versions. https://www.who.int/standards/classifications/classification-of-diseases
35. Zaw, N., Soh, K.: DICOM: a ticking cybersecurity time-bomb in the healthcare industry (2017). https://athenadynamics.com/event/dicom-unknown-vulnerability-cyber-attacks-global-healthcare-industry/

MedBlockSync: A Blockchain Solution for Multi-institutional Healthcare

Jorge Castillo[1(✉)] [iD], Kwabena Aboagye-Otchere[1] [iD], and Qian Chen[2] [iD]

[1] The University of Texas Rio Grande Valley, Brownsville, TX, USA
`jorge.a.castillo01@utrgv.edu`
[2] The University of Texas at San Antonio, San Antonio, TX, USA

Abstract. The integration of Electronic Medical Records (EMRs) into the healthcare industry has revolutionized patient data management by enabling the storage of highly sensitive information. However, the continuous exchange of this information among health institutions to ensure accurate patient care introduces significant challenges related to data dissemination and security. Blockchain technology, with its inherent properties of decentralization, immutability, and transparency, offers a robust solution to these challenges, facilitating secure and efficient data sharing among stakeholders. In this paper, we present MedBlockSync, a robust blockchain system designed for improved data integrity across multi-institutional healthcare organizations. The framework is developed to achieve three key objectives: (1) safeguarding EMR data against cyberattacks, (2) enabling seamless and secure sharing of healthcare information among various stakeholders, and (3) facilitating Internet of Medical Things (IoMT) communication, including real-time data transmission from smart sensors to the blockchain network and EMRs through a secure channel. By incorporating advanced security features into EMRs without necessitating modifications to existing digital health infrastructures, MedBlockSync enhances interoperability among healthcare systems, ensuring both scalability and adaptability in the digital health landscape.

Keywords: Blockchain · Data security · Data sharing · Electronic medical records · Internet of things

1 Introduction

The healthcare industry, renowned for its data-intensive nature, generates, accesses, and disseminates vast amounts of information daily. Electronic Medical Records (EMR) emerged as a centralized solution to manage and store patient data within healthcare institutions. In recent decades, EMR systems have gained widespread adoption, with 96% of US hospitals utilizing them in 2016 [28]. This indicates that EMR technology has become a cornerstone of patient care, capable of handling highly sensitive information, including personal details of patients and their medical records.

© The Author(s), under exclusive license to Springer Nature Switzerland AG 2026
W. Yurcik (Ed.): HealthSec 2024, CCIS 2716, pp. 160–187, 2026.
https://doi.org/10.1007/978-3-032-13800-2_8

The adoption of EMRs has brought numerous advantages to healthcare systems, extending beyond data storage to significantly improving operational efficiency and patient care. One key benefit is enhanced medication management, where EMRs enable healthcare providers to track prescriptions, seamlessly monitor patient's healthcare, and prevent harmful drug interactions through automated alerts that notify clinicians of potential contraindications [29]. Additionally, EMRs streamline billing and insurance processing by automating claims submission, reducing coding errors, and expediting reimbursements, thus minimizing administrative burdens on healthcare providers [44]. Another critical advantage is workflow automation, which optimizes appointment scheduling, clinical documentation, and patient flow management. By digitizing these processes, EMRs reduce manual paperwork, improve resource allocation, and improve overall efficiency in healthcare facilities [37]. These benefits demonstrate that EMRs are not just tools for data archival but essential components in modernizing and improving healthcare delivery.

However, EMR systems were not initially designed for multi-institutional operations, posing challenges when patients transfer between hospitals, leaving their medical records scattered across multiple data silos. To address this issue, the Health Insurance Portability and Accountability Act (HIPAA) was introduced in the U.S. [3]. HIPAA establishes a set of regulations and safeguards information between patients and healthcare institutions, allowing patients to share their medical records with designated third parties, such as family members, friends, or other medical facilities. These regulations are also designed to facilitate legal data requests for healthcare-related research. While HIPAA plays a crucial role in protecting sensitive medical data, it faces scalability limitations (i.e., lengthy legal processes), which contribute to its perception as a slow sharing process. This hinders the research aspect of medical records, potentially impacting advancements in healthcare.

Healthcare 4.0, like Industry 4.0, incorporates cutting-edge technologies such as cloud computing, fog computing, and edge computing into the healthcare sector [49]. This evolution involves adopting revolutionary technology such as the Internet of Medical Things (IoMT) and Blockchain technology [17,31,41,52,55]. Healthcare 4.0 enhances wireless data collection and transmission in healthcare by integrating various IoMT devices with traditional EMR technology, facilitating the sharing of patient data with remote institutions [45]. While IoMT systems enhance data communication and sharing in healthcare, they have also been shown to be highly vulnerable to cyber-attacks, requiring robust authentication schemes to validate or remove compromised devices. In essence, the lack of protection in these IoMT devices further complicates effective patient care.

Furthermore, healthcare information systems are more susceptible to attacks due to the increased centralization of EMR technology. Threats to healthcare industries compromise both the security and privacy of patient data. Attacks targeting the integrity of patient data (such as SQL injection and ransomware) are known to disrupt routine hospital operations and limit the efficiency of healthcare services [16,39,42]. In fact, the Office of Civil Rights received reports of numerous attacks, which affected more than 20 million patients in various healthcare networks [5]. This highlights how current security solutions continue to fall short, leaving healthcare to be one of the most vulnerable industries to cybercrime [36].

It is evident that current healthcare solutions lack robust infrastructure to integrate various technologies. Blockchain, which has recently gained popularity across multiple industries, including security [14,25,51], supply chain monitoring [12,55], and healthcare [10,20,32], has gained traction due to its security attributes, such as transparency and immutability of the ledger. Additionally, the use of smart contracts [1] enables blockchain to function as a *smart* decentralized storage system that operates data rigorously and in a predefined way. According to Sharma et al. [47], blockchain's properties make it an ideal solution for storing, managing, and sharing medical records. This can help bridge the gap between smart devices and smart services in healthcare information systems.

To strengthen security in traditional EMR systems and boost patient anonymity while facilitating medical research, this paper extends our earlier research [13] to further our understanding of the following research questions: i) How can blockchain protect patient data integrity against unauthorized changes? ii) How can access to the blockchain ledger be controlled to support cross-institutional collaboration in medical research? iii) How can IoMT devices be efficiently managed to securely store and retrieve patient data from authorized devices?

Contributions: The following describes our summary of contributions.

1. We propose MedBlockSync, a framework that enhances patient care and medical research by facilitating medical record exchange among healthcare institutions. MedBlockSync ensures the protection of Electronic Medical Records (EMR) technology by providing live backups for medical records across participating institutions. By integrating blockchain technology into existing EMR technology, MedBlockSync allows providers to maintain their current systems without modifications.
2. MedBlockSync offers access control specifically designed for healthcare and research institutions. It provides a multi-level platform that ensures a high degree of patient privacy while securely generating, storing, managing, and sharing medical records.
3. We design an access control methodology for registering and removing IoMT devices as needed. Following initial requests to the framework, smart devices await credential authentication before transmitting patient data to the EMR/blockchain.
4. We implement the MedBlockSync prototype and empirically evaluate its main functionalities. We assess MedBlockSync in terms of device registration, transaction distribution among stakeholders, protection against malicious actors, and the capability to share medical data.

---

[1] Smart contracts are self-executing agreements (i.e., code) on a blockchain that automatically enforce terms when predefined conditions are met.

2   Related Work

This section examines the current blockchain solutions in the healthcare industry, categorizing them according to their functions in securing and sharing data. Furthermore, we delve into the integration of the IoMT and explore methods for securely integrating IoMT devices into existing healthcare information systems.

2.1   Blockchain for Data Security

Blockchain's immutability enables it be a secure way to store medical records. For instance, Li et al. [33] studied data protection systems in healthcare and proposed memory management algorithms. Another successful application is Guardtime, an Estonia-based company that leverages blockchain's immutability to secure patients' medical records [38]. Fan et al. [22] introduced a novel consensus mechanism in blockchain to enhance medical data security, which forms the basis of other works aimed at improving the platform [24]. Fatima et al. [23] conducted a comprehensive review of how blockchain technology enhances privacy and data security in healthcare. Their study focused on its applications in managing patient records, clinical trials, and supply chain operations. [18, 25, 30, 50, 54] also leverage blockchain's immutability to protect medical records.

In our work, we propose the MedBlockSync framework, which prevents unauthorized data modification through the immutability properties of blockchain, thereby asserting the integrity of medical information. Unlike previous research, MedBlockSync incorporates an algorithm which compares data retrieved from the traditional EMR systems with records stored in the blockchain. Upon the detection of discrepancies, the algorithm automatically corrects affected EMR records.

2.2   Blockchain for Data Sharing and Access Control

Facilitating the exchange of patient EMR data between multiple healthcare organizations is essential to perform comprehensive analysis of patient health conditions and driving advances in healthcare. Blockchain technology enables the seamless sharing of data without the need for specific compliance policies. The data shared among network peers is represented as transactions on the blockchain and is replicated across all peers, ensuring the transparency of these transactions.

Blockchain's transparency has revolutionized the secure exchange of patient data among healthcare stakeholders. Wang et al. [53] implemented data access control systems based on blockchain technology to enhance data sharing while safeguarding patient confidentiality. Chen et al. [15] delved into a patient-centric blockchain model in healthcare, highlighting its potential for transparency in sharing health data. Medshare [54] employed access control and provenance mechanisms to ensure the secure sharing of patient medical records. Transparency has also played a pivotal role in medication management, effectively preventing the misuse of counterfeit or inferior medications. For instance, Med-Chain facilitates the secure exchange of medication-specific information between patients, hospitals, and pharmacies [26]. Omar et al. [40] showcased the enhancement of data transparency in clinical trials through the integration of Ethereum's smart contracts. Benchouri et al. [10] and Shae et al. [46] also demonstrated how blockchain technology can effectively prevent the omission of unwanted outcomes or the manipulation of data in clinical trials. Additionally, numerous studies [7,9,19,21,34] have designed blockchain-driven platforms that empower patients to securely share their data.

In contrast to existing studies, our MedBlockSync framework integrates data from all affiliated healthcare institutions through designated *research stakeholders* as part of our proposed access control mechanism. These research stakeholders can access anonymized medical records via keywords (e.g., COVID-19, cardiovascular disease), allowing them to generate datasets for disease prediction and prevention.

2.3   IoMT in Healthcare Information Systems

IoMT devices are crucial in remotely monitoring patient health conditions. They track parameters such as temperature, blood pressure, heart rate, and glucose levels [43]. These devices transmit this medical data to healthcare professionals, enabling them to provide accurate treatments, including medication administration and surgeries. For instance, the VITALS system [8] tracks patients' health by monitoring four physiological indicators. In a separate study, Gunawan et al. [27] developed a heart rate device using the MAX30102 sensor and a detrend method to obtain accurate heart rate data. Song et al. [48] presented a capacitive humidity sensor with exceptional sensitivity to humidity, allowing healthcare professionals to monitor patients' breathing patterns. Ma et al. [35] integrated the Angel sensor with the Alexa Voice Service from Amazon Echo to create a sophisticated healthcare application that captures users' health data and stores it in Amazon DynamoDB. iHome Health IoMT also helps prevent medication misuse by providing medical professionals with a means to monitor heart signal parameters.

However, integrating these IoMT systems into current EMR technology to securely transmit data to medical professionals is challenging. MedBlockSync enables IoMT system integration by implementing mechanisms for registering and authenticating smart devices within the healthcare network. IoMT devices cannot transmit patient data until they undergo proper authentication. Once authenticated, IoMT devices receive designated certificates to securely share health information within the network.

3   Threat Model

The healthcare industry is frequently targeted by adversaries seeking to profit either by selling data, enabling insurance fraud, demanding ransom through ransomware attacks, or even sabotaging the industry to convey a message. These attacks can be executed using different approaches, such as directly modifying data within EMR systems or compromising IoT devices in patients' homes. This section delves into the cyber threats posed to EMRs and outlines the solutions provided by our MedBlockSync framework to mitigate these attacks.

Threat 1: Unauthorized Modification of Patient Records. This threat entails unauthorized modifications to patient records within an EMR system. The adversary injects fabricated messages to compromise the data's integrity. Their goal is to manipulate patient information by exploiting system vulnerabilities, such as SQL injections caused by inadequate input validation, insufficient access control mechanisms, or outdated cryptographic methods. These vulnerabilities pose significant risks to patient safety and undermine the integrity of patient data.

Solution: Automatic data corrections. MedBlockSync securely stores immutable patient records on the blockchain. The information stored is compared EMR data to assert records have integrity. Should MedBlockSync detect any differences between the blockchain and EMR records, the EMR records get automatically updated with data retrieved from the blockchain. By implementing this technology, MedBlockSync enhances data security, ensuring that healthcare providers receive accurate data to make informed decisions and provide the most appropriate treatments or medical procedures for their patients.

Threat 2: Illegitimate Data Monitoring and Alterations Through IoMT Devices. IoMT technology is susceptible to attacks that commonly affect IoT devices, such as shortcomings in encryption and verification mechanisms. Adversaries can exploit these vulnerabilities when IoMT devices transmit medical records or patients' biometric data to EMR systems, potentially compromising privacy and trust in the patient care process.

Solution: Distribution of Certificates to IoMT Devices. MedBlockSync establishes trust among multiple healthcare systems for legitimate IoMT devices by offering a rigorous methodology for certificate registration and distribution. Upon receiving these certificates, IoMT devices are registered in the network, enabling them to securely and verifiably send and receive information. MedBlockSync also incorporates a de-registration feature, enabling the healthcare network to reject messages from specific IoMT devices upon suspicion of intrusion. This functionality is designed to safeguard against attacks aimed at altering patient data.

4   MedBlockSync Framework

This section introduces MedBlockSync, a blockchain-based framework designed to address the critical challenges of security, integrity, and interoperability in healthcare data management. It outlines how MedBlockSync enhances collaboration among healthcare institutions while safeguarding patient records and ensuring robust access control.

MedBlockSync is a blockchain-based framework designed to enhance the integrity, security, and interoperability of electronic medical record (EMR) systems while enabling seamless communication with Internet of Medical Things (IoMT) devices. Unlike traditional databases, which rely on centralized control and are vulnerable to single points of failure, MedBlockSync leverages blockchain technology to ensure data integrity, security, and verifiable transparency in an untrusted environment. This decentralized approach enables cooperation among multiple healthcare institutions while preventing unauthorized modifications and ensuring robust access control. Additionally, MedBlockSync facilitates the secure sharing of anonymized patient records with authorized stakeholders.

As illustrated in Fig. 1, MedBlockSync serves two categories of stakeholders: (1) primary stakeholders, such as medical professionals, and (2) secondary stakeholders, including research institutions. The system is structured into three tiers, each with specific functionalities. The client tier provides an intuitive interface that enables effortless access to electronic medical records (EMRs), blockchain services, and various healthcare features. The logic tier integrates the EMR, Blockchain, and Off-Chain modules, ensuring secure data exchange between stakeholders and supporting other ChainMed services. Finally, the data tier is responsible for storing multi-institutional EMRs, maintaining the distributed blockchain ledger, and managing an off-chain database to securely handle patient records across different institutions. Subsequent sections describe the system structure and stakeholders in further detail.

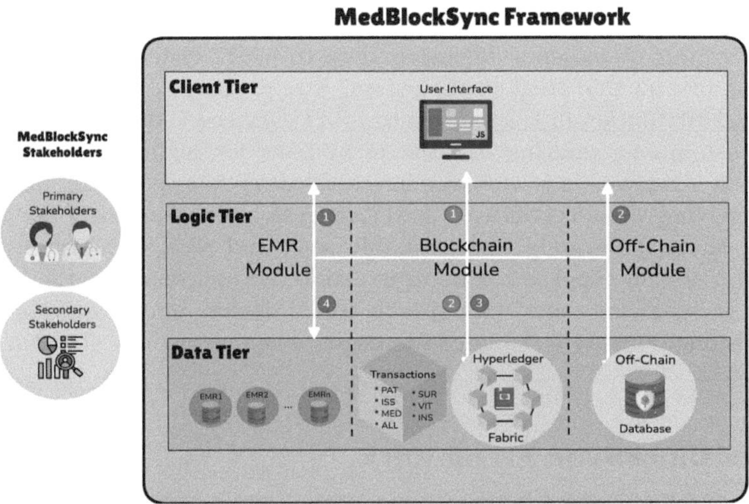

Fig. 1. MedBlockSync overview. Steps annotated represent the basic workflow for each type of stakeholder based on color.

4.1 Stakeholders and Users of MedBlockSync

There are two stakeholders in our healthcare environment; primary and secondary stakeholders. These stakeholders have varying access privileges to the EMR and the blockchain system underneath. Their privileges are determined as follows.

Primary Stakeholders. Primary stakeholders fall into two categories; patients and healthcare professionals. They collect patient data using traditional medical devices and/or IoMT devices. These stakeholders either own the patient's medical record data or provide healthcare to the patients. All primary stakeholders have their access limited to EMRs, traditional medical devices and IoMT devices, and cannot directly access the blockchain. Sample interactions of each category are provided below.

1. <u>Healthcare Workers' Interaction with EMRs:</u> This category includes medical professionals such as clinicians, nurses, doctors, and IT technicians within healthcare organizations. These professionals interact directly with traditional EMRs, performing tasks like patient enrollment, as well as recording and retrieving vital signs. While they do not engage with the blockchain directly, their actions within the EMR system automatically trigger synchronized transactions on the blockchain. This integration ensures that MedBlockSync maintains an immutable record of EMR activities, reducing the risk of data loss or unauthorized modifications.
2. <u>Patients' Interaction with IoMT Devices:</u> Authorized IoMT devices (temperature sensors, smart scales, glucose monitors, etc.) located on site in hospitals and clinics or remotely in patients' homes are integrated within healthcare information systems. These devices are used by healthcare professionals or patients to collect real-time health data. Authorized IoMT devices can automatically transmit patient data to both EMRs and subsequently to the blockchain, ensuring redundancy and data resilience against potential cyber attacks on EMR systems.

Secondary Stakeholders. The secondary stakeholders comprise *research institutions* (e.g. medical schools/universities), insurance companies (both medical and life insurance), and pharmacies. These stakeholders are granted read permissions to access anonymized patient records through the MedBlockSync blockchain. Secondary stakeholders are also known as *auditors* in our environment. Auditors do not directly access EMRs to retrieve patient data. Instead, they utilize transactions stored on the blockchain to generate research datasets focused on specific diseases or medical histories, such as unique medications, allergies, or previous surgeries. These datasets contain only anonymized biometric information that aligns with the specified search criteria. For instance, an auditor may generate a dataset containing solely the biometric data of patients with cancer or those using a particular type of therapy (like chemo). Moreover, auditors can visualize the blockchain's performance metrics, such as transaction load distribution and other important indicators. This feature allows auditors to develop new medical treatments and effectively monitor health-related trends. Typical auditors in our environment will be professors, student researchers, and data scientists.

4.2   MedBlockSync Three-Tier Architecture

The three-tier architecture of MedBlockSync and the interoperability between different stakeholders are illustrated as follows.

Client Tier. MedBlockSync features a user-friendly graphical interface that facilitates seamless interactions with both Electronic Medical Records (EMR) and blockchain networks. It asserts user-based authentication mechanisms endorsed by primary stakeholders to validate the identities of healthcare workers. Authentication may be done via usernames and passwords or ID cards. Authorized users, including IT technicians and doctors, may gain exclusive access to EMRs and healthcare information systems via MedBlockSync's web-based platform. Within this framework, healthcare workers and providers manage the integration of Internet of Medical Things (IoMT) devices, ensuring that legitimate devices securely transmit monitored patients' medical data to the organization's internal network. Secondary stakeholders (auditors), are authenticated via the blockchain module of the MedBlockSync framework to access patient data and transactions stored on the blockchain. While auditors can visualize blockchain data, they are restricted from accessing patient medical records, EMR systems, or healthcare IoMT devices owned by primary stakeholders. The annotated workflows provided by the user interface are highlighted in Fig. 1.

Workflow for Primary Stakeholder. (1) A Healthcare professional selects a specific patient from the EMR system. (2) The Healthcare professional may input in the biometric data to EMR via text (type it), or request a biometric reading from the patient's IoMT devices. (3) MedBlockSync's EMR and blockchain module automatically generate the patient's vitals transactions (VIT), and (4) MedBlockSync updates the patient's medical records in the EMR and blockchain data storages. The healthcare professional may generate other EMR events (e.g., medication/surgery transactions) by following a similar workflow.

Workflow for Secondary Stakeholder. Secondary stakeholders are allowed to access and visualize medical data from the blockchain. An auditor may request blockchain data through the MedBlockSync's user interface (a webpage) by (1) formulating queries to retrieve information of a certain medical disease, and/or (2) submitting queries to obtain a list of blockchain transactions. The MedBlockSync's user interface displays the relevant blockchain transactions. An anonymized data file available for download is also automatically generated containing data collected based on the auditor's query parameters.

Logic Tier. This tier is made up of of three modules: EMR, Blockchain, and Off-Chain. The logic tier processes requests from the user interface then facilitates data transfer to backend services. The three modules are explained further as follows.

Table 1. API event description. Note that this table is adopted from Castillo *et al.* [13].

Event	BCID	Method*	Description
Patient	PAT	GP	Defines the list of available patients by patient id (PID)
Medical Issue	ISS	GP	Defines a medical condition for a specific PID
Medication	MED	GP	Defines the list of medications using PID
Allergy	ALL	GP	Defines the allergies related to a specific PID
Surgery	SUR	GP	Defines the surgeries a PID has had
Vitals	VIT	GP	Defines the patient's vital readings using its ID and appointment ID (EID)
Insurance	INS	GPU	Defines primary and secondary insurance policies that match to PID

* G → GET, P → POST, and U → PUT

<u>EMR Module.</u> MedBlockSync is designed to communicate with many EMR systems by using web APIs regardless of different EMR vendors. With these web APIs, the EMR module can access the essential health information of the patients from the traditional EMR systems including patients' biometric data and medication history. Table 1 lists the EMR API events, their description and relevant Blockchain ID (BCID). The latter being used in the next module. We selected the events relevant to improve patient outcome such as allergies, medical issues, medication, etc. We also include a non-essential API event, namely "Insurance" to provide *auditors* with some additional features that expand their analytic capabilities. For instance, with such data, researchers can determine which insurance company provides the best services to patients. The API events are communicated to the Off-chain module to maintain a record of every event ID. This event ID maps to the corresponding healthcare organization. MedBlockSync leverages the event map to manage many different EMR systems simultaneously. In other words, this record serves as a road map to pair transactions with EMR events.

MedBlockSync is engineered to interact with various EMR systems using web APIs, regardless of the EMR vendor. Through these web APIs, the EMR module may access essential health information from traditional EMR systems, such as patients' biometric data and medication history. Table 1 lists the EMR API events, their descriptions, and corresponding Blockchain IDs (BCIDs), which are utilized in the subsequent module. We have selected events that are relevant for improving patient outcomes, such as allergies, medical issues, and medications. Additionally, we include a non-essential API event, "Insurance," to provide auditors with extra features that enhance their analytic capabilities. With this data, researchers can determine which insurance companies offer the best services to patients. The API events are communicated to the Off-chain module to maintain a record of each event ID. This event ID maps to the respective healthcare organization. MedBlockSync uses the event map to manage multiple EMR systems concurrently. Essentially, this record serves as a roadmap to link transactions with EMR events.

<u>Blockchain Module.</u> This module is responsible for engaging stakeholders with blockchain-related services, particularly smart contracts. It manages interactions involving smart contracts and oversees blockchain identity management for each institution. Blockchain identities are generated by the appropriate membership service provider (MSP), such as Hyperledger Fabric, which assigns cryptographic labels to each institution. Every transaction or query within MedBlockSync is submitted through distinct blockchain identities corresponding to the initiating institution. MedBlockSync's framework interfaces with a single smart contract, the *medical contract*, to facilitate real-time cross-referencing of medical information between EMR systems and the distributed ledger. Patient records are transmitted to the medical contract using the Blockchain IDs (BCIDs) outlined in Table 1, ensuring clear separation between various EMR data types. Further details about the medical contract are covered in Sect. 4.2.

<u>Off-Chain Module.</u> This module connects MedBlockSync to off-chain services provided by IoMT devices. It guarantees patient data security by managing the registration of IoMT devices within the MedBlockSync network prior to biometric data transmission. This module creates a highly controlled environment to protect patient data security. Using distinct MQTT brokers, the module facilitates efficient communication between healthcare systems and IoMT devices. Dynamic MQTT topics are utilized to organize communication among IoMT devices, preventing conflicts during operation. For IoMT device registration, a pairing request with the MAC address is submitted to MedBlockSync, serving as the primary identifier. Upon approval by a healthcare professional (e.g., clinic system administrator), MedBlockSync generates a unique MQTT ID for the device. The device's remote connection configuration profile (CCP) is established. As shown in Fig. 2, the CCP is a JSON object that contains the broker information (IP address and destination port), the username used for communication, and the certificate for the encryption process. Should a registered IoMT device be compromised by cyberattacks, MedBlockSync can automatically deregister the malicious devices, blocking their access to the MQTT broker or MedBlockSync's data tier. Additionally, the Off-Chain Module responds to requests from the EMR module to store critical information, such as the event map, in the off-chain database.

Data Tier. MedBlockSync unifies multiple services within a single framework, with the data tier layer acting as a reliable bridge for other tiers to access essential data stored in the EMR, blockchain, and off-chain databases. Further details for each component in the data tier are explained subsequently.

<u>EMR Cluster.</u> This is a group of standalone EMR systems that may offer different features (i.e., different vendors), but ultimately are fully functional management platforms used medical records. Each EMR is independent and does not share any type of data with one another. The number of available EMRs in MedBlockSync is connected to the amount of medical institutions joining the collaboration. For instance, five hospitals with different EMRs and network structure are looking to enable a collaboration to improve patient care and research. This

```
{
    "ccp": {
        "host": "               ",
        "port": "     "
    },
    "user": "a93ksf109",
    "pem": "-----BEGIN CERTIFICATE-----




                          
                          
                          
                          
                          
                          
                          
    -----END CERTIFICATE-----"
}
```

Fig. 2. CCP of the approved new IoMT device.

new joint network would have an EMR cluster size of 5. The data tier makes sure that all five EMRs are fully operational and willing to communicate with the primary stakeholder they belong to.

This cluster comprises individual EMR systems, e.g., OpenEMR [27], each offering unique features and varying across different vendors. Despite these differences, they collec- tively serve to manage medical records. Each EMR operates in- dependently, ensuring complete data segregation. The availability of EMRs within MedBlockSync depends on the participation of medical institutions in the collaboration. For example, should five hospitals with different EMRs collaborate, the resulting EMR cluster would consist of these five systems. The data tier ensures the smooth operation of all EMRs within the cluster, enabling communication with their respective primary stakeholders.

This cluster consists of individual EMR systems, such as OpenEMR [2], each with its own features and vendor. While these systems vary, they all manage medical records. Each EMR operates independently, maintaining complete data segregation. The EMRs available in MedBlockSync depend on participating medical institutions. For instance, should five hospitals using different EMR systems join MedBlockSync, the cluster will contain those five systems. The data tier facilitates the operation of all EMRs in the cluster, enabling communication with their primary stakeholders.

Blockchain Network. MedBlockSync creates a blockchain network to collectively store multi-institutional medical records. The blockchain is maintained by the institutions of its primary (i.e., healthcare institutions) and secondary stakeholders (i.e., research institutes). Each institution has the freedom to choose the amount of resources (i.e., number of peers) they provide to maintain the network. The blockchain network deployed scales dynamically depending on the size of the collaboration. For example, three health institutions decide to produce a collaboration with a university laboratory. The number of organizations required to build the blockchain of MedBlockSync would be 4. In other words, the sum of all participating institutions represent the pillar of the blockchain network. Further examples are illustrated in Sect. 5.1.

MedBlockSync establishes a blockchain network to store redundant copies of patients' medical records from EMR clusters and provide blockchain services. This network is sustained through collaborative efforts between primary stakeholders in healthcare institutions and secondary stakeholders in research institutes. Each stakeholder determines their contribution to the blockchain network's computing power, typically by counting the number of peers. The scalability of the blockchain network adjusts dynamically based on the size of the collaborating organizations. For example, if three health institutions decide to produce a collaboration with a university laboratory. The number of organizations required to build the blockchain of MedBlockSync would be four. In other words, the sum of all participating institutions represent the pillar of the blockchain network. Further examples are illustrated in Sect. 5.1.

MedBlockSync uses a blockchain network to store redundant copies of patient medical records from the EMR clusters, and to provide blockchain services. This network is maintained through collaboration between primary (healthcare institutions) and secondary stakeholders (research institutes). Each stakeholder determines their contribution to the network's computing power, typically based on the number of nodes they operate. The blockchain network scales dynamically with the size of the collaborating organizations. For example, a collaboration between three health institutions and a university laboratory would result in four participating organizations, and thus four key components of the MedBlockSync blockchain. In short, the total number of participating institutions forms the foundation of the blockchain network. Further examples are provided in Section 5.1.

MedBlockSync generates new blocks by receiving different types of transactions. The transaction type represents a link to a specific EMR event such as patients (PAT), medical issues (ISS), medications (MED), allergies (ALL), surgeries (SUR), vitals (VIT) and insurance (INS). The ledger within the blockchain is operated by the medical contract. Algorithm 1 illustrates the main methods inside the medical contract. This contract operates a ledger that contains different type of transactions such as allergy transactions TX_{ALL}, vitals transactions Tx_{VIT} and more. Every new submitted transaction typically include the transaction type tp, transaction ID id and the raw data RD (if needed). The following explains the main functions of the medical contract.

MedBlockSync's services handles transactions by generating new blocks. Transactions entail EMR data types like patients (PAT), medical issues (ISS), medications (MED), allergies (ALL), surgeries (SUR), vitals (VIT), and insurance (INS). Further details are provided in Table 1. The medical smart contract governs the blockchain ledger of MedBlockSync as outlined in Algorithm 1. This contract allows three type of transactions: inserting new data, retrieving single-type and multi-type data. Additionally, the contract incorporates the transaction's timestamp to filter out outdated transactions that may no longer hold relevance to a particular study. For instance, a researcher might want to access

---

Algorithm 1: Medical contract in MedBlockSync

Data   : Current ledger $\mathbb{CL} = \{Tx_{ALL}, \ldots, Tx_{VIT}\}$
Input   : Transaction ID(s) $id \subset \{1, \ldots, n\}$,
               Transaction type(s) $tp \subset \{ALL, \ldots, VIT\}$,
               Raw transaction data RD
Output: Result set $RD \subset \mathbb{CL}$

// **Method 1:** Insert new data sample
function *insertTransaction(tp, id, RD)*:
    $Tx_{tp_{id}} \leftarrow$ formTransaction(tp, id, RD)
    $Tx_{tp_{id}} \rightarrow Tx_{tp}$
    return *null*
end

// **Method 2:** Get single type data sample
function *queryTransactionByType(tp, id)*:
    Set $Res = \{\}$
    for i *in* id **do**
        $Tx_{tp_i} \leftarrow Tx_{tp}[i]$
        $Tx_{tp_i} \rightarrow Res$
    end
    return *Res*
end

// **Method 3:** Get multi-type data sample
function *queryAllTransactions(tp, id)*:
    Set $Res = \{\}$
    for t *in* tp **do**
        for i *in* id **do**
            $Tx_{t_i} \leftarrow Tx_t[i]$
            $Tx_{t_i} \rightarrow Res$
        end
    end
    return *Res*
end

---

information on penicillin from the past five years to gain insights into the recent implications of penicillin-based allergy treatments. All new submitted transaction must include the transaction type tp, transaction ID id and the raw data D (if necessary). The main functions of the medical contract are explained further in the subsequent methods.

- *Method 1: Insert new data sample.* To insert a new transaction, Med-BlockSync interacts with the *insertTransaction* function to command the contract to generate a new transaction object $Tx_{tp_{id}}$ and store it in the ledger. The ID used to identify the transaction is stored in the event map created by the EMR module.
- *Method 2: Get single type data sample.* A query for this function is formulated using the transaction type and the different IDs. The number of IDs in the request varies with respect to different scenarios (i.e., 1–100, 3–10). The contracts returns a list of transactions matching the original type.
- *Method 3: Get multi-type data sample.* Similar to the previous method, this query is formed by different transaction types and different IDs. The number of transaction types and IDs varies depending on the request. The contract returns a list of transactions that match all types and IDs in the query.

Off-Chain Database. MedBlockSync employs MongoDB, a NoSQL database, to manage all off-chain-related data. This includes auditor user credentials for authentication, an event map for transaction tracking, and a list of authorized IoMT devices. Opting for a NoSQL database enables data storage in JSON documents, which removes the necessity for traditional table structures. The off-chain module holds exclusive control over this database, while other modules must submit requests to add any information that affects their functionality.

MedBlockSync's Functions. In contrast to other blockchain-based frameworks discussed in related works [7,50], MedBlockSync integrates three crucial security features. Firstly, it autonomously protects EMR patient data integrity via self-defense mechanisms (Function A). Secondly, it asserts the availability of patient data for secure sharing and access among various stakeholders (Function B). Lastly, it enforces access control mechanisms to effectively manage IoMT devices and their transmitted data (Function C).

Algorithm 2 outlines MedBlockSync's three security functions, which require cooperation among primary and secondary stakeholders/devices, including healthcare workers (H), IoMT technology (T), and auditors (A), along with patient data (P). MedBlockSync's logic tier, composed of the EMR module (M_E), Blockchain module (M_B), and Off-Chain module (M_O), supervises the execution of these security functions. MedBlockSync facilitates the exchange, reading, and writing of data across the data tier clusters, which include the EMR clusters $\mathbb{D}_E)$, blockchain network $(\mathbb{D}_B)$, and Off-Chain database $(\mathbb{D}_O)$.

Function A: Self-Protecting Data Integrity. This function starts from the self-defense mechanism asserting the integrity of EMR data. Should a healthcare worker (H) query an EMR for patient information, the integrity of the retrieved data is automatically validated by MedBlockSync. This validation process encompasses modules M_E and M_B. $\mathbb{D}_E$ and $\mathbb{D}_B$ for patient data are also concurrently queried in the validation process. MedBlockSync compares the retrieved data from both sources. Granted the data sets match the information from the EMR is forwarded to the healthcare worker (H) since the matching sets indicate data integrity. However, if a discrepancy is detected, MedBlockSync rectifies the situation by replacing the malicious data in the EMR with accurate information obtained from the blockchain to correct a compromised EMR system. This is possible because the blockchain system is immutable and stores precise data. Once corrected, the accurate patient data is transmitted to the healthcare provider.

Function B: Secure Data Sharing. The second security function of MedBlockSync guarantees medical records distributed among stakeholders across different organizations is secure. To start, healthcare workers (H) use modules M_E and M_B to input patient data, creating a collaborative storage system for multi-institutional patient records across $\mathbb{D}_E$ and $\mathbb{D}_B$. Legitimate auditors (A) may then securely access these newly created records via the blockchain network. Auditors receive anonymized data through MedBlockSync's adoption of the Bitcoin privacy model. This model employs pseudonymous identities, formed by combining patient IDs and organization names, to separate the actual identity

---

Algorithm 2: MedBlockSync main logical process adopted from [13]

Input: MedBlockSync stakeholder users H, T and A,
   Patient data $PD = \{pd_1, \ldots, pd_n\}$,
   MedBlockSync with modules M_E, M_B and M_O,
   MedBlockSync data silos $\mathbb{D}_E$, $\mathbb{D}_B$ and $\mathbb{D}_O$,

// **Function A**
① H requests M_E to retrieve a sample $d_{1e} \in \mathbb{D}_E$.
② H requests M_B to retrieve a sample $d_{1b} \in \mathbb{D}_B$.
③ MedBlockSync checks if $d_{1e} \neq d_{1b}$ is satisfied.
④ If satisfied, MedBlockSync enforces data replacement policy $\mathbb{D}_E \leftarrow d_{1b}$.

// **Function B**
① H requests M_E to add $p_1 \rightarrow \mathbb{D}_E$.
② H requests M_B to add $p_1 \rightarrow \mathbb{D}_B$.
③ A requests M_B to retrieve $p_{1b} \leftarrow \mathbb{D}_B$.

// **Function C**
① T requests M_O to add $T \rightarrow \mathbb{D}_O$ with pending status.
② H requests M_O to change the status of T to approved.
③ M_O sends signed certificate to T as proof of identity.
④ H requests M_O to activate T.
⑤ T captures biometrics from patient and submits them to M_O where they are returned to H.
⑥ If T is found to be malicious, H requests M_O to update status of T as rejected.

---

of patients from their respective medical data. This connection occurs at EMR level, where the patient receives medical attention.

Function C: IoMT Access Control. This security function safeguards the registration and activation of legitimate IoMT devices. Healthcare workers or patients may initiate a request to pair a new IoMT device (T) and the healthcare provider's network ($\mathbb{D}_E$) through the Off-Chain module (M_O). After a registered healthcare worker (H) manually approves the pairing request, the IoMT device receives a signed certificate from MedBlockSync, serving as proof of authentication. Subsequently, the IoMT device establishes a connection to the provider's network and is granted permission to transmit real-time healthcare data upon request. Should a malicious IoMT device is detected, healthcare workers may mark the device as "rejected" within MedBlockSync and request MedBlockSync to reject any incoming requests or access by the malicious device (T). Access granted via the prior proof of authentication for the malicious device is revoked, leaving the device isolated.

5   MedBlockSync Evaluation

This section outlines the experimental setup used to evaluate the effectiveness of the MedBlockSync framework. It details the configurations, datasets, and evaluation metrics employed to simulate real-world healthcare environments and assess the framework's performance in addressing identified cybersecurity threats.

5.1 Experimental Setup

MedBlockSync's connectivity allows it to provide services to multiple institutions, depending on the deployment environment. To evaluate the effectiveness of MedBlockSync, we conduct the following three experiments.

1. *Function A: Self-Protecting Data Integrity.* This experiment involves two healthcare institutions, Hospital X and Clinic Y, with one experiencing a malicious attack. An adversary breaches the healthcare network and alters patient records, threatening the integrity of the OpenEMR system and potentially affecting patient outcomes. The experiment will assess MedBlockSync's ability to safeguard medical records by detecting and correcting discrepancies between the compromised OpenEMR and Fabric blockchain systems.
2. *Function B: Secure Data Sharing.* This experiment involves three participating institutions: two primary stakeholders, Hospital X and Clinic Y, and a secondary stakeholder, Research Organization Z. All three participants are authenticated and valid. The objective is to evaluate MedBlockSync's capability to facilitate efficient collaboration by allowing Research Organization Z to retrieve anonymized patient data from Hospital X and clinic Y.
3. *Function C: IoMT Access Control.* This experiment aims to assess MedBlockSync's ability to facilitate secure communication between legitimate IoMT devices and OpenEMR systems while promptly rejecting malicious devices upon detection. A single primary stakeholder, such as a legitimate Hospital X, will demonstrate the registration and de-registration of an IoMT device (e.g., MySignals) within the MedBlockSync framework, showcasing enhanced patient data security.

5.2 MedBlockSync Prototype System

MedBlockSync is a web application built in ExpressJS, a javascript framework used for the development of back-end services. As elaborated in Sect. 4.2, our framework contains three essential modules, namely EMR, Blockchain and Off-Chain modules, which offers streamline communication with different systems and devices. Each module requires the existence of specific components before the prototype can be evaluated. The elements for generating the MedBlockSync prototype are as follows.

OpenEMR System. The OpenEMR project is an open-source EMR system that allows the healthcare organizations to manage patients' medical records [2]. OpenEMR is certified by The Office of the National Coordinator for Health Information Technology (ONC) and is complied with requirements created by the Secretary at the Department of Health and Human Services. OpenEMR is a PHP-based platform that is easily deployed on servers with different operating systems as long as the systems support PHP services. OpenEMR is designed with various built-in APIs to enable headless communication with remote networks such as the EMR module in our MedBlockSync framework. Until 2021 the

OpenEMR system suffered from various cyber attacks including SQL injection and remote code execution [4]. Therefore, vulnerable OpenEMR systems are chosen in this study to validate the security benefits offered by our MedBlockSync framework. The default/original settings of the OpenEMR system are used to conduct various MedBlockSync security evaluation experiments.

Hyperledger Fabric Blockchain. Hyperledger Fabric (Fabric for short) is a permissioned (or private) blockchain that offers a high degree of flexibility and scalability [6]. Fabric is also a container-based blockchain with a variety of components that allow architects to create complex networks with a low degree of difficulty [11]. In contrast to other public blockchains (i.e., Bitcoin), Fabric offers private communication to registered organizations in the form of channels. These *channels* are regulated by the access control policies defined in blockchain ledger.

MedBlockSync relies on a single-channel customized blockchain defined by the amount of collaborative hospitals and research parties. For instance, a network with two hospitals and a research institution requires three blockchain organizations. A blockchain organization is the abstract representation of the institution that wants to participate in the network. Each organization contains an endorsing peer, which is used to propagate transactions from different users (i.e., healthcare and auditor users). All members from every organization in the channel can visualize inserted transactions to create a transparent environment for enhancing the trust of the network. MedBlockSync users are granted cryptographically anonymous identities through the Hyperledger Fabric Membership Service Provider (MSP) [6]. Certificates are issued for each member to access the blockchain and each certification is validated by the appropriate certificate authority (e.g., hospital IT department). The medical contract designed for our prototype is accessed via the Shim API of the Fabric SDK. This contract is built to include the methods described in Sect. 4.2 for the processing of medical records. These three methods reduce the complexity of MedBlockSync by delegating the management of shared medical records to the smart contract.

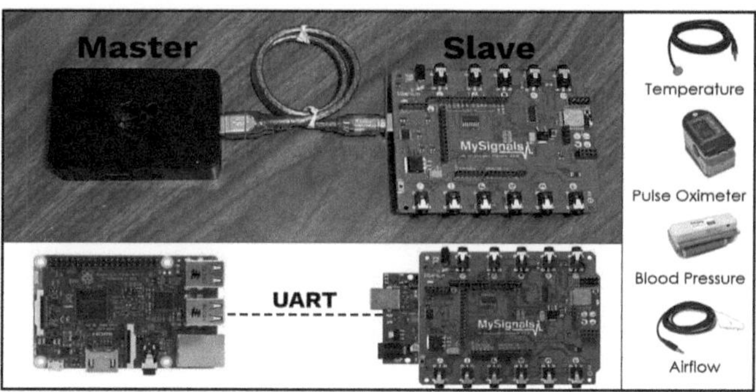

Fig. 3. IoMT prototype with selected sensors.

IoMT Prototype Remote Monitoring System. We configure and develop MySignals devices [1] to create an IoMT remote monitoring system (smart sensors) for conducting our experiments. The MySignals platform is a system offered by Libelium that allows developers to capture a variety of physiological signals, such as oxygen levels and blood pressure. As shown in Fig. 3, our prototype system uses a subset of the available devices including temperature, pulse oximeter, blood pressure and airflow sensors. The selected sensors provide significant health metrics often used as diagnostic and monitoring tools. The IoMT prototype system is designed to work as a two-part system where (a) the *Master* manages the sensor data and incorporates the networking features to behave as a smart device, and (b) the *Slave* represents the medical aspect that retrieves data from the available sensors. The IoMT remote monitoring system communicates with the MedBlockSync framework with three major components. First, an Arduino UNO acts as the main processing unit for the slave to create a responsive and interactive sensory platform via serial communication (UART). Second, the interface with the sensors is operated through the MySignals platform using peripheral communication (i.e., SPI or I2C). All requests for accessing real-time patient's vital data must pass through this component. Finally, a Raspberry Pi 3 acts as the "brain" of the IoMT system that quickly process requests, and transmit sensor data to the server through the Internet. Upon initial booting, the device enters into a blank state. At this stage, the MySignals platform has no virtual identity or recollection of any available endpoints. Once the device is activated by a user (i.e., healthcare technician), it sends the initial request for pairing to obtain a new identity from MedBlockSync as discussed in Sect. 4.2.

5.3   Framework Evaluation

In this section, we evaluate the outcomes of the three distinct experiments to showcase the efficiency of the MedBlockSync framework. The experiments are conducted on a Windows 10 Pro setup, which features an Intel Core i7-9750H processor and 32 GB of RAM. For the Fabric blockchain, we set the block parameters, namely the block timeout and block size, to 1 s and 1 MB respectively. The block timeout specifies how often new blocks are generated in the network, while the block size determines the maximum data capacity of each block in bytes. This configuration ensures that a new block is created every second, and each block can hold up to 1 MB of data.

Blockchain Performance. Figure 4 shows the overall performance analysis of the blockchain in terms of transaction delays and stakeholder-based memory (RAM) consumption. Our first experiment investigates the ability of the framework to process a large amount of data in a single transaction in terms of bytes (B). This determines the amount of patient data that can be sent to the blockchain for every transaction. The experiment is performed by gradually increasing transaction size from 10^3 B (1 KB) to 10^8B (100 MB). Figure 4a illustrates the transaction delay behavior for both blockchain queries and inserts after increasing the transaction size. The delay time is shown to increase exponentially as the transaction size grows larger. Furthermore, we observe that a maximum transaction size of 10^6 B (1 MB) is recommended to avoid significant amount of transaction delays for both queries and inserts. This is because a blockchain's block size is limited (i.e., 1MB), and larger transactions would require multiple blocks to be generated to store its information.

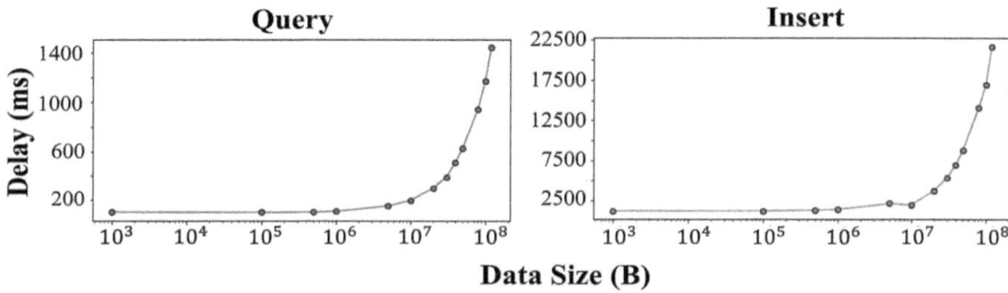

(a) Effect of transaction size in blockchain

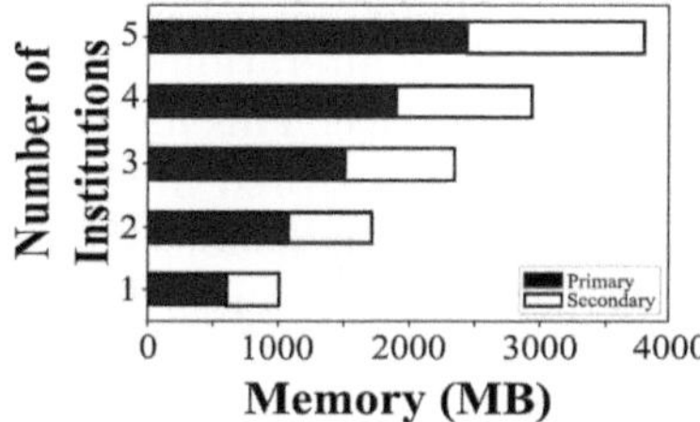

(b) Resource consumption per stakeholder type

Fig. 4. Performance analysis of blockchain.

In contrast to the transaction delay analysis, the second experiment examines the amount of resources each stakeholder consumes from the host computer. This determines the number of institutions you can deploy at the same time within the test network. The experiment deploys one to five different primary and secondary institutions with their respective number of blockchain peers as defined in Sect. 5.2. Figure 4b shows the memory consumption of the different stakeholders in MedBlockSync. Results indicate that primary stakeholders uses almost double the amount of memory comparing with secondary stakeholders. The reason is because primary stakeholders need read and write privileges to the EMR, blockchain and IoMT devices, which requires additional services in the network. These additional services exhaust memory in the host computer. The secondary stakeholders, however, only require read privileges in the blockchain to access existing medical data. This makes their memory consumption to be much smaller in comparison.

Evaluation of Function A. In this experiment we define two medical institutions (i.e., hospital X and clinic Y). One of the institutions (clinic Y) is a victim of an SQL injection attack. The attackers modified the patient's medical records of the institution's EMR system. To evaluate MedBlockSync's performance against data alteration attacks, we pretended to be the attacker to modify one patient's medical record via the OpenEMR's API. This simulated a SQL injection attack that compromises the integrity of EMR. The medical conditions displayed in Fig. 5 represents the patient's medical information before and after being maliciously modified by the attackers. The patient's medical information is an example and does not represent any particular individual.

In this experiment, we assess MedBlockSync's performance in defending against data alteration attacks by simulating a scenario involving two medical institutions: Hospital X and Clinic Y. Clinic Y becomes the victim of an SQL injection attack, resulting in the unauthorized alteration of patient medical records within its EMR system. To evaluate MedBlockSync's ability to detect and prevent such attacks, we simulate an attacker by attempting to alter a patient's medical record through the OpenEMR's API, mimicking an SQL injection attack. The patient's medical record shown in Fig. 5 is an example and does not correspond to any real individual. Figure 5a presents the patient's medical information before and after the simulated attack. If MedBlockSync effectively detects and prevents the unauthorized alteration of medical data, a green success message will appear on the user interface. This message confirms that the Open-EMR information aligns with the data stored in the blockchain ledger, thereby ensuring data integrity and preventing malicious changes.

When MedBlockSync detects and prevents the unauthorized alteration of medical data, the user interface displays a green *success* message. This message indicates that the OpenEMR information matches the data stored in the blockchain ledger, ensuring data integrity and preventing malicious changes.

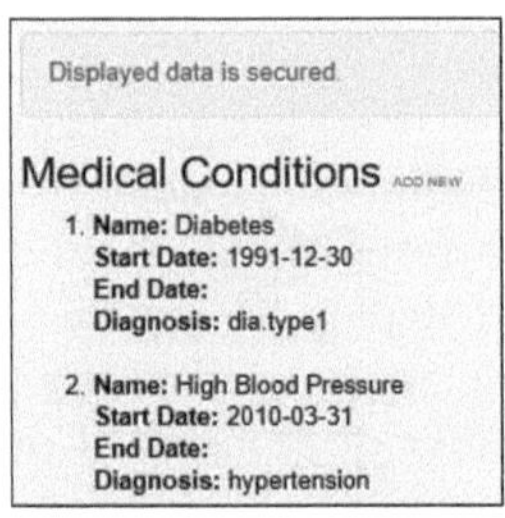
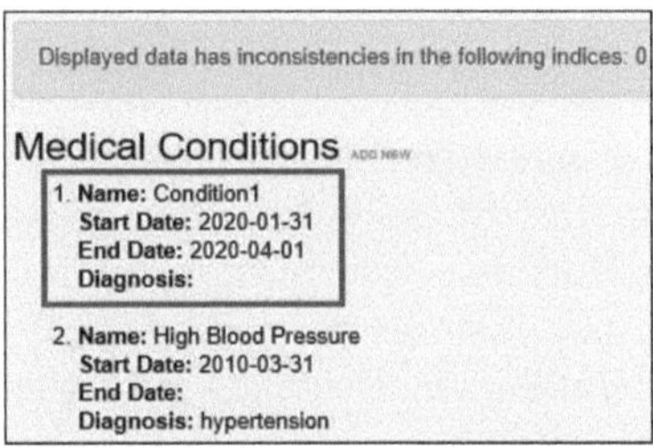

(a) Original data   (b) Data after attack

Fig. 5. MedBlockSync data security functionality sourced from MediLink [13].

Should the OpenEMR data have discrepancies from the data stored in the Fabric blockchain, a red *fail* message is displayed to alert the healthcare worker, as shown in Fig. 5b. This error message indicates that either malicious or internal alterations to the OpenEMR data have occurred without using the MedBlockSync framework, or that OpenEMR is facing a cyber attack. The Fabric

Blockchain may be automatically updated only via modifications to OpenEMR made through the MedBlockSync framework. Thus, cyber attackers or malicious users who compromise OpenEMR systems to alter data would not affect the security of data in the blockchain. In such cases, the user interface displays both the maliciously altered data from OpenEMR and the correct data retrieved from the Fabric blockchain for perusal.

As illustrated in Fig. 5b, the "Condition 1" data within the red box represents the medical information stored in OpenEMR. This data exhibits a different diagnosis and incorrect dates compared to the legitimate medical information stored in the blockchain. If there is a discrepancy between the retrieved medical records from OpenEMR and the information obtained from the blockchain, our MedBlockSync framework automatically restores OpenEMR medical records to the original data stored in the Fabric blockchain.

Evaluation of Function B. In this experiment, Hospital X and Clinic Y, both registered on the blockchain network, submit multiple transactions. Figure 6 illustrates the analysis and distribution of all medical records generated by these institutions. Research Organization Z serves as a secondary stakeholder, acting as an auditor. Unlike the two primary stakeholders, auditors do not submit transactions (data insertion) but instead request access to data stored in the Fabric blockchain.

Figure 6a presents the data sharing functionality of our MedBlockSync. The auditor users are allowed to visualize medical records that have been shared with them. They also can obtain information from the different blockchain operations such as transaction distribution and transaction delays. The left panel seen in the Fig. 6a provides statistics of the blockchain's query and insert operations.

Figure 6a showcases the data sharing functionality of MedBlockSync. Auditors may view shared medical records and access blockchain-related information, including transaction distribution and delays. The left panel of Fig. 6a displays the generated transaction count per institution. These statistics represent query and insert operations on the blockchain. The first column contains four *Parameter* (i.e., maximum, minimum, mean and standard division), which are used to evaluate blockchain's latency. The second column is *Invoke*, which presents the time efficiency to insert a new record (transaction) to the blockchain. The third column *Query*, presents the time efficiency to retrieve data from the blockchain. The number of transactions inserted or queried depend on the participation of healthcare institutions. The right panel displays blockchain storage usage (transaction volume) relative to other participating institutions. Hospital X generates more transactions compared to Clinic Y.

– *Time efficiency for data insertion.* The frequency to generate new blocks depends on the blockchain's block timeout parameter. Our blockchain creates a new block every second (1000 milliseconds). Subsequently, it processes the insertion transaction to the ledger in less than 260 milliseconds. We observe data insertion in MedBlockSync's blockchain takes between 1.14 to 1.26 s, with a mean of 1.16 s and a standard deviation of 0.03 s. This highlights low variance and consistent performance of MedBlockSync blockchain

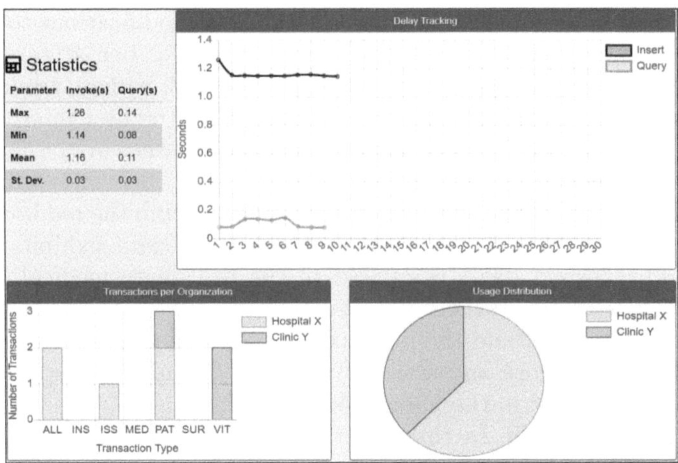

(a) Analysis of transactions for auditor users

```
{                                          {
    "bpd": "70",                               "bpd": "77",
    "bps": "96",                               "bps": "90",
    "head_circ": "23",                         "head_circ": "22",
    "height": "71",                            "height": "69",
    "note" : "",                               "note": "",
    "org": "Clinic Y",                         "org": "Hospital X",
    "oxygen_saturation": "96",                 "oxygen_saturation": "95",
    "pid": "1",                                "pid": "2",
    "pulse": "73",                             "pulse": "81",
    "respiration": "10",                       "respiration": "10",
    "temp_method": "Axillary",                 "temp_method": "Axillary",
    "temperature": "97.5",                     "temperature": "96",
    "waist_circ": "36",                        "waist_circ": "34",
    "weight": "208"                            "weight": "198"
},                                         }
```

(b) Medical records obtained from the query
method

Fig. 6. Analysis of transactions for auditor users. Medical records obtained from the query method.

- *Time efficiency for data query.* Data query in MedBlockSync blockchain is much faster than data insertion, which normally takes 80 to 140 milliseconds. In comparison to data insertion, data query is not bound to the generation of new blocks, which makes the processing of queries much faster. Figure 6a shows a maximum of 0.14 s, a minimum of 0.08 s, a mean of 0.11 s and a standard deviation of 0.03 s for blockchain data query. Similar to the task of data insertion, the small standard deviation of data query indicates data query times are consistent.

The left bottom panel in Fig. 6a demonstrates the amount of transactions produced by each organization. The right bottom panel presents the use of blockchain storage (transaction volume) with respect to other participating institutions. In this Figure, it shows that Hospital X produces more transactions than Clinic Y.

Figure 6b illustrates a sample response from a data query to MedBlockSync. In this experiment, the Fabric blockchain is queried by an auditor for data containing the keyword "penicillin." The medical contract processes the query and returns matching transactions from all participating institutions, namely Hospital X and Clinic Y. Auditors receive anonymized biometric data of patients from all participating institutions, ensuring patient privacy by excluding personal information such as patient names and demographics. This approach allows auditors to analyze patient biometrics without compromising privacy, thereby safeguarding patient data when shared for medical research purposes. Auditors may calculate the number of patients per organization to meet their demands, but the patients are concealed. MedBlockSync therefore can protect patient's privacy when sharing medical research data with different stakeholders.

Evaluation for Function C. This experiment showcases how healthcare workers operate MedBlockSync's Off-Chain module to regulate and manage IoMT devices within a healthcare organization, using Hospital X as an example. This functionality allows healthcare workers to accept or reject patient data submitted by IoMT devices, ensuring control and oversight over the data flow within the organization. Figure 7 illustrates the distinct behaviors of two registered IoMT devices, identified by unique IDs *12b6351316* and *1211279f03*. These IDs are generated based on the security functions introduced in 4.2. Each approved device includes its own MAC address, the date it requested to join the MedBlockSync network, the date it joined the network, its location, and the organization it belongs to. Similarly, every rejected smart device includes its MAC address, the date it requested to join the MedBlockSync network, and the organization it belongs to. If malicious activity has been detected from a registered IoMT device, as presented in Fig. 7, the healthcare providers (users) would remove the suspicious/abnormal IoMT device from the list of approved smart devices. Therefore the rejected IoMT device (i.e., 1211279f03) cannot be connected to the MedBlockSync's network anymore to protect the security and resiliency of the MedBlockSync network.

Should a registered IoT device exhibits suspicious or malicious behavior, healthcare providers have the authority to revoke its approval, as illustrated in Fig. 7. As a result, the rejected device (e.g., 1211279f03) is denied access to the MedBlockSync network, asserting security and resilience in the healthcare information system.

Approved

MQTT ID	Address	Request Date	Join Date	Location	Organization	
12b635f316	54:52:46:78:78:9a	1642438112	1642439085	icu1.hospitalX	Hospital X	Remove

Rejected

MQTT ID	Address	Request Date	Organization	
1211279f03	59:52:a5:78:95:5c	1642439421	Hospital X	Remove

Fig. 7. MedBlockSync IoMT regulation.

6 Conclusion

The rise of telehealth technologies has revolutionized remote healthcare delivery and patient monitoring. This study presents a multi-institutional framework integrated with an IoMT-enabled remote monitoring system, designed to enhance patient safety by safeguarding medical records from cyber threats in a collaborative healthcare environment. MedBlockSync offers a groundbreaking methodology for enhancing the security of healthcare information systems while fostering greater transparency among stakeholders. By enabling the secure storage and seamless exchange of medical records across various entities, including research institutions, the framework ensures data integrity and accessibility. Experimental evaluations affirm MedBlockSync's robustness in leveraging blockchain technology to uphold data security, facilitate granular data sharing, and dynamically regulate IoMT devices. Moreover, its adaptable architecture allows for seamless interoperability with any EMR system, streamlining communication between electronic medical records, blockchain networks, and IoMT infrastructures.

Limitations and Future Work. Although MedBlockSync effectively facilitates the sharing of healthcare records, additional privacy safeguards are required to ensure compliance with diverse federal regulations across different jurisdictions. A more in-depth evaluation of privacy laws is essential to devise robust strategies for protecting medical data. Furthermore, an extensive investigation into MedBlockSync's scalability is necessary, particularly regarding transaction latency and throughput performance, given its reliance on blockchain technology. Equally important is the implementation of proactive detection mechanisms to identify compromised IoMT systems before they engage in data exchange, as maliciously altered patient records, once recorded on the blockchain, become immutable.

Acknowledgment. This research is sponsored by the National Science Foundation under Grant No. 1812599, and SALSI Clusters in Research Excellence (2018–2019). Any opinions, findings, and conclusions or recommendations expressed in this material are those of the authors and do not necessarily reflect the views of the National Science Foundation.

References

1. MySignals platform for e-health application development. http://www.my-signals.com/. Accessed Sep 2020
2. OpenEMR: Fully open-source electronic medical records. https://www.open-emr.org/. Accessed Sep 2021
3. Health insurance portability and accountability act of 1996 (HIPAA) (1996). https://www.cdc.gov/phlp/publications/topic/hipaa.html. Accessed Jan 2024
4. Common vulnerabilities and exploits for openemr application (2012). https://www.cvedetails.com/product/23156/Open-emr-Openemr.html?vendor_id=12269. Accessed Jan 2024

5. Breach portal: Notice to the secretary of HHS breach of unsecured protected health information (2021). https://ocrportal.hhs.gov/ocr/breach/breach_report. jsf. Accessed Dec 2023

6. Hyperledger fabric: a blockchain platform for the enterprise (2021). https:// hyperledger-fabric.readthedocs.io/en/release-2.2/. Accessed Jan 2024

7. Antwi, M., Adnane, A., Ahmad, F., Hussain, R., ur Rehman, M.H., Kerrache, C.A.: The case of hyperledger fabric as a blockchain solution for healthcare applications. Blockchain: Res. Appl. **2**(1), 100012 (2021)

8. Banu, E.A., Rajamani, V.: Design of online vitals monitor by integrating big data and IoT. Comput. Syst. Sci. Eng. **44**(3) (2023)

9. Bautista, J.R., et al.: MediLinker: a blockchain-based decentralized health information management platform for patient-centric healthcare. Front. Big Data **6**, 1146023 (2023)

10. Benchoufi, M., Ravaud, P.: Blockchain technology for improving clinical research quality. Trials **18**(1), 1–5 (2017)

11. Cachin, C., et al.: Architecture of the hyperledger blockchain fabric. In: Workshop on Distributed Cryptocurrencies and Consensus Ledgers, vol. 310 (2016)

12. Castillo, J., Barba, K., Chen, Q.: ChainSCAN: a blockchain-based supply chain alerting framework for food safety. In: International Conference on Science of Cyber Security, pp. 3–20. Springer (2022). https://doi.org/10.1007/978-3-031-17551-0_1

13. Castillo, J., Chen, Q.: MediLink: a secure blockchain framework for multi-institutional healthcare. In: Proceedings of the 2024 Workshop on Cybersecurity in Healthcare, pp. 61–68 (2023)

14. Castillo, J., Rieger, P., Fereidooni, H., Chen, Q., Sadeghi, A.: Fledge: ledger-based federated learning resilient to inference and backdoor attacks. arXiv preprint arXiv:2310.02113 (2023)

15. Chen, H.S., Jarrell, J.T., Carpenter, K.A., Cohen, D.S., Huang, X.: Blockchain in healthcare: a patient-centered model. Biomed. J. Sci. Tech. Res. **20**(3), 15017 (2019)

16. Dameff, C., et al.: Ransomware attack associated with disruptions at adjacent emergency departments in the us. JAMA Netw. Open **6**(5), e2312270–e2312270 (2023)

17. Dilawar, N., Rizwan, M., Ahmad, F., Akram, S.: Blockchain: securing internet of medical things (IOMT). Int. J. Adv. Comput. Sci. Appl. **10**(1) (2019)

18. Du, M., Chen, Q., Chen, J., Ma, X.: An optimized consortium blockchain for medical information sharing. IEEE Trans. Eng. Manage. **68**(6), 1677–1689 (2020)

19. Dubovitskaya, A., Xu, Z., Ryu, S., Schumacher, M., Wang, F.: Secure and trustable electronic medical records sharing using blockchain. In: AMIA Annual Symposium Proceedings, vol. 2017, p. 650. American Medical Informatics Association (2017)

20. Dutta, A.: Real-world applications of blockchain technologies (2021). https://www. analyticsinsight.net/real-world-applications-of-blockchain-technologies/. Accessed Jan 2024

21. Fan, H., et al.: Privacy preserving ultra-short-term wind power prediction based on secure multi party computation. arXiv preprint arXiv:2301.13513 (2023)

22. Fan, K., Wang, S., Ren, Y., Li, H., Yang, Y.: MedBlock: efficient and secure medical data sharing via blockchain. J. Med. Syst. **42**(8), 136 (2018)

23. Fatima, N., Agarwal, P., Sohail, S.S.: Security and privacy issues of blockchain technology in health care—a review. In: ICT Analysis and Applications, pp. 193–201 (2022)

24. da Fonseca Ribeiro, M.I., Vasconcelos, A.: MedBlock: using blockchain in health healthcare application based on blockchain and smart contracts. In: ICEIS (1), pp. 156–164 (2020)
25. Giordanengo, A.: Possible usages of smart contracts (blockchain) in healthcare and why no one is using them. In: MEDINFO 2019: Health and Wellbeing e-Networks for All, pp. 596–600. IOS Press (2019)
26. Gordon, W., Landman, A.: Secure, decentralized, interoperable medication reconciliation using the blockchain. NIST/ONC (2016)
27. Gunawan, R., Andang, A., Ridwan, M.: Performance comparison for hearth rate signal detection for different location in fingertip and wrist using sensor max30102. J. Biomimetics Biomater. Biomed. Eng. **59**, 131–143 (2023)
28. Henry, J., Pylypchuk, Y., Searcy, T., Patel, V.: Adoption of electronic health record systems among us non-federal acute care hospitals: 2008–2015. ONC data brief **35**, 1–9 (2016)
29. Jha, A.K., et al.: Use of electronic health records in us hospitals. N. Engl. J. Med. **360**(16), 1628–1638 (2009)
30. Jiang, S., Cao, J., Wu, H., Yang, Y., Ma, M., He, J.: BLOCHIE: a blockchain-based platform for healthcare information exchange. In: 2018 IEEE International Conference on Smart Computing (Smartcomp), pp. 49–56. IEEE (2018)
31. Khezr, S., Moniruzzaman, M., Yassine, A., Benlamri, R.: Blockchain technology in healthcare: a comprehensive review and directions for future research. Appl. Sci. **9**(9), 1736 (2019)
32. Krawiec, R., White, M.: Blockchain: Opportunities for health care. Tech. rep, Deloitte (2023)
33. Li, H., Zhu, L., Shen, M., Gao, F., Tao, X., Liu, S.: Blockchain-based data preservation system for medical data. J. Med. Syst. **42**, 1–13 (2018)
34. Liang, X., Zhao, J., Shetty, S., Liu, J., Li, D.: Integrating blockchain for data sharing and collaboration in mobile healthcare applications. In: 2017 IEEE 28th Annual International Symposium on Personal, Indoor, and Mobile Radio Communications (PIMRC), pp. 1–5. IEEE (2017)
35. Ma, M., Skubic, M., Ai, K., Hubbard, J.: Angel-echo: a personalized health care application. In: 2017 IEEE/ACM International Conference on Connected Health: Applications, Systems and Engineering Technologies (CHASE), pp. 258–259. IEEE (2017)
36. Mace, S.: Report: healthcare most targeted industry for cyber-crime in 2020 (2021). https://www.healthleadersmedia.com/technology/report-healthcare-most-targeted-industry-cyber-crime-2020. Accessed Jan 2024
37. Menachemi, N., Collum, T.H.: Benefits and drawbacks of electronic health record systems. In: Risk Management and Healthcare Policy, pp. 47–55 (2011)
38. Mettler, M.: Blockchain technology in healthcare: the revolution starts here. In: 2016 IEEE 18th International Conference on E-Health Networking, Applications and Services (Healthcom), pp. 1–3. IEEE (2016)
39. Mitchell, H.: Cyberattack on Alabama hospital linked to 1st alleged ransomware death (2019). https://www.beckershospitalreview.com/cybersecurity/cyberattack-on-alabama-hospital-linked-to-1st-alleged-ransomware-death.html. Accessed Dec 2023
40. Omar, I.A., Jayaraman, R., Salah, K., Simsekler, M.C.E., Yaqoob, I., Ellahham, S.: Ensuring protocol compliance and data transparency in clinical trials using blockchain smart contracts. BMC Med. Res. Methodol. **20**, 1–17 (2020)

41. Paganelli, A.I., et al.: A conceptual IoT-based early-warning architecture for remote monitoring of Covid-19 patients in wards and at home. Internet Things **18**, 100399 (2022)
42. Poulsen, K., McMillan, R., Evans, M.: A hospital hit by hackers, a baby in distress: the case of the first alleged ransomware death (2021). https://www.wsj.com/articles/ransomware-hackers-hospital-first-alleged-death-11633008116?mod=hp_lead_pos10. Accessed Dec 2023
43. Ray, P.P., Chowhan, B., Kumar, N., Almogren, A.: BIOTHR: electronic health record servicing scheme in IoT-blockchain ecosystem. IEEE Internet Things J. **8**(13), 10857–10872 (2021)
44. Reddy, C.K., Aggarwal, C.C.: Healthcare Data Analytics. CRC Press (2015)
45. Rejeb, A., et al.: The internet of things (IoT) in healthcare: taking stock and moving forward. Internet Things, 100721 (2023)
46. Shae, Z., Tsai, J.J.: On the design of a blockchain platform for clinical trial and precision medicine. In: 2017 IEEE 37th International Conference on Distributed Computing Systems (ICDCS), pp. 1972–1980. IEEE (2017)
47. Sharma, A., Kumar, R.: An optimal routing scheme for critical healthcare HTH services—an IoT perspective. In: 2017 Fourth International Conference on Image Information Processing (ICIIP), pp. 1–5. IEEE (2017)
48. Song, Z., Li, S., Hou, B., Cheng, Z., Xue, Y., Chen, B.: High-sensitivity paper-based capacitive humidity sensors for respiratory monitoring. IEEE Sens. J. **23**(3), 2291–2302 (2022)
49. Tanwar, S., Parekh, K., Evans, R.: Blockchain-based electronic healthcare record system for healthcare 4.0 applications. J. Inf. Secur. Appl. **50**, 102407 (2020)
50. Taralunga, D.D., Florea, B.C.: A blockchain-enabled framework for mhealth systems. Sensors **21**(8), 2828 (2021)
51. Taylor, P.J., Dargahi, T., Dehghantanha, A., Parizi, R.M., Choo, K.K.R.: A systematic literature review of blockchain cyber security. Digit. Commun. Netw. **6**(2), 147–156 (2020)
52. Tripathi, G., Ahad, M.A., Paiva, S.: S2HS-a blockchain based approach for smart healthcare system. In: Healthcare, vol. 8, p. 100391. Elsevier (2020)
53. Wang, S., Zhang, Y., Zhang, Y.: A blockchain-based framework for data sharing with fine-grained access control in decentralized storage systems. Ieee Access **6**, 38437–38450 (2018)
54. Xia, Q., Sifah, E.B., Asamoah, K.O., Gao, J., Du, X., Guizani, M.: MedShare: trust-less medical data sharing among cloud service providers via blockchain. IEEE Access **5**, 14757–14767 (2017)
55. Zakari, N., et al.: Blockchain technology in the pharmaceutical industry: a systematic review. PeerJ Comput. Sci. **8**, e840 (2022)

Security and Privacy Framework for Cloud-Based Remote Patient Monitoring and In-place Sensor-Based Care

Sai Shreya Nuguri[1]([envelope]) [iD], Subrahmanya Chandra Bhamidipati[1] [iD], Anirudh Kambhampati[1] [iD], Karan Karthik[1] [iD], Aneesh Calyam[2] [iD], Mahesh Karthik Duvvuri[3] [iD], Mauro Lemus Alarcon[1] [iD], and Prasad Calyam[1] [iD]

[1] University of Missouri-Columbia, Columbia, MO, USA
`{s.nuguri,sb5q6,akwg7,fkwmq,lemusm,calyamp}@missouri.edu`
[2] Rock Bridge High School, Columbia, MO, USA
[3] Carmel High School, Carmel, IN, USA

Abstract. The integration of Internet of Things (IoT) sensors with edge-cloud computing for remote patient monitoring (RPM) offers transformative potential for personalized healthcare. However, this integration introduces critical challenges related to data security, patient privacy, and system scalability. In this paper, we present *Zeus*, a privacy-preserving and secure IoT-based healthcare data management framework for cloud-based remote patient monitoring and in-place sensor-based care. Using a real-world use case of a BodiGuide anklet – a wearable edema monitor for heart failure management, we present a reference edge-cloud architecture that supports secure data collection, transmission via edge gateways, cloud-based analytics and storage, and role-based visualization through an intuitive user interface. Zeus integrates layered security and privacy controls at each stage of the data lifecycle—from collection and transmission to visualization—through a comprehensive risk assessment based on privacy and security threat modeling. Our approach integrates privacy-preserving and security mechanisms such as pseudonymization, role-based access control and data validation to ensure ongoing compliance with healthcare standards. We empirically validate Zeus features during security analysis and privacy analysis featuring structured metrics and quantified risk heatmaps considering attack simulations involving Attempt Likelihood, and Likelihood of Successful Attack combined with Attack Impact. Finally, we perform scalability evaluations using a cloud-based testbed to demonstrate Zeus's ability to handle increasing sensor data volumes and concurrent user loads in RPM environments.

Keywords: IoT-based Healthcare · Remote Patient Monitoring · Data Security and Privacy · Threat Modeling · Cloud Architecture · Risk Assessment

© The Author(s), under exclusive license to Springer Nature Switzerland AG 2026
W. Yurcik (Ed.): HealthSec 2024, CCIS 2716, pp. 188–213, 2026.
https://doi.org/10.1007/978-3-032-13800-2_9

1   Introduction

The use of IoT-based sensor data within cloud platforms in healthcare offers unprecedented opportunities to remotely monitor patient health and proactively manage patient outcomes related to major chronic diseases including heart failure (HF), hypertension, diabetes, and asthma [1]. Figure 1 presents a cloud-based data processing pipeline for IoT-based sensor data to enable diagnostics and treatment of remote patients, bringing a personalized healthcare approach. The data sources can include a diverse array of measurement devices such as blood pressure cuffs, heart implants, hand held spirometers, body patches, and wearables [2]. Following data collection, cloud-based services can facilitate data storage, and analysis/visualization, as well as generation of health alerts to guide proactive interventions e.g., therapy or medication.

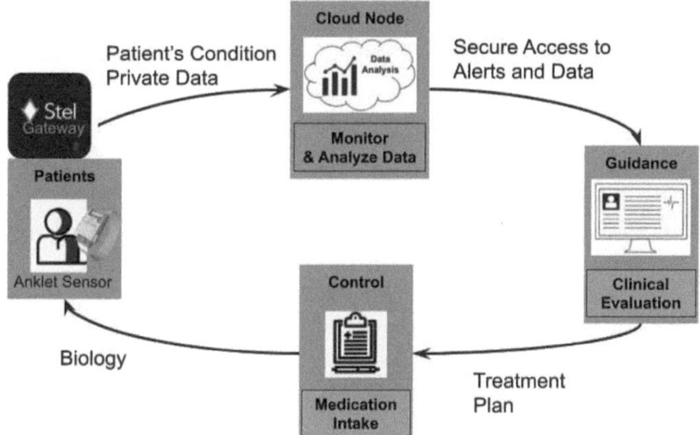

Fig. 1. Overview of the data pipeline for remote patient monitoring involving IoT-based devices for body sensing aimed towards personalized healthcare.

Integration of IoT sensor data and cloud platforms in healthcare applications poses significant challenges [3], including the magnitude and diversity of IoT sensors (the IoT sensor market size exceeded USD 26.14 billion in 2023 and is projected to reach approximately USD 312.22 billion by 2033 [4]), and the heightened sophistication of cyber attacks. These challenges emphasize the need for suitable cloud-based architectures in remote patient monitoring, integrating robust security mechanisms across the entire data pipeline. This encompasses ensuring data integrity, availability, and patient privacy while complying with evolving regulations such as the Health Insurance Portability and Accountability Act (HIPAA) [5], GDPR, and NIST SP 800-188. Scalability and Usability are critical design requirements, especially given the need to serve a growing and diverse patient population through secure and privacy-preserving solutions.

Thus, the Security and Privacy of the data processing pipeline should be end-to-end, addressing relevant mechanisms at every stage to minimize residual risk [6].

Furthermore, rapid device innovation and the integration of diverse clinical data amplify the complexities in designing, implementing, and maintaining robust security/privacy measures. This underscores the challenges faced by healthcare organizations and remote patient monitoring providers [7]. Current approaches often overlook holistic requirements for privacy preservation, real-time threat detection, and secure visualization in IoT-based healthcare applications [8]. There is a pent-up need for next-generation security and privacy frameworks that safeguard healthcare data comprehensively while supporting usability, real-time performance and scalability demands, as well as regulatory compliance requirements.

In this paper, we address the above challenges in remote patient monitoring by developing an IoT-based healthcare data management framework viz., "Zeus" that addresses security and privacy-preserving issues and integrates a cloud-based application for in-place sensor-based care. Specifically, using an exemplar wearable BodiGuide Edema Monitor healthcare use case, we detail a reference architecture and design principles for an open edge-cloud remote patient monitoring that is usable and scalable, while also is compliant with healthcare standards. The BodiGuide Edema Monitor is a proprietary device developed by BodiGuide [9], worn on the ankle to provide peripheral edema monitoring for use in heart failure management. Through an implementation of the reference architecture, we show how our approach can facilitate data transfer through a cellular gateway provided by Stel [10], and leverage cloud-based data analysis and storage on AWS [11], and visualization via a role-based UI portal accessible to patients, caregivers, and physicians.

The Zeus architecture incorporates privacy-preserving techniques such as pseudonymization, query rate-limiting, encrypted data pipelines, role-based access control and data validation to protect sensitive health information throughout the data lifecycle involving collection, transmission, storage, access, and visualization steps. Central to our methodology is a risk assessment based on NIST SP 800-188 that relies on adaptation of the LINDDUN [12] privacy threat modeling and STRIDE [13] security threat modeling methodologies, which enable continuous privacy and security evaluation across the lifecycle steps. Thereby, Zeus is capable to dynamically identify, categorize, and mitigate potential vulnerabilities based on likelihood and impact scores. To validate our Zeus framework, we implement a cloud-based testbed that features simulations of real-world usage scenarios with IoT-based sensor data streams from multiple concurrent users and realistic threat scenarios. Our risk assessment results through security analysis and privacy analysis provide risk heatmaps and threat mitigation mappings to illustrate Zeus's effectiveness in addressing emerging threats in real-time healthcare environments. Our stress-test experiment results demonstrate how our Zeus implementation maintains application responsiveness under increasing data volumes and concurrent user loads in RPM environments.

The remainder of this paper is organized as follows: Sect. 2 presents related work. Section 3 provides a background on our IoT-based healthcare data processing application. Section 4 details the design principles and implementation of the Zeus framework components. Section 5 features the results from performance evaluation experiments focusing on security, privacy and scalability analysis. Section 6 concludes the paper.

2   Related Work

The integration of IoT in healthcare systems has the potential to revolutionize patient care by facilitating closed-loop data management for remote patient monitoring, improving outcomes and reducing errors [14]. However, it also presents challenges in data security and privacy. Hossain et al. [15] focused on security by employing techniques like ECG signal watermarking and user identification codes to customize data protection. By embedding a watermark, their system ensured that the data remained untampered and could be traced back to the correct user. The key advantage of this method is the continuous verification it provides, even during data transmission or storage across various platforms. However, embedding user identification codes directly within the data raises privacy concerns, as it associates sensitive health information with a specific individual, potentially exposing it to unauthorized access.

In contrast, our Zeus framework prioritizes data privacy by utilizing a NIST-aligned pseudonymization process. This approach combines de-identification at the data collection stage with re-identification by authorized users during the data visualization stage, ensuring that privacy standards are upheld consistently throughout the entire data pipeline. Similarly, in [16], authors emphasize security at every stage of the data pipeline and review security solutions (e.g., cryptographic methods and blockchain) for IoT in medical applications to protect sensitive health data. This work aligns with our Zeus framework, which also prioritizes security at every stage of the data pipeline and features a cloud-based architecture to integrate IoT sensors and privacy-preserving gateway hubs in a secure, privacy-preserving, and scalable manner.

Taking data security to the next level, Larson et al. [17] emphasize the need for comprehensive security measures across the entire data lifecycle, from collection to storage and processing. Building on this, Vasserman et al. [18] highlighted foundational security principles for medical application platforms, stressing the importance of maintaining security across all stages of the medical data lifecycle, from collection to storage. Similarly, Anderson [19] further contributed by proposing a security policy model for clinical information systems, which has laid the groundwork for understanding security requirements in healthcare environments. Additionally, Burleson et al. [20] addressed the specific challenges of securing implantable devices. These foundational works influenced the design of the Zeus framework, which integrates these security and privacy considerations to deliver an end-to-end solution that effectively supports remote patient monitoring and care.

Emerging technologies have also been explored to enhance IoT security. Ayoade et al. [21] proposed a blockchain-based decentralized data management system to mitigate risks of single points of failure. Khan et al. [22] introduced a machine learning-based anomaly detection system for real-time monitoring, enhancing patient safety. Giechaskiel et al. [23] and Gazzari et al. [24] explored attacks on IoT devices, underscoring the importance of robust security measures required when using wearable devices. These works have motivated our approach to address the threats and risk assessment aspects related to the integration of the BodiGuide edema monitor and the Stel Vitals hub within an end-to-end solution realized through our Zeus framework. In contrast, our approach in Zeus is novel because we leverage cloud services for secure data movement from the edge and scalable storage to enable: (a) effective analysis of collected patient data in a centralized manner, and (b) pave the way for integrating machine learning algorithms to automate patient monitoring based on heterogeneous data and multiple parameters.

In the context of advancing secure and scalable healthcare IoT systems, it is crucial to examine frameworks that emphasize standards related to conformance testing and robust data handling practices. Yang et al. [25] propose a lightweight and traceable secure mobile health system, tackling the challenges of protecting electronic health records (EHR) through encryption, fine-grained access control, and traitor tracing. This system's dual focus on efficiency and security in mobile health environments aligns well with our Zeus, which similarly prioritizes data privacy and security, scalable data management across a healthcare data pipeline. Additionally, Moosavi et al. [26] deliver a comprehensive analysis of end-to-end security schemes in healthcare IoT, introducing a fog layer to optimize security processing. The focus on end-to-end security in Moosavi et al.'s work is similar to Zeus's focus to safeguard sensitive healthcare data throughout the entire data lifecycle, ensuring secure and efficient data transmission and processing to meet remote patient monitoring demands.

3   IoT-Based Healthcare Application Background

The adoption of IoT technology in healthcare systems introduces a paradigm shift from facility-centered care to patient-centered care. Through the interconnection of devices and sensors that enable real-time continuous monitoring and automated analysis, healthcare providers gain valuable insights into a patient's status. These insights are used to optimize treatment strategies, particularly for managing chronic conditions such as heart failure, diabetes, hypertension, and asthma. For instance, the ability to continuously monitor patients with advanced heart failure at home is crucial for reducing unnecessary hospitalizations and reduce the burden on healthcare facilities for timely interventions. Such remote monitoring empowers patients to manage their conditions more effectively. However, the security and privacy of these interconnected systems remain a significant challenge, especially as the adoption of healthcare IoT grows.

With new technologies constantly being integrated into healthcare systems, the need to implement robust security and privacy measures is more critical than ever. These measures are vital to address the evolving threat landscape and safeguard the sensitive data collected by medical devices, and ensure compliance with healthcare standards. Patient information is not only essential to protect for legal and ethical reasons but is also a cornerstone of patient trust. Unauthorized access to such data can result in significant harm, discrimination, and loss of confidence in healthcare systems, making privacy preservation an absolute priority in the digital age.

The BodiGuide Edema Monitor continuously measures ankle circumference and transmits the data to a cloud-based repository via a Stel cellular gateway, where it is analyzed and feedback is provided to physicians, caregivers, and patients. Ankle circumference is known to be an effective, reliable, and accurate measure of peripheral edema [28]. Continuous monitoring generates a daily edema pattern (as shown in Fig. 2 (a)), which is analyzed to quantify interstitial fluid volume. By tracking fluid retention trends, the device facilitates early interventions, potentially preventing hospital admissions and enabling timely medical responses before a patient's condition worsens. Peripheral edema is a key biomarker in managing heart failure. The wearable edema monitor developed by BodiGuide [29] extends the physician's clinical evaluation of peripheral edema to the home, enhancing self-care and optimizing treatment, thereby reducing hospitalizations and improving the quality of life for heart failure patients.

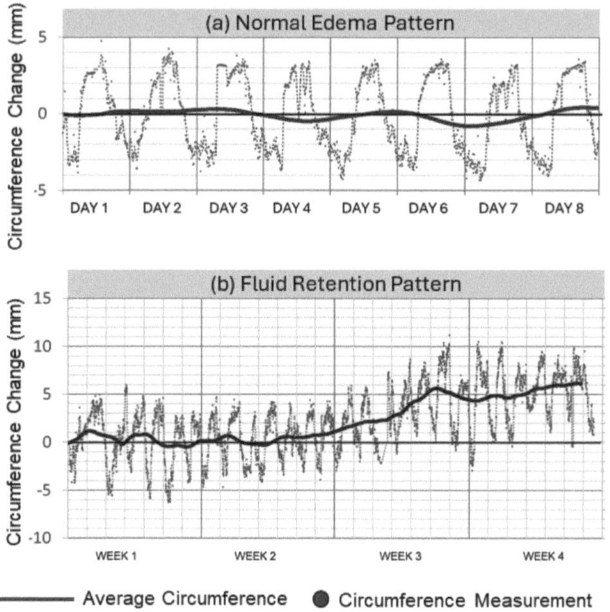

Fig. 2. BodiGuide Edema Monitor tracks and monitors a patient's daily swelling pattern against their normal baseline or "dry" state. The system characterizes variations from normal and provides notifications or alerts corresponding to the type of variation.

As more healthcare providers rely on IoT systems, the increase in connected devices exposes the healthcare infrastructure to new cyber threats. These threats range from unauthorized data access to more targeted attacks that disrupt the functioning of medical devices or compromise the integrity of the data they collect. Therefore, ensuring the security of medical IoT devices and their data pipelines is paramount. A dynamic security framework capable of adapting to emerging threats, incorporating strong encryption, access controls, and real-time anomaly detection is crucial to preventing unauthorized access and data breaches [30,31]. These measures help mitigate risks while ensuring that patient data remains secure across the entire ecosystem.

While addressing security requirements, it is also important for the IoT integration in cloud platforms to be designed to have scalability to handle a large number of concurrent user data streams. Traditional cloud-based architectures often introduce latency and privacy concerns when transmitting high-frequency biometric data from IoT devices. By integrating an edge-computing layer, preliminary data analysis can be performed on local gateway devices before securely transmitting critical insights to the cloud. This approach enhances real-time responsiveness, minimizes bandwidth consumption, and allows faster decision-making for time-sensitive medical conditions such as heart failure [32]. Additionally, edge-cloud interactions reduce the volume of personally identifiable information transmitted over the network, improving compliance with HIPAA and GDPR privacy regulations.

4 Zeus Design Principles

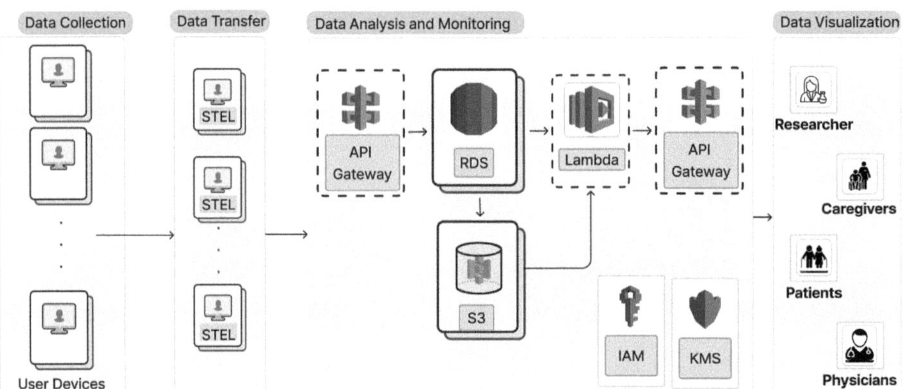

Fig. 3. Zeus Edge-Cloud Architecture integrating BodiGuide Anklet, Stel Gateway and cloud services on AWS.

The Zeus framework architecture, as shown in Fig. 3, is designed to process and analyze healthcare data securely and efficiently. The architecture consists of three primary layers and series of web service components as shown in Table 1. The components enable an end- to-end secure and scalable remote monitoring application through collection of patient data via the BodiGuide Edema Monitor, transfer of the data through edge gateway(s) to a cloud-based repository, processing for data analytics/visualization through a web-portal user-interface. The design foundation of the Zeus framework is established on four fundamental principles: Security, Privacy, Scalability, and Usability. In the following subsections, we expand our description of these guiding pillars and their relevance within the Zeus framework.

Table 1. Edge-Cloud web services in the Zeus framework.

Layer	AWS Component	Description
Edge: Data Collection	BodiGuide Anklet	Captures biometric data and transmits it via Bluetooth connection
	STEL Gateway	Acts as an entry point for securely routing data to AWS cloud services
Cloud: AWS Services	AWS API Gateway	Hosts API endpoints, enabling scalable processing
	AWS Lambda	Data Validation of incoming data from users
	AWS RDS	Stores structured patient data in a managed relational database
	AWS S3	Long-term secure and scalable storage
	AWS IAM	Controls authentication and access policies for secure data handling
	AWS KMS	Encrypts sensitive healthcare data for compliance and security
Visualization: UI	AWS EC2	Hosts the visualization dashboard for researchers, caregivers, and physicians to analyze data insights

4.1 Privacy

Privacy is a fundamental aspect of healthcare data management and a critical factor in remote patient monitoring due to the extensive and often continuous nature of data collection. In the Zeus framework, privacy involves the protection of patient information across the entire data lifecycle, ensuring that personal health data remains confidential, unlinkable to unauthorized parties, and only accessible to designated users for legitimate medical and operational purposes. Privacy within Zeus encompasses both the protection of identifiable information (such as device-linked user profiles) and the anonymization of sensitive health metrics (such as edema data). Privacy measures compliant with NIST SP 800-188 [33] prevent unauthorized linking, re-identification, or disclosure of patient data while ensuring compliance with HIPAA [5] regulatory standards. We employ advanced techniques in Zeus such as decentralized pseudonymization [17], multi-layered encryption, and zero-knowledge storage protocols, aligning with industry standards such as NIST SP 800-188 [33]. Pseudonymization involves processing data so it cannot be attributed to an individual without additional information. Identifiable and de-identified data are stored in separate databases, allowing controlled re-identification by authorized roles.

The Zeus system implementation employs a two-step preprocessing approach: first, the BodiGuide anklet captures and preprocesses data within the device, and second, the Stel Gateway processes and anonymizes the data before transmission to cloud services. This decentralized approach minimizes exposure to potential data breaches by ensuring only processed, non-identifiable information is transmitted. Zeus uses a unique Hub ID and a two-step linking process to associate devices with users securely, keeping user-identifiable information and de-identified health data in separate AWS RDS databases. Access to this data is controlled through AWS IAM features and Lambda functions, ensuring only authorized users can view both identifiable and de-identified information simultaneously.

To proactively address privacy risks, the Zeus framework applies the LIND-DUN privacy threat modeling methodology [26] to systematically identify, assess, and mitigate privacy threats at each data lifecycle stage. This approach enables Zeus to address threats such as Linkability, Identifiability, Non-repudiation, Detectability, Disclosure of Information, Unawareness, and Non-compliance by mapping these risk factors to appropriate privacy-preserving controls as defined in NIST SP 800-188. A LINDDUN risk assessment, as seen in Table 2, was conducted to categorize threats based on their likelihood and impact, identifying major risks through metadata correlation. To mitigate these threats, Zeus employs strict pseudonymization, multi-layer encryption, and role-based access control mechanisms to restrict sensitive data exposure. Additionally, data preprocessing and pseudonymization at the edge minimize linkability, while encrypted identifiers prevent unauthorized re-identification. Transparency is ensured through detailed consent mechanisms, enabling patients to manage their data-sharing preferences and understand the scope of data collection and use.

4.2 Security

The Zeus framework adopts a component-wise security evaluation approach, emphasizing the importance of securing the entire system rather than just individual devices [19]. This approach ensures that every component, from the BodiGuide Edema Monitor to the cloud-based repository on AWS, is secure and compliant with regulatory requirements. Security properties such as integrity, authenticity, and authorization are integral to the system, ensuring that data is protected at all stages of transmission, analysis, and storage [18].

We employ a comprehensive security evaluation to address concerns and attacks on wearable devices highlighted by Gazzari et al. in [24] at every stage of the data pipeline. To secure network segments, Zeus implements private subnets within AWS Virtual Private Cloud (VPC), restricting access to internal resources. Role-based Access Control (RBAC) ensures that only authorized users can perform specific actions, reducing the risk of unauthorized access. Token authentication between services provides an additional layer of security, verifying service-to-service communications and preventing unauthorized API calls. A 2-step approval process is used for device registration, ensuring that only verified devices can connect to the system. Additionally, AWS Key Management Service (KMS) encrypts sensitive data, and AWS Identity and Access Management (IAM) enforces fine-grained permissions for authenticated users. To enhance security, the application administrator is required to associate every new user and device, such as the Stel Gateway hub or BodiGuide Edema Monitor, to ensure that only suitably authenticated and authorized users can access and send data through the pipeline. This step strengthens the IAM process, preventing unauthorized access and securing data at the point of collection.

Table 2. Privacy risk assessment using the LINDDUN privacy threat modeling.

Threat Category	Description	Mitigation Strategies
Linkability	Sensitive health data could be linked across sessions, devices, or users.	Apply strong pseudonymization techniques and enforce minimal data retention.
Identifiability	Patient identities may be inferred from metadata, timestamps, or device characteristics.	Encrypt metadata and limit exposed device information.
Non-repudiation	No clear accountability trail for data access or modifications.	Implement immutable audit logs and access tracking mechanisms.
Detectability	Potential adversaries may detect the presence of user activity even if exact data is hidden.	Use differential privacy and apply obfuscation techniques to activity data.
Disclosure of Information	Unauthorized disclosure of PHI due to weak access control measures	Enforce strict role-based access control and multi-layer encryption.
Unawareness	Users lack control or awareness over how their data is being collected and processed.	Provide real-time consent management and data visibility dashboards.
Non-Compliance	Failure to meet HIPAA, NIST SP 800-188, and GDPR privacy compliance requirements.	Conduct continuous privacy risk assessments and compliance audits.

We use the STRIDE methodology [34] for identifying and categorizing potential security threats within the Zeus framework. In this context, the NIST Pri-

Table 3. Security threats categorized by STRIDE methodology for various components in the remote patient monitoring system.

Threat Type	Components	Threat Description
Spoofing	Edema Monitor/STEL, Developer, User Data, Doctor	Attackers can send fake Edema Monitor data to STEL or AWS, use someone other than the patient to use the Edema Monitor device, impersonate a developer using stolen credentials, or steal a doctor's credentials or identity to access their account
Tampering	Developer, User Data	An attacker could use developer access privilege to modify data, destroy its credibility, modify data via injection attacks, or intercept and alter packets sent to AWS
Repudiation	Developer, User Data	An attacker could exploit a lack of logs/ records on the developer side and operate undetected, or deny modifying data in the database
Information Disclosure	Edema Monitor/STEL, Developer, User Data, Doctor	Attacker may sniff STEL/Edema Monitor packets, use their own STEL to receive Edema Monitor data, release developer credentials to the public, intercept data packets, perform database injection, use social engineering to obtain information from doctors
Denial of Service	Edema Monitor/STEL, Developer, User Data, Doctor	Attacker may physically disable STEL Gateway, employ a (D)DoS on the STEL gateway, perform a DDoS attack on the network, disrupt the application's ability to receive information, perform a DDoS on AWS or our instance, encrypt/delete database data, or physically harm the doctor, preventing service use
Elevation of Privilege	Developer, User Data, Doctor	An attacker could gain access through a developer's credential and reconfigure code to gain higher access, use social engineering or database injection to change privilege levels, or impersonate a doctor to access patient data

vacy Risk Assessment Methodology (PRAM) framework complements STRIDE by providing a structured approach to assess and prioritize the risks identified through STRIDE modeling. Specifically, PRAM guides us in evaluating the likelihood and impact of these threats in a broader context, allowing us to align our security measures with organizational and privacy considerations. Our systematic approach to security ensures a robust defense against various cyber threats. The STRIDE methodology categorizes potential risks into Spoofing, Tampering,

Repudiation, Information Disclosure, Denial of Service, and Elevation of Privilege. The security assessment in Table 3 outlines the security threats identified within Zeus and the corresponding mitigation strategies. By incorporating these security mechanisms, the Zeus framework ensures data confidentiality, integrity, and availability, addressing key security concerns while maintaining compliance with industry standards.

4.3 Usability

Usability plays a crucial role in the effectiveness and acceptance of remote patient monitoring systems. Employing an iterative design approach, we prioritize user requirements and usability throughout the development lifecycle, including frequent user feedback loops and usability testing sessions to refine the system continuously. In our Zeus design, we use role-based access management which ensures that only authorized users with the relevant roles (such as clinical staff, doctors, or caregivers) can access the system, maintaining data integrity and privacy. This also extends to controlling who can visualize or modify sensitive patient data, thereby safeguarding patient confidentiality. Additionally, the system is designed to alert relevant stakeholders about trending events in patient data, providing timely notifications that facilitate proactive care and treatment guidance. Reports on patient status and treatment progress can also be generated to support clinical decision-making.

The system requires minimal intervention from the patient to set up and operate the data sensors, and the UI is designed for ease of use and understanding, facilitating quick access to relevant patient data. The UI, as shown in a snippet for a Patient login in Fig. 4, is intuitively organized with clear visual hierarchies, making navigation straightforward for users of all technical backgrounds and incorporating assistive technologies to support users with disabilities, ensuring inclusivity.

By presenting complex data in a visually appealing and easy-to-understand format, users can quickly grasp trends, patterns, and abnormalities in the health metrics of interest, empowering them to take proactive steps towards better health management and treatment outcomes. Real-time reports and alert notifications of anomaly events are sent to physicians, patients, and designated caregivers, enabling timely interventions. These notifications are customizable, allowing healthcare providers to set specific thresholds and alerts tailored to individual patient considerations. Training materials, including tutorials and FAQs, are readily available to help users quickly become proficient in using the system. Moreover, user feedback mechanisms are also integrated to gather insights for iterative improvements, ensuring that the UI remains adaptive and responsive to evolving user needs. By emphasizing usability, the system not only improves user satisfaction and engagement but also increases adherence to monitoring protocols, thereby enhancing the overall effectiveness of patient care.

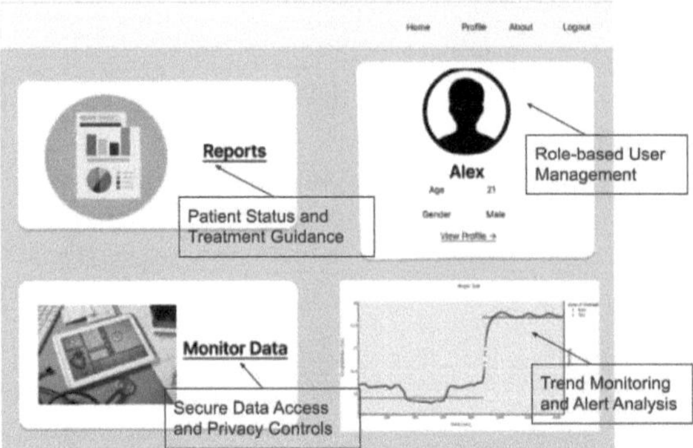

Fig. 4. UI portal displaying the dashboard for patient login; patient has immediate access to relevant reports, profile information, devices, and data collection trends/alerts.

4.4   Scalability

Scalability is an important consideration for the Zeus framework, as it needs to be designed to support high volume of devices, users, and data streams without compromising overall system performance. The scale of the system is dependent on the healthcare environments that range from small clinical practices to large-scale healthcare organizations. The cloud architecture adopted in Zeus as shown in Fig. 3 is inherently scalable, leveraging an edge-cloud model that balances data processing and storage between the edge and the cloud. The edge layer, consisting of devices such as the BodiGuide Anklet and Stel Gateway, performs initial data collection and pre-processing locally, allowing for quick and private data transmission to the cloud. This reduces the amount of raw data transmitted to the cloud, ensuring that only anonymized and processed information is sent for further analysis. By distributing the processing tasks across both the edge and the cloud, Zeus also provides real-time processing capabilities essential in remote patient monitoring.

On the cloud side, Zeus leverages AWS services [11] such as EC2, Lambda, RDS, and S3 to ensure scalability and elasticity. EC2 instances enable horizontal scaling for increased processing power, while Lambda supports event-driven processing for dynamic resource allocation. AWS RDS and S3 provide robust, flexible storage options for large volumes of healthcare data, ensuring high availability and efficient querying. The system employs AWS Auto Scaling to automatically adjust resources based on demand, optimizing performance during high-traffic periods without overspending on cloud resources. This combination of services and modular design allows Zeus to handle fluctuating loads while maintaining uninterrupted performance and cost-efficiency.

5   Performance Evaluation

In this section, we evaluate our Zeus solution across three dimensions: privacy, security, and scalability. First, the privacy evaluation ensures compliance with industry standards, such as the HIPAA Privacy Rule, for protecting sensitive data. Second, the security analysis ensures adherence to industry standards such as the HIPAA Security Rule. Finally, scalability testing examines the system's performance under increasing user load conditions, ensuring it can handle large volumes of data and user interactions without compromising reliability or responsiveness.

5.1   Privacy Analysis

Privacy analysis in Zeus is designed to validate the effectiveness of privacy mechanisms through empirical evaluation, ensuring that patient data remains secure against inference attacks, unauthorized access, and re-identification risks. We first establish the privacy attack goals using the LINDDUN privacy threat modeling methodology [12]. In the context of Zeus, LINDDUN is employed to assess various system components to determine the potential attack goals. These attack goals represent the objectives an adversary might pursue when trying to compromise privacy, such as re-identifying anonymized data, linking pseudonymized records, or disclosing sensitive patient information. Once these attack goals are established, we then calculate the likelihood of these threats occurring. The calculation of likelihood, following the identification of attack goals via LINDDUN, is based on several factors, including the complexity of each attack, the likelihood of an attacker attempting such an attack, and the effectiveness of the system's defenses against it. This is captured through the Attempt Likelihood metric, which is calculated by assessing the probability of different attack motives (e.g., insider threats, external attacks) and the associated severity of each potential attack. Each attack goal identified via LINDDUN is thus evaluated for its likelihood of occurrence based on historical trends, attacker motivations, and the strength of existing countermeasures in Zeus.

The impact and likelihood values were determined using a structured risk assessment methodology based on historical trends, adversary motivations, and technical feasibility. The methodology involves three primary components: Attempt Likelihood, Likelihood of Achieving the Goal, and Impact Score.

1. Attempt Likelihood: The attempt likelihood represents the probability that an attacker will attempt a particular attack. It is calculated using:

$$L_{\text{attempt}} = \sum_{i=1}^{n} P(M_i) \cdot W_i, \tag{1}$$

where:

- $P(M_i)$ represents the probability of each attack motive (e.g., ransomware, insider threat).

- W_i is the assigned weight representing the severity of potential damage for that motive.

This metric assesses the probability that an attacker will successfully accomplish their goal given the current defenses. The combined likelihood is computed as:

$$L_{\text{normalized}} = L_{\text{attempt}} \times L_{\text{success}}. \tag{2}$$

3. Impact Score: The impact score quantifies the severity of consequences if the attack is successful, using the following formula:

$$I = \frac{S_d + S_s + S_r}{3}, \tag{3}$$

where:

- S_d is the data sensitivity score.
- S_s is the system downtime severity score.
- S_r is the reputational damage score.

4. Final Risk Score: The final risk score is calculated as:

$$R_{\text{final}} = \frac{L_{\text{normalized}} \times I}{10}. \tag{4}$$

To quantify the risk of identified threats, Zeus conducted a structured impact and likelihood assessment based on past incident reports, system vulnerabilities, and industry benchmarks. The summary of threat likelihood and impact values is presented in Table 4.

Table 4. Mitigation measures for privacy-related risks.

Location	Attack	Mitigation Technique	Likelihood	Impact	Score
Notification System	Sensitive Data In Alerts	Use vague alerts; avoid sensitive terms	0.56	7.2	4.03
Data Analysis Pipeline	Re-identification from Analysis Outputs	Remove or transform quasi-identifiers	0.42	7	2.94
Notification System	Alert Frequency Traffic Monitoring	Use VPNs and inject dummy alerts	0.42	7.5	3.13
Data Analysis Pipeline	Inference Attacks on Anonymized Data	Aggregate data; obscure patterns	0.30	4.2	1.26
Notification System	Encryption Failures	Apply AES-256 encryption	0.42	7	2.94
Data Analysis Logs	Audit Log Tampering	Use hashed logs and access controls	0.42	6	2.35
Notification System	Pseudonymized Alert Linkability	Rotate pseudonyms per session	0.30	4.8	1.44

Table 5. Privacy Risk Evaluation in Zeus Framework.

Privacy Threat	Impact	Likelihood	Mitigation Strategy
Linkability	High	Medium	Pseudonymization, Data segregation
Identifiability	High	Medium	Controlled re-identification, Key rotation
Inference Attacks	High	High	Data obfuscation, Query rate-limiting
Unauthorized Access	High	Medium	Dynamic RBAC, Multi-factor authentication
Detectability	High	Medium	Privacy-preserving aggregation, Access monitoring
Disclosure of Information	High	High	End-to-end encryption, Access control policies
Unawareness	Medium	High	Privacy notifications, User data transparency
Non-compliance	High	Low	Periodic privacy audits, Compliance monitoring

Zeus's privacy risk distribution analysis categorizes threats into high, moderate, and low-risk segments. A heatmap visualization shown in Fig. 5 highlights the concentration of risks, with high-impact threats requiring immediate mitigation. Key findings include: (i) Sensitive Data in Alerts (High Impact, Moderate Likelihood): requires strict enforcement of anonymization and data minimization policies; (ii) Inference Attacks on Anonymized Data (Moderate Impact, Low Likelihood): managed through noise addition and differential privacy techniques; (iii) Data Packet Interception (High Impact, High Likelihood): addressed through robust encryption protocols and secure data transmission mechanisms.

To address these threats, Zeus implements the following mitigation strategies, detailed in Table 4: (i) Data Masking & Controlled Re-Identification: reduces identifiability risks while allowing authorized users to retrieve necessary patient records securely; (ii) Query Rate-Limiting & Differential Privacy: limits large-scale data aggregation attempts to prevent inference attacks; (iii) Behavior-Based Access Controls: implements continous monitoring that dynamically revokes access upon detecting unusual activity; (iv) Zero-Trust Storage Architecture: enforces strict separation of sensitive data and access logs to prevent misconfigurations leading to data exposure. By integrating these privacy-preserving techniques as summarized in Table 5, Zeus ensures privacy of sensitive patient data, mitigating threats while maintaining regulatory compliance.

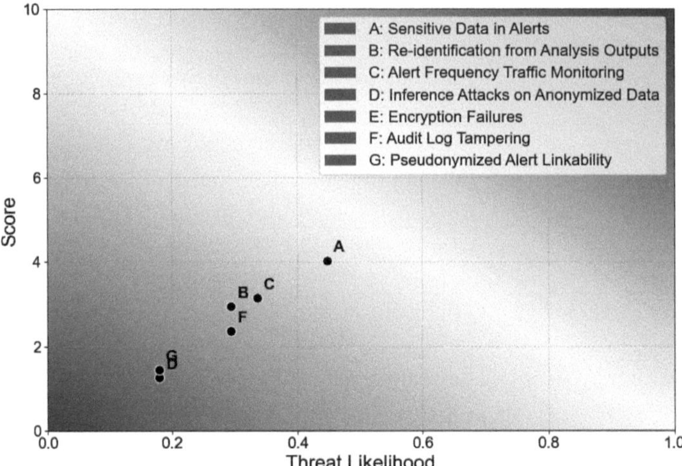

Fig. 5. Major threats in the Overall Privacy Risk Assessment represented as a Heat Map.

5.2 Security Analysis

Our security risk assessment employs the STRIDE threat modeling approach, implemented at each stage of the Zeus data pipeline. This methodology provides a detailed view of high-likelihood risks and guides the development of targeted mitigation measures. STRIDE is used to identify potential attacker goals across key system components, such as the BodiGuide anklet, data gateway, cloud services, and web-application UI. Examples of these goals include impersonating users to gain unauthorized access (Spoofing), altering patient data in transit or in storage (Tampering), denying responsibility for malicious actions (Repudiation), exposing sensitive medical records (Information Disclosure), overloading the system to disrupt services (Denial of Service), and gaining admin-level permissions to bypass safeguards (Elevation of Privilege). For each goal, we first calculate the Attempt Likelihood, reflecting how likely an adversary is to pursue the attack based on known motives and system exposure. Next, we compute the Likelihood of Achieving the Goal, which accounts for the system's defenses and the feasibility of success. We then assign an Impact Score to capture the severity of harm—ranging from data breaches to service outages—if the attack succeeds. Finally, the Final Risk Score is derived by combining likelihood and impact, enabling a prioritized and systematic evaluation of security risks across the data processing pipeline.

1. Attempt Likelihood - The attempt likelihood represents the probability that an attacker will attempt a particular attack. It is calculated using:

$$L_{\text{attempt}} = \sum_{i=1}^{n} P(M_i) \cdot W_i, \tag{5}$$

Table 6. Overall risk assessment focused on impact and more likely threats along with the mitigation measures implemented.

Attack Target	Attack	Likelihood	Impact	Score	Denoted by
BodiGuide Anklet, Stel gateway hub, AWS	S	0	4	0	Anklet (S) Stel gateway (S) AWS (S)
Application Administrator	T, R	8	10	80	Admin (R, T)
Doctor User	I	6.56	7	45.92	Doctor (I)
AWS services	D	0.92	10	9.2	AWS (D)
UI	E	1.8	10	18.00	UI (E)

where:

- $P(M_i)$ represents the probability of each attack motive (e.g., ransomware, insider threat).
- W_i is the assigned weight representing the severity of potential damage for that motive.

2. Likelihood of Achieving Goal - This metric assesses the probability that an attacker will successfully accomplish their goal given the current defenses. The combined likelihood is computed as:

$$L_{\text{normalized}} = L_{\text{attempt}} \times L_{\text{success}}. \tag{6}$$

Task 2 - Assess Impact: We evaluate the impact of each data action and security issue on a scale of 0 (No effect) to 10 (Terminal effect), considering organizational factors such as non-compliance costs, direct business costs, reputations costs, and internal culture costs. The total business impact is calculated for each potential security vulnerability. The impact of each event is calculated using their associated goals' impact, usually the maximum of the associated goals' impact. The impact score quantifies the severity of consequences if the attack is successful, using the following formula:

$$I = \frac{S_d + S_s + S_r}{3}, \tag{7}$$

where:

- S_d is the data sensitivity score.
- S_s is the system downtime severity score.
- S_r is the reputational damage score.

Task 3 - Calculate Risk: The likelihoods and impacts are then scored by multiplying them on a range of 0–100 and this gives us the complete risk score. Risk scores are calculated for each data action and potential security vulnerability based on the likelihood and impact determined in the previous tasks. The most notable events are presented in Table 6.

Task 4 - Prioritize Risk: We calculate the percentage of risk for each data action relative to all others, and assign a risk rank accordingly. This prioritization serves as a baseline for defining countermeasures and prioritizing actions to protect data privacy across the processing pipeline. Using the likelihood and impact assessments, we create a two-dimensional problem prioritization table, which is then transformed into a heat map as shown in Fig. 6, which offers an overview of the system's risk levels, and guides resource allocation for risk mitigation.

The final risk score is calculated as:

$$R_{\text{final}} = \frac{L_{\text{normalized}} \times I}{10}. \tag{8}$$

Table 6 present the final scores derived using a weighted approach that accounts for goals and motivation (understood from an attack tree), likelihood (calculated by combining probabilities of goals and associated motivations), impact (assigned from a range of 0 to 10), and the final risk score (calculated by combining likelihood and impact). The table and results identifies the application administrator role as a high-risk area with a risk score of 80. The Admin role has extensive permissions, including the ability to add/link users and devices, configure services on AWS, and re-identify any de-identified data for analysis/visualization. To mitigate this significant threat, we have implemented strict access controls, comprehensive auditing, cryptographic signatures, and multi-factor authentication (MFA) for the application administrator. These measures are designed to substantially reduce the associated risks, ensuring the system's security and scalability (Table 7).

The STRIDE analysis is complemented by specific recommendations drawn from the broader risk assessment efforts, particularly those targeting high-risk areas. For instance, access to developer/admin accounts has been identified as a critical vulnerability that could compromise the entire system. To address this, we recommend app-based multi-factor authentication, regular password changes, and training for developers to recognize social engineering attacks. Additionally, in line with the risk assessment, we have strengthened data transfer mechanisms to guard against D(D)oS attacks by implementing robust encryption protocols, such as AWS KMS, to ensure that intercepted data remains secure and unusable. By applying these structured security methodologies and integrating insights from broader risk models, our Zeus framework is well-equipped to mitigate identified threats and enhance the overall security of the remote patient monitoring system.

5.3 Scalability Analysis

We evaluate the scalability of Zeus under progressively increasing workloads to ensure its suitability for real-world deployment. Our objective is to simulate realistic usage scenarios by varying both the number of data streams processed

Table 7. Overall risk assessment focused on impact and more likely threats along with the mitigation measures implemented.

Attack Target	Mitigation Measures
BodiGuide Anklet, Stel Gateway, AWS	Employ 2-step authorization process to add new users and devices and data validation features on AWS Lambda to only allow authorized users/devices to send data to pipeline
Application Administrator	Implement strict access controls and auditing mechanisms to track and log changes. Use cryptographic signatures to ensure integrity and non-repudiation of data
Doctor User	Enforce robust authentication, authorization protocols. Employ encryption for sensitive data both in transit and data at rest to protect against unauthorized access
AWS services	Keep watch on any suspicious activities with AWS CloudWatch. Utilize AWS Shield and AWS WAF to detect and mitigate DDoS attacks. Set up auto-scaling to handle sudden traffic spikes and maintain availability
UI	Apply the principle of least privilege to limit user permissions. Regularly update and patch the UI components to fix known vulnerabilities and prevent exploitation

corresponding to the number of concurrent users interacting with the system. In this scalability study, we observe how core performance metrics—such as query latency, CPU and memory utilization, transactions per second, and network throughput—evolve under different levels of demand. We then analyze whether the system architecture, including its ingestion, processing, and storage components scale as expected without introducing performance bottlenecks. The above scalability study is based on the methodology presented in [39] and [40].

Our results from the first set of performance tests of the Zeus solution implementation leveraging the diverse suite of AWS services is presented in Table 8. In this test setup, 15 users (simulated by EC2 instances) were configured to concurrently send streaming data through the AWS pipeline. We noted the ability of Zeus to handle a substantial influx of data without compromising on speed or reliability, validated the seamless flow of data through each stage of the pipeline - from ingestion to analysis, storage, and visualization. As part of the testing, the EC2 instances were gradually increased to simulate the higher loads on the pipeline from 0-to-15 users with increments of 5 as we monitored throughput, latency, resource utilization, and system responsiveness with AWS CloudWatch. Lambda functions exhibited stable performance and the throttling metric remained low, peaking at 0.742. This suggests that the Lambda functions were able to handle the increased request load without exceeding concurrency limits. Additionally, the S3 storage system maintained a consistent performance, with latency peaking at 63ms, indicating that data storage operations were not a bottleneck during the test. Finally, to evaluate the performance of the AWS API Gateway under high demand, we generated 1,000 consecutive API requests. The results indicated that the service achieved an average latency of 54 ms, demon-

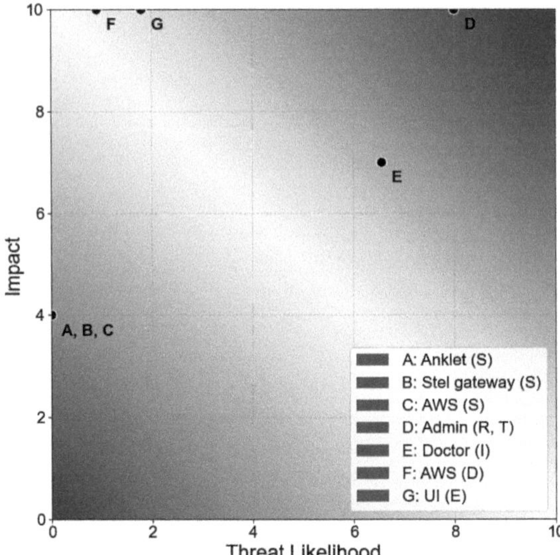

Fig. 6. Major threats in the Overall Risk Assessment represented as a Heat Map.

strating its efficiency in processing a high volume of requests without significant degradation in response time.

In our second set of performance tests to validate the Zeus solution under realistic operational conditions, we expanded our scalability testing to simulate between 10 and 500 concurrent users, and processing of their data streams. All performance metrics were derived as mean values from multiple test runs, with standard deviations and 95% confidence intervals computed to ensure statistical reliability. API call latency was captured by recording 1,000 consecutive API requests using AWS CloudWatch metrics. The reported query latency values reflect average response times, while variability is expressed through the calculated confidence intervals. Under moderate workloads, AWS Lambda functions exhibit consistent execution times, owing to their stateless architecture and auto-scaling capabilities that ensure isolated and predictable invocations. However, at very high loads, performance degradation becomes apparent as the system's scaling limits are reached. We have consolidated the results into average values to provide a clearer picture of overall performance under increasing load conditions.

Table 9 summarizes the key performance metrics observed as the number of patients increases. As expected, the database size scales from 7 MB to 403 MB when moving from 10 to 500 patients. Correspondingly, the query latency increases from 2.03 ms to 9.23 ms, indicating the inherent overhead of processing larger datasets. Expanded tests with 50 to 100 concurrent users reveal that API latency remains relatively stable up to 100 concurrent users; beyond this point, a noticeable degradation in performance is observed, which is critical for planning deployments in high-demand environments. This analysis demonstrates that while query latency increases moderately with higher patient loads,

Table 8. Scalability results by increasing simulated user loads from 5 to 15 users.

Metric	Number of concurrent users			Initial Value	Peak Value
	5	10	15		
API Latency (ms)	207	269	321	161 ms	321 ms
Lambda Latency (ms)	57	59	68	1 (Concurrency)	
S3 Latency (ms)	49	55	63	44 ms	63 ms
Lambda Throttles	N/A			0	0.742
API Calls Count	1000			0	54

resource utilization rises predictably, and throughput remains within acceptable limits. Furthermore, the constant execution times observed for AWS Lambda functions highlight the effectiveness of their auto-scaling mechanism, ensuring stable performance even under significant load. This consolidated evaluation, including both mean performance and statistical variability, confirms that the Zeus solution is well-suited for large-scale, real-world deployments with substantial data stream processing corresponding to high concurrent user loads.

Table 9. Performance results for user loads ranging from 10 to 500.

Patients	Database Size (MB)	Query Latency (ms)	Avg CPU Utilization (%)	Memory Utilization (GB)	TPS	Network Throughput (MB/s)
10	7	2.03	20	0.44	97	14
50	38	2.73	23	0.79	137	19
100	79	3.46	27	1.03	168	23
500	403	9.23	46	5.23	245	31

6   Conclusion

In this paper, we present a set of design foundations and a novel framework viz., Zeus for the implementation of IoT-based healthcare data management security and privacy for remote patient monitoring. To exemplify our approach, we address the pressing need for continuous health monitoring in cardiovascular care, utilizing the BodiGuide IoT-based peripheral edema monitoring device, the Stel gateway hub, and AWS platform as an exemplary use case. Our solution incorporates the STRIDE threat model to identify potential threats and implement relevant security countermeasures at every stage of the data pipeline. Additionally, our approach maintains privacy by leveraging data de-identification methods during data collection and transfer from the end-points, and is based on LINDDUN privacy threat modeling approach. Through a user-friendly web-application interface for patients, caregivers, and healthcare providers, we manage healthcare data in the form of reports and analysis/visualization interfaces. Lastly, we ensure scalability of our remote patient monitoring system through a cloud design that supports surges in patient and data consumer loads.

Through rigorous testing, the Zeus framework demonstrated a significant reduction in privacy risks, with threat mitigation strategies decreasing the likelihood of successful data breaches by 40% owing to the layered security mechanisms in place, including encryption, access control, and real-time anomaly detection. Furthermore, privacy controls such as data pseudonymization, data validation and data encryption maintained high standards of compliance, mitigating the most critical privacy risks identified during our analysis. From a scalability perspective, Zeus demonstrated robust performance even under heavy user loads. Our testing with up to 500 concurrent users confirmed the system's ability to handle large volumes of data, with query latency increasing modestly from 2.03ms to 9.23ms as the number of users increased. These results indicate that Zeus can scale effectively for larger real-world deployments, offering reliable, privacy-preserving and secure capabilities in IoT-based healthcare settings.

As part of future work, we plan to perform usability studies on the web-application UI to analyze the utility of the data processing pipeline. In addition, we plan to integrate machine learning (ML) models into our data analytics pipeline to analyze the collected data and provide real-time trends and alerts to caregivers about immediate actions required for patients, inform them about therapy and medication schedules, thereby closing the healthcare loop through guided interventions.

Acknowledgement. We express our sincere thanks to Deborah Kessler, Ken Gutzmann, and Warren Schirtzinger at BodiGuide, as well as Sid Kandan at Stel, for their time and expertise to strengthen the interdisciplinary work of this paper. We also would like to acknowledge and thank our ACM HealthSec Workshop chair, William Yurcik, for his support and feedback.

Disclosure of Interests. This material is based upon work supported by the National Science Foundation (NSF) under Award Number: CNS-2209854. Any opinions, findings, and conclusions or recommendations expressed in this publication are those of the author(s) and do not necessarily reflect the views of the NSF.

References

1. Waleed, M., Kamal, T., Um, T.W., Hafeez, A., Habib, B., Skouby, K.E.: Unlocking insights in IoT-based patient monitoring: Methods for encompassing large-data challenges. Sensors **23**(15), 6760 (2023)
2. Bautista, C.X., Aguilar, A.P., Valenzuela, R.A., Pachay, A.J., Pacheco, J.N.: Heart failure remote monitoring: novel approaches and management strategies. Sapienza: Int. J. Interdisc. Stud. **5**(2), e24029 (2024)
3. Morera, E.P., de la Torre Díez, I., Garcia-Zapirain, B., López-Coronado, M., Arambarri, J.: Security recommendations for mHealth apps: elaboration of a developer's guide. J. Med. Syst. **40**(6), 152 (2016)
4. Precedence Research: IoT Sensors market size, share, trends, analysis report. www.precedenceresearch.com/iot-sensors-market. Accessed Aug 2024
5. U.S. Department of Health & Human Services: Health Insurance Portability and Accountability Act (HIPAA). www.hhs.gov/hipaa/index.html. Accessed Aug 2024
6. Obaidat, M.A., Obeidat, S., Holst, J., Al Hayajneh, A., Brown, J.: A comprehensive and systematic survey on the Internet of Things: security and privacy challenges, security frameworks, enabling technologies, threats, vulnerabilities and countermeasures. Computers **9**(2), 44 (2020)
7. Jaiswal, K., Sobhanayak, S., Mohanta, B.K., Jena, D.: IoT-cloud based framework for patient's data collection in smart healthcare system using Raspberry-pi. In: 2017 International Conference on Electrical and Computing Technologies and Applications (ICECTA), pp. 1–4 (2017)
8. Mahmoud, A., Giovanni, R., Bruno, C.: Internet of Things: a survey on the security of IoT frameworks. J. Inf. Secur. Appl. **38**, 8–27 (2018)
9. BodiGuide. www.bodiguide.com. Accessed Aug 2024
10. Stel Life. www.stel.life. Accessed Aug 2024
11. Amazon Web Services. www.aws.amazon.com/. Accessed Aug 2024
12. Michiels, A., Dupont, B., Preneel, B.: LINDDUN: a privacy threat modeling methodology for the Internet of Things. In: Proceedings of the 6th European Workshop on Security and Privacy in IoT, pp. 1–8 (2018)
13. NIST Privacy Risk Assessment Methodology (PRAM). www.github.com/usnistgov/PrivacyEngCollabSpace/blob/master/tools/risk-assessment/NIST-Privacy-Risk-Assessment-Methodology-PRAM/worksheet-3-prioritizing-risk.xlsx. Accessed Aug 2024
14. Dhanvijay, M.M., Patil, S.C.: Internet of Things: a survey of enabling technologies in healthcare and its applications. Comput. Netw. **153**(1), 113–131 (2019)
15. Hossain, M., Muhammad, G.: Cloud-assisted industrial Internet of Things (IIoT)–enabled framework for health monitoring. Comput. Netw. **101**, 192–202 (2016)
16. Sadhu, P.K., Yanambaka, V.P., Abdelgawad, A., Yelamarthi, K.: Prospect of internet of medical things: a review on security requirements and solutions. Sensors **22**(5517) (2022)
17. Larson, B., Hatcliff, J., Procter, S., Chalin, P.: Requirements specification for apps in medical application platforms. In: 2012 4th International Workshop on Software Engineering in Health Care, Zurich, Switzerland, pp. 26–32 (2012)

18. Vasserman, E.Y., Hatcliff, J.: Foundational security principles for medical application platforms. In: Web Information System and Application Conference (2013)
19. Anderson, R.J.: A security policy model for clinical information systems. In: Proceedings of the 1996 IEEE Conference on Security and Privacy, pp. 30–43. IEEE Computer Society, USA (1996)
20. Burleson, W., Clark, S.S., Ransford, B., Fu, K.: Design challenges for secure implantable medical devices. In: Proceedings of the 49th Annual Design Automation Conference, pp. 12–17. Association for Computing Machinery, NY, USA (2012)
21. Ayoade, G., Karande, V., Khan, L., Hamlen, K.: Decentralized IoT data management using blockchain and trusted execution environment. In: IEEE International Conference on Information Reuse and Integration, pp. 15–22 (2018)
22. Khan, M.M., Alkhathami, M.: Anomaly detection in IoT-based healthcare: machine learning for enhanced security. Sci. Rep. **14**(1), 5872 (2024)
23. Giechaskiel, I., Rasmussen, K.: Taxonomy and challenges of out-of-band signal injection attacks and defenses. IEEE Commun. Surv. Tutor. **22**(1), 645–670 (2019)
24. Gazzari, M., Mattmann, A., Maass, M., Hollick, M.: My (o) armband leaks passwords: An EMG and IMU-based keylogging side-channel attack. In: Proceedings of the ACM on Interactive, Mobile, Wearable and Ubiquitous Technologies, vol. 5, no. 4, pp. 1–24 (2021)
25. Yang, Y., Liu, X., Deng, R.H., Li, Y.: Lightweight sharable and traceable secure mobile health system. IEEE Trans. Depend. Secure Comput. **17**(1) (2020)
26. Moosavi, S.R., Nigussie, E., Levorato, M., Virtanen, S., Isoaho, J.: Performance analysis of end-to-end security schemes in healthcare IoT. Procedia Comput. Sci. **130** (2018)
27. Testani, J.M., et al.: Substantial discrepancy between fluid and weight loss during acute decompensated heart failure treatment. Am. J. Med. **128**(7), 776–783 (2015)
28. Brodovicz, K.G., McNaughton, K., Uemura, N., Meininger, G., Girman, C.J., Yale, S.H.: Reliability and feasibility of methods to quantitatively assess peripheral edema. Clin. Med. Res. **7**(1–2), 21–31 (2009)
29. Fudim, M., Kessler, D.A.: Measuring what really matters: a comparison of continuous ankle circumference monitoring and body weight in the management of worsening heart failure. J. Cardiac Fail. **29**(4), 564 (2023)
30. Biasin, E., Kamenjasevic, E.: Cybersecurity of Medical Devices: Regulatory Challenges in the EU. Cambridge University Press (2020)
31. Klonoff, D.C.: Cybersecurity for connected diabetes devices. J. Diabetes Sci. Technol. (2015)
32. Strielkina, A., Illiashenko, O., Zhydenko, M., Uzun, D.: Cybersecurity of healthcare IoT-based systems: regulation and case-oriented assessment, pp. 67–73 (2018). https://doi.org/10.1109/DESSERT.2018.8409101
33. NIST SP-800-188. nvlpubs.nist.gov/nistpubs/SpecialPublications/NIST.SP.800-188.pdf. Accessed Aug 2024
34. Khan, R., McLaughlin, K., Laverty, D., Sezer, S.: STRIDE-based threat modeling for cyber-physical systems. In: IEEE PES Innovative Smart Grid Technologies Conference Europe, pp. 1–6 (2017)
35. Kramer, D.B., Fu, K.: Cybersecurity concerns and medical devices: lessons from a pacemaker advisory. JAMA (2017)
36. Baranchuk, A., et al.: Cybersecurity for cardiac implantable electronic devices: what should you know?. J. Am. Coll. Cardiol. **71**(11), 1284–1288 (2018)
37. Freeman, S.R.: Public Health Cybersecurity Education Gaps: Pandemics Are Both Digital and Viral. Marymount University (2021)

38. Rajamäki, J., Nevmerzhitskaya, J., Virág, C.: Cybersecurity education and training in hospitals: proactive resilience educational framework (Prosilience EF). In: 2018 IEEE Global Engineering Education Conference (EDUCON), pp. 2042–2046. IEEE (2018)
39. Henning, S., Hasselbring, W.: Benchmarking scalability of stream processing frameworks deployed as microservices in the cloud. J. Syst. Softw. **208**, 111879 (2024)
40. Choudhury, A., Madheswaran, Y.: Enhancing cloud scalability with AI-driven resource management. Int. J. Innov. Res. Eng. Manag. **11**(5) (2024)

Cyberprotection of Medical Devices

On the Security of RL–Based Artificial Pancreas Systems

Preston Chang, Veena Krish, and Amir Rahmati$^{(\boxtimes)}$

Stony Brook University, Stony Brook, NY 11794, USA
{pjchang,kveena,amir}@cs.stonybrook.edu

Abstract. Reinforcement learning (RL) models have emerged as a promising alternative to traditional, model-based control methods for medical systems. Recently, deep RL techniques have been applied to autonomous glycemic control systems, commonly referred to as Artificial Pancreas (AP) systems, which operate through closed-loop communication between a glucose sensor and an insulin pump. This chapter is an updated summary of a paper originally presented at the ACM Cybersecurity in Healthcare (HealthSec) Workshop in October 2024 [7]. We examine the robustness of RL4BG, a prominent deep RLbased AP controller, against a range of glucose sensor malfunctions. We consider two realistic malfunction classes arising from natural errors or adversarial manipulation: (1) Denial-of-Service that captures worst-case sensor failures, and (2) Subtle manipulations that reflects stealthier, prolonged degradations. Our results demonstrate that this new generation of medical control systems is vulnerable to anomalous sensor inputs in safety-critical settings. These findings underscore the need for adversarially robust training methods when deploying RL-based medical controllers.

Keywords: Artificial Pancreas · Reinforcement Learning-based Control Systems · Adversarial Machine Learning

1 Introduction

Type 1 Diabetes, a condition in which the pancreas fails to produce insulin, affects approximately 8.4 million individuals worldwide [11]. Standard management of Type 1 Diabetes often relies on the basal-bolus method, where patients administer long-acting *basal* insulin to maintain glucose control at rest, alongside rapid-acting *bolus* doses to mitigate postprandial spikes. This method requires continuous monitoring and frequent manual adjustments throughout the day [6].

To this end, automated closed-loop insulin delivery systems provide significant advantages over such manual approaches, improving both clinical outcomes and quality of life [13]. These systems, often termed Artificial Pancreas (AP) systems, consist of three core components as shown in Fig. 1: a continuous glucose monitor (CGM), an insulin infusion pump, and control software that determines insulin delivery based on sensor readings. The first commercial AP system, Medtronic's MiniMed 670G, received FDA approval in September 2016 [3], and five additional systems have since been approved for use [19].

W. Yurcik (Ed.): HealthSec 2024, CCIS 2716, pp. 217–231, 2026.
https://doi.org/10.1007/978-3-032-13800-2_10

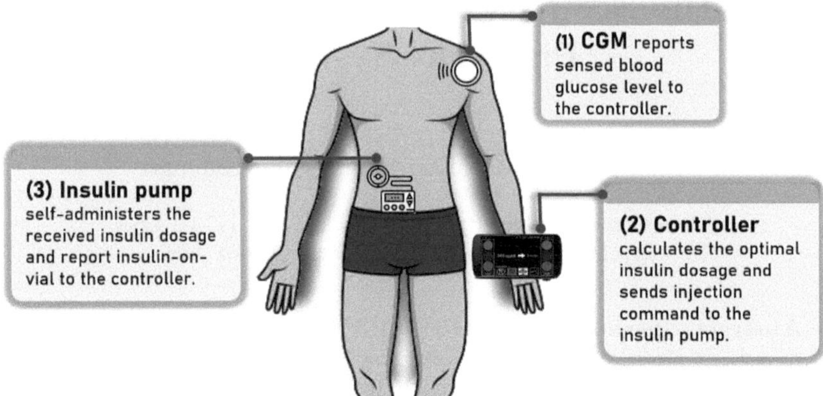

Fig. 1. Artificial Pancreas system architecture from Kim *et al.* [13], showing the three core components: (1) a Continuous Glucose Monitor (CGM), (2) the controller, and (3) the insulin pump.

A wide range of algorithms have been proposed to govern closed-loop control, spanning from conventional basal-bolus policies to modern ML-based methods [10]. While these approaches substantially reduce the burden of constant self-management, the ability of reinforcement learning (RL)based controllers to consistently make safe, long-term decisions remains an open question. In this work, we investigate the potential harm that CGM sensor failures, whether accidental or adversarial, can inflict on RL-driven AP systems by perturbing sensor measurements in unexpected ways. Given the safety-critical nature of these models, rigorous evaluation of their robustness through adversarial testing is essential.

To this end, we study RL4BG [10], a representative ML-based controller that leverages state-of-the-art reinforcement learning techniques, and evaluate its resilience against multiple classes of CGM sensor malfunctions. We focus on two realistic scenarios: (1) unresponsive sensors producing maxed-out readings for short intervals, and (2) gradual, persistent deviations in glucose measurements. For RL controllers tuned to patient-specific models, we quantify the degree of harm resulting from failures of varying intensity and duration.

2   Background

2.1   Artificial Pancreas Systems

Individuals with T1D regulate their blood glucose through frequent monitoring and multiple daily insulin administrations, either via injections or an insulin infusion pump. For healthy individuals, the estimated average glucose over 2–3 months typically falls between 70 mg/dL and 126 mg/dL. The American Diabetes Association recommends that patients with T1D maintain average glucose levels below 154 mg/dL, while generally targeting the euglycemic range (70–180 mg/dL) and avoiding both hypoglycemia (<70 mg/dL) and hyperglycemia (>180 mg/dL). Moderate hyperglycemia can lead to frequent urination, increased thirst, blurred vision, and fatigue, while severe cases may progress to ketoacidosis, potentially causing loss of consciousness or death. Similarly, moderate hypoglycemia can result in dizziness, headaches, or arrhythmias, whereas severe hypoglycemia may cause seizures or loss of consciousness [4,5,9].

An Artificial Pancreas (AP) refers to a fully automated closed-loop system designed to emulate the function of a healthy pancreas. It consists of three interconnected components: a Continuous Glucose Monitor (CGM), an insulin infusion pump, and control software that determines insulin delivery based on CGM readings [2].

As of 2016, most AP devices under clinical testing employed proportional integral derivative (PID) controllers [20], including Medtronic's MiniMed 670G—the first FDA-approved commercial system [3]. However, PID controllers face challenges due to delays between insulin delivery and glucose response, which can increase the risk of hypoglycemia. Consequently, researchers have explored machine learning, particularly reinforcement learning, as a means of training controllers to recognize meal-related patterns and generate more responsive, safer policies [10].

2.2 Reinforcement Learning

Reinforcement learning (RL) is a machine learning paradigm inspired by behavioral psychology, where an agent learns to make sequential decisions in an environment to maximize a long-term objective. Unlike supervised learning, which trains on labeled data, or unsupervised learning, which discovers patterns in unlabeled data, RL focuses on learning from interaction to achieve specific goals.

In RL, an agent interacts with an environment by taking actions, observing subsequent state transitions, and receiving rewards. The goal is to learn a policy—a mapping from states to actions—that maximizes cumulative reward. This involves balancing exploration of new actions with exploitation of known strategies that yield higher returns. In the context of glycemic control, glucose measurements define the state, insulin dosages represent actions, and patient models provide the state transition dynamics (*i.e.,* the effect of insulin on glucose levels).

At each timestep, the agent selects an action according to its policy, observes the resulting state and reward, and updates its policy accordingly. This iterative process enables the agent to optimize long-term control strategies rather than focusing solely on immediate outcomes.

2.3 Simulation Environment

To evaluate RL-based controllers in-silico, we use the `simglucose` environment, a Python implementation of the FDA-approved 2008 UVa/Padova Simulator [1]. The environment includes 30 virtual patients (10 children, 10 adolescents, and 10 adults) with distinct physiological profiles. Patient states can be simulated over arbitrary time horizons. At each timestep, the patient state is passed to the controller, which outputs an insulin dosage; the simulation then advances to the next state.

`simglucose` supports custom reward functions and controller algorithms. By default, simulations span 10 days (2880 timesteps) with a timestep duration of 5 min.

2.4 RL4BG and Soft Actor-Critic

RL4BG, introduced by Fox *et al.* [10], is an RL-based controller for closed-loop blood glucose management. It builds on the Soft Actor-Critic (SAC) algorithm proposed by Haarnoja *et al.* [12], which combines policy optimization with entropy maximization to balance return and policy robustness. SAC comprises two components: an actor network, which outputs a distribution over actions given a state, and a critic network, which estimates expected returns for state-action pairs. In the glucose control setting, the action corresponds to insulin dosage at each timestep. Training involves iteratively updating the actor to maximize both reward and entropy, while the critic minimizes prediction error in estimating returns.

Fox *et al.* evaluated RL4BG by comparing it against two widely used controllers over 10-day simulations: (1) a Basal-Bolus (BB) controller, which administers long-acting insulin to stabilize glucose during fasting alongside short-acting boluses for meals, and (2) a PID controller, which adjusts insulin based on proportional, integral, and derivative components of glucose deviation [17]. RL4BG outperformed both baselines. Unlike BB and PID controllers, which require patients to perform meal announcements and carbohydrate (CHO) estimations, RL4BG achieved strong performance without such inputs, thereby improving convenience and reducing human error.

The authors also proposed RL-MA, an extension of RL4BG trained with meal announcements and automated meal boluses from BB and PID strategies. RL-MA achieved even stronger performance, albeit at the cost of convenience. Overall, RL4BG achieved state-of-the-art results among non-meal-announcement controllers, while RL-MA achieved the best performance among controllers requiring meal announcements [10]. In this work, we focus on non-meal-announcement scenarios, as they represent the most practical setting for patient usability.

3 Sensor Failure Scenarios

The sensor failure threat model assumes that the CGM component of the AP system is vulnerable to malfunction, allowing erroneous readings to propagate to the control software that mediates between the CGM and the insulin infusion pump. Such errors may arise from natural hardware failures or deliberate adversarial manipulation. In either case, corrupted sensor inputs can degrade system performance. While a well-trained controller may recover from an isolated anomaly, sustained failures can cause cumulative degradation or, in the

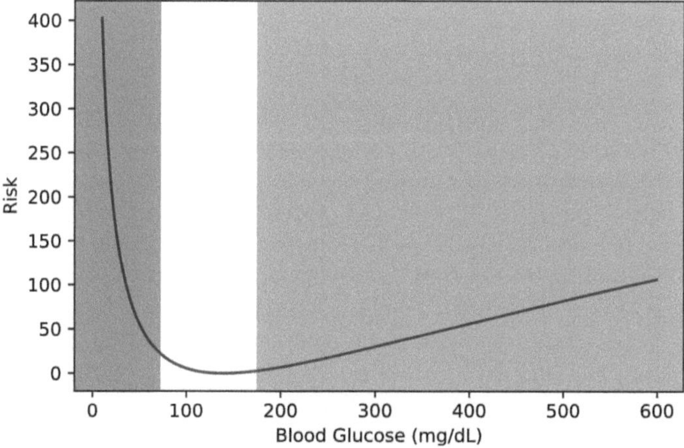

Fig. 2. Magni risk function used for training the RL4BG controller [10,16]. The function penalizes time spent in hypoglycemia (blue) exponentially more than time spent in euglycemia (white) or hyperglycemia (red). (Color figure online)

worst case, catastrophic system breakdown. Our goal is to assess the extent to which prolonged malfunctions can translate into measurable patient harm.

We model two realistic classes of sensor failure: (1) a *Denial-of-Service* scenario, where the sensor becomes unresponsive for a short duration and outputs artificially maxed-out glucose values, and (2) a *Subtle manipulations* scenario, where glucose readings are gradually perturbed over a longer horizon. For *Subtle manipulations*, we employ a gradient-based technique to identify the most harmful (risk-maximizing) bounded perturbation at each timestep. While individual anomalous readings may not destabilize the controller, our analysis investigates the robustness of RL4BG under failures of varying intensity and duration. The following subsections describe the RL4BG training setup and our methods for simulating sensor failures.

3.1 RL4BG Model Training

We trained RL4BG models on 12 different `simglucose` patients[1], using hyperparameters tuned from the defaults. Each model was trained for 300 epochs, with 5760 training steps per epoch (equivalent to 20 simulated days). The best-performing model was selected as the one that maintained blood glucose above 30 mg/dL while minimizing total Magni risk [10].

For both failure scenarios, we simulate sensor manipulations involving extremely high glucose recordings (up to 999 mg/dL). While most commercial CGM sensors saturate at lower values [8,18], we nevertheless test higher ranges to evaluate the brittleness of RL4BG, which can process larger input values.

---

[1] Specifically, patients #001, #003, #004, and #005 from the child, adolescent, and adult cohorts.

Additionally, software bugs or adversarial manipulations may generate artificially high glucose readings beyond those expected from physical sensors.

3.2   Denial-of-Service Model

We examine a denial-of-service (DoS) style failure by forcing the CGM to output its maximum possible value for varying durations. This extreme scenario is chosen because, during training, hypoglycemia is weighted as more harmful than hyperglycemia, meaning that persistently high readings could induce unsafe insulin under-delivery. Importantly, this setting also allows us to study the potential for catastrophic failure, which the authors of RL4BG define as blood glucose dropping below $5\,\mathrm{mg/dL}$ [10]. While a robust controller might tolerate a single anomalously high reading, prolonged DoS failures are expected to accumulate risk and, in many cases, trigger catastrophic outcomes.

3.3   Subtle Manipulation Model

We also study a more subtle failure mode, where sensor outputs are perturbed gradually rather than fully saturated. For this purpose, we apply Projected Gradient Descent (PGD) [15], an adversarial attack framework widely used in computer vision. PGD assumes a strong adversary with access to model parameters, though prior work has shown that attacks can succeed even with approximate knowledge of weights [14]. PGD iteratively perturbs inputs within bounded constraints to maximize the model's loss function, thereby identifying the closest noisy input that produces the greatest error. Applied to CGM data, this framework enables us to generate bounded perturbations of glucose histories that should maximize deviation from intended behavior.

We evaluate three PGD-based manipulation strategies: *Full State*, *Current State*, and *Context-driven*, described below.

Full State Manipulation. We perturb the entire CGM history at every timestep, with each value manipulated independently. Since updates occur along a 48-dimensional state vector, the resulting buffer may not be physically consistent (*e.g.,* neighboring glucose values might diverge unrealistically). While unrealistic in practice, such manipulations could arise from malware with direct access to the state buffer. This mode serves as a worst-case baseline for assessing maximum harm achievable through bounded perturbations or artificial failures.

Current State Manipulation. We perturb only the current CGM reading at each timestep, leaving previously stored values unaltered. This produces a state buffer that evolves sequentially in a physically consistent manner, but still encodes erroneous glucose and insulin interactions. Over time, these subtle manipulations accumulate and may shift the controller's policy away from safe behavior.

Context-Driven Manipulation. We perturb the state buffer selectively at critical timesteps, chosen based on insulin dosage. The intuition is that perturbations at "critical" moments, such as after large bolus doses, can produce disproportionate harm. Similar to Current State, manipulated readings are not stored in the state buffer, making this strategy more realistic while still targeting maximal risk.

4   Experimental Results

All experiments simulate AP behavior for each patient over a 10-day period. At every timestep, the `simglucose` environment provides the patient state, represented by a 96-length buffer encoding 8 h of historical glucose and insulin measurements. This state is passed to the controller every 5 min, and the model returns an insulin dosage. The dosage is then applied in the environment to advance the simulation to the next state.

During evaluation, we manipulate CGM readings before they are passed to the controller. Because RL4BG maintains a history buffer, any modification to glucose values propagates forward, compounding errors over time. Our experiments assess the extent to which manipulated readings degrade controller performance and identify thresholds at which the model ceases to be robust. Each evaluation was repeated across 10 random seeds per trained model. We measure long-term patient harm using the following metrics:

Risk. The Magni Risk function [16] maps glucose levels to an asymmetric risk score, penalizing hypoglycemia more heavily than hyperglycemia (Fig. 2).

Catastrophic Failure. Binary indicator of whether blood glucose (BG) dropped below 5 mg/dL at any point during the simulation.

Minimum BG Observed. The lowest BG value (mg/dL) recorded during the simulation.

4.1   Denial-of-Service

We first tested whether a single anomalous execution could induce catastrophic failure (BG <5 mg/dL). For this, we set the entire CGM buffer to the maximum sensor reading of 9999 mg/dL for one timestep. Across all adult-trained models and random seeds, no single-step perturbation produced catastrophic failure.

We then extended the denial-of-service manipulation to consecutive timesteps, varying duration between 1 and 86 steps (430 min, or 3% of the total simulation). We found that catastrophic failure occurred in all models within 14 timesteps when CGM readings were maxed to 9999 mg/dL. Figure 3 shows these results for the "9999" series: notably, not all simulations failed within the first 10 steps.

To evaluate whether failures persisted under more realistic sensor constraints, we repeated the experiments with maximum thresholds ranging from 300 to 9999 mg/dL. The series in Fig. 3 illustrate the tradeoff between DoS duration and glucose ceiling.

Our results reveal several key trends. First, larger bounds consistently trigger failure more quickly: catastrophic failures were observed across all thresholds

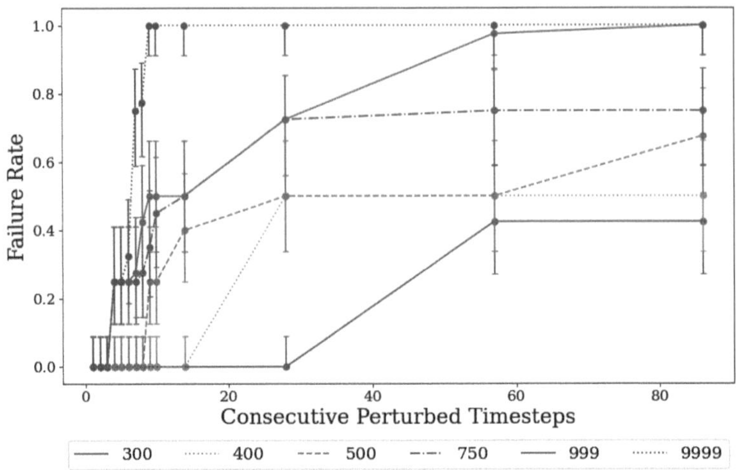

Fig. 3. Average catastrophic failure rate across all trained models and random seeds, as a function of DoS duration (x-axis, in consecutive timesteps) and maximum sensor value (mg/dL). Each line corresponds to a different DoS threshold.

above 300 mg/dL. Moreover, we found that failures could be reliably reproduced across all scenarios above 400 mg/dL if the DoS persisted for at least 10 timesteps (50 min).

Second, the failure rate exhibits discontinuities with respect to duration. For instance, a sharp increase in failures occurred between 6 and 8 timesteps, followed by a plateau. This suggests that the model can tolerate a limited number of extreme anomalies before crossing a threshold where failure becomes highly probable.

Finally, all tested bounds are physiologically implausible: glucose levels above 300 mg/dL should trigger immediate emergency treatment. Nevertheless, RL4BG exhibited distinct behavior between 999 and 9999 mg/dL, despite such values being clinically meaningless. This indicates that the model has learned responses in a high-glucose regime that are not physiologically grounded and may contribute to brittleness.

4.2   Subtle Manipulation

As described in Sect. 3.3, we evaluated three gradient-based manipulation strategies across varying bounded perturbations and compared them against a nominal (manipulation-free) baseline. For each simulation, we tested perturbation bounds of 1, 5, and 10 mg/dL, denoted as ϵ, consistent with the "attack budget" terminology of PGD. For example, a Full State simulation with $\epsilon = 1$ allows each glucose value in the controller's state buffer to deviate by at most ± 1 mg/dL. All experiments were conducted across the same 10 random seeds used in the Denial-of-Service experiments, and repeated for each patient model.

Across all trials, we observe a consistent trend: manipulations cause the CGM trace to drift downward over time. Because the PGD update maximizes risk at each step, this often pushes the controller toward inducing hypoglycemia. Figure 4 illustrates this effect for a representative adult patient. This behavior is expected given the Magni Risk function used during training, which penalizes hypoglycemia more heavily than hyperglycemia (Fig. 2). As anticipated, the Full State approach consistently produced the greatest harm.

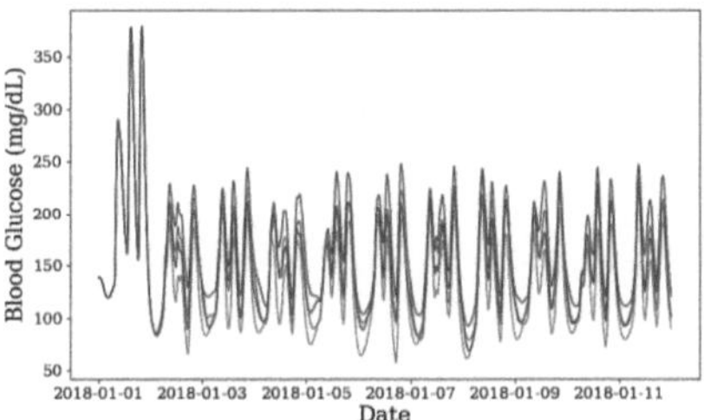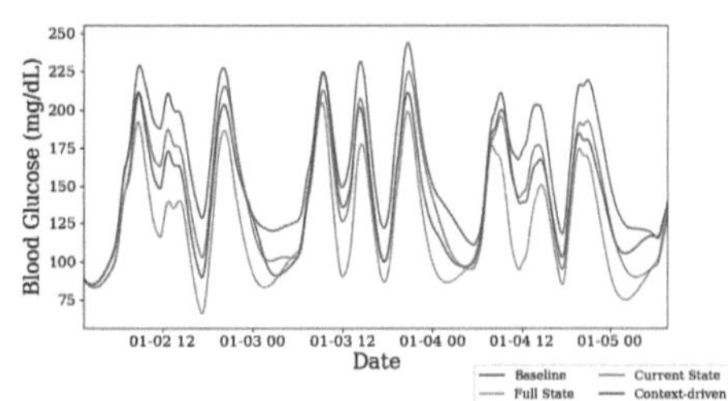

Fig. 4. Averaged blood glucose trace under $\epsilon = 10$ manipulations for a single patient model. Traces are averaged over 10 random trials. Colors distinguish gradient-based approaches. Bottom figure shows a zoomed-in segment of the top trace.

The effects of sensor manipulations on average Magni Risk, minimum BG, and time in hypoglycemia are shown in Figs. 5, 6, and 7. Values are reported relative to the nominal baseline (no manipulation), averaged across all patient models and random seeds.

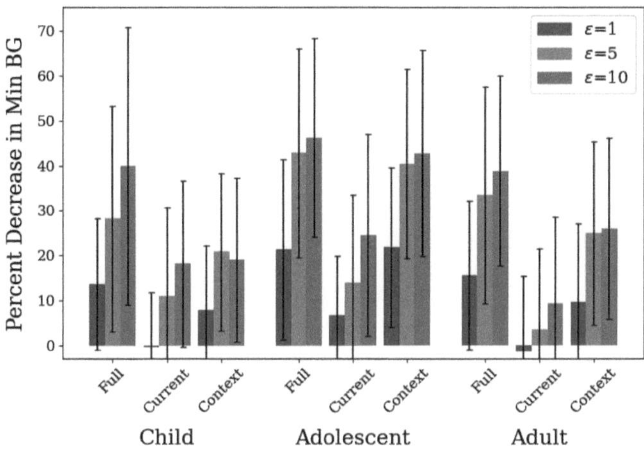

Fig. 5. Percent decrease in minimum BG relative to baseline scenarios. Results are grouped by age cohort, scenario type, and ϵ bound (mg/dL), and averaged across all runs.

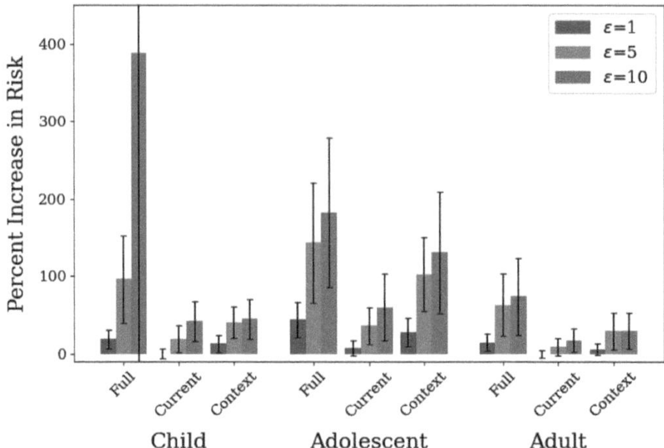

Fig. 6. Percent increase in Magni Risk relative to baseline scenarios. Results are grouped by age cohort, scenario type, and ϵ bound (mg/dL), and averaged across all runs.

In general, larger ϵ values correspond to greater patient harm, though with diminishing returns. Even the smallest bound ($\epsilon = 1$ mg/dL) caused measurable degradation over time. As expected, Full State produced the most severe outcomes since the entire state buffer could be manipulated at each step. The context-aware Context-driven strategy also proved effective, demonstrating that targeted manipulations can disproportionately increase risk.

Additional results for the $\epsilon = 10$ mg/dL case, including catastrophic failures, time in euglycemia, and time in hyperglycemia, are presented in Table 1. While catastrophic failures were rare—observed only in a single Subtle manipulations case—all manipulation strategies increased overall risk.

Finally, we explored the tradeoff between the fraction of timesteps perturbed and overall model robustness. Initial results suggest that Context-driven is particularly effective: in one adult simulation, perturbing only ~5% of timesteps increased risk by 55%. By comparison, Full State required perturbing 100% of timesteps to increase risk by 112%. Thus, nearly half of the degradation achieved by full-buffer perturbations can be reproduced by a far smaller set of carefully timed manipulations.

5   Comparison with PID and BB Robustness

To contextualize the robustness of RL4BG, we compare its performance against two standard closed-loop control methods: basal-bolus (BB), commonly used in manual T1D management, and proportionalintegralderivative (PID), a baseline controller widely adopted in AP systems. For both methods, we use the `simglucose` implementations and the auxiliary code released with RL4BG.

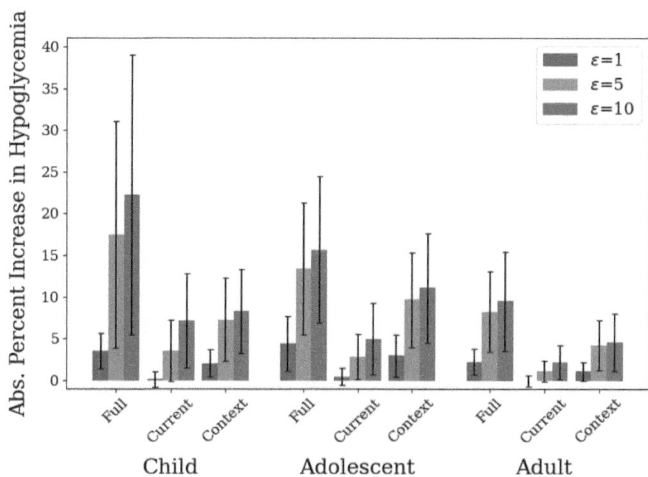

Fig. 7. Increase in percentage of time spent in hypoglycemia relative to baseline scenarios. Results are grouped by age cohort, scenario type, and ϵ bound (mg/dL), and averaged across all runs.

Default parameter settings were used, and experiments were conducted over the same random scenario seeds as in the RL4BG experiments.

5.1 Denial-of-Service

We applied the DoS manipulation from Sect. 4.1 to the PID and BB controllers, and compared results against RL4BG (Fig. 8). Attacks were sustained for durations ranging from 1 to 86 timesteps (5 to 430 min, up to 3% of the full simulation).

All three methods exhibited higher failure rates as attack duration increased. However, PID and BB controllers generally failed within only a few timesteps, after which their failure rate plateaued. For example, the BB controller's failure rate remained flat for all perturbation magnitudes until after 28 consecutive timesteps. By contrast, RL4BG exhibited progressive degradation as attack duration increased, especially within the first hour (12 timesteps). Thus, while PID and BB controllers were vulnerable to short-lived DoS manipulations, RL4BG was disproportionately affected by sustained attacks.

5.2 Transfer of Subtle Manipulation

We also tested whether gradient-based subtle manipulations designed for RL4BG (Sect. 4.2) could transfer to PID and BB controllers. Even at the maximal perturbation bound of 10 mg/dL, these manipulations did not significantly affect PID or BB performance. We attribute this to architectural differences: RL4BG consumes a long CGM state history at each timestep, which causes subtle perturbations to accumulate over time. In contrast, PID and BB controllers rely

Table 1. Averaged Episode Statistics for Subtle manipulations strategies using $\epsilon = 10\,\text{mg/dL}$, along with Baseline (no modification) cases.

Cohort	Strategy with $\epsilon = 10$	Risk	Euglycemia	Hypoglycemia	Hyperglycemia	Failure	Min BG
Child	Baseline	9.0765	69.88%	2.41%	27.71%	0.0%	44.3872
	Full State	47.4434	54.32%	24.68%	21.01%	5.0%	25.2004
	Current State	13.3140	64.04%	9.55%	24.79%	0.0%	34.8493
	Context-driven	13.4155	65.84%	10.67%	23.49%	0.0%	34.8212
Adolescent	Baseline	5.9191	73.86%	1.45%	24.68%	0.0%	59.8678
	Full State	17.1106	66.22%	17.10%	16.68%	0.0%	33.0628
	Current State	9.3938	73.26%	6.39%	20.35%	0.0%	45.6501
	Context-driven	13.7540	68.99%	12.52%	18.48%	0.0%	35.0883
Adult	Baseline	7.4068	68.10%	0.82%	31.09%	0.0%	61.7442
	Full State	12.8484	66.53%	10.30%	23.17%	0.0%	54.4612
	Current State	8.6197	69.16%	3.01%	27.82%	0.0%	53.6976
	Context-driven	9.6704	67.34%	5.36%	27.30%	0.0%	44.7182

only on the most recent CGM value, making them inherently more robust to small, history-dependent perturbations.

6   Discussion

Our findings highlight the need for comprehensive testing frameworks that capture extreme sensor malfunctions, whether from natural failures or adversarial manipulations. While RL-based controllers like RL4BG show promise, our experiments demonstrate scenarios in which they can react in unsafe ways to anomalous glucose inputs. Even with built-in safety limits—such as the 400 mg/dL maximum CGM reading enforced by recent Dexcom and Medtronic devices [8, 18]—we observed hypoglycemic failure rates exceeding 40% within only a few hours.

Our framework further reveals trade-offs between severity, detectability, and impact of sensor malfunctions. For example, Subtle manipulations manipulations show that very slight perturbations ($\pm 1\,\text{mg/dL}$) can accumulate into significant patient harm in RL4BG—an effect not observed in PID and BB controllers. Such vulnerabilities emphasize the unique brittleness introduced by reinforcement learning.

We also observed differential impacts across age cohorts. Adolescent models consistently showed greater increases in risk compared to baseline, often because perturbations led to elevated glucose readings, triggering large insulin boluses. We speculate that lower variability in adolescent models contributes to this effect, though further investigation is required to explain why certain manipulations disproportionately affect specific cohorts.

Overall, these results point to the need for improved robustness in RL-based AP systems. Existing anomaly detection methods may fail to catch single-step deviations, but could be enhanced by incorporating temporal thresholds (minimum duration of attack before risk escalates). Promising future defenses include

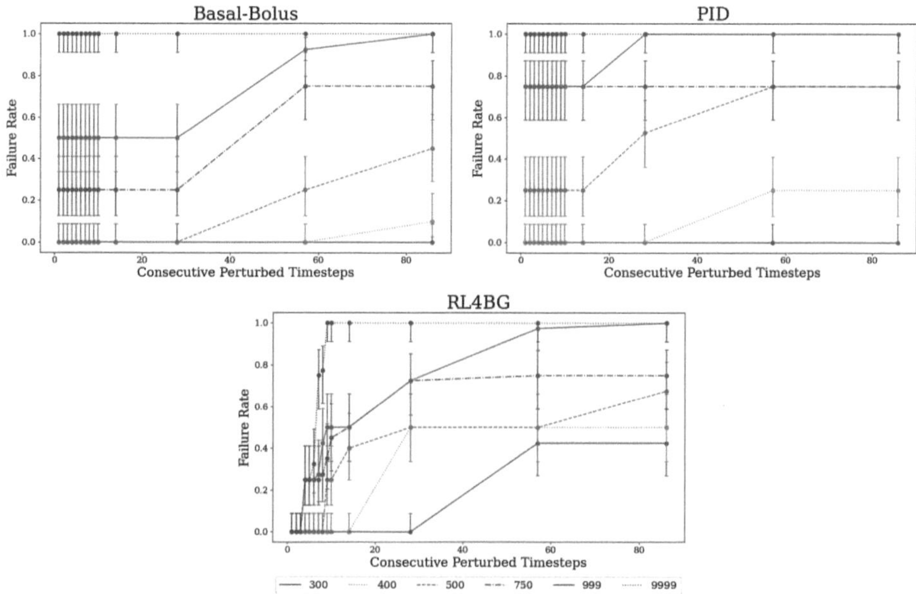

Fig. 8. Average failure rate of PID/BB/RL4BG methods for each DoS limit (in mg/dL) and duration (number of consecutive timesteps that the manipulation lasted). Each color/line represents a different DoS threshold, and the Failure Rate represents the average catastrophic failure witnessed over all models and random seeds.

adversarial training (incorporating manipulated inputs during training), continuous anomaly detection, and runtime safety checks on boundary conditions.

7   Conclusion

In this paper, We introduced two strategies for evaluating the robustness of RL4BG, a representative RL-based AP controller, against sensor malfunctions. Our threat models capture worst-case failures arising from both natural errors and adversarial manipulation. These experiments revealed not only catastrophic failures but also prolonged degradation of performance—both of which present serious risks in safety-critical medical settings.

In particular, we showed that as little as 50 min of an unresponsive CGM sensor was sufficient to universally induce catastrophic failure across simulated T1D patients. We also demonstrated that RL4BG is highly vulnerable to subtle perturbations in CGM values, which can accumulate into significant harm over time.

These findings motivate the establishment of adversarially oriented evaluation practices for RL-based glycemic controllers. While standard testing against random fluctuations may improve generalization to normal glucose variability, it fails to capture the brittleness exposed by anomalous sensor inputs. Our testing framework provides a foundation for such practices and can be applied to future generations of closed-loop AP controllers.

Finally, this work underscores the need for training RL-based systems with robustness in mind. Incorporating adversarial training, anomaly detection, and runtime safety mechanisms will be critical to ensuring that future medical RL models remain safe and reliable under real-world failure conditions.

Acknowledgements. We thank Bill Yurcik for his invaluable feedback during the review process. This work was supported by the Air Force Office of Scientific Research under award numbers FA9550-22-1-0450 and FA9550-22-1-0029. Any opinions, findings, conclusions, or recommendations expressed in this material are those of the authors and do not reflect the views of the sponsors.

References

1. Xie, J.: Simglucose v0.2.1 (2018). https://github.com/jxx123/simglucose. Accessed 16 Feb 2024
2. Artificial pancreas. https://www.niddk.nih.gov/health-information/diabetes/overview/managing-diabetes/artificial-pancreas. Accessed 16 Feb 2024
3. FDA approves first automated insulin delivery device for type 1 diabetes. https://www.fda.gov/news-events/press-announcements/fda-approves-first-automated-insulin-delivery-device-type-1-diabetes. Accessed 16 Feb 2024
4. Hyperglycemia (high blood sugar). https://my.clevelandclinic.org/health/diseases/9815-hyperglycemia-high-blood-sugar. Accessed 16 Feb 2024
5. Low blood glucose (hypoglycemia). https://www.niddk.nih.gov/health-information/diabetes/overview/preventing-problems/low-blood-glucose-hypoglycemia. Accessed 16 Feb 2024
6. Insulin for type 1 diabetes. nhs.uk (2023). https://www.nhs.uk/medicines/insulin/insulin-for-type-1-diabetes/. Accessed 16 Feb 2024
7. Chang, P., Krish, V., Rahmati, A.: Security analysis of RL-based artificial pancreas systems. In: ACM HealthSec Workshop (HealthSec) (2024)
8. Dexcom: Dexcom G7 User Guide. https://dexcompdf.s3.us-west-2.amazonaws.com/en-us/G7-CGM-Users-Guide.pdf. Accessed 30 Aug 2024
9. Dhaliwal, S.K.: Estimated average glucose (EAG). medlineplus.gov. https://medlineplus.gov/ency/patientinstructions/000966.htm. Accessed 16 Feb 2024
10. Fox, I., Lee, J., Pop-Busui, R., Wiens, J.: Deep reinforcement learning for closed-loop blood glucose control (2020)
11. Gregory, G.A., et al.: Global incidence, prevalence, and mortality of type 1 diabetes in 2021 with projection to 2040: a modelling study (2022)
12. Haarnoja, T., Zhou, A., Abbeel, P., Levine, S.: Soft actor-critic: off-policy maximum entropy deep reinforcement learning with a stochastic actor (2018)
13. Kim, J., Oh, J., Son, D., Kwon, H., Astillo, P.V., You, I.: Apsec1.0: innovative security protocol design with formal security analysis for the artificial pancreas system. Sensors **23**(12) (2023)
14. Liu, Y., Chen, X., Liu, C., Song, D.: Delving into transferable adversarial examples and black-box attacks. arXiv preprint arXiv:1611.02770 (2016)
15. Madry, A., Makelov, A., Schmidt, L., Tsipras, D., Vladu, A.: Towards deep learning models resistant to adversarial attacks (2019)

16. Magni, L., et al.: Model predictive control of type 1 diabetes: an in silico trial (2007)
17. Mahmud, F., Isse, N.H., Daud, N.A.M., Morsin, M.: Evaluation of PD/PID controller for insulin control on blood glucose regulation in a Type-I diabetes. In: AIP Conference Proceedings, vol. 1788, no. 1, p. 030072 (2017)
18. Medtronic. MiniMed 780G System User Guide. https://www.medtronic.com/content/dam/medtronic-wide/public/canada/products/diabetes/780g-gs3-system-user-guide.pdf. Accessed 30 Aug 2024
19. Mulvey, A.: FDA clears a new artificial pancreas system. https://www.jdrf.org/blog/2023/05/22/fda-clears-new-artificial-pancreas-system/. Accessed 16 Feb 2024
20. Trevitt, S., Simpson, S., Wood, A.: Artificial pancreas device systems for the closed-loop control of type 1 diabetes: what systems are in development? (2016)

Systems-Theoretic and Data-Driven Security Analysis in ML-Enabled Medical Devices

Gargi Mitra[1]([✉])[iD], Mohammadreza Hallajiyan[1][iD], Inji Kim[2][iD],
Athish Pranav Dharmalingam[3][iD], Mohammed Elnawawy[1][iD],
Shahrear Iqbal[4][iD], Karthik Pattabiraman[1][iD], and Homa Alemzadeh[2][iD]

[1] The University of British Columbia, Vancouver, BC, Canada
{gargi,hallaj,mnawawy,karthikp}@ece.ubc.ca
[2] University of Virginia, Charlottesville, VA, USA
{ddh8jk,ha4d}@virginia.edu
[3] Indian Institute of Technology Madras, Chennai, Tamil Nadu, India
cs21b011@smail.iitm.ac.in
[4] National Research Council Canada, Ottawa, Ontario, Canada
shahrear.iqbal@nrc-cnrc.gc.ca

Abstract. The integration of AI/ML into medical devices is rapidly transforming healthcare by enhancing diagnostic and treatment facilities. However, this advancement also introduces serious cybersecurity risks due to the use of complex and often opaque models, extensive interconnectivity, interoperability with third-party peripheral devices, Internet connectivity, and vulnerabilities in the underlying technologies. These factors contribute to a broad attack surface and make threat prevention, detection, and mitigation challenging. Given the highly safety-critical nature of these devices, a cyberattack on these devices can cause the ML models to mispredict, thereby posing significant safety risks to patients. Therefore, ensuring the security of these devices from the time of design is essential. This paper underscores the urgency of addressing the cybersecurity challenges in ML-enabled medical devices at the premarket phase. We begin by analyzing publicly available data on device recalls and adverse events, and known vulnerabilities, to understand the threat landscape of AI/ML-enabled medical devices and their repercussions on patient safety. Building on this analysis, we introduce a suite of tools and techniques designed by us to assist security analysts in conducting comprehensive premarket risk assessments. Our work aims to empower manufacturers to embed cybersecurity as a core design principle in AI/ML-enabled medical devices, thereby making them safe for patients.

Keywords: AI/ML-enabled medical devices · Security assessment · Safety assessment · System-theoretic security analysis · AI/ML security

1   Introduction

Machine Learning (ML)-driven applications are becoming increasingly popular in the medical field. ML-enabled medical devices (software or software-driven hardware) assist physicians in critical activities such as remote patient monitoring, controlling surgical equipment, automatic drug administration, and preliminary/advanced disease diagnosis [110]. These tasks require high accuracy and reliability, and the loss of either of these can endanger patient safety. However, the use of ML in interconnected medical devices has expanded the threat surface of medical systems [4,20,22,24,59,64,68,71,77,78,80,81,89,124,133] making them more vulnerable to cyberattacks. If an adversary compromises such a device, it can force the ML engine to make incorrect predictions or decisions, which can have catastrophic consequences, such as wrong diagnoses and treatments, leading to severe health complications or even the death of the patient.

Detecting and mitigating cyberattacks in ML-based medical applications is significantly more challenging than in traditional systems for two reasons. First, these applications rely on large datasets and often employ complex, unexplainable models, making their behavior difficult to interpret even for developers. Second, they are highly interconnected with third-party devices that collect patient data for real-time predictions, which are subsequently transmitted to downstream systems or patients and physicians for clinical decision-making and treatment. This high degree of connectivity increases the attack surface, while the complexity of ML models complicates attack detection. Adversaries can exploit the vulnerabilities in the ML models and interface devices to poison training data [88], inject erroneous inputs during inference [49], or modify model parameters through compromised configuration files [126]. We are particularly interested in inference-time false data injection attacks, which are the easiest to execute and most difficult to detect. A recent study on the FDA adverse event reports involving ML-enabled medical devices indicated that over 80% of the reported events were related to data acquisition problems, leading to no data or erroneous data capture [76]. Several studies have also highlighted the vulnerability of data acquisition systems to adversarial examples [20,50,57]. The safety-critical nature of ML-enabled medical devices makes it crucial to identify and address these security vulnerabilities before deployment.

In this paper, we focus on pre-market security risk assessment, which is the process of identifying, assessing the severity of, and mitigating potential security risks in a given medical device before it is approved for market release. This process is crucial for ensuring patient safety, regulatory compliance, and cyber resilience, as well as reducing post-deployment threat mitigation costs. We inspected the publicly available device summaries [118] the manufacturers submitted to the FDA for pre-market approval to determine whether manufacturers conducted security risk assessments for ML-enabled devices. Our investigation reveals that for over 65% of these devices, the manufacturers either do not provide any information about the assessment method in their documentation, or employ inadequate assessment methods (see Fig. 1). In fact, until 2014, no device summary mentioned any security risk assessment. Among the remaining devices,

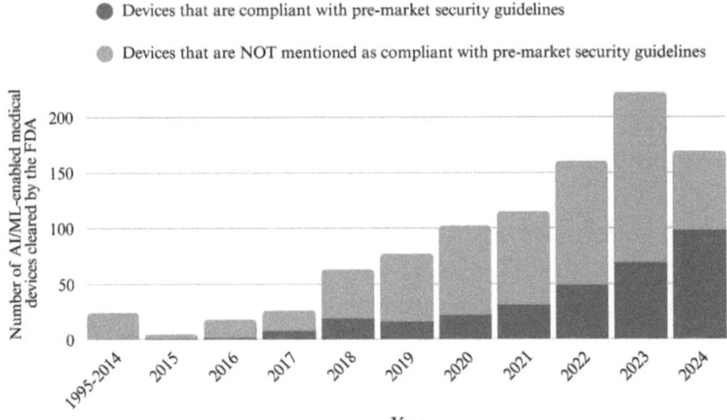

Fig. 1. Growing number of AI/ML-enabled medical devices and the rise of security-awareness among device manufacturers (Data as of April 2025).

a few use proprietary mechanisms that make it challenging to assess the adequacy of their approach, while others utilize existing risk assessment techniques. These techniques, as we discuss in the subsequent sections, are insufficient for securing interconnected ML-enabled medical systems. However, on a positive note, there is a growing security awareness among manufacturers, reflected in the increasing mention of security risk assessments in recent pre-market summaries.

Security practitioners and researchers have made significant efforts in assessing and ensuring the safety and security of medical devices by developing advanced methods for qualitative and quantitative risk assessment (e.g., fault tree analysis (FTA), failure mode and effect analysis (FMEA)) and formal assurance case reports [9,61,62]) and security analysis [14], model-based design and verification [7,16,95], closed-loop validation [63], encryption, and authentication [65]. However, less attention has been paid to the *end-to-end system security* of ML-enabled medical devices by considering the interactions of the ML-enabled device with other interconnected system components. Current security assessment methods primarily focus on algorithm, hardware, software, and firmware vulnerabilities, but they often overlook the *inherent vulnerabilities of the ML models* used in medical devices, how they can be exploited by first exploiting vulnerabilities in interconnected devices, and the potential impact of the ML mispredictions on *patient safety. To bridge this gap, it is imperative to perform a holistic system-theoretic analysis of ML-enabled medical systems.*

In this paper, we first present our experience with developing tools and techniques to automate the extraction of large-scale data on real-world security vulnerabilities and safety incidents for ML-enabled medical devices from public data and knowledge sources. Further, we devise techniques that use this data to enable security practitioners to perform system-theoretic analysis to identify potential threats, new attack paths, and their safety impacts. This will help medical device manufacturers anticipate post-deployment security risks early at design time, assess the severity of the risks, and implement risk prevention and mitigation strategies. For instance, a company developing an ML-enabled device that integrates with third-party commodity off-the-shelf cameras can use our techniques to identify known security vulnerabilities in compatible camera models, evaluate the likelihood of their exploitation, and assess potential risks to patient safety based on previously reported failures and adverse events of both ML-enabled and non-ML-enabled devices with the same functionality. Based on these insights, the company can either implement appropriate security measures and safety mechanisms or provide guidance to users to avoid connecting vulnerable cameras to the device. We demonstrate our tools and techniques on various ML-enabled medical devices, particularly blood glucose management systems (BGMS), as an example of safety-critical personalized devices with a broad and complex attack surface due to their high levels of connectivity and interoperability.

2   Background and Motivation

This section provides the technical background required to understand the subsequent sections and the motivation behind our research.

2.1   AI/ML-Enabled Medical Devices

As of December 2024, the U.S. Food and Drug Administration (FDA) has authorized more than $1,016$ ML-enabled medical devices across 17 different medical disciplines (e.g., Cardiology, Ophthalmology, and Gastroenterology) [110]. These devices can be categorized into two types: Software as a Medical Device (SaMD) and Software in a Medical Device (SiMD). An SaMD is software that can be run on general-purpose computers (e.g., d-Nav for predicting insulin dose for diabetic patients [112]), whereas an SiMD is software that is sold bundled with hardware manufactured by the same company (e.g., GI Genius Intelligent Endoscopy Module [115]). Our analysis of the FDA data shows that while radiological imaging devices are the most common category of FDA-cleared ML-enabled devices (76.5%), safety-critical devices in clinical chemistry (e.g., BGMS), cardiovascular (e.g., arrhythmia diagnosis devices), and neurology (e.g., surgical procedures planning systems) have relatively higher numbers of reported adverse events (see Fig. 5). Unlike radiological devices, most personalized cardiac monitors and BGMS are mobile-based devices used by patients in the absence of continuous medical supervision. Their compatibility with peripheral devices from multiple brands and various communication protocols creates a broad and complex attack surface, making them highly susceptible to false data injection attacks with potentially severe consequences. These factors make such devices a compelling choice for our evaluation. Table 1 shows examples of ML-enabled BGMS, including d-Nav [112], WellDoc BlueStar [117], Dreamed Advisor Pro [114], Dario Blood Glucose Monitoring System [113], and the One Drop Blood Glucose [116] Monitoring System.

Table 1. A study of different FDA-Approved ML-enabled medical devices and their security vulnerabilities that enable false data injection attacks.

Device Name [110]	YoA[$]	Device Function	ML Technique used	Known ML attacks	Possible third-party attack entry points {Known vulnerablity}	Potential impact of mis-prediction
d-Nav System[†]	'19	Insulin dose prediction	Reinforcement learning*	[34]	Android vulnerabilities [31]	Wrong treatment (Fatal)
WellDoc BlueStar[†]	'19	Diabetes management	Light Gradient Boosting Machine*	[15]	Cloud Service API [29]	Wrong diagnosis
Dreamed Advisor Pro[‡]	'19	Diabetes management	Reinforcement learning*	[75]	Blood glucose meter [27]	Wrong treatment (Fatal)
Dario BGMS[‡]	'15	Diabetes management	k-means clustering*	[25]	Android vulnerabilities [31]	Wrong treatment (Fatal)
One Drop BGMS[‡]	'16	Diabetes management	Long short-term memory*	[104]	Bluetooth	Wrong treatment (Fatal)
Mammo-Screen[‡]	'24	Breast cancer detection	Deep learning	[74]	PACS server {[26]} Ⓡ	Wrong diagnosis
CardioLogs ECG Analysis Platform[†]	'17	Cardiac arrhythmia detection	Deep Neural Network (DNN)	[22]	Portable ECG Monitors - {[82]} Ⓛ, Cellular network, Bluetooth	Wrong treatment (Fatal)
GI Genius[‡]	'21	Gastro-intestinal lesion detection	Convolutional neural networks (CNN)*	[58]	Endoscope cameras - {[84]} Ⓡ, Intranet / Internet	Wrong diagnosis
NuVasive Pulse System[‡]	'18	Neurological monitoring	CNN*	[58]	Infra-red sensitive cameras - [125] Ⓛ, {[85]} Ⓡ, Internet	Mistake in surgery (Fatal)
Air Next[‡]	'20	Spirometer	CNN*	[58]	Bluetooth, Internet	Wrong diagnosis
BrainScope TBI[‡]	'19	Brain injury assessment	Regularized logistic regression model	[23]	Internet	Wrong treatment (Fatal)
IDx-DR v2.3[†]	'22	Diabetic Retinopathy Detection	CNN	[58]	This device uses the Topcon NW200 Fundus camera, which comes packaged with a PC running Windows 7 OS. The Windows 7 OS has known vulnerabilities - {[86]} Ⓡ, Internet	Wrong diagnosis (loss of vision)
Iris Intelligent Retinal Imaging System[†]	'15	Storage, management and display of retinal images	Deep Learning	[130]	Same as in the case of IDx-DR v2.3, Internet	Wrong diagnosis (loss of vision)
Paige Prostate[†]	'21	Cancer diagnosis	CNN + Recurrent neural networks	[53]	Medical scanners - {[83]} Ⓛ, Internet	Wrong diagnosis (Fatal)
Tissue of Origin Test Kit[‡]	'18	Malignant Tumor diagnosis	SVM	[77]	Internet	Wrong diagnosis (Fatal)

SiMD, *: Best-guessed ML algorithm, [$] YoA: Year of Approval, Ⓛ: Only locally exploitable vulnerability, Ⓡ: Remotely exploitable vulnerability

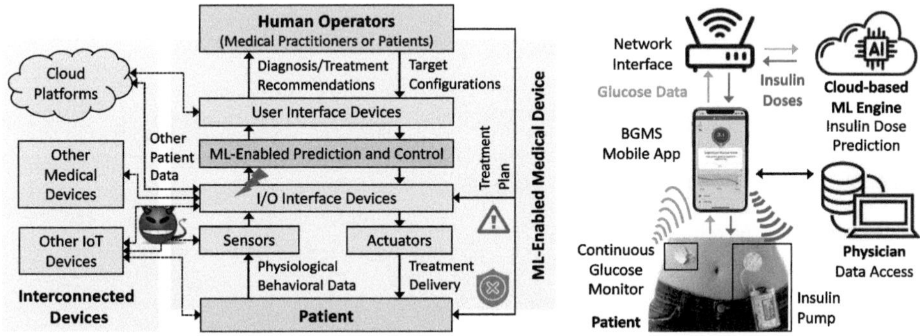

Fig. 2. Left: Typical System Control Structure of Interconnected ML-enabled Medical Cyber-Physical Systems. Right: Example ML-enabled Blood Glucose Management System (BGMS) Authorized by the U.S. FDA.

Interconnected Medical Devices. The ML models in these devices typically receive inputs from multiple sensory devices that collect various physiological data from a patient's body to predict their condition. Moreover, they can interface with third-party software, cloud platforms, and IoT devices, creating a highly interconnected system. For instance, as shown in Fig. 2 (Right), an ML-based diabetes management app such as d-Nav can be installed on a mobile phone. It contains two user-interactive software elements - one for the patient and one for the physician. The system can receive glucose measurement data entered manually into the patient user software or automatically via the cloud from a linked blood glucose meter or continuous glucose monitor (CGM). Some backend components run locally on the phone, while others may be hosted either locally or in the cloud [112].

Interoperability in AI/ML-enabled Medical Devices. In recent years, there has been a growing trend toward enhancing *interoperability*, particularly in AI/ML-enabled medical systems. For example, to promote modular integration across BGMS from different manufacturers, the FDA has introduced a framework identifying three essential components in Automated Insulin Delivery (AID) systems, including Alternate Controller Enabled (ACE) pumps, interoperable CGMs (iCGMs), and interoperable glycemic controllers (iAGCs), that can reliably and securely communicate with digitally connected devices to send, receive, and execute drug delivery commands [35]. Motivated by a broader patient movement towards open and personalized configurations [94,106], several interoperable AID systems have gained FDA approval. Table 2 shows seven FDA-approved AID systems among which five incorporate officially designated interoperable components (ACE pump, iCGM, and iAGC). A recently approved iACG, Tidepool [106], supports a wide range of compatible CGMs and insulin pumps from different manufacturers (such as Medtronic, Tandem, Omnipod, and Dexcom) and is used in a newly FDA-approved AID, called Twiist. Although the current AID devices on the market are not ML-enabled, some of them adopt

Table 2. Examples of FDA-approved Automated Insulin Delivery (AID) systems that support interoperability in connected components. Modified from [66].

AID System	FDA Approval Date	Pump	AGC (Control Algorithm)	CGM
Beta Bionics iLet Bionic Pancreas	05/19/2023	iLet	iLet Dosing Decision Software	Dexcom G6, Dexcom G7
Insulet Omnipod 5	08/26/2024	Omnipod 5 / DASH	SmartAdjust algorithm	Dexcom G6, Dexcom G7
Tandem Mobi	07/11/2023	Mobi	Control-IQ algorithm	Dexcom G6, Dexcom G7
Tandem t: slim X2	12/13/2019	t:slim X2	Control-IQ algorithm	Dexcom G6, Dexcom G7
Medtronic MiniMed 770G	09/01/2020	MiniMed 770G	SmartGuard technology	Guardian Sensor 3, FreeStyle Libre 2 Plus
Medtronic MiniMed 780G	04/21/2023	MiniMed 780G	SmartGuard technology	Guardian Sensor 3, Guardian Sensor 4
Twiist	04/02/2025	Deka insulin pump	Tidepool Loop algorithm	FreeStyle Libre 3 Plus

smart model-predictive control (MPC) algorithms (e.g., SmartAdjust in Omnipod 5 [60], Control-IQ by Tandem t) that are envisioned to use ML in the near future [97]. A similar trend towards growing interoperability in other ML-enabled diabetes management systems is also expected to happen.

This shift towards interconnectivity and interoperability underscores an urgent need for comprehensive system-level security analysis in ML-enabled medical devices. As interconnectivity increases, potential vulnerabilities such as data breaches, insecure interfaces, and compromised control integrity must be proactively addressed through secure-by-design architectures.

2.2 Security Vulnerabilities in ML-Enabled Medical Devices

The draft guidance containing recommendations for AI-enabled device software functions, published in 2025 by the U.S. Food and Drug Administration (FDA) agency, highlights a number of ML risks that are susceptible to cybersecurity threats [111]. These include data poisoning, model inversion/stealing, model evasion, data leakage, overfitting, model bias, and performance drift caused by adversaries. The highly interconnected nature of ML-based medical devices provides a multitude of attack vectors to adversaries. This is also evident from an increasing number of reported recalls, adverse events [9], and security vulnerabilities [1,67,92,128] and demonstrated attacks on medical devices across various clinical specialties [7,19,56,72]. A recent study [1] on over 966 medical devices from 117 vendors found 993 vulnerabilities across medical hardware, operating systems, and software applications. Further, 160 of these had publicly-available exploits that could allow the attackers to target patients and healthcare organizations. The majority of these vulnerabilities were found in health IT applications (741) and moderate-risk devices (292) such as medical imaging and monitoring/telemetry devices and infusion pumps.

2.3   Threat Model

In this work, we focus on false data injection attacks, a significant threat to interconnected medical devices. An adversary can force an ML engine to generate incorrect predictions or decisions by injecting carefully crafted malicious data through the data acquisition system during inference [22,77].

Preventing such attacks in ML-enabled medical devices is particularly challenging due to their interconnectivity with several other peripheral and sensor devices and networks. Figure 2 (Left) shows the various components of an ML-enabled medical system. Adversaries can exploit vulnerabilities in any of the third-party medical and Internet of Things (IoT) devices on the hospital network and/or interface and network devices to find their way into a target ML-enabled device, and inject malicious data into the ML engine even if the ML-enabled device is not compromised. Therefore, it is not enough to secure only the ML-enabled devices. A recent notification by the Federal Bureau of Investigation (FBI) indicated that about 53 percent of connected medical and IoT devices in hospitals have known critical vulnerabilities [92] that could enable such attacks. In our prior work [33], we manually analyzed 15 ML-enabled medical devices across various disciplines to examine their ML models, known vulnerabilities, and potential attack vectors in peripheral devices for false data injection during inference. Table 1 summarizes our findings, revealing that 11 of 15 devices were susceptible to false data injection attacks, with consequences ranging from vision loss to patient death.

2.4   Systems-Theoretic Safety and Security Analysis

Given the highly interconnected nature of ML-enabled medical devices, ensuring their security and safety requires a comprehensive, system-level approach that accounts for complex interactions between components. Modern system-theoretic approaches to safety and security of interconnected devices, such as STAMP (Systems-Theoretic Accident Model and Processes) [69], model accidents as complex processes resulting from safety and security constraint violations due to inadequate controls. Systems are represented as *hierarchical control structures*, with each level constraining the one below and communicating their conditions and behavior to the upper levels. System-Theoretic Process Analysis for Security (STPA-Sec) [131] and Causal Analysis using System Theory (CAST) [69], built upon STAMP, analyze hardware, software, physical systems, and human operators across control layers to pinpoint threat scenarios, security exploits, unsafe actions, and their causal factors. To assess ML-enabled device vulnerabilities, analysts must (i) model the device's control structure and (ii)

Table 3. Summary of State-of-the-Art STPA/STPA-Sec tools (All these tools generate causal scenarios in semi-automated fashion)

Name	Focus	Application Domain
A-STPA, XSTAMPP	Safety	General Purpose
SafetyHAT	Safety	Transportation
WebSTAMP	Safety/Security	Healthcare, Transportation, Chemical Industry
SOT	Safety/Security	Aircraft Systems

identify technologies (e.g., protocols, software, OS, firmware) used in each component.

While several tools support STPA and STPA-Sec across various domains, we assess their suitability for ML-enabled medical systems based on three key features: (i) applicability to security attacks on ML systems, (ii) applicability to the medical domain, and (iii) automation of causal scenario generation. To this end, we evaluate four state-of-the-art STPA/STPA-Sec tools: **(1)** A-STPA [2] and its enhanced version, XSTAMPP [3] assist in linking unsafe control actions to safety hazards and provide graphical aids for control structure creation but require manual causal scenario identification; **(2)** SafetyHAT [18] is customized for the transportation sector. This tool offers a graphical interface, data management, and domain-specific guidewords but lacks automated causal scenario identification; **(3)** WebSTAMP [103] is a web application designed for STPA and STPA-Sec, that provides structured guidance for identifying hazardous control actions and causal scenarios. It has been applied to Glucose Monitoring and Insulin Pumping System, transportation applications [105], and chemical reactors [132]; and, **(4)** SOT [98] – this tool helps systems engineers conduct safety and security analyses by leveraging past knowledge to identify causal scenarios.

In summary, A-STPA, XSTAMPP, and SafetyHAT focus on safety risks from device failures, not malicious attacks. While WebSTAMP and SOT consider security concerns, they still rely on users' knowledge of vulnerabilities and require significant manual effort. Table 3 shows a summary of these tools.

Recent papers such as the survey by Qi et al. [99] explore the use of STPA in learning-enabled systems, and introduce DeepSTPA for analyzing ML lifecycle failures, which is beyond our scope. Other recent papers [90,91,100] explore the usability of Large Language Models (LLMs) in STPA, highlighting the need for human intervention in generating prompts and validating LLM responses. However, none of these studies focus on medical device security.

2.5   Medical Device Databases

The U.S. Food and Drug Administration (FDA) regulates medical devices sold in the US, and maintains several publicly available databases on premarket and postmarket data about cleared and approved medical devices, including device summary information, approval date, user instructions, and information on Premarket Approvals (PMA), Premarket Notifications (510[k]), Adverse Events, and Recalls. We analyze the following FDA databases to extract the information about medical device technologies and their reported safety and security flaws:

AI/ML-Enabled Medical Devices database [110] maintains the information about the FDA-authorized medical devices that incorporate AI/ML across medical disciplines. This data is not comprehensive and only contains releasable information about devices based on information provided in the summary descriptions of their marketing authorization document.

Premarket Notifications (510(k)s) database [118] contains the releasable records of premarket notifications submitted by medical device manufacturers for the devices introduced into commercial distribution for the first time or those reintroduced with significant changes. Each record includes device classification and approval information as well as summaries of device functionality and safety and effectiveness information for more recent submissions.

Recalls database [122] contains records of medical device recalls since November 01, 2002. A recall is a voluntary action that a manufacturer takes to correct or remove from the market any medical device that violates the FDA's laws. Each record in the database contains the information on a recalled device such as the product name, manufacturer name, number of devices on the market, recall class, FDA determined cause, and the human-written textual descriptions of manufacturer's reason for recall and recovery actions taken to correct the device or remove it from the market.

Manufacturer and User Facility Device Experience database [119] **(MAUDE)** is a collection of adverse events of medical devices that volunteers, user facilities, manufacturers, and distributors have reported to the FDA. Each adverse event report contains information such as device and manufacturer names, event type (e.g., Malfunction, Injury, or Death), event and report dates, and human-written event description and manufacturer narratives, which provide a short textual description of the incident, as well as any comments made or follow-up actions taken by the manufacturer to detect and address device problems.

2.6 Vulnerability Databases

We analyze the following publicly available vulnerability databases to identify common threats and security attacks targeting medical devices and peripheral devices:

ICS-CERT Alerts dataset [108] is developed and maintained by Industrial Control Systems Cyber Emergency Response Team and the United States Computer Emergency Readiness Team (US-CERT). US-CERT is responsible for analyzing and reducing cyber threats, vulnerabilities, disseminating cyber threat warning information, and coordinating incident response activities.

MITRE Common Vulnerability Enumeration (CVE) database [87]is a publicly accessible registry of known cybersecurity vulnerabilities, maintained

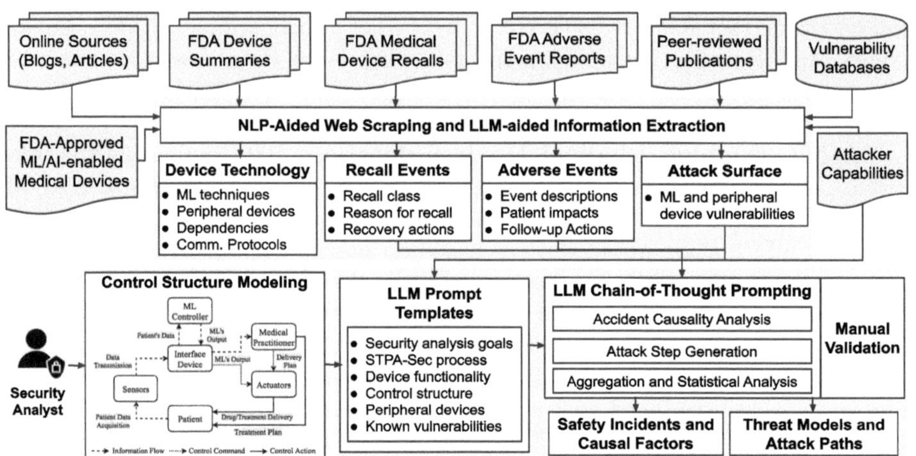

Fig. 3. Overall Approach for Systems-Theoretic and Data-Driven Analysis of Safety and Security of ML-enabled Medical Devices.

by the MITRE corporation. It provides a comprehensive database of vulnerabilities, including those affecting peripheral medical and IoT devices used in medical systems. The data is contributed by software vendors, security researchers, penetration testers, as well as independent researchers.

Despite these publicly available databases, the information on ML-enabled medical devices and the peripheral devices they connect to is only available in a dispersed and unstructured format. It is particularly challenging to (i) extract relevant information on security vulnerabilities and safety impacts from the dispersed data across millions of records in different databases and (2) analyze the free-form natural language text, written by the manufacturers and healthcare professionals, while understanding semantics and the contextual factors involved in the events. In the subsequent sections, we describe how some of the tools and techniques we developed alleviate the aforementioned challenges.

3 Methods

This section presents our framework for performing holistic system-theoretic analysis of ML-enabled medical systems. The framework comprises a suite of Natural Language Processing (NLP) and LLM-aided tools and techniques to assist the systems and control-theoretic security analysis of ML-enabled medical devices. Specifically, we report our experience on the design and validation of tools for semi-automated device modeling and technology identification, information extraction, and systems-theoretic accident causality analysis and attack step generation.

Figure 3 shows an overview of our framework, which consists of three main components.

The **first** component is a device modeling and technology identification technique. It helps security analysts model the interconnections and communications between the ML-enabled medical device and third-party peripherals as a control structure using a generic control structure template for ML-enabled medical devices. It also assists in identifying all technologies used in connected devices that could serve as potential attack entry points.

The **second** component is a set of NLP and LLM-aided web scraping and information extraction techniques to extract and cross-reference the information from publicly available databases. Given a natural language description of an ML-enabled medical device, it extracts key details, including the ML technique used, connected peripherals, and device functionality. Using this information, it scrapes the web for information on relevant ML vulnerabilities that adversaries could exploit to induce misprediction. Additionally, it interfaces with public FDA medical device and vulnerability databases to identify vulnerabilities in similar medical devices and peripheral devices, as well as recalls and adverse events linked to their malfunctions and safety impacts.

The **third** component of this framework is an LLM-based tool that can assist security analysts in systems-theoretic and data-driven safety accident (CAST) and security (STPA-Sec) analysis. This tool integrates the knowledge of CAST and STPA-Sec processes with the extracted information on device technology, control structure, and vulnerabilities and encodes them as customized prompt templates that can guide LLMs in generating (i) a comprehensive list of safety issues and causal factors that could lead to patient harm and (ii) attack vectors that adversaries could exploit to deliberately trigger such safety events.

In the following subsections, we discuss these tools/techniques in detail. We also illustrate how each tool/technique contributes to the overall security assessment, by providing examples of their output when applied to ML-enabled devices, such as the BGMS in Fig. 2.

3.1   Device Modeling and Technology Identification

To identify all possible attack vectors in a given ML-enabled medical system, a security analyst first needs to model the interconnections of the ML-enabled medical device with the peripheral devices, the data flow between various system components, and understand the technology used by various system components. To enable the systems-theoretic security analysis using STPA-Sec (in Sect. 3.3), we adopt the hierarchical system control structures from STAMP (see Sect. 2.4) for this purpose.

System Control Structure Modeling. In our previous work (SAM [54]), we partially automated the construction of the system control structure for ML-enabled medical devices by developing a template control structure that contains typical components and interconnections in an ML-enabled medical system. The security analysts could customize this generic control structure by adding/removing necessary components and interactions to match the description of the system under assessment. Once the control structure is built, the

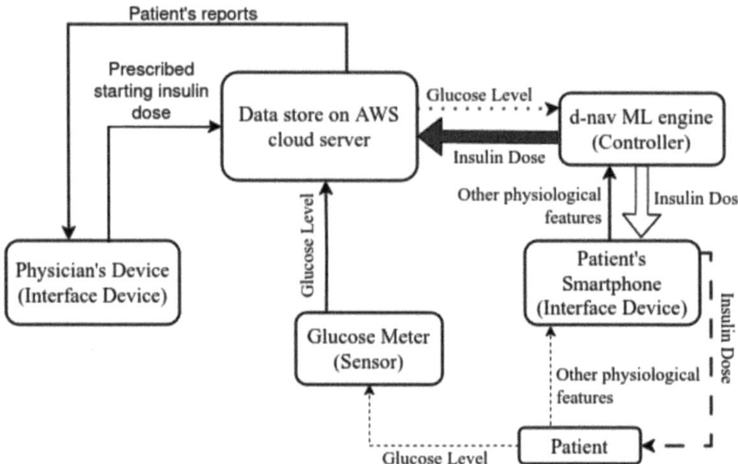

Fig. 4. Control Structure of the d-Nav System. Note that, while setting up the system, the ML engine can be configured to run either on the smartphone or on the cloud server.

security analyst must manually identify the data flows among various system components from the device descriptions. We applied this technique on two ML-enabled medical devices – (1) d-Nav [112], a blood glucose monitoring system, and; (2) ABMD [109], a bone mineral density calculator. We built the control structure and inferred the data flow using the system description provided by the manufacturer, which we obtained from publicly available device summaries submitted to the FDA during the pre-approval process, as well as from information available on the manufacturers' websites. Figure 4 shows the control structure for d-Nav [112], as generated by the technique proposed in SAM. Note that these documents do not follow a standardized format - the information is often dispersed across multiple sites, and the transparency varies across manufacturers. Hence, automating the information retrieval process remains a challenge.

Technology Identification. Once the security analyst builds the control structure, they must identify the technologies used across system components, such as the ML techniques, operating systems, firmware, and communication protocols used by the ML-enabled and connected peripheral devices, to assess the potential security vulnerabilities associated with each of them.

To identify the ML and peripheral device technologies, we have integrated two questionnaires [55] into our toolkit [54], which must be completed by the designers of the ML-enabled device. The first focuses on *compatibility conditions* for each peripheral device in the control structure and needs to be answered by the manufacturer of the ML-enabled device. For example, some blood glucose management systems use Bluetooth to transmit glucose readings from the glucose meter to the glucose management smartphone app, while others require a USB connection for data transfer. Following this, the security analyst must manually identify all commercial peripheral devices that meet the compatibility conditions specified by the ML-enabled device manufacturer. The second questionnaire helps analysts identify the *technologies used in the ML-enabled device, and each compatible peripheral device* by covering key technological and operational factors relevant to medical devices. These questions ensure a thorough assessment of potential attack entry points. The factors are categorized into four groups [54]: (i) Human Interaction – this includes data entry and supervision, data validation, authentication, and anomaly detection; (ii) Communication Protocol – this includes the exact protocol name, version, and whether it uses encryption; (iii) Electromagnetic Susceptibility – this includes whether the device is susceptible to electromagnetic radiation, and if so, what its repercussions would be, and if they have any known shielding or mitigation strategy in place; and, (iv) Dependencies on firmware, hardware, OS, and external libraries. This categorization is based on known attack vectors targeting ML-enabled medical devices [129].

Note that, for a security analyst working for a medical device manufacturing company, obtaining the aforementioned information from the device designers would be straightforward. However, for an analyst working independently or for a third-party company, the manufacturers might be unwilling to provide this information either due to reluctance to spend unnecessary time or effort (as might be the case for peripheral device technologies) or due to confidentiality concerns (as might be the case for ML technique details). In such cases, the analyst can infer compatibility conditions, such as communication links, input devices, and operating systems, from publicly available device descriptions on the FDA website [110] and publicly available information on each peripheral, such as product descriptions on the manufacturer's website. Following this, the analyst could also retrieve a fairly comprehensive list of compatible peripheral devices from third-party information repositories such as TidePool [106]. However, identifying the specific ML technologies used is far more challenging, as most manufacturers do not declare them on their website or do not disclose them publicly at all. To assist the analyst under such circumstances, we have developed NLP- and LLM-aided tools as described in the following subsection.

3.2 NLP and LLM-Aided Web Scraping and Information Extraction

Once the security analyst builds the control structure and identifies the technologies used in the ML-enabled device and its connected components, they must proceed to identify known vulnerabilities in these technologies that might serve as an attack entry point. Today, information about security vulnerabilities, design flaws, and adverse events reported on medical devices is available on the Internet in an unstructured and dispersed manner. This makes it challenging to ensure the coverage of all relevant data during the security assessment process. Our set of NLP-aided web scraping and LLM-aided information extraction tools and techniques assists the system developers and security analysts in extracting and integrating data on all known vulnerabilities and safety issues relevant to the ML-enabled medical device under assessment. This information is also used by our subsequent tools for automated systems-theoretic safety and security analysis.

ML Technology and Vulnerability Identification. In our latest work [32], we proposed MedAIScout, a semi-automated NLP- and LLM-aided tool designed to retrieve information on known ML vulnerabilities relevant to ML-enabled medical devices. MedAIScout works in two steps:

(1) *ML technology identification:* Given a description of an ML-enabled medical device, MedAIScout uses NLP techniques to identify key terms related to the device's functionality, ML model type, and data characteristics. Often, the device manufacturers do not publicly disclose the exact ML technique used in their products. In case the security analyst (MedAIScout user) does not have access to a document containing the exact details (such as in the case of third-party analysts), MedAIScout can analyze available information and infer the most likely ML technique by referencing similar devices documented in existing literature. In this work, we sourced the device descriptions from the publicly accessible pre-market device summaries available on the FDA website [110,118] and peer-reviewed research articles indexed on Google Scholar.

(2) *ML vulnerability identification:* Next, MedAIScout constructs tailored search queries to retrieve peer-reviewed research articles on attacks targeting the device's ML model. MedAIScout uses local LLMs to differentiate between training-time and inference-time attacks and provides context and explanations for each retrieved article's relevance.

Throughout the device's lifecycle, security analysts can use MedAIScout to track emerging ML vulnerabilities. To the best of our knowledge, it is the first automated tool to retrieve known ML vulnerabilities specifically for medical applications. By applying MedAIScout to five FDA-approved ML-enabled medical devices, we found that MedAIScout successfully uncovered relevant vulnerabilities in four devices, thereby substantially assisting in security analysis. For example, when tested on the One Drop blood glucose monitoring system [116], MedAIScout retrieved a peer-reviewed research paper [107] describing an inference-time attack on a similar system. In this attack, an adversary manipulates blood glucose readings at mealtime by compromising the radio communication between the glucose meter and the controller, leading to incorrect insulin dose recommendations. The paper also proposes an appropriate attack detection technique.

Attack Surface Analysis. To capture a comprehensive attack surface for ML-enabled medical devices, we have developed tools for automated searching of public databases and identifying known vulnerabilities in the *peripheral* and *interconnected medical devices*. Comprehensive attack surface analysis is a prerequisite for systems-theoretic security analysis

In our recent work [54], we developed a method for capturing all the known vulnerabilities linked to each technology in every peripheral device used in a given ML-enabled medical device. This method uses the responses about the technological and operational factors used in the peripheral devices from the questionnaires (see §3.1) as search keywords to find known vulnerabilities in the MITRE Common Vulnerability Enumeration (CVE) database [87]. For instance, for the d-Nav BGMS [112], we found that vulnerabilities might exist in a compatible glucose meter [51], Wi-Fi communication between glucose meter and the cloud server [28], the communication between the cloud server for glucose meter and the ML controller [96], Wi-Fi communication between the interface device and the ML controller [28], and Android OS on the interface [31].

In another study [128], we examined cyberattacks targeting hospital networks and interconnected clinical environments. For this purpose, we used two publicly available vulnerability databases – the Common Vulnerabilities and Exposures (CVE) Database [87] and the Industrial Control Systems Cyber Emergency Response Team (ICS-CERT) Alerts database [108]. To automate the collection of information on medical device-related vulnerabilities from ICS-CERT, we developed a tool for crawling the whole US-CERT website and extracting all vulnerability records that contain any medical-related keywords, including generic medical keywords and those describing the common categories and specialties of medical devices, as classified by the FDA Product Code Classification Database [121]. Using this tool, we extracted the vulnerability records reported from 1999 to 2018 that were potentially related to medical devices. We then manually parsed the HTML documents of a final set of 140 extracted records to extract information such as the corresponding CVE IDs, affected product names, and manufacturer or vendor names of products, as well as vulnerability details and backgrounds. Our analysis revealed that the most common vulnerabilities included improper credential management and authentication, weak access control, privilege escalation, and buffer and stack overflows. Furthermore, we found that 18 retrieved vulnerabilities had publicly available exploits. These vulnerabilities were widespread across various medical devices, including insulin pumps, from multiple manufacturers, thereby underscoring the need to consider them in the security analysis of interconnected ML-enabled devices.

Analysis of Recalls and Adverse Events in Medical Devices. In our early work [8,9,11], we developed a suite of NLP tools (called MedSafe [12,13]) for automated extraction, cross-referencing, and classification of records from two public FDA databases: the Medical Device Recalls [122] and the MAUDE (Adverse Event Reports) database [119]. We used these tools to identify all the recalls and adverse events caused by failures in computer-based medical devices,

Table 4. Examples of recalls of AI/ML-enabled medical devices due to software issues that could result in misdiagnosis or wrong treatment (Class II recalls).

Device Name	Approval Panel	Recall #	Reason for Recall	Action Summary	No. of units affected
BodyGuardian Heart Remote Monitoring Kit	Cardiovascular	Z-2479-2020 [42]	The device data being collected and transferred to the monitoring center may not be accurate due to non-validated association between the phone software and the heart monitors, leading to inaccurate evaluation of the patients' condition.	The recalling firm contacted all patients and physicians that had potentially impacted devices. Patients that agreed were sent new devices to replace the affected one to finish their study.	8
Dario BGMS	Clinical chemistry	Z-0260-2020 [40]	The Dario Android App v4.3.0-4.3.2 may experience duplicate logging of a blood glucose level reading.	The firm released Android App v4.3.3. Users were informed about the issue via multiple push notifications and email, asking them to update to the new version.	126,271
Bioplex 2200 ANA Screen	Clinical toxicology	Z-1159-2008 [36]	False negative results due to reagent packs exhibiting low signal.	The firm contacted its consignees, informing them of the issue, recommended that they perform QC testing daily with each reagent pack, and updated the usage instructions.	8,804
Sight OLO CBC Test Kit	Hematology	Z-2173-2024* [46]	The kit shows a bias in the platelet count due to bacterial contamination, which can result in elevated counts with a bias, that results in the test kit performing outside of the device specification.	The manufacturer issued an urgent recall notice to their customers, asking them to discontinue the use of the affected test kits, return the unused kits, and dispose of the used ones.	7,450
UniCel DxH 600 Coulter Cellular Analysis System	Microbiology	Z-2158-2017 [37]	A possible data acquisition disruption may cause some unusual events, that may be incorrectly removed from analysis, which can result in erroneous diagnosis.	The manufacturers sent an Urgent Medical Device Recall letter to customers to inform them of the issue, impact, action, and resolution.	1,408
Incisive CT,(728143, 728144), Software v5.0.0.	Radiology	Z-0640-2024* [45]	Multiple software issues have the potential to lead to misdiagnosis due to image artifacts or incorrect image orientation labels, or need for a CT rescan.	The manufacturer communicated specific details regarding the issue to their customer, as well as advice on actions to be taken. They also promised to install a software upgrade.	828

* indicates that the recalls are in *Open* state as of April 2025, meaning that not all the units have been corrected or removed yet.

Table 5. Examples of adverse events of AI/ML-enabled medical devices with data, interface device, and software related problems that could result in misdiagnosis or wrong treatment (Event Types: Malfunction).

Device Name	Device Function	Approval Panel	Adverse Event # (Year)	Device Problem	Summary Event Description
Zio AT ECG Monitoring System (ZEUS)	Arrhythmia detector and alarm	Cardio-vascular	8356453 [41] (2019)	Application Network Problem	False negative results (missed detection of asymptomatic arrhythmia) due to a BLE (bluethooth low energy) issue.
LINQ II Cardiac Monitor, Zelda AI ECG Classification System	Arrhythmia detector and alarm	Cardio-vascular	20916084 [48] (2024)	Program or Algorithm Execution Problem	An atrial fibrillation episode was adjudicated as false by the artificial intelligence (ai) algorithm.
Dario BGMS	Glucose Test System	Clinical chemistry	18904273 [44] (2022)*	Incorrect, Inadequate, or Imprecise Result or High Readings	Inconsistent and high blood glucose readings, different from other meters or hospital measurements.
HeartFlow FFRCT	Coronary Vascular Physiologic Simulation Software	Cardio-vascular	8269286 [38] (2018)*	False Negative Result	Potential false negative results in FFRCT (Fractional Flow Reserve derived from CT) analysis of coronary arteries due to image quality issues and anatomy uncertainty.
Clarius Ultrasound Scanner	Ultrasonic pulsed doppler imaging system	Radiology	20471171 [47] (2024)	Misconnection	A connectivity issue with ultrasound scanner during diagnostic evaluation in an emergency room, which could potentially lead to significant adverse outcomes.

* indicates several similar adverse events reported for the same device over 2018-2024.

and categorized them by fault class, failure mode, device type, recovery action, and the number of recalled devices. This study was the first automated and large-scale analysis of FDA data on computer-based medical devices and highlighted the key causes of computer failures impacting patient safety. Our findings showed that while software failures continue to be the leading cause of medical device failures, hardware, battery, and I/O issues are also major contributors. Many recalled devices either lacked proper safety considerations during design or their safety mechanisms were inadequately implemented. Later, using these

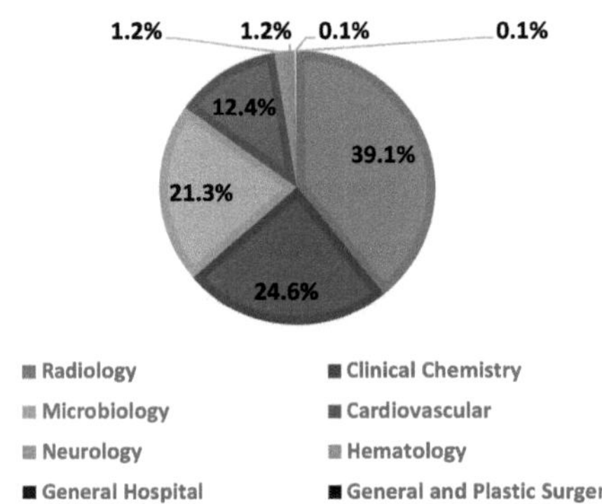

Reported Device Problem	Freq.
Poor Quality Image	421
Not Available (N/A)	295
False Negative Result	103
High Readings	73
Incorrect, Inadequate, or Imprecise Result or Readings	45
Computer Software Problem	42
Inaccurate Information	25
Application Program Problem: Parameter Calculation Error	17
Low Readings	7
Intermittent Program or Algorithm Execution	6
Program or Algorithm Execution Failure	4
Failure to Transmit Record	3
Low Test Results	3

Fig. 5. Left: Adverse Events by Device Category (FDA Approval Panel), Right: Top Reported ML-enabled Device Problems (Data as of April 2025).

tools we extracted all the recalls and adverse events related to BGMS [134,135] and surgical robots [11] and identified most common device malfunctions, examples of security vulnerabilities in different components and device interfaces (e.g., CGMs, insulin pumps, cameras), and the safety impact of device failures and potential harm to patients (e.g., hyperglycemia or injury). For example, we found a Class 1 recall (highest risk level) due to a potential security vulnerability related to the use of the remote controller accessories with the insulin pumps, which affected over 90,000 users on the market [39]. Another Class 2 recall, affecting over 64,000 insulin pumps, indicated the possibility of an unauthorized person connecting wirelessly to a nearby insulin pump to change settings and control insulin delivery due to potential cybersecurity vulnerabilities [43].

More recently, we have applied our techniques to extract and analyze the recalls and adverse events reported on ML-enabled devices and AID systems. Our analysis found over 1,460 adverse events reported for ML-enabled devices over 2015–2024, of which about 92% involved device malfunctions and 7.8% injuries. Although understanding the root causes of the reported events requires an in-depth investigation and consideration of all causal and contextual factors 3.3, these reports provide valuable insights on real problems encountered during the use of devices and how they impacted patient safety. Figure 5 shows the device categories with the highest number of adverse event reports and the top device problems reported over the years. A major part of reported problems (about 60.7%) were related to poor quality and inaccurate inputs/readings and false negative results, which, even if not directly caused by an ML technology, could still impact the ML decision-making results and patient safety. Some examples of safety-critical recalls and adverse events across different device categories are shown in Tables 4 and 5.

In summary, this set of tools and techniques would help a security analyst cover known vulnerabilities in ML models, peripheral medical devices, as well as attack vectors in connected peripheral devices and communication channels, while designing a *secure* ML-enabled medical device. Additionally, it will also help security practitioners design efficient attack prevention and detection techniques.

3.3   Data-Driven Systems-Theoretic Safety and Security Analysis

To predict and proactively mitigate the occurrence of future attacks, it is crucial to not only consider the known vulnerabilities and exploits reported in existing data on past safety and security incidents, but also anticipate for the potential new attacks by considering a more comprehensive attack surface of unknown vulnerabilities or vulnerabilities in other connected devices and the potential attack steps and their safety impacts on patients. To do this, we adopt an LLM-aided and data-driven approach to the systems-theoretic security analysis (STPA-Sec) that incorporates the information extracted from public databases and results from CAST analysis on devices with similar functionality (e.g., a non-ML-enabled device predicate with the same functional specification and use cases as the ML-enabled device) to generate potential attacks steps and their impacts in ML-enabled devices.

Systems-Theoretic Accident Causality (CAST) Analysis. Analysis of real-world safety incidents, including medical device recalls [122] and adverse events [119] can provide valuable insights into how device flaws and security vulnerabilities could lead to system hazards and negatively impact patients and caregivers. However, these incidents are mainly reported by the device users and manufacturers in free-form natural language text, and their analysis requires a semantic understanding of the underlying causal factors. Several previous studies [10,17,21,70,79,93] have shown the advantage of Causal Analysis using System Theory (CAST) [69] in identifying causal and contextual factors contributing to medical adverse events. However, these papers solely focus on the manual causal analysis of single incidents and do not consider security-related hazards and safety-critical vulnerabilities. Such an approach cannot provide a comprehensive understanding of all potential causal factors, including vulnerabilities in IoT and peripheral devices, nor can it yield statistically significant measures of their importance. Additionally, it is not easily scalable to thousands of unstructured adverse event reports on a single device due to the significant human effort required. Therefore, techniques and tools for automated semantic analysis of these reports are needed to extract both safety and security-related causal factors, and summarize key information for CAST analysis.

To facilitate an aggregated CAST analysis, we leverage our NLP techniques for automated classification, summarization, and cross-referencing of large-scale FDA data on recalls and adverse events [8,9,11,33,135]. This information can assist in systems-theoretic analysis of several similar adverse events reported on the same medical device or devices with the same functional specification using CAST to identify the distribution of causal factors and potentially inadequate

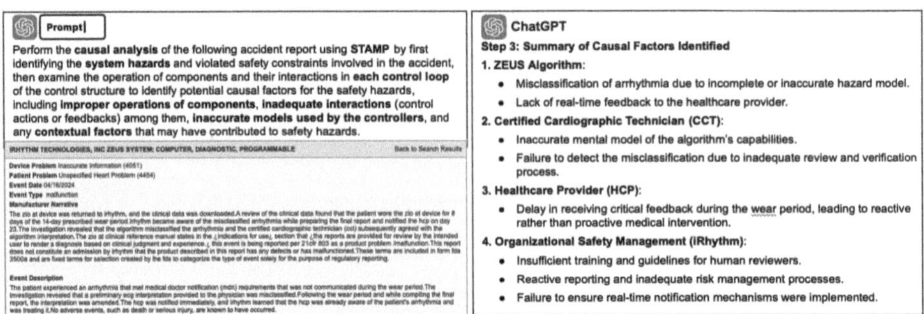

Fig. 6. Example Accident Causality Analysis using STAMP for an FDA-Authorized ML-enabled Medical Device.

safety mechanisms in both system design and operational practices [5,6]. Given a natural language description of an adverse event and the control structure model for a medical device, we first map different sections of the text into different control loops in the system control structure. Then, for each control loop, the set of violated safety constraints is identified. These steps are done through device and medical entity and relation extraction from the text and semantic analysis of causal factors using rule-based parts of speech analysis [5]. Finally, the similar causal factors and safety violations across multiple adverse event reports of the same device can be identified and aggregated for statistical analysis. In [6,11] we performed such an aggregated causality analysis of over 10,000 adverse event reports on tele-operated surgical robots. This analysis identified the most critical causal factors for safety incidents in different models of the same device over a period of 14 years. To further reduce the manual cost of this analysis method, we have recently explored an LLM-aided technique based on customized prompt templates and chain-of-thought prompting [52,127] to decompose the tasks of entity and relation extraction and semantic analysis of causal factors into subtasks that can be performed using LLMs and be later manually validated by security analysts. Figure 6 shows an example of the key causal factors extracted by this LLM-aided technique from an adverse event report [120] for an FDA-authorized ML-enabled cardiac event detection software [123]. The insights on the causes and patient impacts of past incidents can be used for analyzing and specifying the safety impact of the device vulnerabilities.

Systems-Theoretic Security (STPA-Sec) Analysis. In this final step, we analyze consolidated data on the ML model, its functionality, peripheral technologies, and associated safety and security risks to identify how an adversary could inject false data during inference. We developed STPA-Sec for ML-enabled Medical Devices (SAM), a technique for conducting STPA-Sec on AI/ML-enabled medical devices [54]. SAM first assesses the attack surface by identifying all potential attack entry points (Sect. 3.2). Thereafter, it performs STPA-Sec analysis to determine the attack steps. This information would help the

ML-enabled device manufacturer design appropriate security measures or devise advisories for the users.

In the attack step generation step, SAM performs an LLM-aided STPA-Sec analysis to generate the attack steps for a given hazard and an exploitable peripheral device vulnerability. To overcome a human security analyst's limited cross-domain knowledge, we leverage LLMs to automatically identify causal scenarios based on the latest vulnerabilities in the system's underlying technologies. A key challenge in using LLMs is the design of effective prompts to generate optimal task-specific responses. For SAM, the ideal response outlines detailed attack steps exploiting a peripheral vulnerability to inject false data during inference on a given ML technique. To achieve this, we developed the following prompt.

> "Act as a security engineer who has the task of identifying the steps that an adversary follows to cause a security breach in an ML-enabled medical system. *<Description of an ML-enabled medical system>*. *<Definition of security breach>*. You are given a system description, an ML attack, a targeted input peripheral component, and a known vulnerability in the input component. Give a list of steps to show how an adversary can exploit the vulnerability to mislead the ML-enabled component and how that affects the action of the output device on the patient.
>
> **System Description:** *<The SAM user manually writes this description by inspecting information disclosed by the manufacturer.>*
>
> **Data flow:** *<This can be derived from the control structure constructed using the Control structure builder in §3.1.>*
>
> **ML attack:** *<The ML attack identified in §3.2>*
>
> **Targeted input peripheral component:** *<One of the peripheral input devices in the control structure built in §3.1>*
>
> **Targeted technology:** *<One of the underlying technologies in the input device, as identified by the technology identifier (§3.1)>*
>
> **Known vulnerability:** *<Description of the known vulnerability in the targeted technology, as retrieved from the CVE database during attack surface analysis>*"

We observed that explicitly assigning the LLM the role of a security analyst before giving it additional information improves the readability and relevance of the generated results - this is in line with other work in this area [73,101,102]. Similarly, mentioning the data flow provides clarity to the LLM regarding the sequence of data transmission between different components in the system.

By running this prompt for each vulnerable point in the system and each vulnerability uncovered at that point, SAM, regardless of the existence of safety/security margins, generates a comprehensive set of steps an adversary might take to compromise the security of an ML-enabled medical device. Device

Table 6. STPA-Sec output produced by SAM for the attack scenario on d-Nav BGMS, described in $3.3

Step #	Step name	Description
1	Reconnaissance	Identifying the targeted patient's Wi-fi network and its router vulnerabilities
2	Exploitation	Exploitation of router vulnerability to infiltrate the target's network
3	Wi-fi network infiltration	Compromising the connection between glucose meter and cloud server
4	Data interception	Interpreting the data in transit
5	Data tampering	Manipulating the data in transit with a value that would make the ML model mispredict a future blood glucose value
6	Model inversion attack	Compute the manipulated value such that the patient becomes hypoglycemic
7	ML Controller manipulation	Expected reaction of the ML model: Misprediction of patient's future blood glucose level
8	Output device manipulation	Expected reaction of the insulin dose calculator: Computing an insulin dose higher than that required by the patient and sent to the insulin pump or displayed on the d-Nav app
9	Insulin pump misadministration	Expected end result: Wrong insulin dose administered to the patient, either manually or by an automated insulin pump

manufacturers or security analysts can then disregard those that have already been mitigated and develop design recommendations for the remaining ones.

For d-Nav, we selected hypoglycemia as the hazard, and *injecting excess insulin* as the control action that causes it. We consider an adversary who conducts a model inversion attack (identified by MedAIScout [32] in a previous step described in §3.2) on the ML engine to infer sensitive details about a targeted patient, followed by false data injection. This attack would make the ML engine mispredict the insulin dose. To execute this attack, the adversary injects false glucose readings into the Wi-Fi channel that transmits the patient's glucose readings from the glucose meter to the ML engine running in the cloud server. We assume that the patient uses a Wi-Fi router with an unpatched known vulnerability, *CVE-2023-35836* [30], that the adversary exploits for injecting the malicious glucose readings. SAM outputs a list of nine steps for this attack, which are summarized in Table 6. By following these steps, an adversary could inject false data into the BGMS to make it miscalculate the insulin dose.

4   Future Directions and Conclusion

Based on the capabilities of our tools and techniques demonstrated in this paper, and the insights obtained from the experimental results, we would like to expand the scope of our research in the following directions, with a high-level goal of ensuring the security of ML-enabled medical devices by design and efficient post-market security surveillance.

1. Early prediction of vulnerabilities based on existing events - The domain of ML-enabled medical devices has become increasingly competitive, with manufacturers developing ML-enabled devices that offer similar core functionalities as existing non-ML-enabled devices, but with enhanced performance and features such as greater interoperability. As a result, newer devices may inherit existing vulnerabilities in connected devices or similar or more severe vulnerabilities than their predecessor devices. To address this, we plan to develop an LLM-aided technique that analyzes the design of an ML-enabled medical device and, based on known vulnerability data, predicts potential security risks specific to the new device, even without performing STPA-Sec on it. Furthermore, we would expand the scope of our tools and techniques to cover other types of ML-specific attacks in addition to false data injection attacks.
2. Real-time post-market security risk assessment - Our tools and techniques can be extended to support near real-time post-market security surveillance by continuously monitoring large-scale vulnerability databases and performing on-demand risk assessments whenever new vulnerabilities are reported.
3. Designing efficient defense techniques - The output of our STPA-Sec technique can be leveraged to identify the most efficient defense technique in terms of reliability, patient convenience, and cost of implementation.

This paper presents a suite of tools and techniques developed for holistic security risk assessment of ML-enabled medical devices, with a focus on false data injection attacks. We demonstrated the effectiveness of these tools and techniques across multiple ML-enabled blood glucose management systems. The novelty of our tools and techniques are in (i) identifying attack vectors that require exploiting vulnerabilities in third-party connected components to practically execute known attacks on the ML models and (ii) anticipating for the potential safety impacts of such attacks based on the analysis of past incidents on similar devices. This helps security analysts (working for the device manufacturers) assess the feasibility and impact of such attacks more accurately. In the future, we aim to extend our tools to support additional types of ML-specific attacks and facilitate post-market security risk assessments.

Acknowledgments. This research was partially supported by the Natural Sciences and Engineering Research Council of Canada (NSERC), the National Research Council of Canada's (NRC) Digital Health and Geospatial Analytics Program, and the U.S. National Science Foundation (CNS-2146295).

Disclosure of Interests. The authors have no competing interests to declare that are relevant to the content of this article.

References

1. 2023 State of Cybersecurity for Medical Devices and Healthcare Systems. Tech. rep., Health-ISAC (2023). https://info.finitestate.io/2023-state-of-cybersecurity-for-medical-devices-and-healthcare-systems
2. Abdulkhaleq, A., Wagner, S.: Open tool support for system-theoretic process analysis. Universitätsbibliothek der Universität Stuttgart (2014)
3. Abdulkhaleq, A., Wagner, S.: XSTAMPP: an eXtensible STAMP platform as tool support for safety engineering (2015)
4. Albattah, A., Rassam, M.A.: Detection of adversarial attacks against the hybrid convolutional long short-term memory deep learning technique for healthcare monitoring applications. Appl. Sci. **13**(11), 6807 (2023)
5. Alemzadeh, H.: Data-driven resiliency assessment of medical cyber-physical systems. Ph.D. thesis, University of Illinois at Urbana-Champaign (2016)
6. Alemzadeh, H., Chen, D., Lewis, A., Kalbarczyk, Z., Raman, J., Leveson, N., Iyer, R.: Systems-theoretic safety assessment of robotic telesurgical systems. In: Koornneef, F., van Gulijk, C. (eds.) Computer Safety, Reliability, and Security, pp. 213–227. Springer International Publishing, Cham (2015)
7. Alemzadeh, H., Chen, D., Li, X., Kesavadas, T., Kalbarczyk, Z.T., Iyer, R.K.: Targeted attacks on teleoperated surgical robots: dynamic model-based detection and mitigation. In: IEEE/IFIP International Conference on Dependable Systems and Networks (DSN), pp. 395–406. IEEE (2016)
8. Alemzadeh, H., Hoagland, R., Kalbarczyk, Z., Iyer, R.K.: Automated classification of computer-based medical device recalls: an application of natural language processing and statistical learning. In: IEEE International Symposium on Computer-Based Medical Systems, pp. 553–554. IEEE (2014)
9. Alemzadeh, H., Iyer, R.K., Kalbarczyk, Z., Raman, J.: Analysis of safety-critical computer failures in medical devices. IEEE Secur. Privacy **11**(4), 14–26 (2013). https://doi.org/10.1109/MSP.2013.49
10. Alemzadeh, H., Raman, J., Leveson, N., Iyer, R.K.: Safety implications of robotic surgery: a study of 13 years of FDA data on da vinci surgical systems. Coordinated Science Laboratory Report no. UILU-ENG-13-2208 (2013)
11. Alemzadeh, H., Raman, J., Leveson, N., Kalbarczyk, Z., Iyer, R.K.: Adverse events in robotic surgery: a retrospective study of 14 years of FDA data. PLoS ONE **11**(4), e0151470 (2016)
12. Alemzadeh, Homa: MedSafe MAUDE. https://github.com/homa-alem/MedSafe_MAUDE, Accessed 18 Apr 2025
13. Homa, A.: MedSafe Recalls. https://github.com/homa-alem/MedSafe_Backend/, Accessed 18 Apr 2025
14. Almohri, H., Cheng, L., Yao, D., Alemzadeh, H.: On threat modeling and mitigation of medical cyber-physical systems. In: IEEE/ACM International Conference on Connected Health: Applications, Systems and Engineering Technologies (CHASE), pp. 114–119. IEEE (2017)
15. Amich, A., Eshete, B.: Explanation-guided diagnosis of machine learning evasion attacks. In: Proceedings of Security and Privacy in Communication Networks: EAI International Conference, Part I 17, pp. 207–228. Springer (2021)
16. Arney, D., Pajic, M., Goldman, J.M., Lee, I., Mangharam, R., Sokolsky, O.: Toward patient safety in closed-loop medical device systems. In: Proceedings of the 1st ACM/IEEE International Conference on Cyber-Physical Systems, pp. 139–148 (2010)

17. Balgos, V.H.: A systems theoretic application to design for the safety of medical diagnostic devices. Ph.D. thesis, Massachusetts Institute of Technology (2012)
18. Becker, C., Van Eikema Hommes, Q.: Transportation systems safety hazard analysis tool (SafetyHAT) user guide (version 1.0). Tech. rep. (2014)
19. Bonaci, T., Yan, J., Herron, J., Kohno, T., Chizeck, H.J.: Experimental analysis of denial-of-service attacks on teleoperated robotic systems. In: Proceedings of the ACM/IEEE International Conference on Cyber-physical Systems, pp. 11–20 (2015)
20. Bortsova, G., et al.: Adversarial attack vulnerability of medical image analysis systems: unexplored factors. Med. Image Anal. **73**, 102141 (2021)
21. Canham, A.: Examining the application of STAMP in the analysis of patient safety incidents. Ph.D. thesis, Loughborough University (2018)
22. Chen, H., Huang, C., Huang, Q., Zhang, Q., Wang, W.: Ecgadv: generating adversarial electrocardiogram to misguide arrhythmia classification system. In: AAAI Conference on Artificial Intelligence. vol. 34, pp. 3446–3453 (2020)
23. Chen, X., Meng, L., Xu, Y., Wu, D.: Adversarial artifact detection in EEG-based brain-computer interfaces. J. Neural Eng. **21**(5), 056043 (2024)
24. Chen, Y., et al.: Adversarial learning based node-edge graph attention networks for autism spectrum disorder identification. IEEE Trans. Neural Netw. Learn, Syst (2022)
25. Chhabra, A., Roy, A., Mohapatra, P.: Suspicion-free adversarial attacks on clustering algorithms. In: Proceedings of the AAAI Conference on Artificial Intelligence. vol. 34, pp. 3625–3632 (2020)
26. CVE: CVE-2017-14008 (2017). https://www.cve.org/CVERecord?id=CVE-2017-14008, Accessed 18 Apr 2025
27. CVE: CVE-2019-10964 (2019). https://www.cve.org/CVERecord?id=CVE-2019-10964, Accessed 18 Apr 2025
28. CVE: CVE-2020-26145 (2020). https://cve.mitre.org/cgi-bin/cvekey.cgi?keyword=CVE-2020-26145, Accessed 18 Apr 2025
29. CVE: CVE-2020-8933 (2020). https://www.cve.org/CVERecord?id=CVE-2020-8933, Accessed 18 Apr 2025
30. CVE: CVE-2023-3583 (2024). https://cve.mitre.org/cgi-bin/cvename.cgi?name=CVE-2023-35836, Accessed 18 Apr 2025
31. CVE: CVE-2024-43093 (2024). https://www.cve.org/CVERecord?id=CVE-2024-43093, Accessed 18 Apr 2025
32. Dharmalingam, A.P., Mitra, G.: MedAIScout: automated retrieval of known machine learning vulnerabilities in medical applications. In: Red Teaming GenAI: What Can We Learn from Adversaries? (2024)
33. Elnawawy, M., Hallajiyan, M., Mitra, G., Iqbal, S., Pattabiraman, K.: Systematically assessing the security risks of AI/ML-enabled Connected healthcare systems. In: IEEE/ACM Conference on Connected Health: Applications, Systems and Engineering Technologies (CHASE), pp. 97–108 (2024). https://doi.org/10.1109/CHASE60773.2024.00019
34. Elshazly, A.A., et al.: False data injection attacks on reinforcement learning-based charging coordination in smart grids and a countermeasure. Appl. Sci. (2076-3417) **14**(23) (2024)
35. FDA: Product Classification: Interoperable Automated Glycemic Controller. https://www.accessdata.fda.gov/scripts/cdrh/cfdocs/cfpcd/classification.cfm?id=714, Accessed 18 Apr 2025

36. FDA: Class 2 Device Recall BioPlex 2200 ANA Screen on the BioPlex 2200 Multi-Analyte Detection System (2008). https://www.accessdata.fda.gov/scripts/cdrh/cfdocs/cfRES/res.cfm?id=66385, Accessed 18 Apr 2025
37. FDA: Class 2 Device Recall UniCel DxH 600/800 Coulter Cellular Analysis System (2017). https://www.accessdata.fda.gov/scripts/cdrh/cfdocs/cfRES/res.cfm?id=155030, Accessed 18 Apr 2025
38. FDA: MAUDE Adverse Event Report: HEARTFLOW, INC. FFRCT) (2018). https://www.accessdata.fda.gov/scripts/cdrh/cfdocs/cfMAUDE/detail.cfm?mdrfoi_id=8269286, Accessed 18 Apr 2025
39. FDA: Class 1 Device Recall MMT500 (2019). https://www.accessdata.fda.gov/scripts/cdrh/cfdocs/cfres/res.cfm?id=170857, Accessed 18 Apr 2025
40. FDA: Class 2 Device Recall Dario Blood Glucose Monitoring System (2019). https://www.accessdata.fda.gov/scripts/cdrh/cfdocs/cfRES/res.cfm?id=176305, Accessed 18 Apr 2025
41. FDA: MAUDE Adverse Event Report: IRHYTHM TECHNOLOGIES, INC ZIO AT SYSTEM (2019). https://www.accessdata.fda.gov/scripts/cdrh/cfdocs/cfMAUDE/detail.cfm?mdrfoi_id=8356453, Accessed 18 Apr 2025
42. FDA: Class 2 Device Recall BodyGuardian Heart Remote Monitoring Kit (2020). https://www.accessdata.fda.gov/scripts/cdrh/cfdocs/cfres/res.cfm?id=180336, Accessed 18 Apr 2025
43. FDA: Class 2 Device Recall MiniMed Insulin Pump (2020). https://www.accessdata.fda.gov/scripts/cdrh/cfdocs/cfRES/res.cfm?id=175194, Accessed 18 Apr 2025
44. FDA: MAUDE Adverse Event Report: LABSTYLE INNOVATIONS LTD. DARIO BLOOD GLUCOSE MONITORING SYSTEM; GLUCOMETER) (2022). https://www.accessdata.fda.gov/scripts/cdrh/cfdocs/cfMAUDE/detail.cfm?mdrfoi_id=18904273, Accessed 18 Apr 2025
45. FDA: Class 2 Device Recall Incisive CT (2024). https://www.accessdata.fda.gov/scripts/cdrh/cfdocs/cfRES/res.cfm?id=204881, Accessed 18 Apr 2025
46. FDA: Class 2 Device Recall Sight OLO (2024). https://www.accessdata.fda.gov/scripts/cdrh/cfdocs/cfRES/res.cfm?id=207976, Accessed 18 Apr 2025
47. FDA: Maude Adverse Event Report: Clarius Mobile Health Corp. Clarius Ultrasound Scanner; Diagnostic Ultrasound System and Accessories (2024). https://www.accessdata.fda.gov/scripts/cdrh/cfdocs/cfMAUDE/detail.cfm?mdrfoi_id=20471171, Accessed 18 Apr 2025
48. FDA: Maude Adverse Event Report: Medtronic, Inc. Accurhythm Za410 (af); Recorder, Event, Implantable Cardiac, (with Arrhythmia Detection) (2024). https://www.accessdata.fda.gov/scripts/cdrh/cfdocs/cfMAUDE/detail.cfm?mdrfoi_id=20916084, Accessed 18 Apr 2025
49. Finlayson, S.G., Bowers, J.D., Ito, J., Zittrain, J.L., Beam, A.L., Kohane, I.S.: Adversarial attacks on medical machine learning. Science **363**(6433), 1287–1289 (2019)
50. Finlayson, S.G., Chung, H.W., Kohane, I.S., Beam, A.L.: Adversarial attacks against medical deep learning systems. arXiv preprint arXiv:1804.05296 (2018)
51. Garbelini, M.E., Wang, C., Chattopadhyay, S., Sumei, S., Kurniawan, E.: {SweynTooth}: unleashing mayhem over bluetooth low energy. In: USENIX Annual Technical Conference (USENIX ATC), pp. 911–925 (2020)
52. Ge, X., Williams, R.D., Stankovic, J.A., Alemzadeh, H.: DKEC: domain knowledge enhanced multi-label classification for diagnosis prediction. arXiv preprint arXiv:2310.07059 (2023)

53. Ghaffari Laleh, N., et al.: Adversarial attacks and adversarial robustness in computational pathology. Nat. Commun. **13**(1), 5711 (2022)
54. Hallajiyan, M., Dharmalingam, A.P., Mitra, G., Alemzadeh, H., Iqbal, S., Pattabiraman, K.: SAM: foreseeing inference-time false data injection attacks on ML-enabled medical devices. In: Workshop on Cybersecurity in HealthCare (HealthSec), pp. 77–84 (2024), co-held with ACM CCS'24
55. Hallajiyan, M., Dharmalingam, A.P., Mitra, G., Alemzadeh, H., Iqbal, S., Pattabiraman, K.: Sam questionnaires for collecting information on peripheral device technologies (2024)
56. Halperin, D., et al.: Pacemakers and implantable cardiac defibrillators: software radio attacks and zero-power defenses. In: 2008 IEEE Symposium on Security and Privacy (SP 2008), pp. 129–142. IEEE (2008)
57. Han, X., Hu, Y., Foschini, L., Chinitz, L., Jankelson, L., Ranganath, R.: Deep learning models for electrocardiograms are susceptible to adversarial attack. Nat. Med. **26**(3), 360–363 (2020)
58. Hirano, H., Minagi, A., Takemoto, K.: Universal adversarial attacks on deep neural networks for medical image classification. BMC Med. Imaging **21**, 1–13 (2021)
59. Hu, L., et al.: Adversarial training for prostate cancer classification using magnetic resonance imaging. Quant. Imag. Med. Surgery **12**(6), 3276 (2022)
60. Insulet: Omnipod-5 (2025). https://www.omnipod.com/what-is-omnipod/omnipod-5, Accessed 18 Apr 2025
61. Jee, E., Lee, I., Sokolsky, O.: Assurance cases in model-driven development of the pacemaker software. In: International Symposium On Leveraging Applications of Formal Methods, Verification and Validation, pp. 343–356. Springer (2010)
62. Jetley, R., Iyer, S.P., Jones, P.: A formal methods approach to medical device review. Computer **39**(4), 61–67 (2006)
63. Jiang, Z., Pajic, M., Connolly, A., Dixit, S., Mangharam, R.: Real-time heart model for implantable cardiac device validation and verification. In: 2010 22nd Euromicro Conference on Real-Time Systems, pp. 239–248 (2010). https://doi.org/10.1109/ECRTS.2010.36
64. Joel, M.Z., et al.: Adversarial attack vulnerability of deep learning models for oncologic images. MedRxiv **1**, 2021 (2021)
65. Khan, M.A., Quasim, M.T., Alghamdi, N.S., Khan, M.Y.: A secure framework for authentication and encryption using improved ECC for IoT-based medical sensor data. IEEE Access **8**, 52018–52027 (2020)
66. Klonoff, D.C., Ho, C.N., Ayers, A., Abdel-Malek, A.: FDA interoperability designation–creating options for people with diabetes and pump companies: regulatory, technological, and commercial perspectives. J. Diabetes Sci. Technol. (2024). https://doi.org/10.1177/19322968241271304
67. Kramer, D.B., et al.: Security and privacy qualities of medical devices: an analysis of FDA postmarket surveillance. PLoS ONE **7**(7), e40200 (2012)
68. Lal, S., et al.: Adversarial attack and defence through adversarial training and feature fusion for diabetic retinopathy recognition. Sensors **21**(11), 3922 (2021)
69. Leveson, N.: Engineering a safer world: systems thinking applied to safety. MIT Press (2011)
70. Leveson, N., Samost, A., Dekker, S., Finkelstein, S., Raman, J.: A systems approach to analyzing and preventing hospital adverse events. J. Patient Safety **16**(2), 162–167 (2020)
71. Levy-Loboda, T., Sheetrit, E., Liberty, I.F., Haim, A., Nissim, N.: Personalized insulin dose manipulation attack and its detection using interval-based temporal patterns and machine learning algorithms. J. Biomed. Inf. **132**, 104129 (2022)

72. Li, C., Raghunathan, A., Jha, N.K.: Hijacking an insulin pump: Security attacks and defenses for a diabetes therapy system. In: IEEE International Conference on e-Health Networking, Applications and Services, pp. 150–156 (2011)
73. Li, G., Hammoud, H., Itani, H., Khizbullin, D., Ghanem, B.: CAMEL: communicative agents for "mind" exploration of large language model society. In: Advances in Neural Information Processing Systems. vol. 36, pp. 51991–52008. Curran Associates, Inc. (2023)
74. Li, Y., Liu, S.: Adversarial attack and defense in breast cancer deep learning systems. Bioengineering **10**(8), 973 (2023)
75. Lin, Y.C., Hong, Z.W., Liao, Y.H., Shih, M.L., Liu, M.Y., Sun, M.: Tactics of adversarial attack on deep reinforcement learning agents. In: Proceedings of the International Joint Conference on Artificial Intelligence, pp. 3756–3762. International Joint Conferences on Artificial Intelligence Organization (2017)
76. Lyell, D., Wang, Y., Coiera, E., Magrabi, F.: More than algorithms: an analysis of safety events involving ML-enabled medical devices reported to the FDA. J. Am. Med. Inf. Assoc. **30**(7), 1227–1236 (2023)
77. Ma, X., Niu, Y., Gu, L., Wang, Y., Zhao, Y., Bailey, J., Lu, F.: Understanding adversarial attacks on deep learning based medical image analysis systems. Patt. Recogn. **110**, 107332 (2021)
78. Mangaokar, N., Pu, J., Bhattacharya, P., Reddy, C.K., Viswanath, B.: Jekyll: attacking medical image diagnostics using deep generative models. In: IEEE EuroS&P, pp. 139–157 (2020)
79. Mason-Blakley, F., Habibi, R., Weber, J., Price, M.: Assessing stamp EMR with electronic medical record related incident reports: case study: manufacturer and user facility device experience database. In: 2017 IEEE International Conference on Healthcare Informatics (ICHI), pp. 114–123. IEEE (2017)
80. Meiseles, A., Rosenberg, I., Motro, Y., Rokach, L., Moran-Gilad, J.: Adversarial vulnerability of deep learning models in analyzing next generation sequencing data. In: IEEE BIBM, pp. 464–468 (2020). https://doi.org/10.1109/BIBM49941.2020.9313421
81. Menon, K., Bohra, V.K., Murugan, L., Jaganathan, K., Arumugam, C.: COVID-19 diagnosis from chest x-ray images using convolutional neural networks and effects of data poisoning. In: ICCSA, pp. 508–521 (2021)
82. Mitre: Conexus Telemetry Protocol vulnerability. https://cve.mitre.org/cgi-bin/cvename.cgi?name=CVE-2019-6538, Accessed 18 Apr 2025
83. Mitre: Philips MRI 1.5T and MRI 3T vulnerability (1). https://cve.mitre.org/cgi-bin/cvename.cgi?name=CVE-2021-26262, Accessed 18 Apr 2025
84. Mitre: Shekar Endoscope vulnerability (1). https://cve.mitre.org/cgi-bin/cvename.cgi?name=CVE-2017-10722, Accessed 18 Apr 2025
85. Mitre: Sony IPELA E Series Camera vulnerability (1). https://cve.mitre.org/cgi-bin/cvename.cgi?name=CVE-2018-3938, Accessed 18 Apr 2025
86. Mitre: Windows 7 vulnerability (2). https://cve.mitre.org/cgi-bin/cvename.cgi?name=CVE-2019-5921, Accessed 18 Apr 2025
87. Mitre: Common Vulnerabilities and Exposures (CVE) Database (2024). https://cve.mitre.org/, Accessed 18 Apr 2025
88. Mozaffari-Kermani, M., Sur-Kolay, S., Raghunathan, A., Jha, N.K.: Systematic poisoning attacks on and defenses for machine learning in healthcare. IEEE J. Biomed. Health Inform. **19**(6), 1893–1905 (2014)

89. Nielsen, C., Tuladhar, A., Forkert, N.D.: Investigating the vulnerability of federated learning-based diabetic retinopathy grade classification to gradient inversion attacks. In: International Workshop on Ophthalmic Medical Image Analysis, pp. 183–192 (2022)

90. Nouri, A., Cabrero-Daniel, B., Törner, F., Sivencrona, H., Berger, C.: Engineering Safety Requirements for Autonomous Driving with Large Language Models. arXiv preprint arXiv:2403.16289 (2024)

91. Nouri, A., Cabrero-Daniel, B., Torner, F., Sivencrona, H., Berger, C.: Welcome your new AI teammate: on safety analysis by leashing large language models. In: Proceedings of the IEEE/ACM CAIN '24, pp. 172–177 (2024)

92. Office, U.G.A.: Medical device cybersecurity: agencies need to update agreement to ensure effective coordination. Tech. Rep. GAO-24-106683, United States Government Accountability Office (GAO) (2023). https://www.gao.gov/assets/d24106683.pdf

93. O'Neil, M.M.M.: Application of CAST to hospital adverse events. Ph.D. thesis, Massachusetts Institute of Technology (2014)

94. OpenAPS: https://openaps.org, Accessed 18 Apr 2025

95. Pajic, M., Mangharam, R., Sokolsky, O., Arney, D., Goldman, J., Lee, I.: Model-driven safety analysis of closed-loop medical systems. IEEE Trans. Industr. Inf. **10**(1), 3–16 (2012)

96. Palo Alto Networks: 6 New Vulnerabilities Found on D-Link Home Routers (2020). https://unit42.paloaltonetworks.com/6-new-d-link-vulnerabilities-found-on-home-routers, Accessed 18 Apr 2025

97. Pattison, J., Dungan, K.M., Faulds, E.R.: Supporting the use of a person's own diabetes technology in the inpatient setting. Diabetes Spectrum **35**(4), 398–404 (2022)

98. Pereira, D.P., Hirata, C., Nadjm-Tehrani, S.: A STAMP-based ontology approach to support safety and security analyses. J. Inf. Secur. Appl. **47**, 302–319 (2019)

99. Qi, Y., Dong, Y., Khastgir, S., Jennings, P., Zhao, X., Huang, X.: STPA for learning-enabled systems: a survey and a new practice. In: Proceedings of IEEE ITSC '23, pp. 1381–1388 (2023)

100. Qi, Y., Zhao, X., Khastgir, S., Huang, X.: Safety analysis in the era of large language models: a case study of STPA using ChatGPT. arXiv preprint arXiv:2304.01246 (2023)

101. Santu, S.K.K., Feng, D.: Teler: a general taxonomy of LLM prompts for benchmarking complex tasks. arXiv preprint arXiv:2305.11430 (2023)

102. Shanahan, M., McDonell, K., Reynolds, L.: Role play with large language models. Nature **623**(7987), 493–498 (2023)

103. Souza, F.G., Pereira, D.P., Pagliares, R.M., Nadjm-Tehrani, S., Hirata, C.M.: WebSTAMP: a web application for STPA & STPA-Sec. In: MATEC Web of Conferences. vol. 273, p. 02010. EDP Sciences (2019)

104. Sun, M., Tang, F., Yi, J., Wang, F., Zhou, J.: Identify susceptible locations in medical records via adversarial attacks on deep predictive models. In: Proceedings of the 24th ACM SIGKDD International Conference on Knowledge Discovery & Data Mining, pp. 793–801 (2018)

105. Thomas, J., Leveson, N.G.: Performing hazard analysis on complex, software-and human-intensive systems. In: Proc. of the 29th ISSC Conference about System Safety (2011)

106. Tidepool: Supported Devices. https://www.tidepool.org/devices, Accessed 18 Apr 2025

107. Tosun, F.E., Teixeira, A., Ahlén, A., Dey, S.: Detection of bias injection attacks on the glucose sensor in the artificial pancreas under meal disturbance. In: American Control Conference (ACC), pp. 1398–1405. IEEE (2022)
108. US-CERT: Industrial Control Systems Cyber Emergency Response Team (ICS-CERT) Alerts. https://ics-cert.us-cert.gov/alerts, Accessed 18 Apr 2025
109. U.S. FDA: ABMD Software. https://www.accessdata.fda.gov/scripts/cdrh/cfdocs/cfpmn/pmn.cfm?ID=K213760, Accessed 18 Apr 2025
110. U.S. FDA: Artificial Intelligence and Machine Learning (AI/ML)-Enabled Medical Devices. https://www.fda.gov/medical-devices/software-medical-device-samd/artificial-intelligence-and-machine-learning-aiml-enabled-medical-devices, Accessed 18 Apr 2025
111. U.S. FDA: Artificial Intelligence-Enabled Device Software Functions: Lifecycle Management and Marketing Submission Recommendations. https://www.fda.gov/media/184856/download, Accessed 18 Apr 2025
112. U.S. FDA: D-NAV System. https://www.accessdata.fda.gov/scripts/cdrh/cfdocs/cfpmn/pmn.cfm?ID=K181916, Accessed 18 Apr 2025
113. U.S. FDA: Dario Blood Glucose Monitoring System. https://www.accessdata.fda.gov/cdrh_docs/pdf15/K150817.pdf, Accessed 18 Apr 2025
114. U.S. FDA: DreaMed Advisor Pro. https://www.accessdata.fda.gov/cdrh_docs/pdf19/K191370.pdf, Accessed 18 Apr 2025
115. U.S. FDA: GI Genius. https://www.accessdata.fda.gov/scripts/cdrh/cfdocs/cfpmn/denovo.cfm?id=DEN200055, Accessed 18 Apr 2025
116. U.S. FDA: One Drop Blood Glucose Monitoring System. https://www.accessdata.fda.gov/scripts/cdrh/cfdocs/cfpmn/pmn.cfm?ID=K161834, Accessed 18 Apr 2025
117. U.S. FDA: Welldoc Bluestar System. https://www.accessdata.fda.gov/cdrh_docs/pdf19/K190013.pdf, Accessed 18 Apr 2025
118. U.S. Food and Drug Administration: 510(k) Premarket Notification, https://www.accessdata.fda.gov/scripts/cdrh/cfdocs/cfPMN/pmn.cfm
119. U.S. Food and Drug Administration: MAUDE - Manufacturer and User Facility Device Experience. https://www.accessdata.fda.gov/scripts/cdrh/cfdocs/cfMAUDE/search.cfm, Accessed 18 Apr 2025
120. U.S. Food and Drug Administration: MAUDE Adverse Event Report: Irhythm Technologies, Inc Zeus System; Computer, Diagnostic, Programmable. https://www.accessdata.fda.gov/scripts/cdrh/cfdocs/cfMAUDE/detail.cfm?mdrfoi__id=19427744, Accessed 18 Apr 2025
121. U.S. Food and Drug Administration: Product Code Classification Database. https://www.fda.gov/medical-devices/classify-your-medical-device/product-code-classification-database, Accessed 18 Apr 2025
122. U.S. Food and Drug Administration: Recalls, Corrections and Removals (Devices). https://www.fda.gov/medical-devices/postmarket-requirements-devices/recalls-corrections-and-removals-devices, Accessed 18 Apr 2025
123. U.S. Food and Drug Administration: Zeus system. https://www.accessdata.fda.gov/cdrh_docs/pdf22/K222389.pdf, Accessed 18 Apr 2025
124. Vargas, D.V., Su, J.: Understanding the one-pixel attack: propagation maps and locality analysis. In: CEUR Workshop Proceedings. vol. 2640 (2020)
125. Wang, W., Yao, Y., Liu, X., Li, X., Hao, P., Zhu, T.: I can see the light: attacks on autonomous vehicles using invisible lights. In: ACM SIGSAC CCS. pp. 1930–1944 (2021)

126. Wang, Z., Ma, J., Wang, X., Hu, J., Qin, Z., Ren, K.: Threats to training: a survey of poisoning attacks and defenses on machine learning systems. ACM Comput. Surv. **55**(7), 1–36 (2022)
127. Wei, J., et al.: Chain-of-thought prompting elicits reasoning in large language models. Adv. Neural. Inf. Process. Syst. **35**, 24824–24837 (2022)
128. Xu, Y., Tran, D., Tian, Y., Alemzadeh, H.: Analysis of cyber-security vulnerabilities of interconnected medical devices. In: 2019 IEEE/ACM International Conference on Connected Health: Applications, Systems and Engineering Technologies (CHASE) (2019)
129. Yaqoob, T., Abbas, H., Atiquzzaman, M.: Security vulnerabilities, attacks, countermeasures, and regulations of networked medical devices–a review. IEEE Commun. Surv. Tutor. **21**(4), 3723–3768 (2019)
130. Yoo, T.K., Choi, J.Y.: Outcomes of adversarial attacks on deep learning models for ophthalmology imaging domains. JAMA Ophthalmol. **138**(11), 1213–1215 (2020)
131. Young, W., Leveson, N.: Systems thinking for safety and security. In: Proceedings of ACM ACSAC '13, pp. 1–8. Association for Computing Machinery (2013)
132. Young, W., Porada, R.: System-theoretic process analysis for security (STPA-SEC): cyber security and STPA. In: STAMP Conference, pp. 27–30. MIT Press (2017)
133. Yu, J., Qiu, K., Wang, P., Su, C., Fan, Y., Cao, Y.: Perturbing BEAMs: EEG adversarial attack to deep learning models for epilepsy diagnosing. BMC Med. Inf. Decision Making **23**(1), 115 (2023)
134. Zhou, X., Ahmed, B., Aylor, J.H., Asare, P., Alemzadeh, H.: Hybrid knowledge and data driven synthesis of runtime monitors for cyber-physical systems. IEEE Trans. Depen, Secure Comput (2023)
135. Zhou, X., Kouzel, M., Ren, H., Alemzadeh, H.: Design and validation of an open-source closed-loop testbed for artificial pancreas systems. In: 2022 IEEE/ACM Conference on Connected Health: Applications, Systems and Engineering Technologies (CHASE), pp. 1–12. IEEE (2022)

Specialized Healthcare Protection – Genetic Data, Rural Services, & Senior Living

Collaborative, Privacy-Preserving Genomic Research: A Vision and Real-World Deployment

Zahra Rahmani[1], Zebin Yun[2], Nahal Shahini[1], Nadav Gat[2], Yuzhou Jiang[1], Ofir Farchy[3], Yaniv Harel[2], Vipin Chaudhary[1], Erman Ayday[1(✉)], and Mahmood Sharif[2(✉)]

[1] Case Western Reserve University, Cleveland, OH, USA
`{zxr81,nxs814,yxj466,vxc204,exa208}@case.edu`
[2] Tel Aviv University, Tel Aviv, Israel
`{zebinyun,nadavgat}@mail.tau.ac.il`, `{yaniv10,mahmoods}@tauex.tau.ac.il`
[3] Latica, Palo Alto, CA, USA
`ofir@latica.ai`

Abstract. The data revolution presents unprecedented potential for advancements in the healthcare sector, particularly within genomic research. On one hand, the continuous accumulation of large-scale individual genomic data serves as the foundation for the development of artificial intelligence-based innovations and digital health technologies. On the other hand, genomic data raises unique security and privacy risks requiring structured threat modeling and privacy-preserving measures.

This work presents an implementation of a privacy-preserving framework specifically designed for genomic research, integrated into a real-world secure platform for medical data collaboration. The proposed framework addresses critical security and privacy vulnerabilities, enabling the controlled sharing and analysis of genomic datasets while mitigating risks associated with data breaches. By leveraging advanced privacy-preserving algorithms, the framework protects privacy while maintaining data utility. A key aspect of this approach is the strategic trade-offs between data sharing and privacy, providing stakeholders with quantifiable metrics to assess privacy risks and inform data-sharing decisions.

The implementation within a real-world platform encompasses encoding genomic data into binary formats and introducing controlled noise to preserve key statistical attributes. This ensures the integrity of research outcomes while enabling privacy-aware computational analyses. Additionally, the envisioned framework integrates real-time data monitoring and advanced visualization tools, optimizing user experience and decision-making processes. Given the unique characteristics of genomic data, our work underscores the necessity for tailored privacy attacks and corresponding defenses to safeguard sensitive information effectively. By addressing these challenges, the proposed solution aspires to foster a global research ecosystem in genomics, ultimately accelerating breakthroughs in personalized medicine and public health.

1   Introduction

The incremental progress of genomic data collection over recent years has paved the way for transformative advancements in medical research. The advent of cutting-edge technologies, including artificial intelligence (AI), machine learning (ML), and data science, has introduced unprecedented opportunities to conduct medical and genomic investigations. Among others, for example, these innovations facilitate the identification of novel genetic variants, establish correlations between symptoms and underlying causes, and drive the development of personalized medicine. Every healthcare entity, including clinics, research institutions, and medical organizations, possesses unique datasets that hold immense potential for global research initiatives.

Despite these promising advancements, the heightened awareness of data privacy and cybersecurity has emphasized the necessity for reliable protective mechanisms. The safeguarding of patient information and the personal data of clinical trial participants has become a paramount concern. Institutional and regulatory frameworks have been established to mitigate risks related to inadvertent data exposure and malicious cyber threats. Consequently, these protective measures have inadvertently led to data silos, wherein valuable genomic and medical datasets remain confined within the institutions that collected them, rather than being leveraged for collaborative research across multiple entities, thus hindering scientific and technological advancements.

In this study, we articulate a vision for a privacy-preserving framework that enables secure, privacy-preserving genomic collaboration. Our work is supported by a strategic partnership with Latica, an industry collaborator that provides a platform for storing and sharing genomic data. Latica, an American-Israeli startup, has developed an infrastructure that facilitates secure data exchange among healthcare providers, pharmaceutical companies, and research organizations. The integration of real-world genomic use cases and datasets is critical for achieving our research objectives. Furthermore, this study proposes a framework addressing security and privacy concerns within Latica (and similar platforms), ensuring the secure exchange of genomic datasets while minimizing potential risks associated with data breaches. This framework enables researchers on the platform to share their datasets and AI models in a privacy-preserving manner. Additionally, the vision we lay out propose a novel system component that quantifies the trade-off between data utility and privacy costs. Currently, there exists a lack of interpretable tools that accurately assess privacy risks, resulting in uninformed decision-making regarding data sharing. Since stakeholders responsible for these decisions may not possess specialized expertise in privacy and security, it is imperative to develop methodologies that present privacy implications transparently and provide actionable insights.

Overall, this study addresses fundamental challenges in privacy-preserving genomic research, laying the groundwork for a paradigm shift in secure data collaboration. By fostering the development of collective genomic datasets, our approach has the potential to enable AI-driven discoveries, enhance diagnostic accuracy, and advance treatment methodologies for the most pressing global health challenges. To realize this vision, we have already integrated privacy-preserving algorithms into Latica's platform, developed privacy-risk assessment tools, and deployed these mechanisms in high-performance computing environments. Future efforts will focus on rigorous validation of these technologies using real-world genomic datasets, fostering inter-institutional collaboration, and continuously refining privacy-enhancing measures. By doing so, we aim to establish a robust foundation for privacy-aware genomic research, ensuring the secure and responsible application of AI and ML in the field of genomics. It is important to emphasize that while the primary focus of this work is on privacy, cybersecurity remains a crucial component in safeguarding digital assets and maintaining data confidentiality. The protection framework extends to AI models, which form an essential part of the security landscape alongside advanced technological defenses that enhance the integrity of processes and data transmission [20,26,29]. Future research endeavors will explore such cybersecurity dimensions in further depth.

2   Related Work

We examine prior work through three key dimensions: privacy vulnerabilities in genomic data, privacy-preserving methodologies for genomic research, and the intersection of ML and privacy.

2.1   Risks to Genomic Data's Privacy

The issue of genomic privacy has been extensively investigated by various efforts researchers [4,8,23,52,60]. Several studies have demonstrated that conventional anonymization techniques fail to provide sufficient protection for genomic data [27,28,30,39,42,45,59]. Research has further indicated that the identity of a participant in a genomic study can be inferred using a secondary sample, incorporating a subset of their DNA profile in conjunction with clinical study results [19,31,33,55,58,61,64,68]. Additionally, several investigations have explored phenotype-based identity tracing, wherein genetic markers are utilized to predict phenotypic traits, thereby exposing sensitive personal information [3,18,32,41,43,44,46,53,63,70]. These findings highlights the inherent risks in genomic data sharing, particularly when datasets are linked with publicly accessible information. The predictive capabilities of genomic data can be exploited to deduce highly sensitive attributes, including susceptibility to certain diseases and observable traits such as hair and skin color, which may be misused for discriminatory purposes.

Recent studies have further emphasized the threat posed by familial search methodologies, wherein adversaries exploit genetic similarities among relatives to identify individuals [28]. This technique capitalizes on shared genetic markers to compromise individual privacy, raising substantial ethical and security concerns for genomic data-sharing frameworks. The proliferation of public genetic repositories exacerbates this issue, as these extensive datasets can be cross-referenced to re-identify individuals from ostensibly anonymized genomic data.

2.2 Privacy-Enhancing Technologies for Genomic Research

Current methodologies for secure genomic data utilization and exchange predominantly rely on either obfuscation techniques or cryptographic frameworks. Among these, differential privacy (DP) has emerged as a widely proposed approach to mitigate the risks of membership inference attacks when disseminating summary statistics, such as minor allele frequencies and chi-square values [24,38,67]. DP provides a rigorous mathematical guarantee ensuring that the inclusion or exclusion of a single record within a dataset does not substantially alter analytical outcomes, thereby safeguarding individual privacy.

A considerable segment of cryptographic approaches is dedicated to secure genomic sequence comparisons and pattern matching [11,21,34,51,62]. In the domain of privacy-preserving clinical genomics, Baldi et al. introduced private set intersection-based techniques [10], facilitating the identification of shared genetic variants across datasets while maintaining confidentiality of individual-level data. Likewise, partially homomorphic encryption has been proposed for privacy-conscious genomic data analysis in clinical contexts, allowing computations to be executed on encrypted datasets without exposing underlying genetic information [5–7,9]. Additionally, Kantarcioglu et al. pioneered homomorphic encryption methods that support secure genomic research while ensuring data confidentiality [40]. Further advancements include privacy-aware similarity assessment protocols, such as those introduced by Wang et al., who developed private edit-distance algorithms that enable patient similarity identification across multiple institutions to enhance collaborative research while preserving privacy [65]. These cryptographic methods provide privacy assurances and are particularly advantageous in scenarios requiring secure genomic-data processing.

Despite these developments, cryptographic solutions present notable challenges concerning interoperability and scalability. Different genomic-analysis applications necessitate distinct cryptographic protocols, often resulting in security and efficiency limitations when attempting to integrate multiple systems. Moreover, the computational complexity inherent in some encryption techniques poses significant challenges for large-scale genomic studies.

Future research should focus on developing comprehensive frameworks that integrate diverse privacy-preserving mechanisms while optimizing data utility and computational efficiency. The design of flexible frameworks capable of accommodating various genomic research applications is crucial, as is ensuring the scalability required to manage the exponentially growing volume of genomic data generated by modern sequencing technologies. Progress in these areas will enable genomic research to advance without compromising privacy and security.

2.3 Privacy Considerations in ML and AI

Recent advancements in ML have led to an increasing interest in the development of privacy attacks, revealing multiple avenues through which ML models may inadvertently disclose sensitive information either during or after training [15,25,57,69]. Notably, membership inference attacks allow adversaries with access to a trained model to determine whether a specific data record was utilized during training [57]. Similarly, model inversion attacks facilitate the reconstruction of training samples from trained models [25]. Additional threats include but are not limited to unintended memorization of sensitive data [15] and the reconstruction of input-label associations in federated learning environments [69].

Privacy attacks targeting ML models serve as empirical tools for assessing the extent of private data leakage across various settings. However, to date, these techniques have largely remained within the domain of ML privacy research. Our vision (Sect. 3) aims to incorporate these adversarial evaluation methods into the Latica platform, equipping stakeholders with actionable insights regarding the potential privacy risks associated with releasing trained models. Importantly, existing ML privacy attacks have been extensively studied in the context of vision and text domains, whereas their applicability to genomic and medical data remains relatively unexplored. Consequently, it remains unknown whether existing attacks can enable reliable evaluation of privacy risks in genomic datasets, suggesting that domain-specific attack methodologies tailored for genomic and healthcare data may need to be developed.

Researchers have concurrently proposed several approaches to enhance ML privacy [2,12,49,54]. While some of these methods offer empirical improvements without formal privacy guarantees [49], others are grounded in provable privacy frameworks [2,54]. Among these, the differentially private stochastic gradient descent (DP-SGD) algorithm [2] enables model training while adhering to differential privacy principles, thus offering plausible deniability regarding the inclusion of specific records in the training dataset. Within our envisioned framework, such privacy-enhancing mechanisms will be integrated into platform such as Latica's, ensuring reliable data protections during model training.

3   Vision: Secure Collaborative Genomic Research

To tackle the significant issues related to genomic data privacy, we devised an extensive privacy-preserving solution for incorporation into the Latica platform. Our approach utilizes advanced privacy-preserving techniques to guarantee strong privacy safeguards while preserving the utility of shared genomic data.

In our broader vision, Latica acts as a sandbox environment where researchers can securely upload and share their genomic datasets. Our framework and algorithms are seamlessly embedded into the platform, equipping users with tools to analyze and share data without revealing sensitive information. Furthermore, an intuitive interface and advanced visualization tools will be created to enable users to effortlessly manage their datasets and comprehend the privacy and utility levels of shared data. These tools are essential for making informed decisions regarding data sharing and analysis.

3.1   A Privacy-Preserving Genomic Data-Exchange Protocol

We utilized an advanced privacy-preserving algorithm for sharing genomic datasets [36], which functions in two essential phases: data perturbation and utility restoration. Initially, the genomic single-nucleotide polymorphism (SNP) data, with values 0, 1, and 2, is converted into binary form where each SNP value is mapped: 0 to 00, 1 to 01, and 2 to 11, resulting in a binary matrix of dimensions $n \times 2m$. Subsequently, a noise matrix of identical dimensions is generated using a binary-valued XOR mechanism [35], which introduces noise to the encoded data to mask the original genomic sequences. The noise matrix is generated with Bernoulli-distributed values, considering both row (individual) and column (SNP)-wise correlations as detailed in the original study [35]. However, due to the computational demands of the XOR mechanism in large genomic datasets, we have developed an improved version of noise sampling known as efficient binary noise generation [37]. This improvement facilitates the efficient creation of the noise matrix, which is then XORed with the encoded data, resulting in a noisy binary matrix. The noisy matrix is then decoded back into the original SNP space before sharing, although this occurs prior to any utility-enhancing post-processing.

To enhance data utility, especially for genome-wide association studies (GWAS), we include a utility-restoration phase that modifies the minor allele frequencies (MAFs) [16] in the noisy dataset to more closely match publicly available MAF values. This post-processing technique employs an optimal transport method, specifically the earth mover's distance [56], to identify the minimal number of allele flips required to achieve the desired alignment. The procedure is as follows:

1. Compute the minor allele frequency (MAF) $\tilde{\mathcal{M}}_j$ for each SNP j in the noisy (binarized) dataset $\tilde{D}^b$.
2. Calculate the transition from $\tilde{\mathcal{M}}_j$ to the reference MAF $\tilde{\mathcal{M}}_j^r$ using the earth mover's distance, which determines the fraction of alleles to be flipped.
3. Select the precise number of alleles to flip by applying the floor function to the fraction multiplied by the total number of alleles.
4. Randomly choose and flip the required alleles.

This post-processing significantly enhances the reproducibility of GWAS and reduces point error, thereby improving the overall utility of the shared dataset. The robustness of our method is further evidenced by its ability to preserve the privacy of individuals' genomic data while enabling researchers to reliably replicate significant findings.

This dual-stage privacy-preserving scheme is crucial for maintaining the confidentiality of genomic data while ensuring its utility for research purposes. Our implementation within a high-performance computing (HPC) environment guarantees scalability and the capability to handle large datasets. The Latica platform, which functions as a controlled environment for data sharing, integrates this mechanism to allow researchers to securely upload their datasets. The platform's design also facilitates collaborative research by providing secure access to shared datasets and the necessary tools for joint studies. Once datasets are uploaded, Latica's platform applies the privacy-preserving scheme, ensuring the data remains protected while still being usable for advancing personalized medicine and other research initiatives. The use of a privacy budget ϵ enables us to effectively balance the privacy-utility tradeoff, with an optimal range of ϵ between 1 and 1000, equivalent to a privacy budget of less than approximately 0.2 per SNP [37]. This tradeoff is essential for maintaining data utility while safeguarding individual privacy.

Moreover, the verifier, who may be a reviewer in a peer-review process or another researcher seeking to validate the results, can reproduce the researcher's experiments using a sanitized version of the dataset. This process involves calculating the SNP retention rate, a metric that indicates the percentage of SNPs that remain statistically significant in reproduced results compared to those reported by the researcher. The verifier can also utilize public information during this process, potentially applying a relaxed p-value threshold to assess the SNP retention rate. By comparing the retention rate to a theoretical ideal or expected rate, the verifier can evaluate the reliability of the findings. If the difference between the actual and expected rates falls within a specified threshold, the findings are considered reliable. Otherwise, further investigation may be initiated, or additional detailed information may be requested, pending Institutional Review Board (IRB) approval. The public availability of MAF statistics, which is permitted according to NIH guidelines, further bolsters the privacy guarantees of our method, as differential privacy's immunity to post-processing ensures that these statistics do not compromise the overall privacy of the data [22]. Furthermore, Our two-stage privacy-preserving mechanism aligns with existing genomic cybersecurity frameworks, such as the NCCoE's Genomic Data Profile [50], which identifies genomic data integrity, controlled access, and secure storage as primary concerns.

3.2 Privacy-Preserving ML for Genomic Data

A core premise behind Latica's platform is that training ML models on the data accessible through the platform empowers technologists and scientists to create innovative technologies and gain valuable scientific insights. However, as previously discussed (Sect. 2.3), releasing these models poses significant privacy risks. Adversaries might exploit access to the models to deduce sensitive information about individuals' genomic or health data. Therefore, it is crucial to ensure that the models leak minimal to no information about the training data before their release from the platform. To this end, our vision aims to provide stakeholders (both data owners and users) with an automated evaluation system that measures the extent to which models leak information about their training data. Additionally, stakeholders will receive recommendations for potential defenses that can be integrated during training to enhance the protection of the training data.

As previously discussed, various privacy attacks have been proposed and rigorously evaluated against ML models (Sect. 2.3). However, genomic datasets differ significantly from the image or text datasets commonly used in past evaluations [14,57]. Consequently, these differences can affect the effectiveness of attacks. Firstly, genomic datasets typically have relatively small sample sizes, as collecting genomic data remains more costly than collecting text or image data, which can be easily sourced from the internet, albeit not always labeled. Some attacks require auxiliary datasets to train surrogate models that are later used to infer membership [14]. These may be ineffective against genomic models due to data scarcity. Secondly, while there are millions of genomic features—such as Single Nucleotide Polymorphisms (SNPs) [13] that can be ingested by models, the number of useful features in a given dataset is often substantially smaller, with each feature admitting a limited set of values. In contrast, image and text datasets contain significantly more dimensions (e.g., 3,072âĂŞ268,203 dimensions for standard image datasets), each admitting 256 different values [57]. The lower dimensionality of genomic data may reduce overfitting, making certain attacks such as membership inference more challenging [66]. Furthermore, many genomic prediction models (e.g., Ordinary Least Squares, Classical Ridge Regression, Linear regression, Classical Elastic Net, and Bayesian Ridge regression [47]) are inherently more transparent and less prone to overfitting, making them robust choices for genomic data analysis. These attributes ensure that the models provide reliable and interpretable results, even when integrated into privacy-preserving frameworks. Overall, it may be necessary to develop novel attacks specifically tailored for genomic data, and health data in general, to reliably assess machine learning models' leakage. Indeed, as our evaluation of existing attacks showed limited success, we plan to explore new attack directions in future work (e.g., by leveraging augmentations better suited for genomic data [17]).

3.3 Privacy-Risk Communication

Once the risk of private information leakage due to data sharing or ML model release is evaluated, it is essential to communicate this risk to users to aid their decision-making regarding whether to share data or models. To this end, among other factors, it is vital to inform users about the:

1. potential consequences of specific risks (e.g., membership inference);
2. theoretical assurances of the applied countermeasures (e.g., differential privacy mechanisms);
3. empirical evaluation of data leakage (e.g., potential success of membership inference);
4. assumptions underlying the attacks for which the risk is assessed (e.g., whether the adversary possesses auxiliary data); and
5. possible trade-offs between utility and privacy achievable with various countermeasures.

We plan to develop a privacy dashboard that presents such information to stakeholders in a user-friendly manner. Primarily, for usability, it is crucial to optimize both accessibility and runtime. For the former, we intend to rely on established literature that provides methods to describe the complex theoretical guarantees of certain defenses [48] and conduct user studies to identify effective ways to convey metrics estimated by ML privacy attacks that would be understandable to stakeholders with diverse backgrounds and expertise. For the latter, we aim to explore methods to enable prompt assessment of necessary metrics (e.g., by proposing more efficient attacks).

4 Implementing a Proof-of-Concept

We incorporated the privacy-preserving genomic data sharing scheme into the Latica platform and thoroughly evaluated both the privacy and utility of the data using extensive metrics. Our analysis utilized a range of tests, including Average Point Error, Average Sample Error, and Mean and Variance Error, which collectively indicate how well the integrity and statistical properties of the original

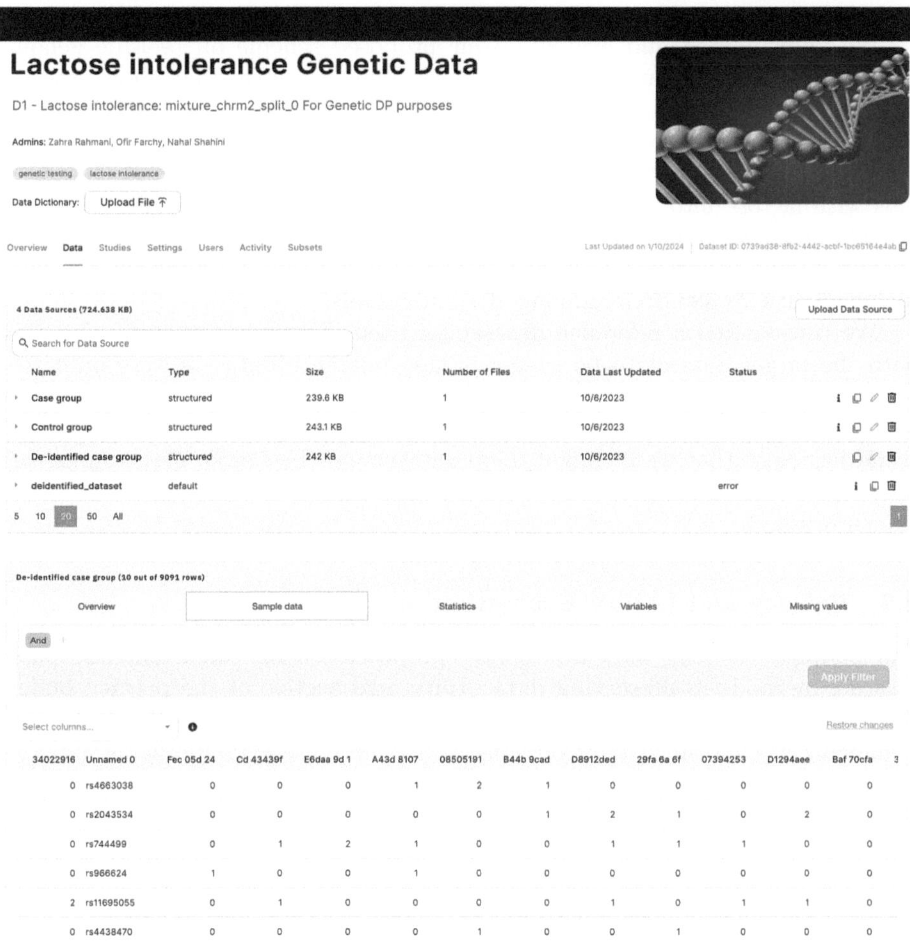

Name	Type	Size	Number of Files	Data Last Updated	Status	
Case group	structured	239.6 KB	1	10/6/2023		
Control group	structured	243.1 KB	1	10/6/2023		
De-identified case group	structured	242 KB	1	10/6/2023		
deidentified_dataset	default				error	

5 10 20 50 All

34022916	Unnamed 0	Fec 05d 24	Cd 43439f	E6daa 9d 1	A43d 8107	08505191	B44b 9cad	D8912ded	29fa 6a 6f	07394253	D1294aee	Baf 70cfa	3
0	rs4663038	0	0	0	1	2	1	0	0	0	0	0	
0	rs2043534	0	0	0	0	0	1	2	1	0	2	0	
0	rs744499	0	1	2	1	0	0	1	1	1	0	0	
0	rs966624	1	0	0	1	0	0	0	0	0	0	0	
2	rs11695055	0	1	0	0	0	0	1	0	1	1	0	
0	rs4438470	0	0	0	0	1	0	0	1	0	0	0	

Fig. 1. The architecture and data flow of Latica's platform.

dataset are maintained post-transformation. The privacy level of the data was assessed using the differential privacy parameter, ϵ, which offers robust privacy protection at various levels.

4.1 Datasets Employed for Evaluation

The datasets utilized for evaluating our privacy-preserving solution consist of a comprehensive collection of genomic data typical of what might be used in advanced medical research. The data encompasses a wide range of SNP variations, representing a diverse genetic background to ensure the generalizability of our results. Before applying our privacy-preserving mechanisms, the genomic data was encoded into a binary matrix format. This preparatory step was crucial for facilitating the subsequent integration of our novel two-stage privacy-preserving algorithm, which introduces controlled noise and leverages publicly known statistics to enhance data quality.

We implemented and evaluated our proposed scheme on real-life genomic datasets from the OpenSNP project [1], a public platform that allows users to share their genetic data, typically derived from consumer genetic testing services. We selected three phenotypes for our study: lactose intolerance, hair color, and eye color. The *lactose intolerance* dataset includes 9,091 SNPs from 60 individuals with lactose intolerance. The *hair color* dataset contains 9,686 SNPs from 60 individuals with dark hair. The *eye color* dataset is larger, with 28,396 SNPs among 401 individuals with brown eyes. Additionally, a **handedness** dataset is included with 28,396 SNPs among 401 individuals.

We constructed a reference dataset for each phenotype, aligning the SNPs with the target dataset to be shared. These reference datasets were built from the remaining data in the OpenSNP project. This thorough dataset selection and preparation ensured that our evaluation was robust and reflective of real-world scenarios. Note that we included these datasets on the Latica platform as users of the platform and ran the algorithms on the platform using these datasets as shown in Fig. 1.

4.2 Privacy and Utility Evaluation

Our findings (see [36]) indicate that the proposed scheme consistently surpasses existing methods in preserving data utility, irrespective of the privacy budget. This strong performance underscores the effectiveness of our two-stage privacy-enhancing mechanism. By introducing controlled noise and employing a distinctive post-processing technique, we achieve an optimal balance between data privacy and usability. This is crucial for advancing collaborative genomic research and personalized medicine. At the same time, the differential privacy framework defends against inference attacks, such as membership inference attacks, by injecting noise and safeguarding SNP value distributions, thereby providing robust privacy protection and high data utility.

4.3   Computational Efficiency Evaluation

The proposed privacy-preserving dataset sharing scheme introduces minimal overhead and exhibits lower computational complexity compared to existing methods. By employing an efficient perturbation technique based on the XOR mechanism, the scheme significantly reduces time complexity by calibrating noise through column-wise correlation of SNPs, thereby accelerating the perturbation process without compromising privacy guarantees. This improvement enables the scheme to manage large genomic datasets practically within a reasonable time-frame.

The scalability of the proposed dataset-sharing solution, when integrated with Latica, is highly promising. Designed to unlock the potential of comprehensive healthcare data, Latica's robust infrastructure facilitates efficient management and distribution of large-scale genomic datasets. The integration leverages advanced data processing and security capabilities, ensuring that the solution can handle increasing volumes of data without performance degradation. The efficient perturbation and utility restoration mechanisms of the proposed scheme maintain low computational complexity, enhancing scalability as the dataset size expands. Consequently, the combined strengths of the platform and the scalable dataset-sharing solution enable effective and secure sharing of extensive genomic data, driving significant advancements in healthcare research.

4.4   Evaluating Existing Privacy Attacks on Genomic ML Models

In a preliminary investigation, we have evaluated the extent to which established ML privacy attacks can assess privacy risks stemming from training and releasing genomic ML models. In particular, we focused on membership inference attacks. To this end, we developed ML models trained on data from OpenSNP. We collected genotype data and filtered out n valid genotypes (that are free of NaN values) to create the dataset. We used n values of 1,000 and 5,000, enabling us to examine how data dimensionality and size affects attack performance. For $n = 1,000$, we obtained 1,207 samples, while, for $n = 5,000$, we obtain 767 samples. We randomly selected a genotype and used it as the label.

For our experiment, we utilized two types of models: Convolutional Neural Networks (CNN) and Multilayer Perceptrons (MLP). To achieve the best performance, we employed grid search to optimize the models' hyperparameters. Specifically, our search space included the following parameters: learning rate (ranging from 5e-6 to 1e-4), criterion type (MSE and CE), architecture (CNN and MLP), number of hidden layers (ranging from 0 to 2), and hidden layer dimensions (ranging from 8 to 32). We tested 14 random genotypes and performed grid search on each individually. For training performance, accuracy easily reaches $\geq 99\%$ in most eases. For test performance, the accuracy reached up to 70%.

For membership inference, we evaluated the different attacks as suggested by Carlini et al. [14]—i.e., tuning each attack to have a False Positive Rate (FPR) of 5% or less, and measuring its True Positive Rate (TPR). In this setting, a

False Positive is a sample that was not in the training set of the target model but predicted as so by the attacker, and a True Positive is a sample that was correctly classified by the attacker as belonging to the training set. We evaluated three attacks differing in their assumptions (i.e. what access does the attacker has, the existence of auxiliary data for the attacker) and the compute required for them. The first attack is based on the Threshold attack suggested by Yeom et al. [66]. In this attack, only the loss of the model is needed, and a sample is classified as a member if the loss for it is below that threshold. This is the baseline attack, as it requires very little and assumes no further knowledge by the attacker.

The second attack is the Augmentation attack, adapted from the attack suggested by Choquette-Choo et al. [17]. In this attack, the attacker generates copies of the sample being attacked, each with random augmentations. For genomic data, the random augmentations are analogues to mutations, and so the change may only be between two adjacent values (e.g. from 0 to 1 but not from 0 to 2). The chance for an augmentation is a parameter set by the attacker, and is independent for each coordinate of the data. All samples are then passed through the model, and if the average confidence of the model is high, the original sample is classified as a member. This attack assumes the attacker may run inference many times on the target model, and also has access to the output model confidence.

The third attack is the offline variant of shadow-models attack suggested by Carlini et al. [14]. In this attack, the attacker trains shadow models with the same architecture as the target model on an auxiliary dataset. For a given sample, the attacker computes the target model's confidence on it, the distribution of confidences of the shadow models and runs a hypothesis test to see whether the first is likely from the distribution of the second. Since all shadow models are trained on data that does not include the sample, the if the confidence of the target model is similar, it suggests that it also did not train on the sample and therefore it is classified as a non-member. Otherwise, it is classified as a member. This attack assumes more than the previous ones, as the attacker requires an auxiliary dataset, with similar distribution to the target dataset.

We find that the TPRs of these attacks are very similar to each other given a specific target model, varying greatly between models. In most cases the TPR of all attacks is below 5% (set to be the FPR), essentially rendering the attacks useless as random guessing may achieve the same result. This is in contrast to previous research, in which the shadow-models attack was found to be the most effective, consistently achieving a higher TPR compared to the other attacks. We posit that this may be due to the differences between genomic data and other data modalities (which these attacks were evaluated on), discussed in 3.2. This result highlights that further exploration of this phenomena is required, and may yield attacks more suitable for this domain, which will better reflect the actual privacy risks of models trained on this data type.

5   Conclusion

In this study, we have demonstrated the feasibility and practicality of a privacy-preserving framework for collaborative genomic research, addressing the crucial need for secure and privacy-preserving data sharing in the era of personalized medicine. By utilizing advanced privacy-preserving algorithms, our solution ensures strong protection of sensitive genomic data while maintaining its utility for research purposes. The collaboration with Latica has been pivotal in validating our approach, illustrating how industry partnerships can enhance the deployment of privacy-preserving data platforms. Our genomic data-sharing method effectively balances the trade-offs between data sharing and privacy, providing stakeholders with transparent tools to evaluate privacy risks and make informed decisions. Our experimental results confirm that the proposed data-sharing framework surpasses existing methods in both privacy protection and data utility, highlighting its potential for broader application in genomic research and other fields requiring sensitive data handling. The integration of real-time monitoring and visualization tools further seek to enhance the user experience, promoting more effective and secure collaboration. Future work will focus on refining the privacy-preserving techniques, suggesting improved privacy-assessment algorithms for genomic ML models, and exploring additional applications in other domains. By continuing to address the unique challenges posed by genomic data, we aim to foster global collaboration and drive significant advancements in personalized medicine and public health.

Acknowledgments. An earlier version of this work has appeared at ACM CCS Workshop on Cybersecurity in Healthcare (HealthSec) 2024. We are deeply appreciative of the anonymous HealthSec peer reviewers and the shepherd, whose detailed feedback and insights have significantly enhanced the quality of this work. We greatly appreciate the world-class peer review provided by established leaders in the field. We would also like to acknowledge Joel Schwartz for his generous support for this project; his contributions have been instrumental to our progress.

References

1. opensnp. https://opensnp.org/
2. Abadi, M., et al.: Deep learning with differential privacy. In: Proceedings of the 2016 ACM SIGSAC Conference on Computer and Communications Security, pp. 308–318 (2016)
3. Allen, H.L., et al.: Hundreds of variants clustered in genomic loci and biological pathways affect human height. Nature **467**(7317), 832–838 (2010)
4. Ayday, E., Humbert, M.: Inference attacks against kin genomic privacy. IEEE Secur. Priv. **15**(5), 29–37 (2017). https://doi.org/10.1109/MSP.2017.3681052
5. Ayday, E., Raisaro, J.L., Hubaux, J.P.: Personal use of the genomic data: privacy vs. storage cost. In: Proceedings of IEEE Global Communications Conference, Exhibition and Industry Forum (Globecom) (2013)

6. Ayday, E., Raisaro, J.L., Hubaux, J.P.: Privacy-enhancing technologies for medical tests using genomic data. In: Proceedings of 20th Annual Network and Distributed System Security Symposium (NDSS) (Short Paper) (2013)

7. Ayday, E., Raisaro, J.L., McLaren, P.J., Fellay, J., Hubaux, J.P.: Privacy-preserving computation of disease risk by using genomic, clinical, and environmental data. In: Proceedings of USENIX Security Workshop on Health Information Technologies (HealthTech) (2013)

8. Ayday, E., De Cristofaro, E., Hubaux, J., Tsudik, G.: The chills and thrills of whole genome sequencing. IEEE Comput. Mag. (2015)

9. Ayday, E., Raisaro, J.L., Hubaux, J.P., Rougemont, J.: Protecting and evaluating genomic privacy in medical tests and personalized medicine. In: Proceedings of the 12th ACM Workshop on Privacy in the Electronic Society, pp. 95–106. ACM (2013)

10. Baldi, P., Baronio, R., De Cristofaro, E., Gasti, P., Tsudik, G.: Countering GATTACA: efficient and secure testing of fully-sequenced human genomes. In: Proceedings of the 18th ACM Conference on Computer and Communications Security, pp. 691–702 (2011)

11. Blanton, M., Atallah, M.J., Frikken, K.B., Malluhi, Q.: Secure and efficient outsourcing of sequence comparisons. In: Proceedings of European Symposium on Research in Computer Security, pp. 505–522 (2012)

12. Bonawitz, K., et al.: Practical secure aggregation for privacy-preserving machine learning. In: Proceedings of the 2017 ACM SIGSAC Conference on Computer and Communications Security, pp. 1175–1191 (2017)

13. Brookes, A.J.: The essence of SNPs. Gene **234**(2), 177–186 (1999)

14. Carlini, N., Chien, S., Nasr, M., Song, S., Terzis, A., Tramèr, F.: Membership inference attacks from first principles. In: IEEE Symposium on Security and Privacy (SP), pp. 1897–1914 (2022)

15. Carlini, N., Liu, C., Erlingsson, Ú., Kos, J., Song, D.: The secret sharer: evaluating and testing unintended memorization in neural networks. In: 28th USENIX Security Symposium (USENIX Security 19), pp. 267–284 (2019)

16. Carlson, C.S., Eberle, M.A., Rieder, M.J., Yi, Q., Kruglyak, L., Nickerson, D.A.: Mapping complex disease loci in whole-genome association studies. Nature **429**(6987), 446–452 (2004)

17. Choquette-Choo, C.A., Tramer, F., Carlini, N., Papernot, N.: Label-only membership inference attacks. In: Proceedings of the 38th International Conference on Machine Learning, vol. 139, pp. 1964–1974 (2021)

18. Claes, P., et al.: Modeling 3D facial shape from DNA. PLoS Genet. **10**(3) (2014)

19. Clayton, D.: On inferring presence of an individual in a mixture: a Bayesian approach. Biostatistics **11**(4), 661–673 (2010)

20. Dayan, O., Wolf, L., Wang, F., Harel, Y.: Optimizing ai for mobile malware detection by self-built-dataset GAN oversampling and LGBM. In: 2023 IEEE International Conference on Cyber Security and Resilience (CSR), pp. 60–65 (2023). https://doi.org/10.1109/CSR57506.2023.10224927

21. De Cristofaro, E., Faber, S., Tsudik, G.: Secure genomic testing with size- and position-hiding private substring matching. In: Proceedings of the 12th ACM Workshop on Privacy in the Electronic Society (2013)

22. Dwork, C., Roth, A.: The algorithmic foundations of differential privacy. Found. Trends Theoret. Comput. Sci. **9**(3–4), 211–407 (2014)

23. Erlich, Y., Narayanan, A.: Routes for breaching and protecting genetic privacy. Nat. Rev. Genet. **15**(6), 409–421 (2014)

24. Fienberg, S.E., Slavkovic, A., Uhler, C.: Privacy preserving GWAS data sharing. In: IEEE 11th International Conference on Data Mining Workshops (ICDMW), pp. 628–635 (2011)
25. Fredrikson, M., Jha, S., Ristenpart, T.: Model inversion attacks that exploit confidence information and basic countermeasures. In: Proceedings of the 22nd ACM SIGSAC Conference on Computer and Communications Security, pp. 1322–1333 (2015)
26. Gandal, N., Moore, T., Riordan, M., Barnir, N.: Empirically evaluating the effect of security precautions on cyber incidents. Comput. Secur. **133**, 103380 (2023). https://doi.org/10.1016/j.cose.2023.103380, https://www.sciencedirect.com/science/article/pii/S0167404823002900
27. Gitschier, J.: Inferential genotyping of Y chromosomes in latter-day saints founders and comparison to utah samples in the HapMap project. Am. J. Hum. Genet. **84**(2), 251–258 (2009)
28. Gymrek, M., McGuire, A.L., Golan, D., Halperin, E., Erlich, Y.: Identifying personal genomes by surname inference. Science **339**(6117), 321–324 (2013)
29. Harel, Y., Gal, I.B., Elovici, Y.: Cyber security and the role of intelligent systems in addressing its challenges. ACM Trans. Intell. Syst. Technol. **8**(4) (2017). https://doi.org/10.1145/3057729
30. Hayden, E.C.: Privacy protections: the genome hacker. Nature **497**, 172–174 (2013)
31. Homer, N., et al.: Resolving individuals contributing trace amounts of DNA to highly complex mixtures using high-density SNP genotyping microarrays. PLoS Genet. **4**(8) (2008)
32. Humbert, M., Huguenin, K., Hugonot, J., Ayday, E., Hubaux, J.P.: De-anonymizing genomic databases using phenotypic traits, pp. 99–114 (2015)
33. Im, H.K., Gamazon, E.R., Nicolae, D.L., Cox, N.J.: On sharing quantitative trait GWAS results in an era of multiple-omics data and the limits of genomic privacy. Am. J. Hum. Genet. **90**(4), 591–598 (2012)
34. Jha, S., Kruger, L., Shmatikov, V.: Towards practical privacy for genomic computation. In: Proceedings of IEEE Symposium on Security and Privacy, pp. 216–230 (2008)
35. Ji, T., Li, P., Yilmaz, E., Ayday, E., Ye, Y., Sun, J.: Differentially private binary- and matrix-valued data query: an XOR mechanism. Proc. VLDB Endowment **14**(5), 849–862 (2021)
36. Jiang, Y., Ji, T., Li, P., Ayday, E.: Reproducibility-oriented and privacy-preserving genomic dataset sharing (2023)
37. Jiang, Y., Ji, T., Li, P., Ayday, E.: Privacy-preserving sharing of genomic datasets for research outcome validation. arXiv preprint arXiv:2209.06327v5 (2024)
38. Johnson, A., Shmatikov, V.: Privacy-preserving data exploration in genome-wide association studies. In: Proceedings of the 19th ACM SIGKDD International Conference on Knowledge Discovery and Data Mining, pp. 1079–1087 (2013)
39. Kale, G., Ayday, E., Tastan, Ö.: A utility maximizing and privacy preserving approach for protecting kinship in genomic databases. Bioinformatics **34**(2) (2017)
40. Kantarcioglu, M., Jiang, W., Liu, Y., Malin, B.: A cryptographic approach to securely share and query genomic sequences. IEEE Trans. Inf Technol. Biomed. **12**(5), 606–617 (2008)
41. Kayser, M., de Knijff, P.: Improving human forensics through advances in genetics, genomics and molecular biology. Nat. Rev. Genet. **12**(3), 179–192 (2011)
42. Lin, Z., Owen, A.B., Altman, R.B.: Genomic research and human subject privacy. Science **305**(5681), 183 (2004)

43. Lippert, C., et al.: Identification of individuals by trait prediction using whole-genome sequencing data. Proc. Natl. Acad. Sci. (2017). https://doi.org/10.1073/pnas.1711125114

44. Liu, F., et al.: A genome-wide association study identifies five loci influencing facial morphology in Europeans. PLoS Genet. **8**(9) (2012)

45. Malin, B.A., Sweeney, L.: How (not) to protect genomic data privacy in a distributed network: using trail re-identification to evaluate and design anonymity protection systems. J. Biomed. Inform. **37**(3), 179–192 (2004)

46. Manning, A.K., et al.: A genome-wide approach accounting for body mass index identifies genetic variants influencing fasting glycemic traits and insulin resistance. Nat. Genet. **44**(6), 659–669 (2012)

47. McDowell, R.: Genomic selection with deep neural networks. Master's thesis, Iowa State University (2016)

48. Nanayakkara, P., Smart, M.A., Cummings, R., Kaptchuk, G., Redmiles, E.M.: What are the chances? explaining the epsilon parameter in differential privacy. In: 32nd USENIX Security Symposium (USENIX Security 23), pp. 1613–1630 (2023)

49. Nasr, M., Shokri, R., Houmansadr, A.: Machine learning with membership privacy using adversarial regularization. In: Proceedings of the 2018 ACM SIGSAC Conference on Computer and Communications Security, pp. 634–646 (2018)

50. National Institute of Standards and Technology (NIST): Genomic Data Project Update Webinar. Presentation slides (2025). https://www.nccoe.nist.gov/webinars/genomic-data-project-update-2025

51. Naveed, M., et al.: Controlled functional encryption. In: Proceedings of the 2014 ACM SIGSAC Conference on Computer and Communications Security (2014)

52. Naveed, M., et al.: Privacy in the genomic era. ACM Comput. Surv. (CSUR) **48**(1), 6 (2015)

53. Ou, X.l., Gao, J., Wang, H., Wang, H.S., Lu, H.l., Sun, H.Y.: Predicting human age with bloodstains by sjTREC quantification. PloS One **7**(8) (2012)

54. Papernot, N., Song, S., Mironov, I., Raghunathan, A., Talwar, K., Erlingsson, Ú.: Scalable private learning with pate. arXiv preprint arXiv:1802.08908 (2018)

55. Raisaro, J.L., et al.: Addressing beacon re-identification attacks: quantification and mitigation of privacy risks. J. Am. Med. Inf. Assoc. **24**(4), 799–805 (2016)

56. Rubner, Y., Tomasi, C., Guibas, L.J.: The earth mover's distance as a metric for image retrieval. Int. J. Comput. Vision **40**(2), 99–121 (2000). https://doi.org/10.1023/A:1026543900054

57. Shokri, R., Stronati, M., Song, C., Shmatikov, V.: Membership inference attacks against machine learning models. In: 2017 IEEE Symposium on Security and Privacy (SP), pp. 3–18. IEEE (2017)

58. Shringarpure, S.S., Bustamante, C.D.: Privacy risks from genomic data-sharing beacons. Am. J. Hum. Genet. **97**(5), 631–646 (2015)

59. Sweeney, L., Abu, A., Winn, J.: Identifying participants in the personal genome project by name. arXiv preprint arXiv:1304.7605 (2013)

60. Telenti, A., Ayday, E., Pierre Hubaux, J.: On genomics, kin, and privacy. F1000Research (2014). https://doi.org/10.12688/f1000research.4089

61. von Thenen, N., Ayday, E., Cicek, A.E.: Re-identification of individuals in genomic data-sharing beacons via allele inference. Bioinformatics **35**(3) (2018)

62. Troncoso-Pastoriza, J.R., Katzenbeisser, S., Celik, M.: Privacy preserving error resilient DNA searching through oblivious automata. In: Proceedings of ACM CCS 2007 (2007)

63. Walsh, S., Liu, F., Ballantyne, K.N., van Oven, M., Lao, O., Kayser, M.: IrisPlex: a sensitive DNA tool for accurate prediction of blue and brown eye colour in the absence of ancestry information. Forensic Sci. Int. Genet. **5**(3), 170–180 (2011)
64. Wang, R., Li, Y.F., Wang, X., Tang, H., Zhou, X.: Learning your identity and disease from research papers: information leaks in genome wide association study. In: Proceedings of the 16th ACM Conference on Computer and Communications Security, pp. 534–544 (2009)
65. Wang, X.S., Huang, Y., Zhao, Y., Tang, H., Wang, X., Bu, D.: Efficient genome-wide, privacy-preserving similar patient query based on private edit distance. In: Proceedings of the 22nd ACM SIGSAC Conference on Computer and Communications Security, pp. 492–503 (2015)
66. Yeom, S., Giacomelli, I., Fredrikson, M., Jha, S.: Privacy risk in machine learning: analyzing the connection to overfitting. In: IEEE 31st Computer Security Foundations Symposium (CSF), pp. 268–282 (2018)
67. Yu, F., Fienberg, S.E., Slavković, A.B., Uhler, C.: Scalable privacy-preserving data sharing methodology for genome-wide association studies. J. Biomed. Inform. **50**, 133–141 (2014)
68. Zhou, X., Peng, B., Li, Y.F., Chen, Y., Tang, H., Wang, X.: To release or not to release: evaluating information leaks in aggregate human-genome data. In: Computer Security – ESORICS 2011, pp. 607–627 (2011)
69. Zhu, L., Liu, Z., Han, S.: Deep leakage from gradients. In: Advances in Neural Information Processing Systems, vol. 32 (2019)
70. Zubakov, D., et al.: Estimating human age from T-cell DNA rearrangements. Curr. Biol. **20**(22), R970–R971 (2010)

What Are the Hazards in Providing Remote Health Services in Rural Australia and How Can We Manage Them?

Ashley Brooks and Arnab Majumdar[✉]

Imperial College London, London, U.K.
{a.brooks15,a.majumdar}@imperial.ac.uk

Abstract. This paper is an updated summary with feedback of a paper originally presented at the ACM HealthSec Workshop held in Salt Lake City October 2024 [12]. The delivery of remote health services in Northern Territory (NT) Australia, presents many communications challenges due to the harsh environment. This poses numerous challenges for the health services provider NT Health, as they have a duty of care for the occupational health and safety of remote health workers (RHWs). While there have been piecemeal attempts to resolve these challenges, this has not been done in a holistic manner, with a notable lack of focus on remote health worker safety. We use a mixed methods approach to identify systemhazards of RHWs as they deliver health services, with a particular emphasis on road safety and an alert and response system that was implemented to improve occupational health and safety. This involved a hazard analysis, using System Theoretic Process Analysis (STPA), of the alert and first response system (involving discussions with NT Health personnel), and a thematic analysis of interviews carried out with staff to understand the effectiveness of NT Health's safety management system and find any notable challenges.

The hazard analysis identified many challenges to effectively implementing an alert and response system due to technological and implementation challenges. At the same time thematic analysis highlighted safety culture challenges, independence and isolation, implementation challenges and inconsistency as potential barriers to an effective safety management system. These findings will only enhance the future occupational health and safety of RHWs and the general population.

Keywords: System safety engineering · rural remote healthcare · STAMP STPA analysis · thematic analysis

1 Introduction

The protection and resilience of critical infrastructure is of paramount importance to national governments. The Centre for the Protection of National Infrastructure (CPNI) defines critical infrastructure as follows, [1]:

'Those critical elements of infrastructure (namely assets, facilities, systems, networks or processes and the essential workers that operate and facilitate them), the loss or

W. Yurcik (Ed.): HealthSec 2024, CCIS 2716, pp. 284–300, 2026.
https://doi.org/10.1007/978-3-032-13800-2_13

compromise of which could result in: a) Major detrimental impact on the availability, integrity or delivery of essential services – including those services whose integrity, if compromised, could result in significant loss of life or casualties – taking into account significant economic or social impacts; and/or b) Significant impact on national security, national defence, or the functioning of the state.'

Such a definition covers key sectors including communication, healthcare and transport. This paper considers the provision of healthcare, i.e. health services in Australia's remote regions of Northern Territory (NT), which involves the need for transport and communications, as an example of such critical infrastructure. The loss or compromise of such infrastructure has profound effects and could result in a significant loss of life or casualties, especially in emergency situations.

Australia's history means that the state and territory governments are responsible for managing threats to life and property within their jurisdictions. They prepare for and respond to emergencies and deliver services such as healthcare [3]. In the Northern Territory this is incredibly challenging given its vast physical size, sparse population, remote locations of many communities, long distances between them and an ever-present harsh climate. At the same time, it is worth noting that ensuring the health and safety of all NT Health employees is a priority for the Department of Health and its NT Regional Health Services.

Traditionally, NT Health has focussed on developing and providing health and safety systems for its employees, and yet numerous hazards still put them at risk and require further improvement. This was shockingly highlighted by the tragic case of a NT Health nurse on duty who was murdered whilst facing numerous hazards on duty, including unreliable communications and lone working [1]. The murder brought to the fore that the activities performed by NT Health employees are typically in very remote locations without reliable communications. In such locations, conducting activities in isolation, with limited external emergency capability and a range of inherent constraints, NT Health needs to adopt the highest practicable preventative controls to protect the health and safety of employees. Through state-of-the-art technology, it is feasible to both:

i) introduce improved real-time monitoring and communications capabilities, and
ii) increase the ability to prevent accidents through technology within the employee's vehicle, which is the main means of communication.

Such technology has the potential to reduce the overall frequency of safety incidents as well as reducing the severity of such incidents.

1.1 NT Health Service Delivery

NT Health consists of five delivery services which manage the NT government's Public Health Care (PHC) services in 51 locations across the territory, Fig. 1. These services are delivered daily by 440 on-site staff employed as: registered nurses and midwives (Remote Area Nurses), Aboriginal and Torres Strait Islander Health Practitioners (ATSIHP), support staff and medical practitioners.

Most of the remote area PHC staff in the NT work and live hundreds of kilometres away from urban areas, in often very small communities accessible only by a four-wheel drive vehicle travelling along unsealed roads which are impassable during the wet

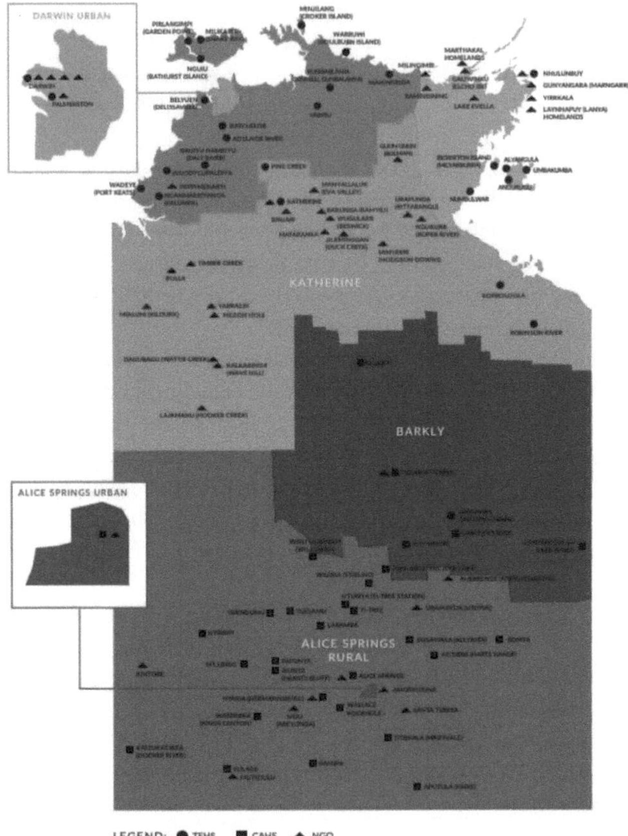

Fig. 1. Map of existing healthcare services in the NT.

season. In the NT, over 70% of the entire road network of 36,000 kms is unsealed, i.e. the roads constructed and formed, but have not been sealed with a hard material such as tar, bitumen, concrete or asphalt. Most unsealed roads in the NT are graded dirt or gravel roads.

Additionally, the NT is unique in the fact that it has a large volume of 'road trains' as illustrated in Fig. 2. Road trains comprise of a large truck or tractor that pulls three or four trailers at a time. The road trains transport all types of goods, including livestock, consumer goods, and fuel.

These factors and the relative isolation of the remote area workplace present a range of health and safety risks which are less critical within an urban operating environment and require a holistic approach to risk management.

The overarching challenge is the geographic separation from many emergencyservices functions which and timely support which may be required in many scenarios. This issue is compounded by communications systems that are less reliable than in urban centres or major communities and the travel times between regional and remote

Fig. 2. Road trains on the roads of the NT.

centres. This scenario presents a complex socio-technical system involving both social and technological components, where a complex system is defined as:

'A complex system is a system in which there are non-trivial relationships between cause and effect: each effect may be due to multiple causes; each cause may contribute to multiple effects; causes and effects may be related as feedback loops, both positive and negative; and cause- effect chains are cyclic and highly entangled rather than linear and separable' [7].

An operation in a socio-technical system can be thought of as one in which people actively interact with technology in order to achieve production goals (i.e., the provision of remote health) through the delivery of services. It is helpful to utilise a systems safety engineering approach when seeking to improve safety outcomes. Two novel systems approaches are [6, 8]:

i) System Theoretic Process Analysis (STPA) - used when conducting a systemic hazard analysis for engineered products, designs and operations,
ii) Functional Resonance Analysis Method (FRAM) - strengths are in specific workplace activities.

Therefore, as this research considers technology interventions and operations within a larger system, STPA is the preferred and chosen approach for this technical part of the hazard analysis.

The challenges outlined require NT Health to ensure a strong focus on developing and implementing robust and reliable preventative controls – as part of the safety management system (SMS) – which reduce the necessity for reactive measures in order to fulfil its obligations as an organisation to ensure a safe workplace. This paper seeks to improve the overall safety of remote health workers from their current levels by taking a systems safety approach, whilst analysing the impact of the introduction of technology interventions. This research will not only impact NT Health as an organisation but also both their remote health workers and remote communities in the territory, by improving safety outcomes (such as reducing the frequency and severity of incidents) and emergency response. It will also impact national governments in their efforts to protect critical national infrastructure and contribute to academic research in systems safety for remote health workers and remote workers, more generally.

1.2 Organisation of the Paper

This paper is organised as follows. In Sects. 2 and 3 we undertake a critical review of the provision of remote health services in Northern Territory as well as methods of system safety analysis for socio-technical systems. This highlights the wider issues surrounding remote health services for NT Health and the selection of an appropriate system-wide safety analysis method (namely, STPA). We analyse challenges faced by occupational health and safety at NT Health, shortcomings in current system in addressing these challenges. This will be undertaken predominantly by means of an analysis of policy and report documents. In Sect. 4 we propose a mixed methods framework that incorporates different analysis methods, e.g., interviews, and hazard analysis tools, to conduct a system safety analysis for the provision of remote health services in NT.

Analysis of the currently implemented system by means of STPA to determine losses, hazards, unsafe control actions, and causal scenarios. This analysis will be used to suggest recommendations for the system to ensure the prevention of losses and hence the improved safety of remote health workers. Section 5 focuses on the application of STPA analysis to remote health workers operations/driving (the alert/response system).

In Sect. 6 we outlined the results of a thematic analysis of interviews conducted with relevant NT Health professionals NT Health's safety management system and its effectiveness to control and mitigate Work Health & Safety (WHS) hazards. We conclude by discussing the implications of the framework and the results, including considerations of operational aspects and governance.

2 Rural Australia

The sheer physical land mass, coupled with a relatively small population of nearly 26 million, makes Australia makes it one of the most sparsely populated nations in the World with only 3.3 inhabitants per square kilometre as of 2021 [2]. In addition, it is a highly urbanised with 85% of the population living in urban areas and about two-thirds in one of the eight capital cities, at an ever increasing rate [10]. In these challenging situations, health workers based in rural and remote environments across Australia depend on other sectors of critical infrastructure in order to work safely and effectively. This includes transport and space-based services (namely telecommunications and navigation/global navigation satellite systems, GNSS). The effective operations and dependability of emergency services are also critical in situations of crisis Fig. 3.

The Northern Territory (NT) of Australia poses particular challenges for healthcare practitioners as they have to work in possibly the most rural/remote region of Australia [10]. They are exposed to such characteristics as climatic extremes, isolation, lack of infrastructure and services and after-hours work. Travelling on roads – a necessary activity for RHW – is a particularly hazardous activity, Fig. 4.

The danger is exacerbated by the lack of telecommunications infrastructure, making any first response, in the event of an accident occurring, a challenge. Knowing these challenges, any hazard or safety analysis must be holistic in its approach. In particular, this applies to implementing any system designed to mitigate these challenges and improve safety for remote health workers. Traditionally, these challenges have been approached in a piece-meal manner resulting in ineffective safety management.

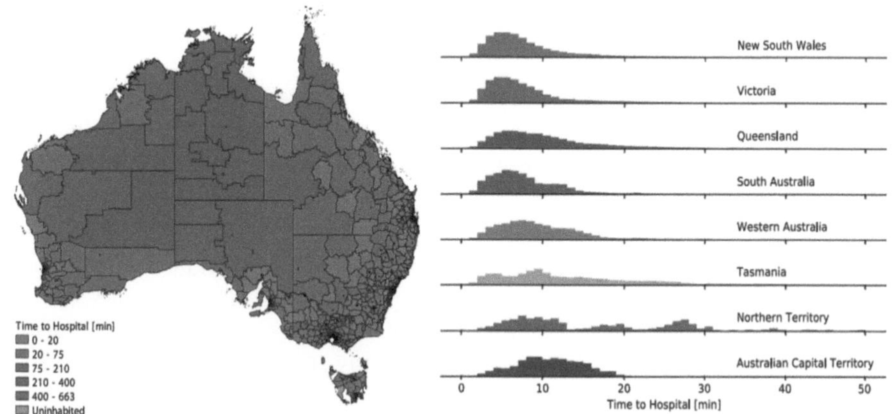

Fig. 3. Driving times to hospitals in Australia.

The following section consequently considers safety and safety management and identifies appropriate tools/methods for performing a system safety analysis.

Fig. 4. Driving hazards on NT Roads

3   Safety Management

All system safety activities (or tasks) can be divided into two broad categories, [11]:

i) engineering – in essence these are associated with the identification and elimination or control of system hazards, in contrast to
ii) management – these ensure that the engineering tasks are performed and to control safety in every aspect of the organisation.

While the traditional form of safety has generally provided assurance after the design of the system, when leverage on the system is poor, system safety imposes a state of safety on the system throughout its life cycle, where costs are minimum. It is desirable to design out potential causes of accidents in the early stages.

Hazard analysis is a fundamental to safety management and begins with hazard identification. While numerous hazard analysis techniques have been developed, these are limited in scope, primarily designed to identify component failures in a linear fashion. For the hazard analysis of complex socio-technical systems, a new technique has been developed to facilitate a system hazard analysis – this technique is STPA, based on systems theory. It is expected that this would be a suitable method for application within NT Health, as it is a flexible tool that can handle hazard analysis (with the aim of loss prevention) effectively for an engineered system.

It's insufficient though to simply conduct a system hazard analysis and identify the hazards). It is also essential to consider how the hazards are managed within the wider safety management system. Therefore, a hazard analysis of a system within NT Health must be combined with an analysis of the organization's safety management system (SMS), typically conducted by means analysis of interviews with relevant personnel.

4   The Technology Challenges Facing NT Health

A unique feature of Northern Territory is that most of the remote primary health care staff work and live hundreds of kilometres away from urban areas, often in very small communities typically accessible only by a four-wheel drive vehicle. Travel on the roads typically involves driving on rough and unsealed roads, as well as at nighttime, in all-weather conditions, and outside of mobile phone (or internet) reception. Unsurprisingly, vehicle accidents are a leading cause of serious injury and death for employees in remote locations in Australia. While driver training and the selection of the correct vehicles can reduce the risk of a collision due to animals, mechanical failure or the actions of other road users remains significant.

While technology cannot eliminate the risk of aggravated assault on a worker, what it can do is to track and communicate with employees during periods of duress and initiate timely emergency responses to life threatening situations. Hence it plays a crucial role in providing a wider safety net for all persons who travel to and for work within the remote regions of Australia.

Based on document analysis, current challenges include:

a) Ensuring safe road travel between communities to attend visits or emergency response in some cases with the risk of vehicle breakdown, accident or injury to employees in transit;

b) Inability to communicate with employees outside of communities due to the lack of a reliable mobile network coverage, with some communities reliant solely on landlines;

c) Inability to communicate with employees when in transit to jobs in order to notify them of a change in job status, new hazards or possible threats while in transit;

d) Lower than desired reliability of satellite phones, coupled with a need to ensure employees are trained and competent in satellite phone use and dialling protocols.

e) At present, electronic mapping in vehicles is unavailable on certain roads, addresses with locations literally "off the map" according to employees in remote area.

f) Emergency response coordination centre being outsourced with no wider visibility of employee travel plans, tasking, or patient-based requirements.

4.1 The Vehicle Tracking and Alert System

In order to address the need to track the location of employees and their vehicles in remote locations, a vehicle tracking and alert system was originally sourced by NT Health. This need was based upon a range of health and safety risks arising from the operations of a highly remote workforce, including: the potential for vehicle accidents including collisions with wildlife, breakdowns and the potential exposure to serious occupational violence. NT Health originally expressed interest in a global positioning system (GPS) vehicle monitoring system, subsequently expanded to include the following alerts:

- Automatic rollover and collision
- Automatic braking and swerving alerts
- Manually activated Duress alerts

Installation was performed by competent automobile electricians under the directions of the provider. Various suppliers were used in all regions as they were available, and equipment was delivered to mechanics and installed in accordance with a checklist of specifications. Installations were subsequently activated and initialised by the provider remotely. Training and procedures were developed by NT Health, and monitoring and alert activation was performed by a third-party NT government agency. However, since implementation, there a few serious incidents have occurred, including two vehicle rollovers and one collision that failed to trigger automatic alerts as required. In addition, several false alerts have been registered. These various incidents all point to the need for a detailed hazard analysis of the system.

5 STPA

The System Theoretic Accident Model and Processes (STAMP) framework is driven by the fact that traditional safety and security approaches are limited by new technology and increasing complexity of systems we build. The role of humans operating these systems is also changing as they supervise increasingly complex automated processes [9]. STAMP applies systems thinking to safety and security (and other system properties) to develop practical methods with tools and processes with the goal to provide more comprehensive, effective and efficient results [8].

STAMP treats accidents as a control problem, not a failure problem, and prevents accidents by enforcing constraints on component behaviour and interactions. An STPA

(Systems-Theoretic Process Analysis) hazard analysis, is based on STAMP and seeks to find inadequate control in a system. A controlled process involves a controller as well as control actions and feedback. This type of control structure forms the basis of an STPA analysis and of the hierarchical control structure model.

In this section, an STPA hazard analysis is presented. While brief explanations will be given accordingly, the reader is encouraged to refer to [8] for further details. The system under analysis is the system designed to provide 24/7 emergency monitoring and first response service to users of NT Health vehicles who have an alert and may need assistance. Once the main purpose of the system is understood, system-level losses and hazards must be identified to proceed with the analysis.

The primary goal of STPA is to prevent losses. In this system the identified system-level losses are:

L1: Loss of first response mission (including resource loss)
L2: Loss of life or serious injury to remote health worker
Once the losses in the analysis have been identified, the system-level hazards can be identified. In this system, these hazards are:

H1: Remote worker does not receive aid/assistance from first response ecosystem [relates to L1, L2].
H2: First response dispatched when not required [relates to L1].
Following this, a control structure model is built capturing functional relationships and interactions of the system in the form of control-feedback loops, as presented below.

5.1 STPA Analysis Main Results

To build the control structure model (Fig. 5), it is necessary to identify the main components (or entities) and consider their roles/responsibilities. For the first response system, the main components identified are: Central Services (CS); NT Health (NTH); Emergency Services (ES); and Remote Health Worker & Vehicle (RHW). The vertical axis (from top to bottom) generally indicates a hierarchy of control and authority in the system, with each entity in the system having control over the entity directly below it. Downward arrows represent control actions or commands, and the upward arrows represent feedback. There may also be other inputs to and outputs from components (often in the form of communication channels). Roles/responsibilities include receiving alerts, contacting others, requesting help, check vehicle status among others. This information is built up from discussion with users and owners of the system and is an iterative process.

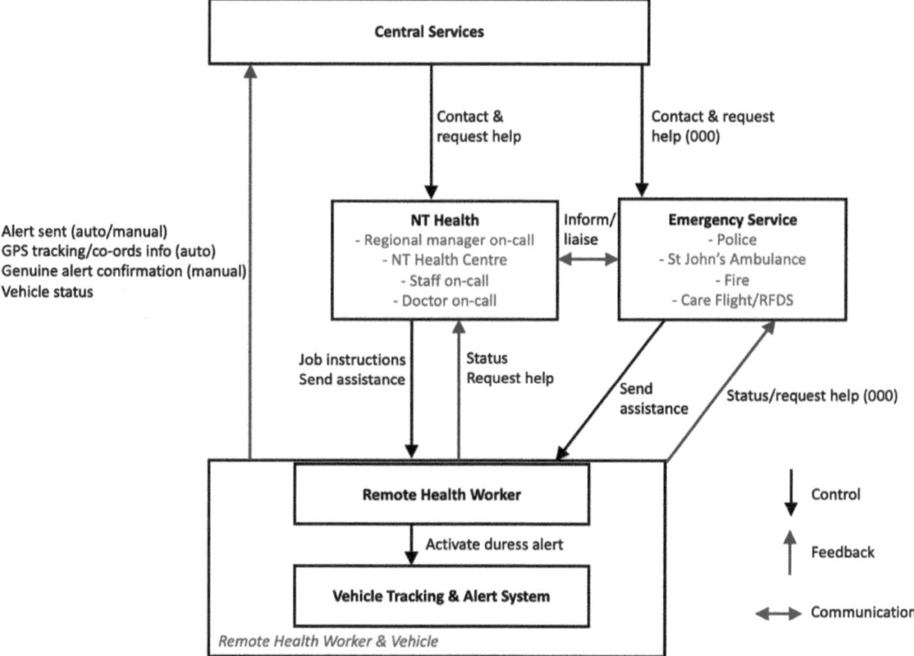

Fig. 5. STPA Control Structure Model for the alert and response system

Using this model, control actions within the control structure diagram were analysed to determine how they might lead to system-level hazards and losses. Following this, the final step was the identification of numerous causal scenarios that could lead to these unsafe control actions (which in turn lead to system-level hazards, and ultimately losses). This included many things, for example, communication errors, faulty equipment, faulty software, misunderstanding of (or conflicting) information or processes. As expected, the scenarios identified included those that have, occurred in the field, as noted in Sect. 4. Namely, alerts not sent and/or not received (by Central Services) as well as the triggering of false alerts.

The analysis highlighted several challenging causal scenarios regarding the implementation and operation of the system, technological or otherwise. Given the number of vehicles and large geographical coverage area, correct installation and calibration may take some time, but must be thoroughly checked. The system is also dependent on adequate satellite coverage (rather than mobile coverage) in the operational environment most of the time, which will remain a challenge. It may be especially difficult to contact the RHW to confirm whether they are in distress or not when they are on the road.

There are also challenges with sending out a first response in a timely fashion due to the large coverage area and limited resources.

The multiple options available from both NT Health and Emergency Services could help in this respect. However, there is also the possibility for confusion and conflict over who should send out assistance due to the location, distance, time, resources, and the believed (or actual) severity of the incident.

Finally, since there are many human controllers involved in the correct functioning of the system, thorough, complete, and consistent training is essential throughout all parts of the system to ensure correct understanding of technology, communications, and processes. This needs to be monitored and reviewed regularly to maintain confidence in the effectiveness of the system.

6   Thematic Analysis

To understand the effectiveness and challenges of safety management with regards to work health and safety at NT Health, semi-structured interviews were conducted. Altogether, five representatives from a range of functions at NT Health were interviewed, and included those who had experience of work health and safety management in NT Health and/or experience working in remote areas. A feature of the interviewees is that they all had many years of remote area nursing experience.

To analyse the data from the interviews a thematic analysis was performed, a presented by Braun and Clarke [11]. This consists of several phases. The first phase involves familiarity with the data by transcribing, reading and re-reading of the data and highlighting initial ideas. The interviews themselves were conducted using Microsoft Teams, which transcribes the interviews using in-built software. Subsequently, to ensure accuracy, these transcripts were checked with the original audio recordings prior to reading. The second phase involves generating the initial codes, formed by identifying a particular feature of the data that is of interest to the analyst. In a systematic manner, the entire data set is assessed so as to identify any interesting aspects that may help form the basis of any repeated patterns or themes.

In the third phase, following the initial coding, themes were identified by gathering all the various codes across the entire data set into similar potential themes. In particular, all the codes are analysed to consider how the different codes may combine together to form any overarching themes. The fourth phase involves reviewing those themes from the third phase and checking their suitability across the entire data set. In this stage it is possible to draw a thematic map of the analysis showing potential themes.

The fifth phase further refines each theme, as well as the overall story the analysis tells, and provides clear definition and names for each theme. Finally, an account is produced through the selection of compelling extract examples, and the analysis is related back to the initial research question.

7   Results of Thematic Analysis

The thematic analysis yielded a total of twenty candidate themes, which were subsequently reduced and refined to four key themes, see Fig. 6. The oval-shaped text boxes represent the following final four themes:

1. Safety culture challenges
2. Independence and isolation
3. Implementation challenges
4. Inconsistency

These themes are discussed below accompanied by relevant interview quotes in italics.

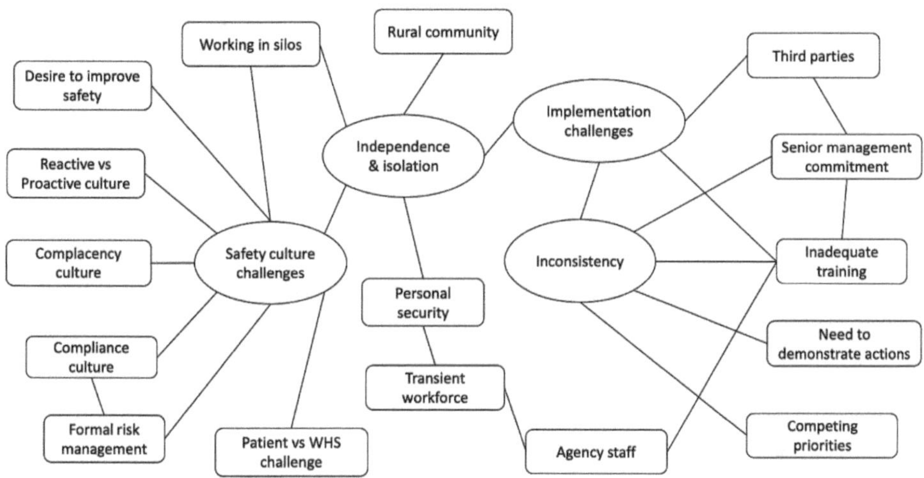

Fig. 6. Thematic map generated from the thematic analysis

7.1 Theme 1: Safety Culture Challenges

Safety culture has been recognised as a critical part of an effective SMS [9]. The interviews revealed both a genuine concern about safety and the desire to improve it, by all participants, though with differing levels of interest.

It wouldn't matter what level you asked at, they will all actually articulate that they're very concerned about safety, with different levels of appreciation for what the priorities should be. I would say that in health specifically, health workers are conducting risk assessments continuously.

As well as the expressed concern for safety, NT Health is also seen to provide the necessary risk reporting systems and tools. As seen in Sect. 4.1, a risk management system is available for all staff.

NT health, so that's the department and the health services, they do resource the health and safety function adequately, so there is a financial investment. The resourcing and the access to systems and reporting tools, incident reporting and investigation tools. All of that is in play and available.

Yet, despite the concern and commitment for safety and general resourcing and tools for risk management, the interviews reveal an organisation with a reactive culture, moving from crisis to crisis. This is believed to potentially lead to assigning blame (a blame culture).

In my experience, they're quick to, again, because they are reactive, they are quick to assign blame because that's the easy and instinctive thing to do.

Another feature revealed was a tendency to be complacent with risk at times. If everything always goes right, then it is assumed to continue this way. It was suggested that those with considerable working experience in remote environments are now simply immune to the known issues and have become desensitised.

If you have more senior, or you know longer serving, supervisors and managers who have spent a lot of time working in those remote communities, they have become desensitized to some of the issues that younger employees find absolutely traumatic.

Unsurprising for a well-regulated health organisation is the emphasis on compliance. However, care needs to be exercised to not only focus on this when managing safety.

There is a focus on endeavouring to be compliant with the legislative requirements. The financial aspect is more of a focus, whereas the work health and safety is added on.

7.2   Theme 2: Independence and Isolation

The second theme is independence and isolation, AS RHW work in very isolated and remote environments. Interestingly for some, such autonomy is an attraction. However, there is a tendency to contain issues and manage independently, and a reluctance to escalate issues accordingly.

Certain attributes to the job that actually attracts certain people that really appreciate significant autonomy as a result of the distances and the remoteness of some of these locations. Teams are generally very tight knit and resistant to notifying outside, so there's a behaviour there around containing it themselves and only escalating when they have to.

The term 'tyranny of distance' was used on several occasions to emphasize the extremely difficult environment in which remote health workers operate – namely lack of appropriate funding, communications and infrastructure. Another feature to note is the distance from professional support, which may even include no access to police or fire services.

The definite challenges we have in addition to that tyranny of distance and the poor communications I think is just the general funding as well and infrastructure that goes into these communities because they're very expensive to maintain.

The many challenges with driving and communications are also apparent.

So isolation and remoteness is one, from an operational perspective, the remote community workplaces challenge by the need to travel often long distances sometimes at night, in adverse in an adverse environment adverse in respect to road conditions whether the conditions, heat, rain, poor roads, lots of animals and livestock accessing the road while you're driving. Poor communications due to almost no mobile phone reception. In fact, you know, guaranteed no mobile phone reception in in a large part of the work environment.

Perhaps of increasing worry are the impacts of isolation on mental health and well-being.

Clear statistical information or data that we can say that isolation has an effect on mental health and well-being.

7.3   Theme 3: Implementation Challenges

In this particular theme, it was noted that some systems fail to be implemented adequately to their required standard. Hence the systems cannot be used as intended. This seems to be particularly relevant to implementing technology and pose considerable challenges given the vast disparate nature of the health services provision across NT.

The downside to that, is that some of those systems are poorly implemented and as a result of that, the use of those systems is not what it was intended to be.

In certain cases, there is no systematic approach to implementation with regards to training (on new technology, or systems). The approach taken may be to learn on the job or teach yourself, without sufficient reinforcement on the learning of information, or if the system is implemented and used by staff as intended. The lack of systematic implementation was also referred to with the use and availability of satellite phones, a key communications tool in remote areas.

It was not a systematic approach. Again, it was something that should have been a real priority and then supported by a good, you know, a good period of time, of making sure that the information had sunk in and that the systems that you'd spoke about were, you know, being used and staff knew what to do.

7.4   Theme 4: Inconsistency

The final theme is that of inconsistency, whilst overlapping with the other three themes, was identified as an important theme in its own right. Firstly, leadership plays a vital role in the quality of health and safety in the communities which varies somewhat, with some showing more interest in WHS than others.

In my experience working in this space, I find that the quality of health and safety outcomes in each community, and so this is in each community, is determined by the individual leadership of the staff or the managers in those communities, or the managers supervising those communities.

Equipment is procured sometimes with very little consideration for WHS. In addition, installation is rarely comprehensive – this may be particularly challenging given the large geographic expanse of NT.

If it has been done historically, it's not well communicated. Any new equipment brought in certainly from my perspective, I push the training and I push for the safe work procedures. I can't say uniformly for the whole of work, health and safety that happens. So there are requirements to have a GPS installed, but we are now finding that some vehicles are being deployed to whoever ordered them without these things in them, so there is variation… there is a standard specification for these things, but there are pathways where they're not being followed.

Finally, all interviewees agreed that incidents (and safety information, more generally) are well reported "upwards", generally through the Riskman system. However, often the resulting actions are inconsistently reported back "downwards", to close the loop. This effects the overall confidence and perceived value by staff in the reporting mechanisms.

From what I can say that there was a system in place prior, but it wasn't effective, so information regarding safety is reported up to, up the echelons. But there needs to be more reporting back down. So it's a 360 degree. That doesn't happen very often from a reporting process.

7.5 Summary

Following semi-structured interviews with NT Health staff relating to the effectiveness of the SMS, a thematic map was created in order to derive connections between areas of interest, revealing four main themes. These themes provide invaluable insights that affect managing WHS at NT Health in general, as well as in the implemented alert and first response system, and in any future implemented systems, designed to support and increase safety for remote health workers. By combining both the STPA hazard analysis and thematic analysis, a holistic analysis, which can be used to ensure the effective implementation and operation of systems such as the alert system, as well as to recognize limitations and any necessary controls.

8 Conclusions

At the outset, the authors commend Northern Territory (NT) Health for providing health-care in one of the harshest and most dangerous environments on the planet. The very nature of the problem of work (occupational) health and safety of remote health workers (RHW) in Northern Territory, indeed in rural regions across the globe in general, poses considerable challenges including: climatic extremes, isolation, lack of infrastructure and services, and after-hours work. Furthermore, an unavoidable hazard in the NT is the long distances that need to be traversed on unsealed roads. Adding to this is the lack of a reasonable and robust telecommunications infrastructure, making the task of any first responders, should an accident occur, extremely challenging. Consequently, we took a 'mixed methods' research approach to this problem.

Initially, a STPA Analysis was performed to capture system hazards of the system of interest (the first response socio-technical system). In order to understand the safety management system (SMS) and its effectiveness with regards to WHS and the system of interest, we conducted semi-structured interviews with key NT Health staff members. A thematic analysis of the transcribed interviews provided the appropriate level of detail required.

The very nature of the problem, the quality of the data provided, the sheer physical vastness of NT and the relatively few experts with experience of the remote healthcare system in NT means that this methodology is a robust and reliable mixed methods approach.

The STPA analysis showed that many different scenarios could lead to unsafe control actions, which lead to hazards and ultimately losses. These scenarios include technological, human and organisational factors. One of the benefits of using an STPA analysis is that it can identify a comprehensive range of factors.

When considering driver related aspects, there is a need to apply sensitivity and inclusion in remedial measures, given the unique demography of the NT with a large indigenous population. This poses a considerable challenge in that The NT is incredibly diverse, with over a hundred nationalities and over 140 social, cultural, and religious organisations. According to a 2016 census, there are 74,546 Indigenous people in the NT, approximately 30.3% of the NT population,13] representing the highest proportion of Indigenous people in the country in any state or territory. The Indigenous peoples of Australia, also known as Aboriginal and Torres Strait Islander people, in reality comprise hundreds of groups each with their own distinct set of languages, histories and cultural traditions [14]. Indigenous people tend to live together in small populations in communities, also referred to as homelands or outstations, in remote areas where on lands over which they have traditional ownership or have historical knowledge [15]. It is estimated that there are 500 communities with a total of 2,400 homes across the NT. Finally, over 100 Indigenous languages and dialects are spoken, [16] with considerable differences in the grammatical structures, concepts, and vocabulary of these languages. Typically, in each community, the same language or dialect is spoken.

With this in mind, amongst the measures to be considered therefore are:

a) road safety education conducted in differing indigenous languages,
b) a long-term commitment within NT to teach road safety in rural, remote areas of Australia to the indigenous citizens and seek to change the culture of road safety.

Whilst efforts underway to do this by various volunteer organisations, the fully-funded involvement of the NT government is a pre-requisite for this to be successful.

Several aspects of the response system are particularly important and will require the support of a well-functioning SMS.

i) Consistency – ensuring the correct installation and calibration of the alert system across all NT Health vehicles.
ii) Training of staff on any new equipment in vehicles, e.g. the alert system and satellite phones.
iii) Infrastructure gaps – extending to lack of satellite equipment availability or not carrying equipment. This includes first response contact staff at NT Health who will require continuous access to a phone (and, moreover, possibly a satellite phone).
iv) a high turnover of staff and high use of agency staff in rural and remote communities. This creates challenges for safety, particularly in terms of adequate training, including knowledge on new equipment/technology.

The interviewees highlighted the problems posed by safety culture, noting repeatedly the very reactive nature of the SMS, compounded by formalised processes which hampered flexibility. The best solution for NT Health in such cases would be to revamp the safety culture of its remote health working, using the experience of workers in the field to develop a more flexible, proactive system. Furthermore, once any new system (technological or otherwise) or SMS is in place, education, and training of the staff is essential. It is important to note a continual effort is needed to prevent a return to the reactive nature of the SMS.

Acknowledgments. This research would not have been possible without the support and collaboration with NT Health staff. Sincere gratitude goes to all, for their support and advice along the way. Many thanks also to the HealthSec peer reviewers and their invaluable feedback which has enhanced the quality of this paper.

Disclosure of Interests. The authors have no competing interests to declare that are relevant to the content of this article.

References

1. CPNI.: Critical National Infrastructure | CPNI. Retrieved December 31, 2022 (n.d.). https://www.cpni.gov.uk/critical-national-infrastructure-0
2. Australian Government: Critical Infrastructure Resilience Strategy: Plan (2015). www.itsanhonour.gov.au
3. ABC News. Gayle Woodford: Man charged with murdering "popular" outback SA nurse - ABC News. Retrieved December 31, 2022 (n.d.). https://www.abc.net.au/news/2016-03-27/gayle-woodford-man-charged-with-nurse-murder/7278140
4. INCOSE: System Special Cases (2022b). https://www.incose.org/about-systems-engineering/system-and-se-definition/system-special-cases
5. Leveson, N.: Engineering a Safer World: Systems Thinking Applied to Safety. MIT Press (2012). https://doi.org/10.7551/mitpress/8179.001.0001
6. Hollnagel, E.: Brief introduction to FRAM (2016). https://functionalresonance.com/brief-introduction-to-fram/
7. Australian Bureau of Statistics: Regional population (2022b). https://www.abs.gov.au/statistics/people/population/regional-population/latest-release
8. Population Australia: Population of Australia 2022 (2022). https://www.population.net.au/
9. Roland, H.E., Moriarty, B.: System Safety Engineering and Management. John Wiley & Sons, Inc. (1990) https://doi.org/10.1002/9780470172438
10. Leveson, N.: A new accident model for engineering safer systems. Saf. Sci. **42**(4), 237–270 (2004). https://doi.org/10.1016/S0925-7535(03)00047-X
11. Braun, V., Clarke, V.: Using thematic analysis in psychology. Qual. Res. Psychol. **3**(2), 77–101 (2006). https://doi.org/10.1191/1478088706qp063oa
12. Brooks, A., Majumdar, A.: Mixed methods analysis of system hazards in the provision of remote health services in Rural Australia: combining STPA analysis and thematic analysis to identify and manage hazards. In: Proceedings of the ACM Workshop on Cybersecurity in Healthcare (HealthSec), Salt Lake City, UT, USA (2024). https://dl.acm.org/doi/pdf/10.1145/3689942.3694739
13. Australian Institute of Health and Welfare (AIHW): The health and welfare of Australia's Aboriginal and Torres Strait Islander peoples. Canberra, AIHW (2015)
14. NT Government. Services to remote communities and homelands (2022). https://nt.gov.au/community/local-councils-remote-communities-and-homelands/services-to-remote-communities-and-homelands. Accessed 20 Mar 2025
15. NT Government. Aboriginal languages in NT. https://nt.gov.au/community/interpreting-and-translating-services/aboriginal-interpreter-service/aboriginal-languages-in-nt. Accessed 20 Mar 2025

Computer Security Issues in Continuing Care Retirement Communities: A Resident's Perspective

John McHugh[1] and William Yurcik[2]

[1] Assurance Labs, Inc., Gaithersburg, MD 20886, USA
mchugh@cs.unc.edu
[2] Centers for Medicare and Medicaid Services (CMS), Baltimore, MD 21244, USA
William.Yurcik@cms.hhs.gov

Abstract. As the "baby boomer" portion of the U.S. population ages, the need for different types of living communities increases. At the HealthSec 2024 workshop we first presented the personal experience of the first author who lives in a continuing care retirement community, identifying technology opportunities for three healthcare challenges: (1) Signs-of-Life, (2) Signs-of-Health, and (3) human asset management. This paper extends this previous work with the feedback we received at the HealthSec 2024 workshop.

While we discuss technology solutions ranging from no technology up to artificial intelligence, along with these technology solutions are corresponding security and privacy risks. We feel it is important to raise these healthcare challenges in order to focus attention, stimulate research investment, and encourage innovation for senior living environments.

Going forward, we suggest researchers seek the involvement of residents in geriatric living environments to serve as "participant observers" helping to determine the appropriate technology solutions and risk management tradeoffs to address the unique healthcare challenges presented by the demographics of our aging population. We would also encourage researchers from other countries with different senior care health systems and social cultures to join us in what to this point has been a U.S. centric study effort.

Keywords: cybersecurity · geriatrics · assisted-living · senior-living · risk management

1 Introduction, Demographic Change, and Healthcare Implications

In this paper, an expansion of our earlier work, [11] we discuss the demographic reality in the U.S. population which is leading to healthcare challenges to senior

---

W. Yurcik—Official Organizational Disclaimer: "The views presented herein do not represent the views of the Federal Government.".

© The Author(s), under exclusive license to Springer Nature Switzerland AG 2026
W. Yurcik (Ed.): HealthSec 2024, CCIS 2716, pp. 301–325, 2026.
https://doi.org/10.1007/978-3-032-13800-2_14

living environments. We are blessed to have the experience of an accomplished cybersecurity researcher who lives in a retirement community to share direct observations from his living environment. Of course this is but one data point of observations amongst millions but as you will see the healthcare challenges for which we provide insight about are key and generalizable to all senior living environments. Specifically, the three senior living healthcare challenges we focus upon are (1) Signs-of-Life, (2) Signs-of-Health, and (3) human asset management. For each of these senior living healthcare challenges we will discuss the available technologies, benefits, and risks associated with their use.

In the U.S. a large part of the population is becoming senior (over 65 years old) and the younger generation (20–40) are having children at lower rates. With increasing life expectancies and declining birth rates, the number of Americans aged 65 and older is projected to increase from 58 million in 2022 to 82 million by 2050 (a 47% increase), and the 65-and-older age group's share of the total population is projected to rise from 17% to 23%. [18] It is predicted that in 2034 that the old will outnumber the young in America. [6] This demographic shift is not unique to the U.S., other nations such as Japan and Italy have even larger population shifts. [9]

This demographic shift has significant implications for the U.S. healthcare system and in particular senior living facilities. Demand for overall healthcare services will grow dramatically, the nature of the healthcare services will have to conform to geriatric needs, and healthcare delivery will need to adapt to different settings. [7,12] According to the National Council on Aging (NCOA), almost 95% of adults 60 and older have at least one chronic condition, and nearly 80% have two or more chronic conditions. [13] Chronic conditions limit a person's ability to perform daily activities, causing them to lose their independence, and result in the need for a continuum of care ranging from in-home care to assisted living to institutional full-time care.

The good news is that aging happens gradually over time allowing for accommodation. Also, the range of physical/mental well-being has infinite variations between persons as well as infinite variations in the same person over time. [6]

This paper focuses on independent and/or retirement living, which is different from assisted living or skilled nursing in that while independent/retirement living does provide prepared meals and housekeeping, it does not include nursing oversight on-site. If a medical emergency occurs at an independent/retirement living facility, emergency medical services have to be contacted to arrive on-site. We note that during the period between the preparation of [11] and the conference at which it was presented, the facility in which the first author resides was hit by Hurricane Helene. Although the facility did not experience major damage, the storm exposed additional risks as discussed below.

2   My Continuing Care Retirement Community

Continuing Care Retirement Communities (CCRCs) are a retirement housing option that operates as an insurance plan. The average entry age of a senior in a

CCRC is 78 years old. [14] Many states regulate CCRCs. In North Carolina (NC), they are regulated by the State Department of Insurance under Ch. 58, Article 64 of the general statutes. The primary thrust of this regulation is to ensure the fiscal stability of the CCRCs. [17] To enter a CCRC, residents must be capable of living independently and financially able to pay the associated entrance and monthly fees for, at least, their expected lifetime. CCRCs offer varying levels of healthcare including independent living in apartments or stand alone "cottages;" assisted living facilities for those in need of help with the usual activities of daily living (dressing, bathing, etc.), and skilled nursing home facilities for those needing constant medical attention.

The first author is a CCRC resident and any first-person references in the paper reflect his observations/opinions. His CCRC, Carolina Village (CV) in Hendersonville, NC, was founded in 1974, and operates as a non-profit, 501(c)(3) organization. It provides services to the community and is also exempt from property taxes. At CV, independent living (IL) is provided in apartments and "cottages" with 1 to 6 dwelling units in each. Independent Living Services (ILS) acts as a 24/7 gatekeeper providing minor medical services, blood pressure checks, dressing changes, etc. and calling EMS when necessary. The associated assisted living facility is called the Care Center (CC), and the skilled nursing facility is called the Medical Center (MC).

In return for a substantial entrance fee and a monthly fee that does not change with the level of care, the CCRC undertakes to care for the resident at any needed level of care for life, even if the resident exhausts his or her financial resources. We joke that the best-case scenario for a CCRC is a resident who dies in IL just as the amortization of the entrance fee completes (a few years) and the worst case is a new resident who suffers an illness or injury soon after entering and spends several decades in the MC. The best case scenario for a resident is to be able to live an active and productive life in IL for many decades, dying suddenly and painlessly before needing assisted living or nursing care. This is also a near optimum scenario for the CCRC which puts considerable effort into keeping its residents able to live independently.

CV has about 550 total residents. While the numbers change almost daily, about 50 residents appear to reside in the CC, about 20 in the MC and the remainder in IL. Residents may reside temporarily in the MC or CC while recovering from illness, surgery, or accidents and then return to their IL unit. The minimum entrance age is 62. The age range is 62–103 with an average age of 85 and 5 residents over 100.

CV has expanded a number of times with the most recent expansion in 2019 adding about 160 new residents in a new apartment block and additional "cottages", in this case a mix of duplex and sixplex buildings. I live in one of the new sixplexes which are built into a hillside, so the two lower units and the four upper units are all ground floor, but on different streets. It took me a bit of effort to get the address handled correctly by Google Maps and Amazon has delivered my packages to Unit 2 on the upper level rather than to Unit 2 on the lower level despite their being on different streets.

2.1 Carolina Village Communications Infrastructure

CV provides internet and basic cable TV to its residents as part of the monthly fee. Traditional landline telephone is available in older parts of CV, but newer parts will get a VOIP service that depends on the internet being up. Unable to port my home number to the local (AT&T) exchange, I have a wireless base station that serves my local handsets. Many residents rely on cell service entirely.

Wi-Fi is available throughout the community, but my impression is that the service in the older parts of the village is limited. The IT staff is installing fiber and Ethernet in the older buildings and service is improving. The long-term plan is to provide a router in each unit giving each one its own private address space. Residents also have the option of getting service from commercial providers, including the local cable company and many do.

CV is adjacent to the I-26 highway and the regional provider, ERC Broadband, provides CV with a connection to their long-haul fiber that connects Asheville to Atlanta. The CV network is NATed[1] to 192.168/16 from this connection, so our traffic usually appears to originate in Atlanta. This causes problems with web sites for chain stores with branches here and in Atlanta.

The most recent CV expansion was built with fiber optic loops through the new buildings and CAT-6 Ethernet and Cable TV coax from the communications cabinet in the garage to the individual rooms. The fiber loops run through an 8-port gigabit switch in each unit. Because of the loop through, the switch must be on for the loop to work. There is no UPS/backup power in the units, so power outages take out the Internet for all units on the loop. One of the IT department workers says that they now realize that individual fibers should have been "home run"ed from each unit eliminating the loop risk. In my case, one port of the fiber switch feeds my gigabit router/access point and the rooms with computer equipment are fed via Ethernet from it. These include my office, the guest room, and the entertainment cabinet in the living room. My Wi-Fi access point supports password protected user and guest access. Speed tests on the wired network in the unit typically show download speeds in excess of 800Mbps and upload speeds in excess of 900Mbps.

Ironically, shortly after I retired, the local phone company where I lived in the woods outside Saluda, NC, some 5 wire miles from their central office, replaced their 40-year-old buried copper with home run fibers to every residence. Having made do with 1–3 Mbps DSL for my last 10 working years, I then had access to higher speed 100Mbps at a lower price!

2.2 Carolina Village Computer Usage

Surprisingly, CV is somewhat technology averse. Many things that could be done with computers are done manually and it is clear that the village's own use of computers is somewhat haphazard.

---

[1] NAT is Network Address Translation. A NAT device maps externally routed IP addresses to internal IP addresses eliminating the need to assign a new externally routable IP address to every new/modified host on the inside network.

Event signup sheets are posted on a physical bulletin board in the main building. I live approximately half a mile from this bulletin board. Requests to allow signups on-line were rejected with the excuse that doing so would be unfair to residents who do not use computers and/or smart phones.

There is no database of resident information that can be queried to create emails for specific groups. In May, I received an email inviting me to a Mother's Day event. When I questioned this, I was told that it was not possible to restrict a mailing to women only. I also received an email schedule for washing inside windows in the main building. Apparently, it is not possible to send emails selectively by location either.

The business office is unable to take payments by EFT although I can allow them to draft my monthly fees from my account and they will send me the bill by email rather than stuffing it in a crack in the front door as they used to do.

There is no Chief Technical Officer (or similar position) and no data processing department or individual in charge of CV office computing. Recently, the IT department has instituted policies that attempt to ensure that current software versions and security patches are installed on all CV office machines. There still seems to be no one on the staff with a mission of determining how to effectively incorporate currently available software and software centric business practices into the CV business operations.

When the dining halls reopened after pandemic closures, a tablet-based ordering system from FullCount[2] replaced the pencil-and-paper system used previously. Although the FullCount system allows on-line ordering and the ability of residents and their families to track meal balances, ordering histories, note allergy and dietary restrictions, etc. CV limits its usage to the Point-of-Sale (POS) terminal and tablet-based components. Apparently, many of the features are available only at extra cost, but they might pay for themselves in reduced manual effort, (e.g. the need to staff phones to take orders for much of the day).

2.3   Carolina Village Website and Village Hub

CV has a public web site[3] and a resident site,[4] which is partially accessible by non-residents. The public site is almost exclusively a marketing tool, but it does have a job listing and application page. This is the page that should come up if you do a search for "Carolina Village". It is professionally done, but despite having a current copyright date some of the information is out-of-date.

The Village Hub is intended as a primary means of one-way communication from the management to the residents and to a limited extent, between residents. Each resident is given an account. According to the resident handbook, available on the hub to residents and guests alike:

Each resident will be given a personal username and password for logging in to the Hub.

---

[2] https://www.fullcount.net.
[3] https://www.carolinavillage.com/.
[4] https://www.mycvhub.com/.

- Username is cv.firstname.lastname Example: John Smith = cv.john.smith
- The password will usually be the resident's birth month and day, as 4 digits. Example: July 3 birthday = 0703

So much for security! There are a number of interactive screens available on the campus that show the Hub. The resident directory, not available to guests, is available on those screens. Many residents have their birthday (often without the year) on their Hub page which can be accessed quickly to provide enough information to compromise accounts. The "Resident Celebrations" page, available on the public screens, has monthly pages listing residents and their birthdays. A few camera pics with a cell phone and enough information is provided to quickly compromise accounts. In addition, the listing for the current month appears on the physical bulletin board in the main building. Compromise of a single account allows an intruder to access all resident information on the Hub and the ability to compromise any account having the default password.

There are a few things that could be damaging and that require login as a specific user. You could edit the user's personal page, perhaps replacing the user's description of a career as a schoolteacher with one describing a career as an ax murderer! There are a number of forms that could be submitted that have the potential for causing damage. The Absence Notification Form is discussed below. You could create a bogus event and reserve a room, fill out a bogus comment card or submit a bogus work order. Fortunately, the USPS "Hold Mail" form requires either physical identification or a USPS account.

The hub does not include the capability for the user to change his or her own password. This is deliberate under the theory that the residents are unable to remember passwords and allowing arbitrary passwords that are then forgotten would place an undue burden on staff who would be constantly changing passwords.

The Hub is a product of Touchtown. Touchtown was acquired by Uniguest,[5] a company that specializes in "Connected Content, Deployed Everywhere, Engaged Audiences". It would appear that the role previously served by the Village Hub, a simple web interface easily usable by seniors, has been subsumed by Uniguest's suite of Community Apps. The Touchtown Village Hub app and similar ones are available on Amazon and various other app stores. The internal structure of the Hub is opaque. It resists common website cloning tools. Many of the internal links appear as long random strings and these appear to vary with time. This may be an effort to prevent external links to internal nodes. [10]

Developing applications for the Hub is beyond the capabilities of the CV staff. A few third-party applications have been partially integrated. It is possible to enter work orders which are handled by TheWorxHub[6]. Entering a work order results in an acknowledgment email containing a link to the actual work order, but the link requires login to TheWorxHub and residents do not have an account

---

[5] https://uniguest.com/.
[6] https://www.brightlysoftware.com/.

there. Absence Notification Forms (ANF) let ILS know that a resident will be away overnight so that the failure to check-in (see Sect. 3.1) does not cause alarm. ANFs and comment forms can be filled and submitted through the Hub. Until recently, these were Google Forms, but have been changed to use Microsoft 365 (MS365) forms. Although both Google and MS365 forms allow pre-population of forms, CV personnel lack the skills necessary to do this. The justification for switching to MS365 forms was a claim that Google forms are not HIPAA[7] compliant while MS365 Forms are. This is misleading, at best. [1,2] None of the information collected on these forms requires HIPAA compliance and it is possible to use either in HIPAA compliant ways. CV staff may use MS365 to collect HIPAA sensitive information. This might justify the switch but the process is not straight forward. [3,4]

The initial implementation in MS365 exposed what I consider a serious security issue. The Google forms implementation sent an email acknowledgment that the form had been submitted. This feature is not available in MS365 but the resident was initially offered the option of saving a copy. Selecting this option pops up a MS365 login window, something that is useless for residents who do not have a MS365 account. When I selected this window, the login window was pre-populated with an email address that I have at the University of South Florida where I have a courtesy appointment. The only MS application that I have on my Mac is a copy of the MS Teams client that I use for meetings with colleagues at USF. Apparently, having this email gives me a MS365 account, but there is no reason for the MS365 form filling app, running from the Hub in my browser to know of it. The account and password are in my Chrome password manager, but nothing should associate this with MS365. When I installed Firefox, and used it to fill the form, the problem persisted. The option to save a copy has been removed, but I will not trust MS365 forms until I can understand where it is getting the account information.

3   Healthcare Challenge One: Signs-of-Life

There many healthcare challenges associated with living in a CCRC. The discussion that follows focus on three of these, Signs-of-Life in this section followed by Signs-of-Health and Human asset management in the subsequent sections.

Healthcare challenge number one is Signs-of-Life - determining if a CCRC member is (or is not) experiencing a life-threatening medical emergency or death. Due to the demographics of people living in CCRCs, it is likely that they will experience disabling medical emergency events at significantly higher rates than the general population. Since emergency medical services are not on-site and must be summoned, response time may be the difference between life and death. Many residents live alone and, if they are unable to summon help, they may die before anyone is aware of a problem.

---

[7] The Health Insurance Portability and Accountability Act (1996) sets federal standards to prevent disclosure of sensitive health information without patient consent.

Human beings manifest they are alive by the following five Signs-of-Life indicators: (1) breathing, (2) Maintaining a body temperature of about 37°C, (3) excreting waste, (4) moving, and (5) responding to their environment. Signs-of-Life can be sensed using any or all of these indicators. One, or more Signs-of-Life signals that appears to be abnormal, interrupted, or absent, is an indication that something serious is wrong and must be investigated immediately.

3.1 Signs-of-Life Technology Opportunities

There are a variety of ways for detecting Signs-of-Life that range from no technology use to completely automated AI solutions. For some time, CV has provided residents with pendants that can be carried and have a button that can be pushed to summon help, but these require that the resident carry the pendant and be able to activate it. Pull cord call systems are also installed in each resident's unit. The following description is from the Resident Handbook.

RESIDENT SAFETY SYSTEMS

Emergency Call System

- Each resident is provided an emergency call button on a pendant, which will direct help to any location on campus. Residents are urged to wear their pendants while on the Carolina Village campus. To activate the pendant, hold the button down for three seconds. IN THE EVENT OF A PENDANT ACTIVATION, RESIDENTS SHOULD REMAIN WHERE THEY ARE LOCATED IF IT IS A SAFE LOCATION; the emergency call system is equipped with a tracking device to bring emergency help to the resident. Moving locations could slow the response time. There is a $250 fee for replacing a lost pendant or for upgrading from an older pendant to a new pendant.
- Every apartment and cottage is equipped with an emergency call system with a pull cord in every bathroom and fire/smoke protection. Residents should pull this cord all the way down in the event of a medical need. ILS will respond.

Other popular tracking technologies such as Apple Air Tags operate in this space but they are problematic. Apple Air Tags are designed to track belongings, not people, and Apple has taken steps with several disclosures, privacy warnings, and alerts designed to prevent unwanted people tracking. It is illegal to track people without their consent in many jurisdictions. Even with consent, there are still problems: a person must physically have the Apple Air Tag with them, Apple Air Tags run on batteries with limited lifespans, and Apple Air Tags use Bluetooth technology to communicate and must be near iPhones, iPads, and Macs to provide current location information.

In general, any technology involving short range wireless communication will suffer from similar problems. Alert systems using cell phone based technology avoid some of these problems. "Smart Watches" often include fall detectors and the like. These typically use the associated cell phone as a relay and depend on it being present and functioning.

Carolina Village Apartment Ring Checker. The residents themselves created a system for checking on apartment dweller well-being twice each day. Residents were asked to hang a colorful fabric "ring", provided shortly after move-in, outside their doors by 9:00 PM and to remove it by 9:00 AM the next day. A volunteer, the "ring checker," checked each morning and evening and knocked on the door if the ring had not been placed or removed by the appointed time. If there was no answer, ILS/Security would enter the apartment to check on the resident. Residents were supposed to notify the ring checker and ILS of an overnight absence. A red ring indicated the unit of the current hallway "ring checker."

The ring check system started in 1975 and used for 49 years. It was credited with saving many residents who had falls, heart attacks, strokes, serious illness, and other health issues which left them alone and incapacitated.

JNL Daily Check-In Button. Recently, the ring checker system was replaced with a wireless alert system from JNL Technologies.[8] The installed units are part of their Nurse Call system marketed under the name "Quantum." The JNL devices replace one of the earlier emergency call devices in each unit. In addition to the call function activated by a pull cord, they have a green check-in touch area that the resident is supposed to touch once a day between 5:00 AM and 10:00 AM providing a daily Sign-of-Life. If the signal is not received at ILS by 10:00 AM, ILS calls the resident and sends someone to the unit if there is no answer. Although this functionality is part of the emergency call system described above, the integration is not mentioned in the handbook nor is the fact that pushing the red area on the box is equivalent to pulling the cord.

This system is described in the Resident Handbook as follows:

Check-In Program

- In addition, each apartment and cottage is also equipped with a check-in system. Residents are encouraged to push the green check-in button once daily between 5:00 a.m.–10:00 a.m. If a resident does not check in during this timeframe, an ILS team member will call to ensure safety and well-being.
- The Check-in system is voluntary, but all residents are strongly encouraged to participate. Opt-out forms can be obtained from the ILS office.

When the check-in device was installed in my unit, my wife and I opted out. After she died, I opted in, asking the ILS director about his experience with the system. Apparently, there were "teething" problems that have been resolved. On one occasion, my check-in did not go through, and I was gone for the day by the time ILS checked.

The check-in system is useful and necessary in a place like CV, especially among the cottages where it is easy to isolate. A friend of ours died not long after we moved in. She experienced stomach pains, but did not seek attention

---

[8] https://jnltech.net/.

for them, dismissing them as indigestion. She collapsed on the floor of her unit with what turned out to be a severe intestinal infection. It was several days before her next-door neighbor became concerned and went in to find her. After surgery, a hospital stay and some days in the MC, she seemed to be recovering, but the damage was too advanced, her condition worsened, and she died. Since this event, I have been considering ways in which the JNL system could be supplemented with automatically reported data.

Hurricane Helene exposed another flaw in the system. While the main building, the MC and the CC have some backup power, the cottages do not. The older cottages were without power for about 3 days and the newer ones, fed from a different distribution line, were without power for about 2 days. The store and forward routers in the cottage area had UPS backup but that failed after a few hours rendering the entire check-in and call system for the cottages inoperative. I was away during this period, but I understand that ILS went door to door daily checking on the well being of residents. Given that CV had a winter storm power outage of several days shortly before the new cottages were built, the failure to provide backup power there seems strange.

The check-in system was initially implemented as a twice a day system with the evening check-in being between 5:00 p.m. and 10:00 p.m. ILS started calling non-responders at about 10:30 p.m. with predictable results; irate residents who forgot to check-in awakened from sleep in the middle of the night. Whether better training and a trial period where residents are reminded of their failure to press the green button sometime on the following day might have resolved the issue is unknown, but the notion of requiring residents to press a button to prove that they are alive seems a bit awkward and we wonder if there might be better ways to achieve the same goal. Before we do that, let's look at possible modifications to the existing system that would make it easier to use reliably. Note that all of the proposed modifications would require both hardware and software modifications but that the availability of low-cost micro controller components would allow out-of-band prototype development and evaluation with minimal investment, obviating the requirement to modify the installed units until the utility of the modifications has been demonstrated.

The goals of the suggested modifications are twofold. The immediate goal is to make the manual system more comfortable for the user by providing immediate feedback when it is used so that the user knows that the message has been sent and received and to provide prompts for required check-in interactions. By turning off the prompt when the check-in has been accomplished, the user is reassured that that the interaction occurred. When the same action is required day-after-day, it is easy to forget whether you took the action already today, especially if an unusual event interrupted your normal routine. There is no harm in pushing the check-in button again if you cannot be sure that you did it earlier, but the presence of too many days with multiple check-ins might also serve to help diagnose the onset of other mental difficulties.

Feedback: When the check-in button is pushed, a green LED turns on momentarily and a beep is heard. This appears to come solely from the local unit.

If this is the case, allowing two-way communication with the unit would have the light and sound controlled by the central station to which the user unit reports. Having the button push light the LED and make the beep while the acknowledgment flashes the LED several times and modulates the beep provides assurance that the signal has been received. Similar behavior should be provided for the red call button.

Prompting: Check-in is required during a certain time window. A prompt light (blue, yellow, or a shade not easily confused with green.) could appear at the start of the check-in period and turn off when the check-in is acknowledged. Failure to check-in during the time window should modulate or flash the prompt light until either it is reset by a late check-in, or the next check-in period starts. It should be possible to suspend this feature remotely in response to a scheduled absence by the resident. Prompting could be implemented locally, without remote access, but changes in the time window would require reprogramming of each unit.

The current check-in alert units are battery powered, proposed changes would increase battery drain and require modification and/or redesign of the units. Unless the manufacturer can be convinced of the need for these modifications, they are unlikely to happen. As an alternative, feedback and prompting could be provided via an alternate channel, say via Wi-Fi. Each unit in the village has Wi-Fi access and suitable micro controllers with Wi-Fi capabilities are available for about $5 each in reasonable quantities. The feedback / prompt units need not be battery powered and could be simply located in the same room as the alert unit. Such units could allow more elaborate reverse communications, e.g. a prompt light at the beginning of the check-in period and a loud alarm near or at its end if no check-in has been performed.

3.2   Additional Signs of Life Sensors

The objective of signs of life sensors is to capture activities by a resident that indicate that the resident is present and engaged in normal activities. Theses sensors primarily capture such activities and confirm that someone, presumably a resident is active in the unit. Other information from these sensors can also contribute to signs of health discussed in the next section.

Toilet flush: An occupied unit will probably have multiple toilet flushes per day. For most toilets, it should be possible to sense the motion of either the flush arm or the valve float using a reed switch and magnet or a mercury switch and use this to generate an appropriate RF signal. These are good candidates for battery operation.

Door and/or drawer openings: In these cases, we want to detect the movement of the door or drawer rather than its open or closed state. Movements can probably be detected using magnet/reed switch combinations positioned so that the switch is momentarily activated by the motion of the monitored item. Sensors activated by a momentary switch closure can be designed to draw current only briefly when activated. It may be possible to add such sensors to refrigerator and microwave doors. These are good candidates for battery operation.

Current draws/voltage swings: Manually activated appliances such as coffee pots, microwaves, electric ranges, etc., draw current while in use. Units that are not programmable or activated by a timer are potential candidates for generating Signs-of-Life. In addition, sensors could be added to light circuits controlled by wall switches to sense when the light has been turned on or off. These can be mains powered as the appliances require mains power. Battery powered sensors could also be placed in or near light fixtures to sense the presence or absence of light

Motion detectors: Motion detectors provide indications of activity in a living space. Modern versions claim to be able to distinguish between human and pet movements and should be suitable if adequate coverage can be ensured. Inovonics makes a motion detector suitable for Signs-of-Life monitoring. Battery life is extended by allowing the detector to sleep for a period of two to six hours after reporting motion.

Remote Controls: Many entertainment systems and appliances use remote controls. Radio frequency remote signals can probably be captured and used to generate Signs-of-Life. Some radio remotes use Wi-Fi while others use other bands. Infrared remotes are more problematical as they are directional, but placing additional sensors near intended targets could be effective in capturing usage.

Home Security Sensors: The home security industry provides a variety of door and window sensors, but most of these signal continuously when the monitored object is left open and are probably not suitable for use on interior doors or on windows and doors left open for ventilation. Nonetheless, signals from a home security system might provide additional Signs-of-Life.

Smart Home Integration: The units in the most recent addition (Clear Creek Cottages) to the CV were designed around 2016 and initially occupied in 2019. By the design time, smart home integration was well established, and Amazon Alexa had been available for several years. Wireless light switches have been available since the early 2000s but none of these technologies were included in the Clear Creek design, however ceiling fans with lights use a battery operated remote built into a wall switch.[9]

In most integrated smart home systems, command devices communicate with a hub which controls the lights, appliances, etc. In designing a smart home for elderly residents, any interactions that go through the hub or that can be detected by the hub have the potential to emit Signs-of-Life indicators. As "smart" appliances become more common, it should be possible to include them as potential sensors. It may be possible to sense the use of these units

---

[9] This seems to have been an afterthought (or perhaps a response to a failure to install a 3-wire line from the switches to the fixtures). In addition, number of awkward light switch locations could have been avoided by the use of wireless switches and the added cost probably recovered in reduced wire and wiring costs.

by sniffing their network traffic. To the extent that their traffic leaves the village, a single monitor (or a monitor per ISP) could cover the entire village. Even though the traffic is encrypted, the fact that it occurs at all may be sufficient to use for our purposes, especially if the return traffic results in a communication to a controlled device within the environment. [8]

Entry and egress monitoring: are special cases. If a unit is unoccupied, there should be no Signs-of-Life. Single occupancy unit occupancy is a binary property, but units occupied by a couple can have 2 (or more), 1, or 0 occupants at any given time. The sleep periods of the motion detectors discussed above complicate occupancy determination and it may be worth considering mains powered motion detectors that could report the lack of motion as well as the presence of motion more frequently. Location services, (e.g. cell phone GPS) might be used to confirm that a resident has left the unit but is subject to a false negative if left behind. Vehicles with location service offer another occupancy alternative but could manifest a false positive if moved without the occupant. This is an area that requires research.

Signal Integration: Residents interact with the staff of the village in many ways. Ordering a meal creates entries in the dining system that could be also used to show activity (and possibly location). Access to the gym is controlled by a fob that must be clicked to unlock the door. Some exercise equipment requires a user specific card to set it up for that individual. Sensors at the gates open automatically for cars with owner specific bar codes. Adding signals from resident activities outside the dwelling unit could provide a more complete picture of resident activity. It might be possible to develop a phone app that would send a sign of life alert whenever the phone is used.

3.3   Associated Risks with Signs-of-Life Solutions

The sensor boxes provided by JNL are battery powered. They use low power 900MHz band spread spectrum transmitters from Inovonics.[10] The transmitters send periodic "heartbeat" signals that allow the system to self-organize and to detect failed units. The signals from a group of alert units are aggregated and forwarded by repeater units that have battery backups. The signals ultimately wind up at a computer monitoring system in the ILS office. The transmitters draw 5 micro amps average from the nominal 3.0 Volt battery for hourly sensor heartbeats and an additional 15 micro amps average at a 1 alert per hour rate. Maximum transmit current draw is 100 milliamps. Each unit can transmit a primary and a secondary alarm in response to a contact closure. In addition to the sensor heartbeat, the transmitter can send a "low battery" alarm when the battery voltage drops to 2.6 Volt. Battery life with hourly heartbeats and once a day check-in should be several years. CV Maintenance does periodic battery replacement and responds to low battery alerts.

The current check-in mechanism has a latency of up to nearly 30 hours. If a resident becomes incapacitated immediately after a check-in at the 5:00 AM

---

[10] https://www.inovonics.com/.

start of the check-in period, ILS will not become concerned until well after 10:00 AM the following day. For some types of incapacitations this is likely to be fatal while it is tolerable but undesirable for others. Because it requires positive action on the part of the resident, false positives are unlikely and false negatives relatively easy to resolve. As additional sensors are added, latency is reduced. Sensor redundancy minimizes the importance of false negatives but exacerbates the impact of false positives. Fortunately, many of the proposed sensors are unlikely to have false positives though a toilet float sensor could create a false positive in a leaky toilet while a flush arm sensor would not. The heartbeats used with the check-in sensors are probably not needed with most of the proposed sensors due to redundancy. Having no input from a given sensor for extended periods may indicate failure of the sensor. Most units at the village receive housekeeping services once every two weeks and the housekeepers could be instructed to test suspect sensors (e.g. flush all toilets, open and close doors and drawers).

Sensory overload is a potential problem. Sending a "Signs-of-Life" more than once or perhaps twice an hour is probably unnecessary. As experience is gained with the system, we will probably learn how often Signs-of-Life occur under normal circumstances and will be able to calculate intervals between signals that should cause concern if exceeded. Local aggregation of signals could be used to keep the loads on the reporting network reasonable. Depending on the sensors used, the interval of concern may vary by time-of-day, day-of-week, and by occupant. It is also likely that some customization will be needed. Some residents cook regularly while others eat most of their meals out. Some are night owls while others go early to bed and get up early. Some sleep through the night, while others are up frequently.

This brings us to our second healthcare challenge, the potential to use fine-grained activity sensor data captured over long periods of time in order to monitor physical and/or cognitive decline.

4   Healthcare Challenge Two: Signs-of-Health

The failure of Signs-of-Life to be received when expected indicates a possible medical emergency requiring immediate response. Challenge number two, which we call Signs-of-Health, requires analyzing the patterns of behavior indicated by the Signs-of-Life signals to determine if changes in the patterns over time indicate changes in the physical and/or mental health of a CCRC resident.

The concept of "Activities of Daily Living" (ADL) has been a cornerstone of nursing since the 1950s. [15] as shown in Fig. 1, ADLs are the essential activities individuals must perform to live independently, such as eating, bathing, dressing, and managing personal hygiene. These foundational tasks provide a helpful framework for assessing Signs-of-Health.

$$\text{Total Dependence} \Leftarrow \qquad \Rightarrow \text{Total Independence}$$

1. **Maintaining a safe environment**
2. **Communicating**
3. **Breathing**
4. **Eating food and drinking fluids**
5. **Eliminating body wastes**
6. **Personal cleansing and dressing**
7. **Controlling body temperature**
8. **Mobilizing**
9. **Working and playing**
10. **Expressing sexuality**
11. **Sleeping**
12. **Dying**

Fig. 1. The 12 Activities of Daily Living (ADLs)

CCRC staff in key positions, such as housekeeping, should be trained to recognize and report ADL changes in residents. This may not be easy since residents may conceal health problems for fear of being asked to transfer to another setting to accommodate their changing health status. However, many health problems, if detected earlier, can be medically managed to enable a CCRC resident in living independently to continue to do so.

Indicators of Signs-of-Health that may be observed without medical testing include:

1. Balance and Stability (Fall Hazards)
2. Care Refusal
3. Wandering or Exit Seeking
4. Isolation/Lack of Engagement/Altered Reality
5. Lethargy/Loss of Appetite
6. Weight Loss
7. Confusion
8. Bathing and Dressing

4.1   Signs-of-Health Technology Opportunities

While the primary Signs-of-Health technology opportunities are related to house-keeping and dining hall observations and tracking, we next identify 13 other sensor-enabled technology opportunities.

4.2   Sensors for Signs-of-Health

As noted above, many ADLs have the potential to generate sensor signals similar to the manually generated Proof-of-Life check-in signal. The aggregation of these signals offers the opportunity to model an individual residents behavior and changes in the behavior may provide an indication of the resident's health. In addition, some of these and other sensors such as those described below may provide direct indications of health status. This is largely an area for research at the present time. Good candidates include the following:

Fall and occupancy sensors: We have recently become aware of occupancy and fall detection technology from Gamgee, a Dutch company, that may be well suited as a Signs-of-Life indicator. [5] While this approach appears to be in early stages of development, it could, if successful, serve multiple roles. The technology detects perturbations in the Wi-Fi field due to motion or the presence of objects. As a fall detector, it claims to be able to detect falls and raise an alert without the need for an attached fall sensor. As a home security sensor, it is claimed to be able to identify which known individuals are present and to be able to detect the presence of strangers. As far as we can tell, the company has not yet developed a proof-of-concept prototype. The system would use Channel State Information as input to machine learning algorithms that would provide fall detection and occupancy information. Similar work seems to exist elsewhere, as well.

Sleep sensors: A "weight-on-bed" sensor or "motion-in-bed" sensor is useful for both Signs-of-Life and Signs-of-Health. Some of the current smart watch sensors (FitBit, Apple Watch) provide sophisticated sleep signal analysis. For users like me who use a CPAP or similar machine, the nightly usage reports are a useful input for Proof-of-Health. Many such machines report usage via a cell phone chip embedded in the device.

Smart Socks: There has recently been an explosion in human sock development as sensor monitoring devices for both Signs-of-Life (blood flow, heart rate, sweat levels) and Signs-of-Health (temperature, movement). Temperature differences in one foot relative to the other may also indicate a sign of inflammation as a precursor to other problems such as an early detection of a foot ulcer.

Automated Assistants: Robots for elder care can help elders with ADLs such as mobility, medication management, and cognitive stimulation. They can also provide emotional support with companionship and reducing loneliness, and improve safety through communications. Robots can also be a mobile platform for all other Signs-of-Life, Signs-of-Health sensors. While Japan has had a continuous and growing investment in robots for elder care, the body of research evidence currently suggests that robots may actually result in more work for caregivers, not less.

Smart Chairs: Sensors embedded in chairs can capture health status from sedentary residents. Sedentary behavior (sitting) is a pervasive activity across all age groups, characterizing many home activities and other settings (especially work settings). Sedentary behavior has been increasing in time proportion to other activities of daily living and unfortunately this sedentary lifestyle corresponds to an increased risk of metabolic diseases, heart disease, type 2 diabetes, musculoskeletal diseases, incorrect posture, obesity, social isolation accompanied by anxiety and depression, cognitive and functional decline, and poor quality of life. [16] Sensors of multiple types embedded into seats can track sedentary behavior (time proportion of the day sitting) and vital signs while sitting (heart rate, respiration rate, blood pressure).

Other signal integration: Food service is another opportunity to recognize and report Signs-of-Health. Automated food service logs could monitor resident dining hall engagement to determine regular eating patterns via dining hall attendance tracking, healthy meal choices via meal tracking, etc. The use of gym equipment controlled and monitored by resident specific cards is another source of Signs-of-Health.

Other: Other suitable sensors exist or may require some development effort. Identifying such sensors or recognizing other suitable Signs-of-Health and developing sensors for them is an area for future research.

The opportunity to collect sensor observation information over a long period can provide indications of changing health status and using this information to create individual models of behavior is the key response to the Signs-of-Health Challenge.

Many older individuals, especially those in residences such as CV, tend to develop fairly consistent routines. Some of these are forced by the structure of the environment. At the village, meals are available in (or from) the dining facilities at specific times. Trash pickups (for those of us in the cottages) occur on specific days. Classes, lectures, and other group activities occur on a scheduled basis. In my own case, I tend to rise between 5 a.m. and 6 a.m., put in eye drops, shower and dress, and then eat breakfast in the dining hall at around 7:00 a.m. most days. I take out my trash immediately before or after breakfast on trash days and leave CV in my car to hike with non-village friends several times a week. I try to be in bed between 9:00p.m. and 10:00 p.m. To the extent that these patterns can be captured through Signs-of-Life and Signs of Health observations, they can be used to create a rough model of current "normal" behavior as an indicator for Signs-of-Health.

If I become acutely ill or injured, my behavior may change abruptly, and it will become obvious that my behavior is inconsistent with the model. My behavior could also change abruptly for other reasons, but the change, if recognized could be a cause for concern and a possible "Are you OK?" message from ILS. As I age, I expect that my model will drift and that this will also be the case for most residents. Perhaps I will go to bed earlier (or later), change the time I wake up and get up, stop eating breakfast in the dining hall, hike less frequently, etc. I may forget whether I have pressed the manual check-in button and press it sometime later to be sure.

Individual models and their drift may prove useful in accessing slow changes in physical/mental health status. These changes are often subtle, but, if combined with the results of medical exams, either the annual "wellness exams" covered by Medicare or symptoms or event-driven medical interventions, may provide insight into changes in health status that are a part of the aging process. Systematic capturing of activities associated with everyday life (ADLs) and using them to create individual models of these activities, (e.g. using machine learning, etc.) could help to identify the onset of physical/mental changes and lead to timely interventions and/or effective accommodations. This will require a holistic approach, integrating detailed observations with clinical results.

4.3   Associated Risks with Signs-of-Health

Signs-of-Health are not without risks. These run the gamut from "Can it be done at all?" to perceived and real loss of privacy to gross misinterpretation of the model resulting in inappropriate or even damaging treatments.

The overall goal of Signs-of-Health at a place like CV is to keep residents living independently with a good quality of life for as long as possible. Under the current system family and/or staff often recognize that an individual resident needs a higher level of care and help to ease the transition. Some residents realize that they are no longer capable of functioning independently and seek transfers from IL to the CC while others persist in a state of denial well past the time when they should make the transition. We think that careful, fine-grained observation of resident behavior, possibly done with the assistance of AI, has the potential to support this goal if it can be done safely and accurately.

Intuitively, creating individual behavioral models and using them to track changes in behavior due to aging and due to changes in physical and mental health status is appealing. Whether this can be done effectively using only externally visible aspects of behavior such as those gathered by Signs-of-Life sensors is an open question. Even if it can be done, issues of privacy and efficacy must be addressed. As far as the authors are aware, the gathering of this kind of data for this purpose has not been done and research in the area should begin with a series of small pilot studies.

While the Signs-of-Health observations are invasive, the observations can be distilled in such a way as to show a monitor nothing more than the current occupancy status of the resident's unit and the elapsed time since the last Sign-of-Life signal. As the observations become more frequent, detailed, and diverse, the risks to privacy increase. The creation of an individual model of behavior is itself an invasion of privacy in the eyes of some subjects of such modeling. If such an effort is to be undertaken, the nature and purpose of the modeling needs to be clearly understood by the participants, subjects and users alike. If such projects are to be undertaken, the involvement of ethicists and social scientists is absolutely necessary, and it must be demonstrated and documented such that the subjects of this kind of modeling understand the risks as well as the possible benefits involved and that coercion to participate is forbidden.

Once the system is in place and aggregating information on residents, the risks multiply. The objective of the system is to use long-term fine-grained information about the behavior of individual residents to model their behavior and detect variations in the behavior that could be indicators/predictors of changes in physical/mental health status. This is a laudable goal, but the concentration of so much personal data in an easily usable form lends itself to potential abuses ranging from blackmail to withholding treatment in cases where the model indicates an untreatable condition requiring expensive measures to prolong life. We are not suggesting that these sorts of abuses would happen but that the aggregation of data, per se, creates risks of this kind.

There are a great many unknowns and substantial uncertainty associated with the development and use of models of this type. For a model of behavior to be useful, it must be the case that, in the absence of influences that perturb the behavior, that observed behaviors going forward are generally within the envelope of behaviors predicted by the model. Some individuals living in retirement facilities lead very regular, repetitive, lives and will probably be easy to model while others may seem to have few regular activities and, from the point of view of the Signs-of-Life data appear to live chaotic and unpredictable lives. While it may be possible to create partial models for some aspects of these resident behaviors, they may not be sufficient for Signs-of-Health unless we can show that their chaotic lifestyle is, in itself, an indication of health. In my own case, my behavior has changed greatly since the deaths of my wife in January 2024 and our dog in April 2024. My bed and rising times are less regular. I travel more frequently.

The risk of misinterpretation is possibly the most serious risk associated with this sort of modeling. Reaching an erroneous conclusion that a resident is suffering from a serious physical/mental problem and treating on the basis of this conclusion alone could be disastrous, however we have seen numerous cases in other areas where an erroneous interpretation of computer data has resulted in disastrous courses of action.

Inadequacy or inaccuracy in the models creates additional risks. A system of the type proposed will be breaking new ground and there is a tendency to place unwarranted trust in models produced by machine learning or artificial intelligence. In most cases, the phenomena being modeled are too complex to be fully understood. Machine learning excels at finding patterns, but not at producing understanding, and the specific patterns recognized may not represent the entire picture. The risk is that we associate specific patterns with certain outcomes based on limited experience and later learn that the same patterns can be associated with different outcomes. Acting on earlier experience may be wrong in other cases. Since we will be working with individuals, it is important not to transfer experience based on one resident (or a group of similar residents) to others without understanding causal relationships.

Finally, there is the risk that the situations being observed are so complex that the data collected by the system has no useful predictive value even for the resident from whom it was collected.

5   Healthcare Challenge Three: Human Asset Management

Healthcare Challenge number three is Human Asset Management which is keeping track of all CCRC people including CCRC staff, CCRC residents, CCRC visitors, CCRC deliveries. There are multiple motivations for this function:

- CCRC staff for management purposes to make sure facility work is being appropriately staffed and functioning
- CCRC residents to track resident patterns and to be aware if a resident is either on-site with Signs-of-Life or on-site with no Signs-of-Life

(unseen/unresponsive) or off-site to return at an expected day/time or missing off-site without notification as a possible Silver Alert[11]
- CCRC visitors for security, match visitors to specific CCRC residents, and to track/monitor/manage possible infection control as required for public health
- CCRC deliveries for security, vendor work supply management, and to track/monitor/manage possible infection control as required for public health

There needs to be an automated centralized logging system to record and track every person entering or exiting from the CCRC. This logging system can also be used for:

- Daily CCRC scheduled on-site activities and events including schedule changes
- CCRC reservation calendar for future events
- Transportation requests for future services or immediate services on a first-come, first-served basis.
- Sign-up log records for CCRC off-site activities

The fiber plus a few point-to-point Wi-Fi links supports a network of video cameras that monitor the area around the back gate and other public areas for people movement. There are also cameras in public areas of the older parts of the village. Post pandemic, CV built a gatehouse at the front entrance that is manned 24 hours a day. Since it is possible to walk into the village from many places this seems to be an appearance response to an undefined threat rather than a substantive one.

During Covid, temperatures were taken of all residents and staff when they entered CV, and visiting was restricted. Residents were, however, free to come and go. The largest resident outbreak of Covid occurred when a number of residents went off site to attend a 2020 Christmas event at a local church.

As noted earlier, there is no centralized database that can provide focused communications for human asset management purposes. Sign-ups for activities are done manually. Events intended for subgroups of residents are announced to the entire community. While certain staff members have specific roles, e.g. transportation organizer, room reservations, etc., requests go to individuals, not to roles and, if the individual is away, requests often go unanswered.

5.1 Human Asset Management Technology Opportunities

CV's approach to human asset management for both residents and staff appears to be haphazard. There is no database of residents that could form a basis for

---

[11] A Silver Alert is a public notification system that alerts when an elderly person/senior citizen is missing from a care facility without notice. The intent of the Silver Alert is to help locate the missing person quickly. Each state has their own protocol for activating a Silver Alert. Silver Alerts may be broadcast on a variety of media including radio, television, cable, social media, and state transportation signage.

storing, organizing, accessing and using information about the residents, collectively or individually. It is not clear what the situation is with respect to staff. Staffing, especially for low level positions is difficult. At the time [11] was written, CV was trying to hire an HVAC technician offering \$18–\$24/h. Indeed.com showed an average of \$27 for the area which may explain the problem.

The issue of visitors is more complex. When I moved to CV in 2019, there was no front gate, and the back gate was only closed for a period from late evening until early morning. Temporary access restrictions appeared during Covid, and a manned gate house installed after, turning CV into a gated community. The back gate is closed and activated by a vehicle decal or a keypad. Many residents, especially those from "up north" approve because it makes them feel safe. Visitors now must announce themselves at the front gate but, as far as I can tell, no ID is required, and no visitor log kept. Once on campus, visitors are free to roam and neither the MC nor CC normally has any access controls.

Infection control is haphazard. During Covid, CV announced the cumulative number of cases, but not the current count. They claimed that HIPAA prevented them from identifying cases among either residents or staff and they made no visible attempts to try to identify and warn people who had been in contact with confirmed cases during their contagious, pre-diagnosis period. It appears that many of the CV cases came from staff or from residents who went to off campus gatherings. During a meeting with residents during Covid, management responded to requests for more information about resident and staff infections by saying that they we are not accustomed to sharing this sort of information with residents. At the time of writing, early March 2025, the village has a Norovirus outbreak (25 active cases identified) and, again, there is no useful information about the victims that would allow other residents to judge whether they are at elevated risk.

There is an opportunity to introduce technology in the form of a DBMS with components to deal with both resident and employee aspects of the problem. The only tricky aspect of the problem is the need to accommodate the ability of residents to move temporarily between levels of care, e.g. from IL to MC to CC and back to IL. This should be possible without losing the information relevant to IL so that it does not have to be reentered when the resident returns to IL. Given this, we can posit a set of data associated with each resident that includes basic demographic information, historical records for payments, work orders, dining, etc. Independent records exist for a number of these items, but the proposed system will either subsume and replace the existing records or (more likely) federate them so that their contents can be accessed and processed from a common interface.

A human asset management system may also unify other aspects of resident life such as signups for excursions or events, reservations for CV facilities, transportation requests, etc. Management has resisted automating these on the grounds that it would be unfair to residents who do not use computers. This group is getting smaller, and nothing precludes setting aside a portion of the signups for residents who do not use computers.[12] In addition it should be possible to develop signup applications for the large screen monitors that appear in public places and design them in such a way that even non computer users can make use of them (as many do for the Village Hub). CV uses small fobs for access to the gym, pool, and similar facilities and it should be possible to use the same tokens to sign into such a reservation application.

5.2   Associated Risks with Different Human Asset Management Solutions

The goal of a human asset management system solution is to capture movement about CV facilities in a unified automated system. This would include all staff, visitor, delivery, and resident movement (e.g. off-site, gym, pool, library, group activities). These multiple stakeholders do not have needs that align so there is an inherent tension and risks in both tracking and restricting movement.

Aside from the check-in system and a requirement for notification to ILS in advance of overnight absences, no effort is currently being made to track the comings-and-goings of residents. Synergistically, a Signs-of-Life system would be much simplified if it were possible to know whether a dwelling unit was empty or occupied. I am personally not inclined to announce my departures or expected return times and think that being required to do so would be an invasion of my privacy.

The current CV human asset management system is inefficient from communications viewpoint for both staff and residents. The inability to select an appropriate subset of residents to receive communications wastes both staff and resident time and materials. For example, when irrelevant announcements are printed and distributed to all residents rather than to the affected subset. In addition, this creates an associated risk that notifications that are important to a specific group are ignored by residents fatigued by a flood of irrelevant communications.

Billing and payment are cases in point. For many of my recurring bills, I can sign up with my bank to get electronic bills and then schedule a payment which the bank ensures arrives by a date I specify. The norm at CV appears to be paper bills delivered by hand to resident units with payment by check. As far as I can tell from talking to my bank, allowing CV to draft my account results in the bank sending a physical check to CV in response to the draft with an uncertainty as to the date that it will be presented and paid.

Proposals for revamping the CV human asset management system would require substantial changes in the way CV operates including addition/retraining of staff members to obtain the needed data processing skills. Building and installing the system could be done under contract although it is also possible that residents having relevant skills could help, if CV would allow them to do so.

---

[12] Having staff transcribe the manual entries, if getting everything into one place is desirable.

CV has numerous surveillance cameras in public places, and at the risk of becoming "big brother", it is possible to identify residents using AI face recognition and record their movements. Doing this would be considered privacy invasion by many, however, if this could be done effectively, this would provide a comprehensive system for human asset management. However, this would also represent a contentious tradeoff between healthcare, privacy, and freedom of movement.

6 Summary

This paper is based on the observations of a participant resident and seeks to serve two purposes: (1) to look at the personal experiences of the first author, McHugh, as a resident in a Continuing Care Retirement Community (CCRC) and (2) to consider how more advanced computer technology, up to and including individual modeling and the application of AI, could improve the quality of life for residents of such facilities. The observations are specific to a single CCRC, Carolina Village (CV) located in western North Carolina. The first author is also an established computer security researcher whose late wife was active in public health outcomes research.

That said, we suspect that our observations are applicable to other CCRCs and to other senior living models, since the problems that we observe are not unique. Indeed, many of them were observable at other facilities my late wife and I considered before choosing CV. There is a tendency at CV (and at other facilities with which we have experience) for the management to dismiss the ideas and experiences of residents as not being relevant to their current situations or from some notion that because we are in a retirement community we are incapable of being useful. Never mind that another resident in my sixplex is a member of the NC State Transportation Board and that other residents have substantial responsibilities in local charitable organizations, government oversight commissions, etc.

CV celebrated its fiftieth anniversary last year. It has a well-deserved reputation as one of the best facilities of its kind in the area and many of its senior employees have been with CV for many years as there is a tendency to promote from within and to hire relatives of current employees. This may go a long way towards explaining its relatively slow adoption of automated approaches for areas like record keeping, billing and the like. There seems to be no one tasked with looking at areas where the adoption of new technology might improve service and/or reduce costs.

CV has good communications backbone connectivity and an adequate network infrastructure for residents with ubiquitous Wi-Fi and wired/fiber optic connections in the newer units. The administration's use of computer technology is minimal. There is no centralized resident database and relatively trivial operations such as generating emails to selected subgroups of residents is not possible. Many tasks that could be easily done on-line (e.g. event sign-up, ordering carry out meals, etc.) are done manually or by phone, the rationale being that allowing this on-line would be unfair to non-computer users.

A web-based system, the Village Hub is used to communicate with residents and has limited facilities for residents to enter work orders, absence forms, etc. Security is minimal and resident accounts and passwords are easily guessed.

Using technology to improve resident safety and quality of life presents a number of challenges. A recent check-in system allows residents to inform the Independent Living Services (ILS) staff that they are alive and well once a day. ILS will contact any participating resident who fails to check-in, but one who becomes incapacitated immediately after a check-in may not be contacted for more than a day.

We considered a number of possible "Signs-of-Life" sensors that could substantially reduce this response time and discuss the potential risks from using this approach. Assuming that a Signs-of-Life system was deployed, we then address the question of whether changes in patterns of Signs-of-Life indications can be used to detect changes in physical/mental health status so that early interventions can be made. We call this "Signs-of-Health" and it is an area for future research. Integrating a Signs-of-Health system into the operations of an organization such as CV would be a major undertaking given the relatively primitive use of information technology.

The deployment of a Signs-of-Health system presents numerous risks. If a Signs-of-Health system could be effectively/efficiently implemented, the attendant risks associated with the resulting aggregation of sensitive personal information and the uncertainties associated with modeling individual behavior raise important tradeoffs between healthcare and privacy.

Implementing a human asset management system to improve safety and efficiency within an assisted living community represents similar challenges to deploying a Signs-of-Health system. While physical barriers and concierge gateways can be implemented and supported with automation, such deployments raise important tradeoffs between healthcare, privacy, and freedom of movement.

There is much potential research going forward. We foresee next steps in two directions: (1) building a research community with expertise in aging, sensing, and other related fields; and (2) comprehensively exploring assisted living facilities across the U.S. to learn and systematically document different living situations, healthcare challenges, and associated solution risks.

Acknowledgement. The first author would like to thank the staff at Carolina Village for making it a wonderful place to live and especially Kevin Parries, Jon Renegar, Brent Thomas, Jordan Webber, and Ed McDade for making this paper possible. Both authors would like to thank Dr. Elise Bolda for her insightful comments on the earlier version of this paper.

Disclosure of Interests. We have no competing interests in the work reported here.

References

1. Alder, S.: Is Google Forms HIPAA compliant? https://www.hipaajournal.com/google-forms-hipaa-compliant/ (Dec 10 2023), URL valid as of 20 Feb 2025

2. Alder, S.: Is Microsoft Forms HIPAA compliant? https://www.hipaajournal.com/is-microsoft-forms-hipaa-compliant/ (Sep 16 2024), URL valid as of 20 Feb 2025
3. Alder, S.: HIPAA risk assessment. https://www.hipaajournal.com/hipaa-risk-assessment/ (Jan 6 2025), URL valid as of 20 Feb 2025
4. Alder, S.: How to make Microsoft Office 365 HIPAA compliant. https://www.hipaajournal.com/microsoft-office-365-hipaa-compliant/ (Jan 6 2025), URL valid as of 20 Feb 2025
5. Ali, M., Hendriks, P., Popping, N., Levi, S., Navee, A.: A comparison of machine learning algorithms for wi-fi sensing using (csi) data. Electronics **12**(18) (2023), https://doi.org/10.3390/electronics12183935 as of 21 Jan 2025
6. Dowling, M., Kenney, C., , Carney, M.T.: The Aging Revolution. Skyhorse Publishing (2024)
7. Eggleston, E.M., Finkelstei, J.: Finding the role of health care in population health. Journal of the American Medical Association **311**(8), 797–798 (2014), https://doi.org/10.1001/jama.2014.163 as of 21 Jan 1015
8. Jackson, R.B., Camp, T.: Amazon echo security: Machine learning to classify encrypted traffic. In: IEEE 27th International Conference on Computer Communication and Networks (ICCCN). pp. 1–10 (2018)
9. Kaneda, T., Greenbaum, C., Patierno, K.: 2019 world population data sheet. Population Reference Bureau, available at https://www.prb.org/wp-content/uploads/2019/09/2019-world-population-data-sheet.pdf as of 21 Jan 2025
10. Lesavich, S., McHugh, J.: Deep-linking may mean deep legal trouble. In: Second IASTED International Conference Law and Technology (LawTech'2000. San Francisco, CA USA. (2000)
11. McHugh, J., Yurcik, W.: Position paper: Personal experience in the technology opportunities and associated risks of healthcare challenges in a Continuing Care Retirement Community (CCRC). In: ACM Cybersecurity in Healthcare Workshop (HealthSec'24). Salt Lake City, UT, USA (October 2024), available at https://doi.org/10.1145/3689942.3694752 as of 20 Feb 2025
12. National Academies of Sciences, Engineering, and Medicine (ed.): Aging, Function, and Rehabilitation - Proceedings of a Workshop. National Academies Press (2024)
13. National Council on Aging, (NCOA): https://www.ncoa.org/, URL valid on 21 Jan 2025
14. Pearce, B.W.: Senior Living Communities: Operations Management and Marketing for Assisted Living. Independent Living, and Continuing Care Retirement Communities. Johns Hopkins University Press, Memory Care (2024)
15. Roper, N., Logan, W.W., Tierney, A.J.: The Roper-Logan-Tierney Model of Nursing. Elsevier-Health Sciences Division (2020)
16. Salice, F., De Vellis, M., Barbieri, A.G., Masciadri, A., Coma, S.: Nonintrusive monitoring and detection of sitting and lying persons: A technological review. IEEE Open Access (December 2024), https://ieeexplore.ieee.org/stamp/stamp.jsp?arnumber=10771771
17. Span, P.: When the retirement community goes bankrupt. New York Times Health Section, available at https://www.nytimes.com/2025/01/18/health/retirement-community-bankruptcy.html (January 2025), published Jan. 18, 2025. Updated Jan. 22, 2025. URL Valid on 20 Feb 2025
18. U.S. Census Bureau: 2023 national population projections tables: Main series. https://www.census.gov/data/tables/2023/demo/popproj/2023-summary-tables.html (2023), URL valid on 21 Jan 2025

Author Index

A

Aboagye-Otchere, Kwabena   160
Alarcon, Mauro Lemus   188
Alemzadeh, Homa   232
Alvarez, Carlos Guerrero   130
Amit, Guy   86
Anantharaman, Prashant   130
Ayday, Erman   267

B

Beg, Aamish A.   130
Bhamidipati, Subrahmanya Chandra   188
Borodchuk, Danylo   130
Brooks, Ashley   284
Brooks, Ian   113

C

Calyam, Aneesh   188
Calyam, Prasad   188
Castillo, Jorge   160
Chang, Preston   217
Chaudhary, Vipin   267
Chen, Qian   160
Chien, Aichi   67

D

da Silva Avelino, Rodolpho   113
de Miranda, Fabio Roberto   113
de Moreas Batista, Andre Filipe   113
Dharmalingam, Athish Pranav   232
Duvvuri, Mahesh Karthik   188
Dykstra, Josiah   33

E

Elnawawy, Mohammed   232

F

Farchy, Ofir   267

G

Gastner, Michael T.   113
Gat, Nadav   267
Gettinger, Andrew   130

H

Hallajiyan, Mohammadreza   232
Harel, Yaniv   267
Hough, Douglas   33

I

Iqbal, Shahrear   232

J

Jiang, Yuzhou   267

K

Kambhampati, Anirudh   188
Karthik, Karan   188
Kim, Inji   232
Krish, Veena   217

L

Levy, Moshe   86
Locasto, Michael E.   130

M

Majumdar, Arnab   284
McHugh, John   301
Mirsky, Yisroel   86
Mitra, Gargi   232

N

Neumann, Peter G.   3
North, Stephen   113
Nuguri, Sai Shreya   188

P

Pattabiraman, Karthik   232
Pluta, Gregory   113

R
Rahmani, Zahra   267
Rahmati, Amir   217

S
Sami Saydjari, O.   33
Schick, Andreas   113
Shahini, Nahal   267
Shapiro, Rebecca   130
Sharif, Mahmood   267
Smith, Sean W.   130
Sullivan, Natalie   19

T
Tian, Yuan   67
Tilley, Laura   19

V
Varadharaju, Vishnupriya   130

Y
Yun, Zebin   267
Yurcik, William   3, 19, 113, 301

Z
Zhu, Yunzheng   67